Reubin O'D. Askew and the Golden Age of Florida Politics

FLORIDA GOVERNMENT AND POLITICS

LAWTON M. CHILES, JR.
Center for Florida History
AT FLORIDA SOUTHERN COLLEGE

UNIVERSITY PRESS OF FLORIDA

Florida A&M University, Tallahassee
Florida Atlantic University, Boca Raton
Florida Gulf Coast University, Ft. Myers
Florida International University, Miami
Florida State University, Tallahassee
New College of Florida, Sarasota
University of Central Florida, Orlando
University of Florida, Gainesville
University of North Florida, Jacksonville
University of South Florida, Tampa
University of West Florida, Pensacola

Reubin O'D. Askew

AND THE GOLDEN AGE OF

FLORIDA POLITICS

Martin A. Dyckman

Foreword by David R. Colburn and Susan A. MacManus

University Press of Florida

Gainesville · Tallahassee · Tampa · Boca Raton

Pensacola · Orlando · Miami · Jacksonville · Ft. Myers · Sarasota

LAWTON M. CHILES, JR.
Center for Florida History
AT FLORIDA SOUTHERN COLLEGE

Published in cooperation with the Lawton M. Chiles, Jr.
Center for Florida History at Florida Southern College
Copyright 2011 by Martin A. Dyckman
Printed in the United States of America on recycled, acid-free paper.

16   15   14   13   12   11   6   5   4   3   2   1

A record of cataloging-in-publication data
is available from the Library of Congress.
ISBN 978-0-8130-3571-0

The University Press of Florida is the scholarly publishing agency for the State
University System of Florida, comprising Florida A&M University, Florida
Atlantic University, Florida Gulf Coast University, Florida International Uni-
versity, Florida State University, New College of Florida, University of Central
Florida, University of Florida, University of North Florida, University of South
Florida, and University of West Florida.

University Press of Florida
15 Northwest 15th Street
Gainesville, FL 32611-2079
http://www.upf.com

In memory of Bill Gillespie, Marshall Harris, Ken Myers,
Jim Redman, Bill Sadowski, and Roland Page,
who should have lived to write this book.

CONTENTS

FOREWORD

Florida has held a unique place in the American mind for more than six decades. For many retirees, its environment has been like a healthy elixir that allowed them to live longer and more vigorous lives; for others, it served as a place of renewal where all things were possible; and for immigrants, it offered political freedom and access to the American dream. Historian Gary Mormino described Florida as a "powerful symbol of renewal and regeneration." Others have suggested that, if Florida had not been available to Americans after World War II, they would have been much poorer for it. Those who watched the 2000 presidential election unfold, however, wondered if that were in fact so.

During World War II, Americans from all walks of life discovered Florida through military service, and it opened their eyes to the postwar possibilities. With the end of the war in August 1945, Florida veterans returned home, where they were soon joined by hundreds and then thousands of Americans who were ready to pursue a new life in the Sunshine State. In the sixty years between 1945 and 2005, 17 million people moved to Florida, increasing the state's population to 18.5 million people in 2005.

Florida's population growth, the settlement patterns of new residents, and their diversity had a profound effect on the state's place in the nation as well as the image Floridians had of themselves. Prior to 1940, Florida was the smallest state in the South and one of the poorest in the nation. Its society and economy were rural and agricultural, biracial and segregated. Most residents lived within forty miles of the Georgia border, and their culture and politics were consequently southern in orientation. Like its southern neighbors, Florida was a one-party state with the Democratic Party dominating politics from the end of Reconstruction in 1876 to 1970.

All that changed in the sixty years following World War II. By 2005—in less than an average life span today—Florida became the largest state in the region, the fourth largest in the nation, a senior haven, and a dynamic multiracial and multiethnic state. Most Floridians now reside closer to the Caribbean than they do to Georgia, and, for most of them, their image of themselves and their state has changed dramatically to reflect this new geographic orientation.

As Florida changed, so too did its politics. Voters threw out the Constitution of 1885 in favor of a new document that would speak to the needs of a new state in 1968. They then gradually abandoned the Democratic Party in favor of a dynamic two-party system. By the 1990s, Republicans took their expanding constituency and their control of the districting process following the 1990 census to secure majorities in the state legislature and the congressional delegation. These were remarkable political developments and reflected the transformative changes in the state's population. However, in statewide races for governor, U.S. senator, and elected cabinet positions, as well as in presidential contests, Democrats remained competitive with their Republican counterparts, in large part because they held a 6 percent lead in registered voters (42 percent to 36 percent for Republicans).

Such a politically and demographically complex and diverse population has made Florida today something other than a unified whole. The political maxim that "All politics is local" is truer of Florida than of most other states. For example, those who reside in north Florida share little in common with those living in central or south Florida, and vice versa. While those residing in southeast Florida see themselves as part of the "new America," those in north Florida view Miami as a foreign country. Ask a resident what it means to be a Floridian, and few, if any, can answer the question. Ask a Floridian about the state's history, and even fewer can tell you that it has operated under five different flags or that its colonial period began much earlier than that of New England or Virginia. Perhaps one in ten or twenty can tell you who Democrat

LeRoy Collins was, despite Republican Jeb Bush's acknowledgment of Collins as the model for all governors who followed him. It is literally a state unknown and indefinable to its people. Such historical ignorance and regional division become major obstacles when state leaders try to find consensus among voters and solutions that address the needs of all citizens.

An essential purpose of this series is to put Floridians in touch with their rich and diverse history and to enhance their understanding of the political developments that have reshaped the state, region, and nation. This series focuses on the Sunshine State's unique and fascinating political history since 1900 and on public policy issues that have influenced the state and nation. The University Press of Florida is dedicated to producing high-quality books on these subjects. It is also committed to publishing shorter essays of twenty-five to fifty pages in this series that address some of the immediately pressing public policy issues confronting Florida. As part of this series, the University Press of Florida also welcomes book manuscripts on the region that examine critical political and policy developments that had an impact on Florida.

In this volume, Martin A. Dyckman, retired associate editor of the *St. Petersburg Times* and award-winning columnist and author, recounts the life and the governorship of Reubin O'Donovan Askew and the politics of his era. Although Dyckman has as much to say about the politics of this period from 1966 to 2005 as he does about Askew, he has given scholars and students of history and politics the first in-depth study of the person whom many think is a transformative figure in Florida and southern politics. Dyckman has also provided readers with insightful views on a whole host of eclectic Florida politicians from the serious to the bombastic and many others in between.

For Dyckman, the crucial developments of this era that enabled Florida to enter the golden age of state politics took place at its beginning with the federal decision to end segregation in public facilities and at the polling place together with the federal court-mandated reapportionment which ended "the eight-decade reign of rural legislators." Almost overnight, Florida transitioned from a legislature that identified with the political and cultural values of rural, north Florida to one that spoke to the needs and concerns of urban, south Florida. It was a sea change in the way Floridians governed themselves and viewed their future.

Dyckman's book takes readers from the governorship of the frequently outrageous Claude Kirk, the first Republican governor of the twentieth century, to the governorship of Jeb Bush, the foremost Republican governor of his time. Its focus is principally on Askew, a Democrat, his Democratic successors, and legislators who redefined state politics in the era from 1970 to 1996 and sought to resolve some of the most pressing policy issues facing modern Florida. Rated by scholars as one of the ten best governors of the twentieth century, Askew sought, among many other things, to restore the public's waning confidence in its government by insisting that it be fully transparent. One of his major contributions to state and national politics was the 1976 "Sunshine" initiative that requires officials and candidates to disclose their personal finances. Askew also addressed directly the public's anxiety about race relations, including the integration of schools and busing, by making clear that his administration embraced the rights of all citizens and all children. He appointed the first African American to the state cabinet and the first to the Florida Supreme Court.

Dyckman makes clear that, although Askew entered the governor's office with a mandate following the debacle of the Kirk years, and although he had a sizable Democratic majority in the legislature, he often needed votes on the other side of the aisle to pass his major initiatives from education to the environment. This was, in fact, an era when bipartisanship existed, even as Republicans sought to wrest control of the state from Democrats. That bipartisanship, Dyckman reminds readers, made it possible for Florida to address some difficult and thorny issues. By the mid-1990s, much of this spirit of cooperation collapsed as term limits and redistricting heightened partisanship at the expense of the needs of citizens. How Florida politics was transformed from an era of bipartisanship to one of intense political conflict is an important theme running through Dyckman's study, and not just for state politics but for national politics as well.

This is a rich and rewarding history of a state that was at the center of political change in the nation and of a governor who guided Florida into this modern era with skill and foresight. Dyckman tells the story with insight and colorful detail. It is a must read for Floridians and for scholars and students of state politics who seek to understand the changes that redefined Florida in the golden era.

David R. Colburn and Susan A. MacManus
Series Editors

1

THE BIG BANG

All reunions are nostalgic; this one was especially so. The forty sport-shirted men seated with their wives beside the swimming pool at an Orlando hotel on a balmy October evening in 2002 shared a unique experience. The last time the man at the lectern had addressed them was from the podium of the Florida House of Representatives twenty-eight years before. T. Terrell Sessums still appeared the same—as tall, professorial, and taciturn as when a reporter wrote of him that if the world ended he would be found standing calmly in the rubble, assessing his next move. The colleagues to whom he was speaking were also their recognizable old selves, despite some expanded waistlines and hair that was graying or gone. But for them the world *had* ended, at least the part that had been their special bond. Florida politics had changed almost beyond recognition since their time in Tallahassee. Sessums remarked on the difference. "I have a little difficulty remembering which of you were Republicans and Democrats. They don't have that problem any longer," he said.[1]

Their common bond was having served in the House from 1971 through 1974, the flowering of what came to be remembered as the Golden Age of the Florida Legislature. The decade of the 1970s was distinguished by progressive politics and a constructive two-party system. By 2002, however, the Golden Age was as evanescent as Camelot. Only one in four Floridians was native to the state, whose population had doubled since Sessums's speakership. Such circumstances are not conducive to collective memory; new citizens saw Tallahassee as a capital so thoroughly defined by partisan differences and party discipline that

Speaker of the House Johnnie Byrd, a Republican elected from the same county that Democrat Sessums had represented, remarked matter-of-factly that his members were "like sheep in a way . . . looking for someone to tell them what to do."[2]

Only two people at the reunion were still in the capacities they had filled during the Golden Age. One was Representative Jerry Melvin of Fort Walton Beach, who had served twenty years as a Democrat, sat out sixteen, and returned in 1994 as a Republican. The other was the author, capital bureau chief of the *St. Petersburg Times* from 1969 to 1976, residing once again in Tallahassee to write his editorials and columns. We agreed that the politics of the present had changed for the worse from the politics of the past. "I don't think it was directed to be partisan, like it is now," Melvin said.[3] When the Golden Age inaugurated Florida's modern two-party system, Democratic and Republican leaders shared an agenda in which partisan disputes were incidental rather than paramount. They worked hard to keep it that way.

"It was the greatest time in my life . . . the greatest time of [all] our lives as far as I'm concerned," said Richard A. Pettigrew, the other former Speaker present that night. Pettigrew, a liberal Democrat, had a friendship transcending party differences with House Republican leader Don Reed. It contributed to the passage of dozens of bills on which they agreed even when many of their own party members did not. Legislators of both parties followed their example, forming cross-party friendships that are conspicuously rare today. The most common complaint among Republicans was not that they could not pass bills but that Democrats would grab the credit.[4]

The Golden Age was the product of a peaceful revolution, a court-ordered reapportionment that overthrew the eight-decade reign of rural legislators who, with few exceptions, were racially and economically reactionary. That their successors accomplished so much owed immeasurably to the remarkable, once-in-a-generation leadership of a man who had left the legislature to defy the seemingly impossible odds against his being elected governor. The biography of Reubin O'Donovan Askew and the history of the Golden Age are inseparable.

Askew was governor of Florida from January 1971 to January 1979. In 1981, a paper presented to the Southern Political Science Association placed Askew among the "ten outstanding governors of the 20th Century," along with such luminaries as Robert La Follette, Woodrow Wilson, Alfred E. Smith, and Terry Sanford. Although Askew breathed life into what had been a nonexistent Democratic Party organization, his relations with the legislature were essentially nonpartisan; unlike his most conspicuously partisan successor, Jeb Bush (1999–2007), Askew cultivated both sides of the aisle. This was a necessity as well as a virtue, because Askew could not count upon—nor did he expect—Democratic legislators to follow in lockstep. Discipline as dogma did not occur to him, and it would not have occurred to any leaders of the 1970s to characterize their rank and file as "sheep."[5]

The Golden Age was remarkable for how far the legislature progressed in a very short time. Until the 1960s, it had been by at least one quantifiable measure the nation's worst. Under a constitutional formula unchanged since 1924, rural areas that made up less than 15 percent of the population could elect a majority of both houses. The Senate ruling clique, which *Tampa Tribune* editor James Clendenin famously nicknamed the Pork Chop Gang for its 1950s resistance to fair apportionment, were segregationists who would have closed the public schools but for Governor LeRoy Collins's 1957 veto, were deeply suspicious of the fast-growing coastal areas, and saw their responsibilities through the eyes of the special-interest lobbyists and bureaucrats upon whose advice they depended. The House of Representatives was nearly as reactionary. The legislature's noblest contribution that decade was to agree with Collins on establishing community colleges within fifty miles of every Floridian. They were of enormous worth as Florida's population more than tripled in the ensuing half century. In Askew's judgment, an urban legislature probably would have had different priorities.[6]

The legislature was overwhelmingly Democratic in name if not in spirit. This was a legacy of the Civil War and Reconstruction. The Democratic Party itself was, in effect, a shell corporation; political scientist V. O. Key Jr. famously wrote in 1949 that the Florida story was "every man for himself. . . . Florida is not only unbossed, it is unled." Democratic primaries—restricted to white voters before 1948—were the only elections that mattered. Governors built personal campaign organizations that dissolved upon victory because the constitution did not allow consecutive terms. Most power belonged to six officials known collectively as the Cabinet, who were not subject to term limits, were seldom opposed for reelection, and rarely risked their sinecures to run for governor or U.S. Senate. Democratic nominees, taking the general elections for granted, gave no thought to party organization, an indifference that the Republicans would exploit. Some county supervisors of elections automatically enrolled new voters as Democrats, warning them that to register Republican would waste their votes and perhaps their reputations. When Kenneth H. "Buddy" MacKay Jr. of Ocala returned from the Army and attempted to register as a Republican, the Marion County supervisor told him that doing so would "disgrace your family" and enrolled him as a Democrat. Many years later, MacKay would conclude a distinguished political career as Florida's last Democratic governor of the twentieth century.[7]

Pork Chop rule ended with a series of U.S. Supreme Court decisions that eventually forced the 1965 state legislature to reapportion with relative fairness. Askew, one of a handful of northern Florida legislators who supported equitable apportionment, managed the Senate bill. It eliminated or merged the districts of several of his friends, among them Senator Doyle Carlton Jr., a Collins ally, who later contributed $1,000 to an Askew opponent in 1970. Askew had stood for fair apportionment since his first Senate term, when former Senate president Dewey Johnson admonished him that "you've got a bright future, but it's going to be short . . . if you don't get right" and threatened to prevent construction of the University of West Florida, slated for Askew's hometown of Pensacola.[8] In the 1966 elections held pursuant to Askew's bill, Dade residents could vote for twenty-eight legislators elected county-wide and found more than four hundred names on their local ballots. The legislators had barely taken their seats at a special session in January 1967 when the U.S. Supreme Court ruled the plan unconstitutional because districts varied in population by as much as 40 percent, a spread that "can hardly be deemed '*de minimis*.'" The decision meant that states would have to justify *any* deviation from mathematical equality. The High Court sent the case back to a three-judge district court at Miami, which, out of patience with the legislature, ordered new elections and commissioned Manning J. Dauer, a University of Florida political science professor, to write a new plan. Dade, the largest county, would now have nine senators and twenty-two House members, all elected at-large. Hillsborough County shared eleven House members with three small counties that each formerly had its own. Only six single-member districts remained in the Senate and only three in the House.[9]

When the legislature convened in April 1967, 67 of the 119 House members were first-termers. Of the 48 senators, 25 were freshmen, although 13 of them had been in the House. The 92 newcomers were the most in Florida's modern history, exceeding even the 83 seats that changed hands when a term-limits initiative took its first toll in 2000. After the 1966 campaign, Dade freshman Bob Graham had been given a coveted seat on the House Appropriations Committee for his timely support to elect Ralph Turlington Speaker. The special election in March 1967 disposed of every senior Democrat on the higher education sub-committee, making Graham chairman by default. It was the first rung on his ladder to the governor's office twelve years later. The few return-ing legislators included a leadership cadre of urban progressives—Pet-tigrew, Reed, and Sessums among them—who had been stifled under rural rule. With the new members, they reinvented their state. "They were some of the most brilliant members in Florida's history. They came refreshed, young, eager to change the world. They did change the world of Florida," said environmentalist Nathaniel P. Reed.[10]

By the time Askew left office in January 1979, they had replaced Florida's obsolete 1885 constitution, a goal that had eluded Collins's best efforts; reorganized the judiciary and the executive branch; made the governor rather than the elected Cabinet responsible for the state budget; stopped cities from dumping raw sewage into the environment and created effective, enforceable pollution controls; established a pio-neering system of water-management districts; enacted restrictions on development and requirements for land-use planning; begun the purchase of environmentally sensitive land for recreation and preser-vation; limited campaign spending and required effective disclosure of campaign contributors; passed an open-meetings law and strengthened the public-records statute; registered lobbyists; stopped the commercial dredging and filling of bays and estuaries; enacted a tax on corporate profits and repealed the sales tax on household utilities and residential rentals; made the judiciary nonpartisan and provided for appointing rather than electing the appellate bench; created an ethics commission and required public officials to disclose their financial assets and liabilities; ordered due process in rule-making and other administrative procedures; passed a deceptive trade practices act modeled on federal law; instituted no-fault divorce and auto insurance; given utility consumers an advocate before the Public Service Commission and switched its membership from election to appointment; granted home rule to cities and counties; created a statewide juvenile justice system; required treatment rather than jail for alcoholics; protected the civil rights of the mentally ill; rewritten the school code to more nearly equalize spending between rich and poor counties; reformed property taxation; demanded effective regulation of nursing homes; capped the small-county shares of state racetrack revenue; redistributed gasoline taxes to help growing counties; and taxed the mining of phosphate and other minerals. The capitol in those years was an abattoir for sacred cows. The significant failures were few. Florida's refusal to ratify the proposed Equal Rights Amendment doomed the amendment's prospects for becoming part of the U.S. Constitution. In a spasm of homophobia, the 1977 legislature made Florida the only state that explicitly forbade gays and lesbians from adopting children. The tax base, heavily dependent on retail sales and residential construction, remained inadequate and left the state exceptionally vulnerable to swings in the national economy.

But the successes at the time eclipsed the shortcomings. "Government in Florida," wrote Jack Bass and Walter De Vries in *The Transformation of Southern Politics*, "was transformed almost overnight into a system far ahead of any other in the South in terms of its responsiveness to specific issues and its institutional ability to respond." What Dade representative Marshall Harris called "the ferment of reapportionment" conditioned him and others to think, "Hey, this legislature which has never done anything might finally begin to act on behalf of the people." They did not think of themselves as unique, though history would. "These were new faces thrust into an old institution, without ties—no ties to the leadership, no ties to the lobbyists, no ties to the old cabinet officers who had been there from time immemorial. They were brand new on the scene and they felt they were taking a fresh look at the institutions," Pettigrew said in 1985. There was also, as MacKay would remark, "a consensus for reform in the business community," excepting only a few diehards who tried to thwart Askew's tax reforms.[11]

The reforms that were fundamental to all the others improved the legislature itself. Before reapportionment, members worked without staffs, offices, or printed copies of bills and amendments. The legislature tacitly outsourced its fact-finding and bill-drafting functions to the lobbyists and bureaucracies. Members were paid only $100 a month and met for only sixty days every two years. Senate committee chairmen could "meet" by themselves, their pockets full of proxies signed by the absent members. By 1970, however, Rutgers University academician Alan B. Rosenthal could write that no other legislature "has made as much progress as Florida's." His account described the Florida legislature as having "emerged as the very picture of health . . . matched by few in the nation." The new leadership had provided, among other things, for professional staff, member offices, computers, printed bills, a public record of committee deliberations and roll-call votes, and interim committee meetings to prepare legislation in advance of the annual sessions specified by the 1968 constitution. The Senate adopted open hearings and due process in voting on whether to remove officials suspended by the governor. The auditor general and his staff now worked for the legislative branch instead of the executive. Members had increased their pay to $1,000 a month. In 1971 the Citizens Conference on State Legislatures ranked Florida's first nationally in independence and fourth-best overall; it was the only southern state among the top twenty-five. Speaking at a seminar during his seventh month as governor, Askew said that the legislature's independence was a tonic for the executive branch. He remarked, however, that "I'm beginning to think we have the most independent legislative branch since Parliament beheaded the king."[12]

2

CLAUDIUS REX (1966–1970)

Both Reubin Askew's election and the legislature's newfound independence owed greatly to a man who had intended neither result. He was the governor before Askew, Claude R. Kirk Jr. Bombastic, flamboyant, and carefree in his use of public money to indulge and promote himself, Kirk gave the legislature plenty of grist for its investigating committees and provided a perfect contrast for an opponent so serious, studious, and abstemious that the *New York Times* labeled Askew "Florida's Supersquare." Indeed, Askew said it was Kirk's conduct that set his mind to running against the incumbent.[1]

Kirk's poor legislative relations began moments after Florida's first Republican governor in ninety-four years began his inaugural address outside Florida's old capitol on January 3, 1967. It was wet and cold in Tallahassee; many legislators were already in a poor frame of mind when Kirk startled them by saying he would call them into special session six days later to adopt a new constitution. Kirk, forty-one years old, was an insurance executive who had not held public office and disdained its protocol. He had not alerted Senate president Verle A. Pope of St. Augustine or House Speaker Ralph Turlington of Gainesville, who were embarrassed to admit to the news media that the governor had not forewarned them of the special session. Nearly as stunning was Kirk's announcement that he had hired a private investigator, George Wackenhut, to direct a "governor's war on crime" that would be financed by private contributions. He escorted a beautiful blonde woman, whom he would not identify, to his inaugural ball that night and left on a vacation barely twelve hours after taking office. Having begun badly, Kirk's relations with the legislature steadily degenerated over budget issues, his ethics, and a statewide teacher strike, and hit bottom when he vetoed a legislative pay raise that Republican legislators insisted he had promised to accept.[2]

Kirk biographer Edmund F. Kallina Jr. accurately described the governor's style as "the politics of confrontation." Kirk reveled in insulting Pope, a man widely revered as the "Lion of St. Johns" (his county) for his unyielding opposition to special interests and the Pork Chop Gang. Kirk called Turlington "stupid," an assessment shared by no one else. He ridiculed Superintendent of Public Instruction Floyd T. Christian, who had once been a coach, saying that Christian "could do everything with a football except sign it." Kirk's persistent feud with U.S. representative William C. Cramer of St. Petersburg, the state's senior Republican officeholder, contributed to the defeats of both of them in 1970. Kirk claimed that Cramer had schemed to replace him on the 1966 ticket when it became obvious that Democratic incumbent Haydon Burns was vulnerable.[3]

Many people shared Kirk's desire for a new constitution, which was being recommended by a blue-ribbon commission. The state's 1885 constitution, which had been adopted to erase the liberal reforms of post–Civil War Reconstruction, was functionally obsolete for a fast-growing state of nearly 7 million residents. It made the governors weak by limiting them to single terms and forcing them to share power with six other officials elected statewide—the so-called Cabinet. By 1969, depending upon who was counting, there were between 170 and 220 legally distinct state agencies, some run by the governor, others by individual Cabinet officers, and the rest by boards comprising the governor and Cabinet members. The constitution precluded home rule for cities and counties, limited regular sessions of the legislature to sixty consecutive days every other year, and befogged the judicial system with widely varying jurisdictions in different counties. It had been patched with 151 amendments; voters had rejected 63 others, including three token reapportionments proposed by the Pork Choppers. Even so, a considerate or prudent governor would have given Florida's part-time legislators more than six days to reschedule their business affairs before convening a special session. He would also have waited for the U.S. Supreme

Court's impending action on the legislature's current apportionment. The members had barely assembled on January 9 for Kirk's special session when the Court declared the legislature unconstitutional, leaving it powerless to act on anything but another reapportionment. When the Senate closed its doors, supposedly to discuss gubernatorial appointments, four reporters who suspected the real subject was reapportionment refused to leave the galleries. Senators raged at them, and the sergeants at arms led them forcibly out of the chamber, but the publicity ensured that it would be the last such secret session.[4]

Kirk had run against conservative Democratic senator Spessard Holland in 1964. Kirk knew he would lose but intended to make himself known for the governor's race two years later.[5] He won the 1966 nomination for governor almost by default, easily defeating one opponent in the Republican primary. Few people thought Burns could be defeated, least of all in the new off-year election schedule that the Democrats had set up after a Republican candidate polled 40 percent on Richard Nixon's coattails in 1960. It allowed the governor elected to a two-year term in 1964 to run for a full term in 1966. Seeking a major accomplishment on which to campaign, Burns—nicknamed "Old Slick" when mayor of Jacksonville—persuaded the legislature to send the voters a $300 million road bond issue in a November 1965 special election. To get the necessary supermajorities for an off-year referendum, Burns traded questionable roads and other pork-barrel projects for members' votes, employing what Senator Ed H. Price Jr. called "the roughest and toughest" organized lobbying he had ever seen. A group of legislators whom Burns called "the Dirty Dozen"—among them future governors Askew and Lawton Chiles—rallied voters to reject the plan, humiliating Burns and exposing his weakness. Six months after the referendum, Burns lost the 1966 nomination in a rematch runoff with Miami mayor Robert King High.[6]

High's victory was Pyrrhic; it left the Democrats bitterly divided. The 1966 Democratic primary, as historian David Colburn describes it, was "a repeat battle between Democratic voters of North Florida, representing natives, Crackers, and racial conservatives, against those of South Florida, representing migrants from the Northeast, refugees from Cuba, and political moderates and liberals." Although the sectional conflict had defined Democratic primaries since 1954, Kirk was the first Republican whom conservative Democrats considered a plausible alternative. Kirk promised Florida "no advance or increases in taxes of any kind" and relentlessly labeled High an "ultraliberal." To some voters, that was a coded message about segregation, still prevalent in Florida. Many whites resented President Lyndon Johnson's historic Civil Rights Act of 1964 and Voting Rights Act of 1965. Burns refused to endorse High and helped Kirk, who won with 55 percent. High carried only eleven of the state's sixty-seven counties.[7]

That day, Republican legislative candidates took advantage of the 1966 apportionment to win twenty-two seats in the House and ten in the Senate, a significant increase over their 1965 total of twelve seats. Inspired by Kirk's victory, they ran many more candidates in the special reapportionment election four months later. Helped by low voter turnout, they took 39 seats in the 119-member House and 20 in the 48-member Senate, enabling them to sustain Kirk's vetoes by voting en bloc. "The big things were the popularity of Kirk and the unpopularity of President Johnson," said Kenneth Plante, an Oviedo businessman who defeated Florida's first female senator, Democrat Beth Johnson of Orlando. The chairman of the appropriations committee, the third most influential position in the Senate, was among nine senators who had won in November but lost in March. Pope insisted that Askew replace him. It became the genesis of Askew's rise to the governorship.[8]

Kirk took office owing nothing to the lobbies that were accustomed to controlling the Democrats they had helped to elect. Many of the legislature's new leaders were similarly unencumbered; Kirk's administration had the potential to be progressive and successful like none before. When the mood was right, he could be eloquent, persuasive, even charismatic. Senator Louis de la Parte Jr., a Democrat who worked well with Kirk on human services issues, once said of him, "I don't want to get in the same room with that guy. I'm afraid he might charm me." Kirk's disdain for rules and his flair for showmanship could serve good purposes on occasion, as when in 1970 he flew down to the Florida State Prison and removed two boys, age fourteen and sixteen, who had been sent there by a harsh judge. En route to the prison, Kirk admitted to Charlotte Maguire, an assistant secretary of the Department of Health and Rehabilitative Services, that he had no idea where to relocate the boys. She reminded him that the Division of Youth Services, thanks to de la Parte, had a new halfway house near Tallahassee. The public liked what Kirk did that day. But Kirk also wasted many opportunities due to his lack of tact and discretion. The 1976 *Almanac of American Politics* called him "a man whose flamboyance seemed to have degenerated into asininity."[9]

Kirk's "war on crime" was a ten-month fiasco that bagged only a relatively few corrupt or incompetent county commissioners and sheriffs and left Wackenhut to write off $280,000 that Kirk owed. However, it had the constructive result of prodding the 1967 legislature into creating what is now the Florida Department of Law Enforcement. The agency replaced the Florida Sheriffs' Bureau, which had been run by elected sheriffs, some of whom bore investigation themselves. Although the constitution of 1968 and the reorganization act of 1969 were enacted on Kirk's watch, those historic achievements could have been even better had the governor conducted himself with more diplomacy and less confrontation.[10]

Kirk's record on the environment was the luminous aspect of his administration. The governor took his lead on natural resources from Nathaniel Pryor Reed of Hobe Sound, an early recruit to his campaign whose financial independence enabled him to devote his life to protecting Florida's environment. Reed came to Kirk's attention by way of his opposition to Cramer's faction. Although Reed and Kirk seemed to have little in common, Reed found that Kirk's sense of humor "tickled my ribs." He marveled at Kirk's ability to function despite excessive consumption of alcohol. If he had any serious misgivings about the man, he sublimated them to his strong dislike of Burns, who was no environmentalist. "Claude basically was a populist," Reed said of him years later. "He was a lousy conservative Republican. That was all an act, all of that thunder and lightning." Whether Kirk was sensitive to the environment before he met Reed is open to question, but he did listen to Reed and followed his advice. Reed took only a dollar a year in salary as Kirk's environmental adviser and as chairman of the newly created Air and Water Pollution Control Board.[11]

Kirk had made generalized campaign promises, notably, to "make Florida first in the nation in education," which would be impossible to reconcile with his anti-tax pledge. Like Ronald Reagan a few years later, Kirk professed that lower taxes would yield higher revenue. When the media pressed for details, he referred elusively to still-unwritten "white papers." His new campaign adviser, a veteran Republican professional named Robert Lee, saw to it that the white papers would be both bulky and late, which discouraged the media from looking too closely into them. Having learned only during a Kirk speech that he was supposed to be writing white papers on the environment, Reed could not find the time to prepare them. Kirk's showmanship and Lee's strategy concealed the candidate's inexperience and unfamiliarity with Florida government. "He didn't even know how many members there were in the legislature, he didn't know what Cabinet officers there were, he didn't know anything about state government. And he didn't bother to learn a whole hell of a lot about it while he was governor. He spent a lot of time enjoying being governor," Don Reed said later. He conceded, however, that Kirk had the benefit of "super advice" from Nathaniel Reed and some others.[12]

In 1967, Florida cities were discharging raw sewage into the Atlantic Ocean, the St. Johns River, and other waterways. "Dilution was the 'cure' for pollution," Nat Reed said. That was stopped. Florida was notorious for selling its submerged sovereignty land to developers who clogged estuaries and destroyed marine habitat by building subdivisions on dredged-up sand. That ended also, largely because of the Randell-Thomas Act of 1967, which required the governor and Cabinet to consider the environmental impact of such projects. Another measure forbade the sale of state-owned submerged land when "contrary to the public interest." When a delegation of developers asked Kirk to water down the restrictions and rid himself of Reed, Kirk replied, "Gentlemen, there's plenty of work in the Bahamas." Under Reed's tutelage, Kirk reversed his support for Islandia, a proposed grandiose development in Biscayne Bay, and endorsed the 1968 federal action that protected the bay by creating the Biscayne National Monument. Kirk and Reed also influenced the Nixon administration to halt construction of the environmentally hazardous Cross-Florida Barge Canal and thwarted further construction on what would have been a massive "jetport" in the Everglades, limiting its one completed runway to use as a pilot training facility.[13]

Nathaniel Reed, education adviser Charles Perry, and legal assistant Wade Hopping were the principal Kirk aides who maintained good relations with the legislature. They were non-ideological and unafraid to tell Kirk when they thought he was wrong. Reed and Askew often found themselves leaving the capitol building at the same late-night hours and struck up a casual friendship, with Reed enlisting the senator to sponsor much of his legislation. The two men were nearly the same age—Reed thirty-four, Askew thirty-nine—and shared a devotion to nonpartisan public policy. Their relationship confounded Kirk, not merely because Askew was a Democrat. "He's a mumbler," Kirk complained to Reed. "Why don't you pick a powerhouse in the Senate to represent you? Picking a guy from *Pensacola*? Pensacola is in *Alabama*!" Reed replied simply that Askew was effective at passing Reed's bills. "He is like one of those great Presbyterian elders who come into your life," Reed said of Askew years later. "His motivation, the purity of his motivation, and that focus that he could put on the problem were really astonishing."[14]

LeRoy Collins had questioned the role of the Cabinet, but Kirk was the first governor to be openly hostile to it. In the summer of 1967 he began calling it "the committee." Decrying the personal and staff time invested in briefings for its weekly meetings, Kirk began to attend only every other week and threatened to withhold his signature from checks authorized in his absence. At Secretary of State Tom Adams's urging, the Cabinet continued meeting weekly, forcing Kirk to end his biweekly boycott. As governor, Askew eventually persuaded the Cabinet to meet every other week. Although other states elected multiple executives, Florida was unique in the extent to which they governed collectively. The 1885 constitution provided for a five-member board of education on which the elected secretary of state, attorney general, treasurer, and superintendent of public instruction would have votes equal to the governor's. (The agriculture commissioner and comptroller were not members of that board.) Subsequently, the legislature employed the Cabinet system for many new functions. All six Cabinet officers sat with the governor on boards managing state institutions and natural resources. Moreover, the comptroller was also the state banking commissioner and the treasurer became ex officio the insurance commissioner; the roles were rich in patronage and potential for abuse. The Cabinet was notable also for close ties to the Pork Chop Gang. Adams himself had been a Pork Chop senator. A former Senate president, W. Randolph Hodges of Cedar Key, headed the Cabinet's marine resources agency. The governor's exclusive patronage was limited to building roads; issuing liquor licenses; staffing the motor vehicle, hotel and restaurant, racing, and development commissions; and making appointments to state and local boards and vacant local offices. Telephone, power, and gas companies were regulated—more in theory than in fact—by an elected three-member commission whose senior member, Jerry Carter, once described himself as "a cheap politician—the only kind my constituents can afford."[15]

Many younger Democrats opposed the Cabinet system. Their leader was Richard Pettigrew, an idealistic thirty-six-year-old lawyer who in November 1970 would become the first Speaker of the House from Miami and only the second from southeast Florida. His political science studies at the University of Florida made him as passionate about reorganizing government as some of his peers were about football. He favored "a strong chief executive and a counterbalance, a strong legislative body." So did Don Reed, the House Republican leader. But to their mutual dismay, Kirk's conduct as governor was an obstacle to reforming the system. The month after his inauguration, Kirk, a divorced father of four whose alimony and child support exceeded his salary as governor, had married the "Madame X" of his inaugural ball—Erika Mattfeld, a German-born divorcée he had met in Brazil. After their delayed honeymoon in Europe, the *St. Petersburg Times* revealed that the state had paid for their airline tickets. Kirk complimented the reporter and reimbursed the cost. By year's end the House was investigating the Florida Development Commission, a tourism and industrial promotion agency under the governor, in reaction to a *Times* report that the agency's $90,000-a-year contract with New York publicist William Safire was secretly intended to promote Kirk for the 1968 Republican vice-presidential nomination. Bill Beaufort, the commission's former chairman, confirmed the hidden intent of the contract. "The governor pushed the contract across the desk for me to sign," Beaufort said. "We felt that the advertising value to the State of Florida and all the development from that would be well worth the money that would be spent." Beaufort quit when Kirk installed his press secretary as the commission's executive director. Kirk had been governor less than three months when he set his sights on the White House. In the fall, he had the commission mail twenty-five thousand Christmas cards, many of them to Republican Party officials in other states. He ordered a large set of china emblazoned with his personal seal, a stylized eagle, for the governor's mansion and flew eagle flags on his chauffeured limousine. Floridians even found the governor's face staring at them from elevator inspection cards.[16]

Kirk wanted to be the 1968 running mate for former vice-president Richard M. Nixon. When Kirk realized that Nixon did not want him, he abruptly endorsed New York governor Nelson Rockefeller for the presidency. That outraged Florida Republicans who were loyal to Nixon or considered Rockefeller too liberal; at the nominating convention, Rockefeller won only one of Florida's thirty-four votes: Kirk's. When the Florida Republican Party eventually stopped paying for Kirk's travel on a leased jet, he established a personal slush fund called "The Governor's Club." He tried to keep the contributor list secret, but the Florida Supreme Court forced him to divulge to a legislative committee the names of 233 donors of funds totaling $420,680. State contractors, liquor licensees, and appointees to various boards dominated the list, resulting in the Senate's refusal to confirm Kirk's transportation secretary, Michael O'Neil, who had helped set up the Governor's Club. Kirk also lost his battle for control of the Florida Republican Party. He was unable to block the election of C. W. Bill Young, a Cramer ally, as Senate minority leader, and after he put Nathaniel Reed up to opposing Cramer for a seat on the Republican National Committee, Reed wisely withdrew.[17]

Kirk was beginning to squander the friendship of Don Reed, who had named one of his children after the governor. Reed described a cognac-fueled argument with Kirk concerning William Murfin, a Cramer ally who was state Republican chairman: Kirk "leaned over and drew his finger across the carpet . . . and told me that if I was with Murfin, I was obviously against him. I laid a few expletives on him and walked out. . . . He felt he was king and that was that." Kirk's thirst for alcohol, an open secret in Tallahassee, contributed to his problems with the legislature. Representative Frederick H. Schultz, House Speaker during Kirk's final two years, told of seeing Kirk consume the equivalent of twelve martinis during a meeting at the mansion one night. "You couldn't trust what he told you," Schultz said, "because he felt if it was in his best interest to do something else, he'd do it."[18]

Service in the legislature during Kirk's first year cost most members more than they had expected. The budget dispute outlasted the sixty-day regular session and kept them intermittently in Tallahassee until August, for a total of 102 calendar days. The duration strained marriages as well as finances; Peter Dunbar, an aide to Don Reed, subsequently counted thirty-seven divorces among members of the House. Most of those marriages might have survived the casual affairs that were known to occur during two-month sessions in Tallahassee, but as Don Reed once observed to a reporter, "Five months was long enough to fall in love." The legislature also worked on the constitution during that long summer but eventually gave up.[19]

As a parting gift to James E. "Nick" Connor, the last Pork Chop Senate president, the 1965 session had voted to build a psychiatric hospital in his rural home county, Hernando. Critics dubbed it Hernando's Hideaway, the title of a tune from the musical *Pajama Game*. The first bill introduced in the newly reapportioned 1967 House was a measure by Representative Kenneth Myers, a Miami Democrat, that repealed Hernando's Hideaway. The legislation substituted two new facilities in urban settings, as mental health professionals advocated. Amid other post–Pork Chop reforms, the legislature enacted codes of ethics for lobbyists, legislators, and state employees; required governmental public boards and commissions to meet in public; and revised the gasoline tax to spend more on urban roads. In some ways, however, the special interests proved as influential under the new regime as under the old. A paper company lobbyist wrote generous tax breaks into the pollution control legislation, the phosphate industry fought off a severance tax, and the legislature created a private government for the exclusive benefit of Walt Disney World, the tourist attraction that would transform central Florida. Pope and Turlington, who described themselves as "sort of a bridge between the old and the new," had given some key committee assignments, notably in finance and taxation, to legislators whom the *St. Petersburg Times* described as "old hands attuned to the special interests."[20]

The longest-running, costliest battle was over education financing. A series of Kirk vetoes frustrated the legislature. The House voted 105–1 to override a veto affecting universities and junior colleges, but the Senate held firm for Kirk. Meanwhile, public school teachers insisted upon pay raises they thought Kirk had promised, but he was adamant against tax increases. The Florida Education Association threatened a statewide teacher walkout. In June the National Education Association censured Kirk (undoubtedly to his delight) and urged teachers elsewhere to boycott jobs in Florida. There was a tense confrontation in Kirk's office with Democratic legislators including Pope, Turlington, and Askew over Kirk's televised claim that he had recommended a better budget than the legislature's. As the lawmakers saw it, Kirk's budget was some $35 million in the red (the constitution forbade deficit spending). Turlington called Kirk a "very clever man," with a tone in his voice that made clear it was no compliment. Kirk challenged him: did he mean what he implied? Yes, Turlington said, he did. As Askew remembered the incident, Kirk was proposing to "balance" the budget by double-counting some projected savings and by issuing bonds that would require a referendum. "I said, 'It's unbalanced, let's not do this,'" Askew recalled. "He said, 'Well now, senator, you say it's unbalanced. I say it isn't. Who do you think that truck driver is going to believe, me or you?'" Kirk's cynicism, Askew said, "shook me to the core." Like many another senator, Askew had thought casually about eventually running for governor. That afternoon, he began to think about it seriously.[21] To embarrass Kirk, the House Democrats called up a budget bill that matched Kirk's dollar-for-dollar and prepared to pass it on the spot, forcing Republican leaders—who understood fiscal reality much better than Kirk did—to stage a brief filibuster. The legislature soon passed the bill, and Kirk uncapped his veto pen. "Claude Kirk," Turlington said, "is the only governor in my eighteen years in government to get exactly the budget he has asked for. I can't understand why he vetoed parts of his own bill." The Democrats' turn at showmanship irked Don Reed, who was beginning to regret having helped Turlington secure the speakership. Although the Democrats had righteous objections to many of the forty-five vetoes Kirk signed that year, including one that blocked Medicaid implementation in Florida, their hands were not spotless. When Manatee County's Democratic delegation tried to rename the Sarasota-Bradenton Airport as the Bradenton-Sarasota Airport, it became a partisan issue. Only six House Democrats joined the Republicans in opposing it. Kirk vetoed that bill, too.[22]

The two-year budget finally enacted in August was plainly inadequate, and the teachers were still threatening mass resignations. At a special session in January and February 1968, Kirk proposed to raise the sales tax from three cents on the dollar to five if voters would agree to replace the Cabinet education structure with an appointed board and superintendent. Although it refused to link the issues, the legislature authorized a referendum on an appointed superintendent and board. Floyd Christian, in what the Democrats hailed as a noble gesture, consented to "let the people decide." The legislature approved a fourth cent of sales tax, the repeal of some exemptions, and higher taxes on cigarettes. At the time it was the largest tax increase in Florida history, and it happened on the watch of a governor who had promised no new taxes. But the teachers union thought it did not earmark enough money to the public schools and turned in approximately thirty-four thousand resignations. On February 19 roughly half of Florida's teachers were absent from class. Flouting his education adviser's urgent advice to stay in Tallahassee, Kirk was in California when the walkout began. He visited Disneyland, where he shook hands with a mechanical ape and wisecracked, "Verle Pope, I believe." According to Kirk, the trip was essential "to finish bringing Disney World to Florida." Although the teacher walkout was extremely unpopular with the public, so was Kirk's absence, and many voters took that memory to the polls in 1970. The schools remained open with parents and others volunteering as teachers, and the strike collapsed within three weeks. The effects persisted. Some school boards refused to rehire teachers who had resigned. Biographer Edmund F. Kallina Jr. wrote that the episode "inflicted lasting damage" on Kirk and "poisoned the atmosphere and destroyed what little chance was left for real educational change."[23]

During a special session on the constitution in June 1968, the legislature withdrew the pending amendment that would have put Kirk in charge of education governance. It was obviously foredoomed at the polls. Don Reed, unwilling to "whip a dead dog," said he would not push for Cabinet reform in the new constitution. A *St. Petersburg Times* editorial predicted sourly that the new constitution would do "little for anyone." Twenty-eight lame-duck legislators, defeated in the May 1968 primaries or voluntarily retiring, returned in June to vote on the new constitution. The session put to rest the dreams of some south Florida legislators of moving the seat of government to a central location near Orlando. The consensus was to replace the old capitol building instead; Tallahassee's fire marshal warned that had the building belonged to the city he would have shut it down. The need was undeniable; some offices and committee chambers were in windowless attic rooms without emergency exits.[24]

Kirk had no discernible influence on the content of the new constitution, which was not subject to his veto. In eight days, the legislature concluded a debate that had begun under Governor LeRoy Collins in 1955, and the key votes of thirty-seven to nine in the Senate and ninety-four to sixteen in the House were comfortably greater than the necessary three-fifths. But as the *St. Petersburg Times* had predicted, it was more bland than bold. It acknowledged the Cabinet, unmentioned by name in the 1885 constitution. Florida would remain the only state with a constitutional ban on taxing incomes or estates, a relic of a short-lived Florida land boom in the 1920s. New ceilings on local government taxing rates would make budgeting more difficult for cities, counties, and school boards. The homestead property tax exemption, adopted to rescue homeowners during the Great Depression, was retained and expanded to include condominiums and cooperative apartments, and was doubled (to $10,000) for people over sixty-five. A motion to lower the voting age to nineteen failed. There was no attempt to act on court reform. However, there were important structural innovations: annual legislative sessions; mandatory reapportionment every ten years based on population, with automatic review by the Florida Supreme Court; two terms for governors; an elected lieutenant governor (since 1885, the Senate president had been the designated successor); stronger home rule for cities and counties; and a requirement that the legislature reorganize the executive branch. In a rare act of self-sacrifice, the Senate agreed to give up eight of its forty-eight seats in the next redistricting. The most significant changes allowed the new constitution to be amended without the consent of the legislature. These procedures included a voter initiative process and appointment of a revision commission to meet in 1978 and every twenty years thereafter. The commission's amendments would go directly to the ballot. A third new method, a constitutional convention summoned by voter petition, has not been invoked. The new constitution was, as Senator John E. Mathews Jr. remarked, the product of "twelve to fifteen years of tribulation" during which the Pork Choppers had blocked repeated efforts by Collins to weaken their control. Conceding the new constitution to be imperfect, Pope rationalized that it "will serve as a vehicle for later constitutional reforms." For Lawton Chiles, it was analogous to breaking a big rock. "You don't break that big rock with one lick, you chip away at it," he said. Yet he failed to persuade his friend and customary ally, Louis de la Parte of Tampa, who said he was weary of hearing "it's this or nothing" and was particularly critical of the income tax, property tax rate limitations, and voting-age outcomes. "We can all say we're for quality education but we've done nothing in the constitution to let the Legislature handle it properly," de la Parte said. Although Askew disapproved of the product, he voted in favor of letting the voters decide. Most newspapers endorsed the constitution, but not the *St. Petersburg Times* or the *Orlando Sentinel*, which objected to a lieutenant governor as "nothing more than an expensive office boy for the governor." The *Miami Herald* expressed the prevailing media viewpoint: the November 5 vote would be "perhaps the last chance in this century." The *Tampa Tribune* pronounced it a net gain for good government but deplored the tax restrictions and the inaction on the judiciary.[25]

The new constitution was presented to the voters as three separate questions. They were ratified narrowly and with little enthusiasm. Some 55 percent agreed to the basic document incorporating most of the changes, but the total vote of 1.1 million was barely half the turnout in the more dramatic contests for the U.S. presidency and the seat of retiring U.S. senator George Smathers. With nearly 58 percent, Congressman Edward Gurney became the first Florida Republican elected to the

Senate by popular vote, defeating LeRoy Collins. He won in much the same style as Kirk had, by portraying his opponent as "Liberal LeRoy" and hammering daily at "crime, law and order, and taxes." The Senate race, like the contest for Florida's electoral votes, played out against a national backdrop of urban riots, the memorably divisive Democratic National Convention at Chicago, and deepening domestic strife over the war in Vietnam. It appeared to some that Kirk's election had been no fluke. The Republican tide failed, however, to carry the party's three state supreme court candidates—among them Wade Hopping, whom Kirk had appointed to a vacancy three months before. Kirk, meanwhile, had overplayed his hand in a vainglorious attempt to control the state Senate, where the Republicans lost four of their twenty seats and failed to oust Kirk's priority target, Verle Pope. The Republicans gained three seats in the House, preserving the veto-sustaining power they had just lost in the Senate. It would not take long, however, for Kirk to squander that advantage.[26]

3

THE DOUBLE CROSS
(1969–1970)

The new constitution required the legislature convening in April 1969 to rebuild the entire Florida government for the first time since the aftermath of the Civil War. By July 1 there could be no more than twenty-five departments in the executive branch apart from those specified in the constitution. That the job was completed without another long, hot summer in Tallahassee was a tribute to two remarkable Democratic politicians: Richard A. Pettigrew, chairman of the House committee on reorganization, and Frederick H. Schultz, the Speaker, who backed him up despite withering pressure from the Cabinet.

Schultz, age forty, was an independently wealthy Jacksonville businessman and banker who had nearly been thrown out of Princeton University for breaking "pretty much all of the rules that they had." The mature Schultz was a skilled legislator and an outstanding Speaker whom the Republicans credited with the bipartisanship they had found lacking before he took the gavel. Schultz gave the Republicans an office near his own, proportional representation on most committees, and an accommodation that Minority Leader Don Reed described as "Wherever we can agree, we will agree. If we can't agree, instead of playing games with us, let's get it out on the floor and get it over with and get back to the important things." Schultz served later as vice-chairman of the Federal Reserve.[1]

Pettigrew and Schultz, House members since the first reapportionment in 1963, had been friendly rivals for the Speaker's term that

Schultz won. Pettigrew was virtually assured of succeeding him. When Schultz offered him the chairmanship of the reorganization committee, both men understood that the task would jeopardize Pettigrew's ambition to be Speaker, but neither could imagine anyone else for the job. Pettigrew had already sacrificed greatly to remain in the legislature. A March 1967 opinion by the Florida Bar's ethics committee had forced him to choose between leaving office and resigning from the prominent law firm where he had begun his career ten years earlier. The ruling, since repealed, deemed it improper for a legislator's law partner to lobby the legislature even if the lawmaker abstained, as Pettigrew did, on the lobbyist's issues. A senior partner in Pettigrew's firm held the lucrative Hialeah racetrack lobbying account. Ironically, the firm had intended for Pettigrew to capitalize on his legislative experience by becoming the Hialeah lobbyist eventually. Instead, he chose to leave the firm. With duties in Tallahassee taking most of his time, it would be a long while before his law practice prospered again. For the seven years he remained in the legislature, his wife, Ann, made many of their children's clothes.[2]

The Cabinet members remembered Pettigrew as a foe of their institution during his service on the Constitution Revision Commission. In March 1969, Pettigrew's consulting firm, Booz, Allen, and Hamilton, confirmed the Cabinet's fears and aroused scores of lobbies by recommending a strong-governor reorganization. The governor would be responsible for eighteen departments, including an appointed board to regulate utilities, insurance, and banking. The Cabinet would retain no collective function except the Board of Education, and then only until the constitution could be amended again. The report said the Cabinet system was "incomprehensible to the public" and that its members were not publicly accountable for many of their actions. Doyle Conner, the commissioner of agriculture, dismissed it as recommending little "of practical value in Florida." In the Senate, Cabinet allies controlled the counterpart to Pettigrew's committee. Senator Mallory Horne of Tallahassee, a former House Speaker, called the report "subjective orientation falling just short of fraud." He accused the consultants of writing reports "the way those who pay them want them written."[3]

The Senate intended to consolidate agencies under the governor and Cabinet collectively, reducing the governor's already limited authority.

A substantial bloc of House Democrats had the same objective. Carey Matthews, Schultz's majority leader, spoke of "rising sentiment for the Senate approach, or major portions anyway." Matthews had a conflict of interest in that regard; he had earned more than $200,000 in fees from a failing casualty insurance company that Treasurer/Insurance Commissioner Broward Williams should have shut down. Matthews eventually resigned his seat and was sentenced to probation on federal fraud charges. Legislators involved in state-chartered banks were equally sensitive to the comptroller's objections to reorganization. Nearly every legislator heard from constituents in the insurance and banking industries who were responding to Cabinet members' appeals for grassroots lobbying. Even cemetery owners lobbied; Comptroller Fred O. "Bud" Dickinson Jr. regulated them as well as banks. Although Republican legislators were subject to the same lobbying, they backed Pettigrew to a greater extent than many of his fellow Democrats did. Don Reed had served with Pettigrew on the Constitution Revision Commission and shared his low opinion of the Cabinet system. So did Kirk, of course, but that was no help.[4]

Kirk had not objected while legislators, freed from the old constitution's $1,200-a-year salary limit, were considering a pay raise. Because of annual sessions and the new interim committee meetings, their jobs were now part-time more in theory than in fact. They were already evading the ceiling with $600 a month in unvouchered expense allowances; the leadership promised to require documentation in exchange for a salary increase. Schultz and his deputies, wary of the governor, let Reed introduce and manage the pay raise, which he had assured them Kirk would accept. Schultz said he had heard the same promise from Kirk himself. On April 17 the House voted seventy-eight to thirty-eight to set the pay at $12,000 a year. The Senate agreed the next day; fourteen Democrats and only three Republicans voted no. Among the opponents were Askew and Fred Karl, a highly respected former House member, who warned his colleagues, "If you vote for this you aren't coming back except on a visit."[5]

Kirk still had said nothing; his silence was becoming as ominous as the vehement opposition of the state's most pro-Republican newspaper, the *Orlando Sentinel*, which called the pay raise "an inflationary and ruthless raid on the public treasury" and "gluttonous feeding at the public trough." The editorializing was not confined to the opinion pages; its news coverage of the "legislative relief bill" was consistently one-sided, bristling with pejoratives such as "whopping," "pell mell," "greased," "plush," and "goodies." The newspaper printed mail-in coupons and two front-page petitions against the raise. Reed reiterated to the House that Kirk had promised Republican legislative leaders there would be no veto. C. W. Bill Young, the Senate minority leader, affirmed Reed's account of the meeting. A few hours later, however, Kirk asked for permission to address a joint session the next day. After briefly acknowledging the legislators' hard work, his speech cut to the quick. To the citizens, Kirk said, it appeared the legislature had acted with "almost indecent haste and no attention to public feeling." Legislators deserved more money, he said, but not that much. He said legislators were profiting from the laws they passed, putting their families on the payroll, ignoring purchasing and budgeting processes that applied elsewhere, drawing expense money by committee policy instead of by law, and auditing everyone's spending but their own. The public expected him to veto the bill, Kirk said, and so he would. Should the legislature adopt certain reforms, such as a law that "will remove conflicts of interest rather than paper them over," Kirk said, the public would be more tolerant. Although there was truth in his criticisms, the speech was political theater calculated to embarrass the legislature. Kirk did not seem to care whether the veto would stick; either way, the public would applaud him for it and the legislators would bear the blame.[6]

There was no applause when he had finished until some citizens in the gallery began to clap and a few legislators followed desultorily. Kirk had hardly left the House chamber when Reed, his face tense with fury, took the microphone to apologize to members who had relied on his faith in "the man downstairs." Young complained that Kirk had "painted every member of this legislature as a thief." Republican leaders began referring to Kirk's "Duck's Nest" mansion at Palm Beach as "the Rat's Nest." Representative Marshall Harris of Miami, a Democrat and close Pettigrew ally, complained that Kirk had "killed reorganization." Pettigrew called off a committee meeting that day, fearing that the members would fulfill Harris's prediction. Pro-Cabinet senators gloated. If Kirk had not doomed reorganization, he had clearly obliterated the party lines in the legislature, if only for the moment. As one of only four twentieth-century governors who had not served in the legislature, Kirk was insensitive to the institutional pride and loyalties of its members. It was accepted—indeed, expected—that the House and Senate would quarrel and that governors occasionally would veto legislation, but for Kirk to flaunt his veto in their faces was unforgivable. Most legislators believed Kirk had broken his word, and they could not forgive that either. "I have no further confidence in his integrity whatsoever," said Senator Joseph A. McClain, a Tampa Republican and former law professor. Two months later, McClain's secretary wrote to Askew to encourage him to run for governor and to offer her help. "That's when the Republicans in the legislature and Kirk split ways. It led to his eventual defeat. . . . Some of us were not sorry," said Bill James, one of Reed's successors as minority leader. Although Kirk insisted that he had promised no more than a "reasonable" raise, his defense was unpersuasive. As Kirk biographer Kallina points out, Kirk had said nothing before the bill was passed to contradict Reed's public statements that he would accept it. The *Orlando Sentinel*'s Tallahassee bureau chief, D. G. Lawrence, acknowledged that Kirk had given "at least tacit approval" to the raise, perhaps assuming the legislature would act first on the expense accounts and nepotism issues. But to Reed, and indeed to others, the salary increase was an essential institutional reform.[7]

Senator Bill Gunter, an Orlando Democrat who opposed the raise, advised Kirk to let tempers cool before sending his written veto message to the House. Kirk ignored him, setting up a showdown the day after the speech. As leaders lined up votes to override the veto, the *Tampa Tribune* asked why legislators of either party "would have expected anything else from a governor whose record is most notable for political expediency." Fifteen House members and five senators who had opposed the pay raise switched sides to help override the veto by votes of eighty-nine to twenty-three and thirty-five to ten, well above the two-thirds necessary. Schultz made a personal appeal that colleagues credited with changing votes. The pay-raise issue "was never an important one," Schultz said, but it was no longer the question: "The issue is clearly that the governor of this state questioned the integrity of every man and woman on the floor of this House. . . . [H]e clearly challenged the independence of the legislative branch. . . . This may be the most vital issue that you will ever have to vote on in this body. I ask you for your unanimous vote to override the governor's veto." In both houses, more Democrats than Republicans backed the governor. Askew, who disdained appeals to emotion and was regarded by other legislators as somewhat aloof, argued in support of the veto. Although Kirk's remarks were unjustified, Askew said, "The fact remains it was not a good bill last Friday. It is not a good bill this Friday." The *Orlando Sentinel* outdid itself. "Judas betrayed Christ for thirty pieces of silver," said its editorial. "But times have changed. The cost of living is up. So is inflation. . . . Judas never enjoyed his ill-gotten gains. Neither will the members of the House and Senate who voted to override." Despite the newspaper's prediction, most pay-raise supporters won their next campaigns. Thirteen legislators, most of whom had supported the raise, were defeated in the 1970 party primaries. Don Reed overcame two opponents; one of them, whom Reed suspected of having Kirk's backing, talked about almost nothing but the raise. The Florida Supreme Court unanimously rejected Kirk's implausible legal challenges to the raise. The episode ended Reed's friendship with Kirk. Yet Reed would say five years later that Kirk "probably did more for the state of Florida, either knowingly or unknowingly, than any governor has ever done."[8]

Kirk's veto speech had not killed reorganization after all. At Louis de la Parte's insistence, the Senate agreed to put the governor rather than the Cabinet in charge of the agencies for prisons, welfare, youth services, psychiatric hospitals, mental retardation, and health. He argued that these functions, lacking powerful clients, needed the governor to be singularly responsible for them. The Senate rejected every other attempt to enlarge the governor's authority at the Cabinet's expense and threatened to leave the governor with even less to do. It seemed to one of Pettigrew's legal aides, Jim Joanos, that the Cabinet was obsessed with control of the state's fledgling computer operation. "People were trading away a lot of things to keep that computer. I think the notion was whoever had control of computers had control of information," he said. Casting votes he would later regret, Askew was part of the pro-Cabinet bloc. Following a series of "strong governor" votes in the House, the comptroller and agriculture commissioner confronted Schultz at a meeting arranged by Pat Thomas, the state Democratic chairman. Reporters were kept out, but it was evident afterward on the faces of Dickinson and Conner that Schultz had stood his ground. As the Speaker recalled the confrontation, the two Cabinet members argued, "My God, you want to give Claude Kirk more power?" Schultz said he conceded Kirk to be "the worst governor we ever had" but had expressed his confidence that Kirk would not be reelected. Pettigrew was making the same case to legislators: "There's no way he's going to get reelected, and I want to create something so the next governor can be effective." However, the Cabinet members' concerns had less to do with Kirk than with the patronage power that they did not want to yield to even a Democratic governor. "They had convinced all their employees that this was a terrible thing," Schultz said.[9]

Pettigrew and Schultz would have lost the fight in their own chamber but for Reed and the Republicans. The pro-Cabinet Democrats caucused at one tense point and threatened to oust the Speaker. Although Schultz refused to weaken the House bill, he placated the mutineers by giving them three of the eight House seats on the conference committee to reconcile the House and Senate reorganization bills. Among the conferees was E. C. Rowell of Wildwood, who had been the last rural Speaker. Rowell, a masterful parliamentarian who humorously relished his image as—in his words—"the mean, wicked old man," had already tried to prevent Pettigrew from succeeding Schultz. As all of the Senate conferees were pro-Cabinet, Pettigrew could count on only five of the sixteen votes on the conference committee. So he simply bypassed it. He suspended its meetings and took his case privately to Senate president John E. Mathews Jr., warning him that reorganization was headed for "a big train wreck" for which the Senate would be blamed. Mathews, more sympathetic to reorganization than most of his Democratic colleagues, arranged for Pettigrew to negotiate individually with a series of influential senators: de la Parte on social services, Horne on personnel issues, Wilbur Boyd on education, and Lawton Chiles on budgeting. Chiles offered the breakthrough compromise, agreeing to make the governor solely responsible for proposing and managing a balanced state budget. The Cabinet would vote on fund transfers but the governor's influence would be paramount. This was a hugely important reform. Acting as a budget commission, the Cabinet had been adopting whatever its members wanted with no thought of how to pay for it all, which made its recommendations useless to the legislature. "Of the priorities in reorganization, that was the most important one," Pettigrew said. The Cabinet members did not seem to appreciate the significance.[10]

Although it took two weeks to reconcile the House and Senate bills, the reorganization cleared the legislature in the last week of the session on votes of 102–4 in the House and 41–0 in the Senate. The major compromises included creating the Department of Health and Rehabilitative Services as the nation's largest state agency, encompassing prisons, health, welfare, and all other social services; splitting environmental authority, with the governor responsible for a Department of Pollution Control and the governor and Cabinet collectively supervising parks, state lands, and saltwater fishing under a Department of Natural Resources; centralized revenue collection under a new governor-Cabinet agency; and purchasing, state aircraft, vehicles, and building management under another such agency. Legislators who did not read the bill closely found out later that the disposition they had approved for the five-member state Road Board, one of the choicest patronage plums, replaced it with a secretary directly appointed by the governor. Regulated professions, each with its own board, were grouped under a secretary. A Department of Community Affairs was created; it would be important in the state's subsequent efforts to manage growth. The comptroller remained in charge of regulating state banks, the principal source of Dickinson's political influence and campaign funds. For similar reasons, the treasurer continued as insurance commissioner. The Game and Fresh Water Fish Commission, which had constitutional status, was left alone, a decision that would take three decades to reverse. The parole commission was exempted also. The Public Service Commission drew a pass because of a Florida Supreme Court advisory opinion defining it as "a part of the legislative or the judicial branch of government" rather than the executive. That curiously ambiguous description gave the electric, telephone, natural gas, and trucking industry lobbyists the argument they needed to keep the legislature from reforming utility regulation as part of the reorganization bill.[11]

This time, Kirk knew when not to veto. "There is no question that this is the best that can possibly be accomplished, recognizing that you will be here next year and that democracy is an ongoing thing," he told a Republican caucus. But he signed the bill in private, denying its sponsors the customary opportunity to be photographed with the governor, pen in hand. Pettigrew told the press that Kirk himself had been the greatest obstacle: "We did it notwithstanding his posture of hostility toward the legislature and of arbitrary action which made strengthening the office of governor very difficult under the circumstances."[12]

With less publicity, the session had also adopted a court reform amendment (which the voters would reject); granted home rule to cities and ordinance-making powers to counties; applied the state conflict-of-interest law to local governments; approved urban renewal subject to local referendum; enacted a model planning and zoning code; reformed welfare to eliminate the veto power of local boards that were unfriendly to minorities; established uniform, population-based pay scales for county commissioners, sheriffs, and other constitutional officers; strengthened the nepotism law; and begun a one-year experiment with suspending "sovereign immunity," the doctrine that governmental agencies could not be sued for causing injury. "We have accomplished everything we set out to do," Schultz told the House. Turning toward Pettigrew, he added, "It was your session." The Speaker also lauded Don Reed in a direct response to an *Orlando Sentinel* editorial headlined "Reed Is a Jerk." Schultz said the minority leader had done "an outstanding job not only for his people but for all the members of the House of Representatives." The House gave Reed a standing ovation.[13]

Kirk argued bitterly with the Cabinet over two of the five new agency heads. He had one vote, they had six. One important appointment was his alone to make. Ray Osborne, his lieutenant governor, would double as head of the newly created Department of Commerce, in charge of workers' compensation and other labor issues as well as the promotional functions of the former Development Commission. The legislation allowed Kirk to designate Osborne without Senate confirmation. That was the end of reorganization in the Kirk era. Pettigrew refused to try for more in 1970. "This is an election year, and nerves are still rubbed raw," he said.[14]

There would be more than enough election-year drama anyway. Kirk was about to pick a fight with a power greater than the Florida Legislature. The issue was the busing of children to desegregate schools, a remedy increasingly being applied by federal judges across the South. Most Florida politicians campaigning in 1970 were anti-busing. None spoke as radically as Kirk, who told the U.S. Supreme Court he would order school boards not to comply. Although Kirk never said anything to reflect a visceral racism, he was an opportunist and a cynic with an instinct for exploiting controversial issues. By April 1970, Kirk knew he would have two potentially strong opponents in the Republican primary, state senator Louis A. "Skip" Bafalis of Palm Beach, and Jack Eckerd of Belleair, wealthy founder of a drugstore chain bearing his name. Either would be attractive to Republican voters who could no longer stomach Kirk. On a Sunday evening two days before the opening day of the 1970 legislative session, he set out—or so he thought—to make voters ignore Bafalis, Eckerd, or anyone else who might run against him. He abruptly suspended the Manatee County school superintendent and the five school board members. Florida's governor was now defying federal authority as brazenly as had George Wallace of Alabama, Ross Barnett of Mississippi, and Orval Faubus of Arkansas. He personally took over the superintendent's desk, where he countermanded the Manatee busing plan and seemed to be enjoying himself hugely. Since Kirk had already allowed Volusia County's board to comply with a federal judge's order, his April 5 coup in Manatee was a complete surprise. Addressing the legislature when the 1970 session began on April 7, Kirk said it was "ludicrous" to accuse him of defying the judiciary; he said he was simply trying to force the U.S. Supreme Court to rule on the issue of "forced busing" (the Court definitively upheld busing in a North Carolina case a year later). It was irrational, Kirk argued, to reassign children so late in the year. Like most other southern politicians, he neglected to explain why he had not opposed busing during the generations when it was a matter of black children being transported past nearby white schools. At Tampa, U.S. District Judge Ben Krentzman had no sympathy or patience for Kirk's rationalization. It had been sixteen years since the U.S. Supreme Court had declared racial school segregation to be unconstitutional. The Manatee case had been litigated since 1965. Moreover, Manatee would already have been in compliance but for Kirk's earlier interference in the proceedings. Krentzman ordered Kirk to appear in person, declared the school board and superintendent reinstated, and set a new compliance deadline of April 16.[15]

Openly defiant, Kirk suspended the school officials once again, escalating the situation dangerously by returning to Bradenton with ninety armed state law enforcement agents and Manatee deputies. The U.S. attorney for the district charged that Kirk had threatened to fire on federal marshals. Kirk did not exactly deny it; "Physically, we will resist only to the extent that they attack us," he said. In a fruitless petition to the U.S. Supreme Court, he warned of a "grave danger of loss of life." Refusing to attend a hearing before Krentzman, Kirk left for Tallahassee, leaving behind a note to his staff in Manatee that said, "If you're shot and bleeding, you will lie there and bleed until you hear from me." Krentzman held Kirk and two aides in contempt and imposed a fine of $10,000 a day. He added, however, that Kirk could void the fine by complying with the desegregation order. According to S. Curtis "Curt" Kiser, a Kirk legal aide at the time, the governor had a secret promise from H. L. Hunt, an archconservative Texas oil billionaire, to pay the fines for him however long Kirk wanted to hold out. (In 2009, Kirk said he had no memory of such an offer.) But to the surprise of many and the disgust of some, Kirk abruptly gave up the fight three days later, allowing 2,617 children to be bused to different schools. Kirk claimed in a televised speech that he had won, that the government had agreed to a modified court order. In fact, the Department of Justice had agreed only to ask the Department of Health, Education and Welfare, which had formulated the plan, to take another look at it. State representative Jerome Pratt, a Manatee Democrat, was irate over Kirk's surrender and said the governor had perpetrated "the cruelest hoax in America." Fortunately for Kirk, his about-face was crowded off many front pages by the crisis aboard the crippled *Apollo 13* spacecraft, whose crew returned safely.[16]

Kirk's next move amounted to civil war in the Florida Republican Party. It was set up by the U.S. Senate's April 8 vote to reject the Supreme Court nomination of G. Harrold Carswell of Tallahassee, a judge of the Fifth U.S. Circuit Court of Appeals. Carswell's detractors considered him segregationist and mediocre. To his supporters, Carswell and the South had been traduced by northern liberals. To Kirk, it was a political opportunity. In a coup orchestrated by Kirk and Senator Edward Gurney, Carswell resigned from the appeals court to run for the U.S. Senate seat of retiring Democrat Spessard Holland. His opponent in the Republican primary was Kirk's perceived nemesis, William C. Cramer, whom Kirk suspected of encouraging Eckerd to run for governor. Ray Osborne was already opposing Cramer for the nomination, but Kirk thought Carswell's candidacy would be stronger and persuaded his lieutenant governor to withdraw. Nothing went as planned; Cramer trampled Carswell in the primary with 63 percent of the vote. Many of Cramer's supporters voted against Kirk in his primary; after Kirk won a runoff, they openly backed Askew against him in November. Many of Kirk's partisans refused to support Cramer, who lost in November to state senator Lawton Chiles.[17]

Meanwhile, the reorganization dispute continued to fester in the House. A pro-Cabinet bloc claiming forty members—roughly half the majority party—styled themselves "Florida Conservative Democrats" and threatened to overthrow Pettigrew as Speaker-designate. Representative Miley Miers of Tallahassee intended to be their candidate at the formal vote in November, and he negotiated with the Republicans to form a coalition. The House now had what amounted to a three-party system: some forty announced conservative Democrats, thirty-seven nonaligned liberals and moderates, and forty-two Republicans. Despite his personal friendship with Pettigrew, Reed encouraged the plot. "Oh, it's great, it's great," he said. "I think it puts us in the catbird seat." He hoped that if the conservative Democrats were desperate enough, they might vote to put a Republican at the rostrum. "We thought we would either have a speaker, or a piece of one," he said later.[18]

One of the 1970 session's most significant issues concerned a bill that the sponsor did not expect to pass. Ralph Turlington, chairing the House Appropriations Committee, held hearings on a proposed net-worth tax to replace the token fees Florida charged corporations for the privilege of doing business. Turlington's pretext for hearing the bill was to fill an $83 million hole in the school budget. Another committee had primary jurisdiction of tax legislation, but it was chaired by James H. Sweeny Jr. of Volusia County, the longest-serving House member and a constant friend of business lobbies, who would have killed the net-worth tax without a hearing. Turlington bypassed him by walking over to the clerk's desk when the bill was introduced and taking custody of it himself. A reporter wrote of the lobbyists at the hearing that "their manner verged on arrogance" while Turlington's twenty-three-year-old research aide, Greg Johnson, explained the bill. Johnson's documentation included a senior honors thesis that Steve Pajcic, a young protégé of Schultz's, had written at Princeton University on the need for a corporate income tax in Florida. The lobbyists, smugly confident that Turlington could not pass the bill, could not foresee that his hearings, Pajcic's thesis, and Johnson's research would become the foundation of Askew's campaign a few months later and of the corporate profits tax that voters would approve in 1971. The debate over the education budget, featuring a new formula to try to equalize spending between rich and poor counties, occasioned two of the most memorable put-downs in legislative lore. Marshall Harris, author of the school plan and a notably effective debater, appealed to the Republicans to vote for the bill because it would help them get reelected. "My people do not want a log-rolling type of deficit financing. They want fiscal responsibility," replied Representative Lewis Earle of Maitland. "If that's all you gathered out of my remarks," Harris retorted, "I don't think even I could help you get re-elected." After Representative Don Nichols of Jacksonville challenged Reed to "lay aside your greed" and "heed the need of these school children," Reed replied swiftly, "Now I know how the Philistines felt after they were slain by the jawbone of an ass." The legislature passed the bill. Unsurprisingly, Kirk vetoed it. This time, the veto was overridden.[19]

The Senate grudgingly agreed to let the voters decide on four-year terms for House members. The voters rejected that along with constitutional amendments to let eighteen-year-olds vote and be considered legally adult. The electoral outcomes were favorable for a long-sought amendment to permit the sale of state-owned submerged land "only when in the public interest" and for an amendment authorizing up to $100 million in pollution control bonds. Reacting to a damaging oil spill in Tampa Bay in 1969, the legislature empowered the state to hold shippers responsible for cleanup costs. It was the nation's toughest such law; sponsor Bill Young called it a "landmark." The legislature enacted

Askew's bill to elect judges on nonpartisan ballots, but Kirk vetoed it. However, Kirk did not veto legislation setting spending limits on political campaigns. It allowed gubernatorial candidates to spend no more than $350,000 in the primaries and as much again in the general election. As an incumbent, Kirk could easily have raised more than $700,000, but he could not have outspent Eckerd, a multimillionaire who had already given nearly $1 million to his own campaign before the law took effect. The spending ceiling profoundly influenced Florida politics before the U.S. Supreme Court declared such laws unconstitutional six years later. Without it, Askew almost certainly would not have been elected governor. The legislature, reacting to Kirk's Governor's Club, also voted nearly unanimously to require elected officials to disclose gifts worth more than twenty-five dollars. But it failed to pass a related bill empowering the secretary of state to audit candidates' campaign finance reports. Under pressure from school boards complaining of higher insurance premiums, the legislature refused to extend the one-year waiver of sovereign immunity. It adjourned with seven hours to spare after enacting a major reform of the nursing home laws which opened up previously secret inspection reports, authorized the Division of Health to close deficient institutions, and repealed a blanket exemption for older facilities. Kirk vetoed both the appropriations bill and the school formula and called a special session a week later to enact a new budget. He called the legislation fiscally unsound, unconstitutional, and "based upon the fallacy that more money means more education." The vetoes were overridden with decisive votes from three Republicans who broke ranks in the House and two who did so in the Senate. As with the pay raise, Kirk asked the Florida Supreme Court to foil the legislature. Once again, he lost. He objected that lawmakers had conditioned the entire education budget on passage of Harris's new school formula, which he argued violated a constitutional provision against making or changing laws in an appropriations bill. The court held, however, that "Appropriations may constitutionally be made upon matters or events reasonably related to the subject of the appropriation."[20]

A federal district court upheld a new law requiring officeholders to resign upon running for other positions with overlapping terms. It was the handiwork of House members coveting the seats of the nine senators running in 1970 for governor, Cabinet, and Congress. Askew, having decided to leave the Senate even if he should lose the governor's race, supported the bill. When he delivered his resignation to Kirk, Kirk told him "Good luck, but I hope the Democrats don't have the sense to nominate you; you're the most dangerous man in the race." The three-judge federal court that upheld the law in part also ruled it inapplicable to candidates for federal office. The U.S. Supreme Court overturned that precedent in a Texas appeal twelve years later, and Florida reinstated its original law.[21]

4

A MOTHER'S SON

In May of his last year as governor, Askew was working late at the capitol when he was alerted to an emergency at the home of his press secretary, Paul Schnitt. Schnitt's father, visiting from St. Petersburg, had died suddenly of a heart attack. Askew's security guard sped him to the residence, where the governor found the younger man weeping beside Samuel Schnitt's body. Askew cradled him in his arms. Be thankful, he said, that you had a father for whom you could grieve.[1]

The moment was a rare window into the immense void in Askew's own life. Although it was well known that he had been raised by a single mother whom he adored, little was ever said about his father. That was a painful subject. On the only occasion that Askew could recall ever seeing his father, an event "burned in my memory," Leo Goldberg Askew Sr. had slammed a door in his face.[2]

Reubin O'Donovan Askew was born on September 11, 1928, in Muskogee, Oklahoma, the youngest of six siblings. The pregnancy was unexpected and evidently unwelcome by the father. The parents divorced two years later in the teeth of the Great Depression, the marriage wrecked by Leo's alcoholism and infidelities. Alberta Askew was thirty-three years old. She had no job prospects, only a fourth grade education, and no relatives of her own in Oklahoma. A year later, when Reubin was three, Alberta attempted to shame Leo into sending support money. She sent the children to his house with a message delivered by Mollie, the eldest sister. "If you're not going to help us like you're supposed to, we're going to come live with you," she said. Leo Sr. shoved Leo Jr., thirteen years old, out the screen door and slammed it. Thereafter, Askew recalled, his mother "bent over backwards trying to avoid me having any bad feelings toward my father. All I remember her saying is, 'Reubin, you'll understand that sometimes men and women can't live together, but remember your father is a good man.'" Askew said she "surrounded me with love and my oldest brother did everything he could when I was growing up to make up for there not being a father in the home. . . . I do not remember an insecure moment in my life growing up." Reubin's siblings were not so forgiving. Mollie, twelve years older, and Leo Jr. told him "some pretty sad stories," particularly about Christmas times when their father had been "just falling down drunk." Although his three older brothers eventually kept in touch with Leo Sr., Reubin never again heard his voice or heard from him in any other way. The announcements he sent of his graduations from high school, college, and law school went unanswered. Leo Askew Sr., having remarried, died before his son was elected governor of Florida. Reubin eventually visited his grave and met Leo's stepson, who was a Baptist missionary "and thought wonders of his stepfather."[3]

Alberta Nora O'Donovan was born and raised in Pensacola. Her father was a Roman Catholic immigrant from Ireland. Her mother was an Episcopalian born near Tallahassee. Alberta was brought up in her mother's faith. Leo Goldberg Askew grew up in Pittsburg, Texas, bearing a given name that honored a Jewish merchant who was a friend of Leo's gentile father. Nora and Leo met at Pensacola, where he was with the Navy, first as an enlisted man and later as a civilian sheet-metal worker. Having married just before World War I, they moved to Muskogee after Pensacola's military-dependent economy collapsed at war's end. During the Depression that began the year after his youngest son's birth, Leo was a motor pool supervisor for the Oklahoma National Guard. Although he sent little cash to his family, he was obligated to pay for the provisions Alberta charged at a grocery store a half block from her rented home. He may not have noticed how much flour and sugar and how many eggs went on the tab. Alberta was baking pies to sell to friends, relatives, and neighbors to raise money for other necessities. Reubin's job, the first of many, was to deliver the baked goods. He remembered the home in Muskogee as "always clean, almost to the point of being immaculate. . . . We did not have much, but we stayed clean. Mother knew how to stretch meals and we ate things that you just would not think today made much sense. For instance, we would literally have spaghetti and mashed potatoes. We would mix some of it, only because it was filling. We did not have a lot of meat and we ate a lot of rice and beans. . . . We did not eat many eggs." Yet he did not consider himself to be poor.[4]

The family's existence at Muskogee was tenuous socially as well as financially; there were friendly relations with only one of Reubin's paternal uncles. After the divorce, his paternal grandmother wanted little to do with the five grandchildren. Even so, Askew reflected on his childhood as nearly idyllic. "I cannot ever remember an insecure moment in my life growing up, because my mother and family provided a surrounding for me that was probably as happy as you could want for a child," he said. In 1937, when Alberta took the three youngest children—Roy, Bonnie, and Reubin—by bus to Pensacola for a vacation, Mollie, the eldest, took it upon herself to make the move permanent. She gave up the rented house, sold her mother's furniture, and sent their other possessions to an aunt's house in Pensacola. It was an audacious act for a twenty-year-old, and she told Reubin that she had "sat down in the middle of the empty house and cried, hoping she had done the right thing." His great regret was that she had not sent along his prized marble collection. At first, Alberta Askew was furious with her daughter. Soon, however, she realized that they were better off for the strong support of her relatives in Pensacola. Among other things, they provided a sizable clientele for nine-year-old Reubin's new magazine route. Reubin was responsible for paying the household water bill out of the fifty cents to a dollar he earned every week. Every sibling worked and had a designated fiscal responsibility. Sometimes they could keep the rest of what they earned, sometimes not. Alberta taught Reubin that the only way to keep money in his pocket was to not spend it. "So I grew up pretty frugal. I still am," Askew said more than seventy years later. His mother also opposed gambling so strongly that she would not allow him to keep the marbles he won from other children. What he saw in Pensacola reinforced her teaching. Slot machines were legal in Florida in 1936 and 1937; at almost every grocery store or gasoline station, the future governor saw poor people losing their food and rent money. His profound disgust for gambling would have historical consequences. Alberta worked in a sewing room run by the Works Progress Administration, a New Deal agency, and later became assistant housekeeper at the San Carlos Hotel, where she supervised many African American maids. "Having struggled herself, she had empathy for them and their plight," Askew said. The experience contributed to his liberalism on civil rights as well as to what he expected of others. After he reviewed their financial disclosure forms, "Some otherwise bright lawyers never became judges in Florida under me because they were not charitable," he said.[5]

Although she had been raised Episcopalian and had baptized her children as such, Alberta Askew joined the Christian Science church in Oklahoma, where two of her brothers-in-law were practitioners, and raised her family in that faith. The future governor would remain a Christian Scientist until he was in law school, when he contemplated marriage and parenthood and decided he could not conscientiously deny medical care to his children. It was a difficult decision that wounded his mother and the eligible young women among Pensacola's Christian Scientists. For himself, Askew chose the Presbyterian Church because of its "educated ministry, and also the theology," but he remained sensitive to Christian Science's strong teachings against tobacco and alcohol. Family experience reinforced the doctrine: his brothers Leo and Johnny became alcoholics like their father. Leo overcame the disease; Johnny did not, and died of it. When Reubin experimented with tobacco in the Army, a few puffs on a pipe left him dizzy, sick to his stomach, breathless, and convinced that once was enough. Acknowledging that he drank occasionally during a subsequent tour as an Air Force officer, he said it was "just to satisfy myself it wasn't what I wanted." Although Reubin and Donna Lou Askew had toasted their early wedding anniversaries with white wine, with parenthood they became teetotalers. The governor's mansion was famously dry during the Askews' residency. A Capital Press Club skit made light of the apple juice that had been served to reporters at a mansion pizza party. When it dawned on Vice-President Spiro Agnew, being honored at a mansion luncheon in 1971, that there would be no wine, he turned to a fellow guest and asked incredulously, "Is he serious?"[6]

The youthful Askew had traded in his magazine business for a newspaper route and held a series of other jobs that were typical of children of his era. He shined shoes, bagged groceries, worked in clothing stores, and clerked at Sidney Shams's grocery store. As he delivered groceries to a black café at the edge of the business district, he realized that there was no other place downtown where an African American could be served a meal or even a cup of coffee. He remembered that experience as the foundation of his opposition to segregation. He was a supervisor for Shams by the time he graduated from Pensacola High School. He joined a home guard unit during World War II when he was only fifteen, thinking his mother's consent made it legal. As governor, he saw documents revealing that his age had been falsified as seventeen. He did not remember doing that. The commanding officer and executive officer could have been responsible; they were his first cousins.[7]

Askew's adolescence was not all work. He found time to join the Pensacola High School Band. On learning that it had two sousaphones and only one sousaphone player, Askew bargained with the director to let him "carry that thing around" if he would teach him music. But for the "really complicated pieces, I would just fake it." He also sang in the glee club and the youth choir of the First Baptist Church. He appeared in two Little Theatre productions but turned down one role because it called for him to kiss a girl onstage. Although he had no scruples against kissing, he was too shy to do so in front of an audience, or to change costumes in front of women without wearing basketball shorts over his underwear. And he refused to read a line with "god damn" in it; the director allowed him to say "dammit" instead. His subsequent military service did not desensitize him to blasphemy, and he would not tolerate it in the governor's office. When a visiting legislator exclaimed "Jesus Christ, Reubin, you can't do that," Askew rebuked him sharply. Then, fearing he had overdone it, he added, "Besides, to you, it's 'Holy Moses.'" The legislator was Jewish.[8]

Askew formed early friendships in Pensacola's Jewish community, notably with Abe Levin, proprietor of a luggage and pawn shop, whom he came to regard as a surrogate father, and with Levin's son David, a future Askew law partner and department head. His Boy Scout troop met at a synagogue. Later, political foes would target him for anti-Semitic attacks based on his Jewish-sounding first name and his law firm. The tactics backfired.[9]

School, work, a newspaper route, the Scouts, the theater, the band. Where did he find the time? It became a lifetime pattern of working long and hard—as Nathaniel Reed would note at the capitol in 1967—and of overachieving. Into his eighties, Askew would still teach public administration to graduate students at Florida State University. Although he could remember no childhood sense of insecurity, the absence of a father—compounded by the father's willful neglect—had molded his character unmistakably. "Even to this day, he is still trying to prove himself," remarked Lance deHaven-Smith, a faculty colleague at Florida State. "If you ask him about his teaching he'll tell you how he's taught at every university in the state and driven 90,000 miles doing this. Why would you be worried about proving yourself when you've been a two-term governor? It's like every day he has to go out and convince himself he's been a good person." The ambition had been evident even during Askew's youth. He knew long before college that he wanted to be a lawyer and to go into politics, although he could not recall why. "People used to say, 'That child talks so much he's got to become a lawyer,'" Askew told an interviewer. "I also knew that lawyers didn't have to work on Sunday." As for so much else, he credited his mother. "I said I wanted to be one and she said, 'Well, you can be one. You have just got to pay the price. . . . [A]nd you have just got to work hard to do it.'" She taught him also that "if you are going to do a job, you need to do it well." Over the years, he said, "she instilled tremendous confidence in me." To an Associated Press reporter preparing a pre-inauguration profile in January 1971, the governor-elect's mother described him as "the most determined boy I've ever seen. Anything he did, he had to do perfectly, even if it was just cleaning the yard." Although he was the youngest, "the rest of the children kind of looked up to him. . . . He never gave me one bit of unhappiness. Oh sure, I had to spank him once in a while. But, who'd want a boy you didn't have to spank?"[10]

Askew's self-confidence, self-assurance, competitiveness, and occasional stubbornness would be noted by the news media as well as by his staff and political colleagues. The governor's mansion had a tennis court, where Askew hated to lose almost as much as in a fight over legislation. Jean Pride, the wife of his press secretary, was a superb tennis player. After losing a singles match to her, Askew joked, "That's the last time you're going to play on *this* court." And it was. To House Speaker Fred Schultz, Askew came across as "very strong-minded and sometimes wrong but never in doubt." As his peers at Pensacola remembered him, "When the rest of us were talking about sports and girls, Rube was talking about being governor. We used to kid him, 'Here comes the governor.'" On the eve of his inauguration, Askew conceded that "I have had so many people tell me that, perhaps I did make such a statement." His military service was emblematic of Askew's drive to excel. When he enlisted at age seventeen, he chose one of the Army's toughest and riskiest branches, the airborne infantry. "I was a tall, skinny kid, six feet two and a half inches, only 165 pounds when I graduated from high school," he said. "Maybe I was trying to prove something to myself." Or perhaps to his family; his three brothers had seen combat in World War II. Training itself could be dangerous. At Fort Benning, Georgia, a fellow trooper from Pensacola was accidentally hanged by his harness after parachuting into a tree. He had told Askew of a premonition and had gone to the company commander who insisted he jump. Askew went home for the funeral, distressed by what he knew and angry at the officer, whom he thought should be court-martialed. Alberta Askew begged him to quit the Army. "No, Mama, I can't do that," he said, assuring her it was a freak accident. As it turned out, the Army contributed more to Askew's career than mere self-fulfillment. It sent him to Carlisle Barracks, Pennsylvania, to learn how to conduct the indoctrination lectures known as troop information and education. It helped him greatly in college, law, and politics "because it taught to me to speak on my feet." At Carlisle he befriended a black soldier who had been denied admission to a medical school, and was dismayed to learn that there was a quota system to limit African American and Jewish enrollments. Askew served not quite twenty months in the Army, rising to the rank of technical sergeant and taking early release in May 1948 to enroll at Florida State University (FSU) with an educational subsidy under the GI Bill of Rights.[11]

FSU had been the Florida State College for Women until 1947, when the legislature voted to make it coeducational along with the all-male University of Florida at Gainesville. Askew was one of some five hundred men in the company of thirty-five hundred women and soon became prominent in campus society. He joined the Delta Tau Delta fraternity, where about two-thirds of the brothers were ex-GIs, and the Cavaliers, a national men's dance society. He dated extensively—for the most part going to on-campus dances—under a neo-Victorian conduct code that imposed curfews only on the women, expelled only women for drinking, and forbade women to wear shorts or slacks on campus. He was "pinned" twice, which meant giving his fraternity pin to a young woman as a ceremonial commitment somewhat beyond steady dating but short of engagement. Honoring a recently established FSU tradition, his fraternity brothers threw him into Westcott Fountain, a campus landmark, each time. But neither relationship outlasted his enrollment. Askew majored in public administration, which he chose as an applied science that "prepares you for a job." To supplement the government stipend of seventy-four dollars a month, he worked in the main dining hall and took various off-campus jobs. One was in a Schwobilt clothing store on the street level of a Tallahassee office building owned by Leon County's state senator, LeRoy Collins, a future governor who became a role model for Askew. Askew was the campus chairman for Collins's 1950 reelection campaign. Askew was elected sophomore class president, lost a close race for student body president, and won it on his second attempt the following year. He was tapped for Gold Key, a campus honorary, and Omicron Delta Kappa, a national leadership society. Campus politics introduced him to his first negative press; he quarreled with the editor of the *Florida Flambeau*, the student newspaper, and with Jerry Thomas, a future Florida Senate president and gubernatorial candidate who wrote columns critical of him. He said the experience nearly soured him on politics. Askew defeated Thomas—not for the last time—when they were candidates for king of the junior-senior prom.[12]

Student government also brought Askew into confrontation with Florida's reactionary racial politics. Reacting to a lawsuit filed by five African Americans who had been denied admission to University of Florida graduate schools, the 1951 legislature voted to deny funds to any state college that became desegregated. Amidst that controversy, the Florida Student Government Association, meeting at the University of Florida with black delegates present, adopted a resolution favoring desegregation throughout Florida higher education. After Askew and fellow FSU delegate Alan Head supported the resolution, the Florida

State student council disassociated itself from their "uninstructed" actions, and Askew found himself in trouble with the state Board of Control on two counts. State law and board rules prohibited biracial meetings on a campus; not only had he attended one, but he had invited the association to convene subsequently at FSU, subject to administration approval. As he might have guessed, the permission would be denied. Askew was summoned to FSU president Doak S. Campbell's office for a harsh grilling by a board representative. "The law's wrong," Askew insisted. He was fortunate not to be expelled, which was the fate of a graduate student who invited African Americans to the FSU campus several years later. The university system remained rigidly segregated until September 1958, when the University of Florida admitted its first black law student in obedience to a federal court order.[13]

Askew had enrolled in the Air Force Reserve Officers Training Corps at FSU, partly because it entailed a twenty-eight-dollar monthly stipend and also because "it seemed like the thing to do, and we forgot what the R stood for." The Korean War began while he was a rising senior, and Askew went directly from graduation to active duty as a second lieutenant. He spent two more years in uniform, most of the time running an aerial photography laboratory in France, mustering out as a captain. He understood that the Air Force was systematically mapping "every inch of Europe" to prepare for a possible nuclear war with the Soviet Union.[14]

On his release in 1953 he enrolled at the University of Florida College of Law, where he found that "the easiest course I had . . . was tougher than the hardest course I had as an undergraduate. The intensity was just tremendous. . . . I did not know what studying was as an undergraduate." Askew received his first D grade despite scoring sixteenth out of forty-four in an evidence course. "'It was a healthy D,' the professor said. 'In fact, I think you were the top D.'" Overall, however, his grades were good enough for him to make the staff of the *Law Review*, which he thought was "probably worth more than any course I had." As at FSU, he held several part-time jobs. He cleaned dining-hall tables and worked banquets. He was also a counselor at a freshman dorm where he first encountered James Bax, a future department head under Kirk and Askew, and put him on report for shouting out a window. He was elected president of his law school first-year class but lost a race for summer student body president by only three or four votes. He failed also to make Blue Key, an organization that dominated campus politics, controlled homecoming festivities, and was considered an indispensable connection for anyone contemplating a career in state politics. "Florida Blue Key ran everything that was runnable outside the [university] administration," said another politician who had tried and failed to make it. Blue Key favored candidates who had been University of Florida undergraduates; his having been student body president at rival Florida State did not help Askew's chances for membership.[15]

Askew had little time for social life in law school and was still unattached when he graduated in January 1956. While waiting for the bar examination he worked as a field representative for the FSU Alumni Association. At an educators' convention in Miami where FSU president Campbell was to speak, Askew encountered Donna Lou Harper, a new first grade teacher recently graduated from FSU, six years his junior. They had met casually at a homecoming event in Tallahassee more than a year earlier, and she had agreed that he could write to her. He never did, although he insisted that he had sent her a Christmas card. At Miami, though, it was love on second sight, if only on his part. They went to dinner that night. The next day they went to church together and took a Sunday drive to Key Largo. Two weeks later she accepted his invitation to Circus Weekend, one of the major events at FSU. During that visit she was startled to hear Askew inquire "how soon I could get ready for a wedding." Whose wedding? "Your wedding," he said, insisting that she go with him to Moon's Jewelry Store—a Tallahassee landmark—to pick out the engagement ring she would want if she were to be married. "I didn't know he was going to go down Monday and put money on it," she said. On the next Mother's Day weekend, when she was visiting her parents at Sanford, Askew arrived, elated by the news that he had passed the bar exam. Had she made up her mind yet? he asked, adding that "I'm getting married in October. I hope you're the one." That night, she said, "I had a little prayer session" in which she thought of all the things that were important in a marriage. "I went down my little list and got to the end and inside I heard this little voice; 'He's everything you think is important, that you wanted in someone. What's your problem?'" They were married in August, not October, as he began his legal career as an assistant Escambia County prosecutor, earning $450 a month. Two years later he went into private partnership with his friend David Levin, specializing in negligence and domestic relations. It was a point of pride that "I got an awful lot of couples back together." They adopted their daughter, Angela, in 1961 and their son, Kevin, two years later. As governor, he was known as an insistent matchmaker. Paul Schnitt's marriage to Virginia Ellis, a *St. Petersburg Times* reporter in Tallahassee, was one example. "She was a Christian Scientist and he was Jewish, and he wasn't sure how that would work," Askew said. "I pushed him hard. I said, 'Don't pass up a chance to marry that woman, she's rare and exceptional.'" Other staffers noted Askew's paternalistic urge and understood its origins. Because Askew had lost his own father, speechwriter Jim Bacchus once said, "He was really an extra father to many of us."[16]

5

REUBIN WHO? (1968–1970)

After signing the Civil Rights Act of 1964, President Lyndon Johnson famously revealed to aide Bill Moyers his fear that he had "handed the South to the Republicans for our lifetimes."[1] Although Johnson narrowly won Florida that year, the state seemed to fulfill his prediction soon enough with the Kirk and Gurney victories in 1966 and 1968. Even so, perceptions of an unstoppable "Republican Revolution" overlooked the extent to which Democratic disunity within Florida and urban riots and campus unrest across the nation had tilted the scales atypically and perhaps only temporarily. Stirring the ashes of former governor LeRoy Collins's loss to Gurney, Democratic pollster Pat Caddell, a protégé of Fred Schultz, concluded that Florida voters still preferred Democratic issues and Democratic candidates, provided they did not appear to be "old," "corrupt," or "complacent." They wanted new faces and "a new populism which is neither right nor left."[2]

Earlier in 1968, Steve Pajcic, a twenty-two-year-old Princeton University student from Jacksonville, had submitted a senior thesis advocating a corporate income tax as the fairest means for Florida to raise urgently needed revenue. The university judged his extensively documented 158-page paper to be the year's best on domestic policy. More importantly, it altered the course of Florida history by helping to elect Reubin Askew governor and by providing the empirical foundation for his tax reforms. After serving eleven years in the legislature and running for governor, Pajcic still thought that his thesis "had more impact on state government than I ever did."[3]

Pajcic, another of Schultz's protégés, had studied Florida taxes during summer employment at the state budget office. Through contacts there, his thesis made its way to Gregory W. Johnson, a University of Florida intern with a Senate tax subcommittee, who was working separately to prove that Florida overtaxed the poor to benefit the rich. Johnson discussed it with his friend Eugene Stearns, a Florida State University law student who was working for Richard Pettigrew. They conceived a "Fair Share" tax reform campaign to elect a progressive to the governor's office on an independent ticket in 1970. The candidate they had in mind was Talbot "Sandy" D'Alemberte, a lawyer and second-term House member from Miami. He toyed with the idea but abandoned it as quixotic, partly because "I realized that I was not at all known in Florida."[4]

Askew was equally unknown except in his Pensacola-based district and at Tallahassee. The capital's journalists, lobbyists, and legislators admired his personal behavior and his courage on race and reapportionment issues. One colleague called him "the original Boy Scout of the Senate." Syndicated columnist Allen Morris wrote that Askew's management of a 1963 redistricting bill—on only his nineteenth day in the Senate—made him a "marked man" to angry Pork Choppers. His problem was that he was almost totally unknown among the massive populations of central and south Florida where the 1970 election would be decided. In a state awash with new residents, many did not know who their own legislators were, let alone who represented the most remote part of the state. No one from Pensacola had ever run for governor. An early poll showing Askew's name recognition at 3 percent may have overstated it. Media and politicians alike took for granted that the Democratic nomination for governor would be decided in a second primary between Attorney General Earl Faircloth, who had been a legislator from Miami, and Senate president John E. Mathews Jr. of Jacksonville, both of whom had run statewide before. A Florida maxim at the time held that "you run once to get known, twice to get elected." That had been true of five of the six previous governors. In April, the Capital Press Club's annual skits featured a song that began, "If you don't know who is a Reubin Askew, you begin to see his plight." Before his confrontation with Kirk, Askew had aimed his ambition no higher than perhaps

running someday for Congress, where he expected that civil rights issues would make his Washington career a short one. As for governor, "I
did not think anyone from Pensacola had much chance." Yet in November 1970 he would be the last man standing. The "Fair Share" tax reform
plank had done for him what had been intended for D'Alemberte.[5]

Askew's improbable political ascent began in 1958 when he defeated
five opponents for the state House seat of a friend, J. B. Hopkins, who
was challenging incumbent senator Philip D. Beall Jr. Such elections
often turned more on personality and connections than on issues or
advertising. So it was with Askew, who had the benefit of his mother's
large family, which "stretched from one end of Pensacola to the other,"
as well as connections acquired through Jaycee and United Way activities. His runoff opponent tried unsuccessfully to exploit the race issue
by claiming that his own voters were "decent," a code word for white.
When an irate heckler called Askew a "nigger lover," he replied, "The
trouble is I don't love them enough. The difference between you and me
is that I'm trying to overcome my prejudices and you're not."[6]

The freshman legislator broke his lance against the beverage lobby
when he called for stricter regulation of alcohol. Mallory Horne, who
became Speaker after Askew left for the Senate, recalled that he "seldom spoke; it was almost as if he was afraid to step out front." Yet he
could be bold when necessary; in his first term Askew helped Collins and
Speaker Thomas Beasley deflect a torrent of segregationist legislation.
Askew took cues on how to vote from veterans he respected, particularly Ralph Turlington of Gainesville and Robert Mann of Tampa. He
watched the electronic voting displays on either side of the Speaker's
rostrum to see whose lights showed red and green. "The half dozen I
looked up to almost always voted the same way," he said. He attracted
the notice of Allen Morris by refusing a lobbyist's gift of a copy of Morris's *Florida Handbook*, a definitive guide to state government. Askew
did not think he should accept even innocuous gifts. Morris knew of no
other legislator whose scruples were as exacting. When Horne decided
to nail down his future speakership, Askew refused to commit his vote
because he thought new members should wait to observe the candidates
in action. "It was pretty damn naive but a real pragmatic point, and that
sort of epitomizes Reubin," said Horne. "He marched to his own band

more than any elected official I ever saw." Every Democrat who was not a freshman traditionally became chairman of something. Askew's second term found him in charge of the Committee on Executive Business, which, for lack of anything to do, rarely met. Askew took it as an opportunity to uphold the vetoes Collins had signed after the 1959 session; the hearings Askew held resulted in sustaining each veto.[7]

Having been reelected without opposition in 1960, Askew ran two years later for the Senate seat. It had been in the Beall family for all but four years since 1946. Race was more of a factor this time. The militantly segregationist White Citizens' Council supported Beall, who had tried to make it a felony to teach at a desegregated school. Beall himself could not say much about race; he was counting on black support he thought he had secured with gifts of cash and liquor to people he considered influential in the black community. Askew met with African American clergy, challenged them to repudiate the corruption, showed them Beall's voting record, and won the greater share of the black vote. Making an issue of Askew's stand on reapportionment, Beall called him the "second senator from Dade County." The tactic backfired. Askew cited unsuccessful legislation Beall had introduced to make Miami Beach a separate county and contended that casino gambling had to be the ulterior motive for a senator from Pensacola to try to split Dade County. Beall later told journalist Don Meiklejohn that he was fated to lose the election because he had divorced and remarried, had moved out of Escambia, and was drinking "a little more than a politician from Escambia County could afford."[8]

Askew saw that lobbyists had more influence in the Senate than he had witnessed in the larger House. Describing the only Pork Chop retreat he had attended, he recalled that "the lobbyists were there. Anybody needed a drink, it was there. If they needed a smoke, it was there. If you had to blow your nose, someone handed you a Kleenex." Having isolated himself from the Senate power structure, Askew was never considered one of the more influential senators. His "loner" reputation persisted after the courts purged the Pork Choppers. "Nobody thought Askew was up to being governor," said Jim Apthorp, his first chief of staff. "The people in control of the Senate, including [John] Mathews, didn't like him. He struggled with being one of the 'good old boys'; he wasn't one." Askew thought himself a friend of Mathews, a highly regarded lawyer who had run fifth among six candidates for the 1964 Democratic gubernatorial nomination, and had qualms about running against him in 1970. "I really thought so highly of Mathews that I had a hard time thinking I would be a better governor," he said. Mathews himself made Askew's decision easier. Knowing what Askew had in mind, the new Senate president told him that his committee assignments would depend on his loyalty. "To the Senate or to you?" Askew inquired. "To me," Mathews said. Refusing the pledge, Askew drew what seemed the most difficult and politically unrewarding job available, that of chairing the committee to revise the constitution's judicial article, which the 1968 session had not even attempted to do. "That's when I realized he didn't really feel any sense of kinship to me," Askew said. "It freed me up of feeling badly about running against Jack." He also had encouragement from Joseph Cresse, the assistant budget director, who told him he would make a better governor because "Mathews explains in great detail but won't take a position." Even so, Askew agonized over the race. As he worried aloud one night over running up a crushing campaign deficit, Donna Lou told him it was time to decide. "You know what your problem is?" she said. "You've run out of excuses."[9]

Many legislators supported Mathews. Only a few, notably Representative Marshall Harris of Miami, were for Askew. Askew did have significant help from one of the ten most influential Floridians, Chester Ferguson. He was a Tampa lawyer and Board of Regents member who headed the vast Lykes family business interests. Like many others, Ferguson doubted that anyone could be elected governor from Pensacola; he encouraged Askew to be the running mate of Metropolitan Dade County's mayor, Chuck Hall. When Askew rejected that idea, Ferguson offered Askew a position in his law firm at either Miami or Tampa, which would provide the advantage of a large population base from which to campaign for governor. Askew, guarding his independence, turned that down too. Eventually, Askew said, Ferguson persuaded John Pace, "the wealthiest guy in Pensacola, that I really had a shot at it." Pace led an effort to raise the $100,000 that Askew thought he needed to start a viable campaign. The drive came up short at $80,000, but Askew decided that it was enough in light of the new campaign spending limit. A joke soon made the rounds: "Pensacola will have no United Fund this year. Reubin got it all."[10]

The 1970 campaign was the first in which gubernatorial candidates were required to name a lieutenant governor, and they had to do so by the qualifying deadline. That nearly kept Askew out of the race. His first choice, former state senator Beth Johnson of Orlando, declined. So did Maurice Ferré, a Hispanic legislator and businessman at Miami. Either choice would have been a first for Florida. Jon Moyle, a West Palm Beach attorney who had worked for Governor Farris Bryant, agreed to be Askew's running mate if he could find no one else. He was even less known than Askew and did not believe that he could help Askew win. Eugene Stearns noticed Askew and George Sheldon, his legislative aide, dining alone one evening. "It was the most pathetic thing you ever saw, they couldn't draw flies. They had no support outside of Pensacola," Stearns said. There was also little backing at Tallahassee, despite its large population of Florida State alumni who presumably would be enthusiastic about electing one of their own to statewide office for the first time. With only one exception "we drew a complete blank in this area," another FSU alumnus wrote after the election. "The general feeling was you were a fine fellow . . . but you didn't have a chance at election and they didn't want to be identified with a loser in this politically-oriented community."[11]

Askew was tempted briefly to abandon his own campaign to become Faircloth's running mate. It was a cheerless prospect. Askew had misgivings about Faircloth's environmental record and resented how he had forced Collins into a ruinous runoff for the Democratic U.S. Senate nomination in 1968. After thinking overnight, he turned Faircloth down. "I realized there that for a minute I was willing to do something to be lieutenant governor I wouldn't do to be governor," he told Sheldon, adding, "We're going to run the kind of race I want to run. We're going to come in fourth, probably."[12]

The filing deadline was only days away when Askew announced to widespread surprise that Secretary of State Tom Adams had agreed to be his candidate for lieutenant governor. It was the most improbable of political marriages. Adams was an unsuccessful dairy farmer who had found fame if not fortune as a Pork Chop senator. He represented thinly populated Clay and Baker counties from 1956 to 1960, when the rural clique backed him in a successful race for a rare vacancy in the office of secretary of state. In his first legislative campaign he had been taken blindfolded to a Ku Klux Klan rally where whatever he said "passed the test." For most of the 1960s the question was not whether Adams would run for governor, but when. He became an effective administrator known for hiring bright, politically promising young men, and it was assumed that there was an invincible "Adams Army" of supporters. Unknown to the public, Adams still had a sizable 1960 campaign debt, swollen by interest on principal he could not repay. In June 1969 he announced that he could not raise enough money to campaign for governor "without scratching somebody's back" and would not run even for reelection. The media initially treated him as an upstanding victim of corrupt campaign practices, but the halo was tarnished when banks began filing lawsuits that revealed the old debt. Adams toyed with resigning early to look for opportunities to repay the debt but reconsidered after other Democrats, horrified that Kirk might appoint his successor, started a fund-raising drive for him. The press skits lampooned him as "Tin Cup Tom."[13]

Sheldon, a recent graduate of Florida State University, had been working part-time for Adams and was about to go to work full-time for Adams's deputy, Jim Smith, when Askew recruited him to be his Senate aide. Troubled by the Faircloth flirtation and by Askew's poor prospects of enlisting an effective running mate for himself, Sheldon and Smith thought Adams might be the answer. They told Askew and Adams that each wanted to see the other. It was not true, but the trick worked. As they had hoped, Askew asked Adams to run with him. Adams refused at first, saying he wanted to concentrate on paying off his debt so that he could run for another office in four years. "Four years from now," Askew told him, "you're going to be as old as yesterday's newspaper." Askew respected Adams as the "most able Cabinet member . . . he was standing up routinely to Kirk" and had misgivings only over Adams's debt. Adams misled him, claiming that it amounted to only $65,000 and that some of it might be forgiven.[14]

The partnership with Adams, who said "old heads must support bright new faces," gave Askew's campaign its first appearance of viability. The odds were still long but no longer impossible with a veteran politician like Adams on board. Adams's debt was the most obvious problem—not simply that he owed money, but that it revealed spending which had not been reported as the law required. Askew rationalized that many other politicians were similarly culpable but not as candid. Capitalizing on Adams's reputation as an administrator, Askew said that Adams would act as a chief of staff. Eventually, he would regret saying so. Even with Adams, however, the campaign lacked a platform to distinguish it dramatically from those of the other Democrats. Askew stood for good government issues such as nonpartisan election of judges and financial disclosure, which he emphasized by releasing his income tax returns. But that would not be enough.[15]

The next big surprise was decisive. Again, the Adams staff was involved. Stearns and Johnson, disappointed that D'Alemberte would not be their tax reform candidate, discussed their frustration with Smith, Adams's deputy. It occurred to Smith that Askew might be their man. He arranged for Stearns and Johnson to present the tax reform case to Adams, who liked it, and then to Askew. Askew had voted in the Senate against a corporate income tax; when he heard what the meeting would concern, his campaign coordinator, Elmer Rounds, said later, "he almost turned around and walked away." On reading a white paper that Johnson had assembled from his research and Pajcic's thesis, Askew realized that he had been misled by Florida's business lobbyists; legislators were depending for their information upon the people opposing tax reform. It was the first time he had seen an independent analysis on an issue opposed by special interests. The tax reform platform Askew announced on August 5, 1970, set him apart from the other three Democratic candidates—Mathews, Faircloth, and Chuck Hall—as well as from Kirk and the two Republicans opposing the governor's renomination. Askew proposed a corporate "profits" tax, taking care to avoid the buzzword "income." He called also for a severance tax on the powerful phosphate mining lobby and the repeal of "morally wrong" loopholes— among them the sales tax exemption for car rentals, and property tax exemptions for private clubs with profitable bars and restaurants. He proposed to repeal the sales tax on household utilities and long-term residential rentals. "For the same reasons that it is unfair," he said, "our tax structure is unproductive, and consequently state government has been almost totally inadequate to deal with such pressing problems as pollution, education, and the myriad unanswered problems of our mushrooming citizenry." As soon as they could recover from their own surprise, his opponents steered the news media to the audio recording of Askew's Senate speech against a corporate income tax. On that occasion, February 15, 1968, he had complained that "There seems to be something permeating the halls that if you don't vote for this you don't have the guts to stand up to big corporations. . . . How can you single out one segment of the business community?" Askew responded that he had changed his mind; he was now persuaded that corporations should be taxed even if partnerships and sole proprietorships could not be.[16]

His campaign consultant, Miami mayor David Kennedy, had devised a strategy for the Democratic primary that focused on eighteen counties. The goal was to run second to Faircloth and defeat him in a runoff. It meant that his entire primary campaign would be against Mathews. They assumed that Hall, unknown outside Dade, would place fourth even though he had a north Floridian running mate, former Democratic state chairman Pat Thomas of Quincy. Mathews and Faircloth also played the geographical balancing game. The Jacksonville senator chose North Miami mayor Elton Gissendanner. Faircloth, a Miamian, enlisted George Tapper, a former Pork Chop senator from Port St. Joe. That left the Askew-Adams ticket as the only one without roots in Dade, the state's largest county, but it turned out not to matter.

Askew, forty-one years old when he filed, was the youngest and most photogenic of the Democratic candidates. He was ideally suited for television. His only outward flaw was a facial tic, the blinking of one eye, which appeared when he was fatigued; he was usually able to control it when he was on camera. Faircloth and Mathews, though not obese, looked rotund; a newspaper feature on Faircloth likened him to "a grownup Gerber baby." Askew worked crowds better than Mathews, whose candidacy attracted more approval than enthusiasm. Mathews's competence, which even his opponents respected, was much greater than his charisma.

Askew declared strong positions on campaign reform and the environment. He promised to use "every available means" to reroute the Cross-Florida Barge Canal, already under construction, away from the sensitive Ocklawaha River. Environmentalists contended that the canal would contaminate the Floridan aquifer, source of much of Florida's drinking water. If research supported that objection, Askew said, he would ask the federal government to halt the canal. On that issue, he was at odds with almost all of Florida's leading Democrats, including his own running mate. Adams had cultivated the waterways lobby and was one of the canal's most ardent boosters. Underscoring a difference with Mathews, Askew reminded voters that he had opposed the legislative pay raise.[17]

Tax reform remained Askew's major theme. Mathews, attempting to minimize the issue, said he could run a responsible government without any new taxes. Greg Johnson found a 1968 newspaper article that quoted Mathews as saying it eventually would be "inevitable" to extend the sales tax to groceries. Two weeks before the primary, Stearns, Johnson, and Rounds decided it was time for a bold stroke. For a month, Askew had been stagnant in opinion polling, three points behind Mathews. On a day when they knew Askew would not be able to call in from the campaign trail to approve the day's proposed press statement, they issued one referring to Mathews as "Food Tax Jack." It was the sort of one-liner the media love; it was quoted widely, deeply offending Mathews and his supporters. Askew, too, was upset and rebuked his staff. "If that ever happens again, attacking one of my friends without my approval, I'm going to quit this race that day," he said. Mathews complained that the 1968 remark was quoted out of context; he said he had been warning of what Kirk's proposed budget might necessitate. Even so, Mathews refused to declare that he would never consent to taxing groceries. He said instead that he would never agree to it "until all other sources of revenue have been exhausted." He said he could not make a categorical promise because "It's not in my nature." Although it was uncharacteristic of Askew to call names, he did not retract "Food Tax Jack." Considering how narrowly he edged past Mathews in the voting, the label may well have been the decisive stroke. Mathews thought so and recalled for the media that his father had been defeated for reelection to the Senate a year after voting for the original sales tax in 1949. The Askew campaign statement, Mathews said, "was completely false, and he knew it was false, and I think he's ashamed of it."[18]

Meanwhile, another dark horse had been surging out of obscurity. He was state senator Lawton Chiles, one of four candidates opposing Farris Bryant, a former governor, for the Democratic nomination to succeed retiring U.S. senator Spessard Holland. Knowing that he could not raise much money, the forty-year-old Chiles decided on a low-cost strategy to make himself familiar to the voters. He rented a camper, drove to Century, a sawmill town in Escambia County near the Alabama line, and on March 17 began walking. He said he would walk all the way to the Florida Keys, more than eight hundred miles, before the campaign ended, pausing only for the legislative session. An aide drove the vehicle, where Chiles spent his nights and wrote daily newsletters describing his travels and conversations with people along the way. Even close friends were taken by surprise. When state senator Wilbur Boyd heard about it, he drove out to the Panhandle to find Chiles in sweat-stained khakis, plaid sports shirt, and work boots, marching along a lonely road. "Lawton, listen," Boyd pleaded. "Everybody thinks you're crazy." Chiles smiled. The well-educated lawyer who talked like a country boy had sensed the nation's souring mood amidst the seemingly endless Vietnam War. More than anything, the people wanted their politicians to listen. "Walkin' Lawton," as everyone soon called him, would listen. He became a media sensation. Fred Schultz, another of the Senate candidates, quietly renamed his campaign newsletter, which had been titled "Flying with Fred," and gave up his airplane for a motor home.[19]

With a week to go, upsets that had recently seemed impossible now appeared within reach. In Volusia County, where the *Daytona Beach News-Journal* had been one of the first papers to endorse him, Askew gave an outdoor barbecue that attracted at least twenty-five hundred people—and many more mosquitoes—on a hot, humid night. Chiles was there. Noting the size and enthusiasm of the audience, Chiles joked that he and Askew had an agreement: "He can come walking the roads with me anytime, and I can come work his crowds." Askew himself was less confident than he appeared, but on September 8 he came in second to Faircloth, edging Mathews out of the runoff by a margin of

20,280 votes. In polling 206,333 votes statewide, Askew led Mathews in thirty-six of the sixty-seven counties, finishing first in twelve, including Alachua, Brevard, and Leon. He carried Escambia, his home, with 71.4 percent, even though the *Pensacola News Journal*, disapproving of Adams, had endorsed the Mathews ticket instead. Mathews led in six counties. He won Duval, his home, with only a 41.6 percent plurality. Had Mathews been able to carry Duval by the same margin as Askew took Escambia, he would have been Faircloth's opponent in the September 29 runoff. Faircloth's tally was 227,412, just under 30 percent. Seven of every ten voters had opposed the presumed front-runner.[20]

Chiles's star was also ascendant that night. He ran a strong second in the Senate primary, with 24.6 percent to 23.0 percent for Schultz and 31.3 percent for Bryant. Chiles made the runoff by a margin of 12,555 votes. What the media were already calling the "new face" phenomenon made for dour faces at Claude Kirk's election-night headquarters. His supporters were less concerned that the incumbent governor had been forced into a runoff with drugstore millionaire Jack Eckerd than by the prospect of facing Askew in November. Having polled 47.7 percent to Eckerd's 38.4, Kirk was in little danger of losing the runoff. But as he had said to Askew himself, he knew who his most dangerous opponent was. His opposition research folder on Askew was empty.[21]

"Overnight, the underdogs became the men to beat," wrote Bill Mansfield, the *Miami Herald*'s capital bureau chief. Faircloth tacitly acknowledged that. He had scarcely mentioned Askew before the primary. Now, he challenged him to debate. Faircloth won endorsements from Hall and from the embittered Mathews, who said he was "convinced the attorney general better understands the problems of the state than does Reubin Askew." However, Hall's running mate, Pat Thomas, endorsed Askew, as did most of the newspapers that had preferred Mathews. If the primary campaign had been lackluster, the ensuing three weeks made up for it. Faircloth berated Askew for choosing the debt-ridden Adams, and Askew accused Faircloth of accepting contributions from the liquor industry and favoring a controversial dredge-and-fill project. The liveliest issue was Askew's proposed corporate profits tax. "He now condemns what he once thought fair and he now praises what he once condemned," Faircloth said in a televised debate. To confuse voters, Faircloth began airing commercials that showed him stamping "veto" on a personal income tax, a prospect that Askew explicitly opposed. Faircloth overplayed his hand when he charged that a corporate tax would inflate the price of goods and services in Florida. Following a suggestion Askew credited to Jay Landers, whom Adams had brought to the campaign, Askew's staff purchased identical shirts from Sears stores in Florida and Georgia. As Askew told Florida voters, Sears was paying $500,000 a year in Georgia income taxes but only $2,000 under Florida's archaic licensing tax. Yet the shirts cost the same six dollars in each state.[22]

Askew won the September 29 runoff with 57.6 percent of the total vote. His 447,025 votes were more than double his count three weeks before. He had beaten Faircloth two to one in the battle for Mathews's and Hall's supporters, and he came within a whisker of taking Dade County, Faircloth's home base, where the attorney general led by less than a single percentage point. Askew carried Escambia, his home, by a margin of six to one. Faircloth conceded swiftly and endorsed Askew against Kirk. Mathews endorsed him, too; there would be no Democratic fratricide this time. Chiles, meanwhile, crushed Bryant with 66 percent of the vote and looked forward to doing the same to Cramer, who had beaten Carswell nearly two to one. The runoff set up the scenario most feared by the realists in Kirk's administration. Encountering Askew at an airport, Kirk's chief of staff, Lloyd C. Hagaman, conceded he would be the next governor. There were few remaining "DemoKirks," and Hagaman was not waiting for the election to start looking for a new job. Kirk, having easily defeated Eckerd, needed a new angle against Askew, but there was no mud for him to throw. He tried to tell voters that Askew's election would hurt President Nixon's chances of carrying Florida again in 1972, that Askew was too liberal, and even that he was too nice, too much of a "Momma's boy," to be governor. Kirk tried to tarnish Askew as a supporter of pornography, a preposterous claim linked to some clients whom Askew's former law partners had represented. And of course he attacked the proposed corporate tax. "If $300 million in new taxes is tax reform, then I'm Prince Valiant," Kirk said. "Claudius Maximus yes, but Prince Valiant no." That and other remarks played to Askew's advantage by underscoring the contrast in their personalities. Kirk outraged many voters by complaining that a newspaper had sent only a "lady reporter" to cover his speech and by writing off a racial disturbance at Quincy as "just another Saturday night in Gadsden County."[23]

"I want to bring dignity to the governor's office," Askew said. Reporters tried in vain to get Askew to react to the "Momma's boy" issue. He was waiting for the right moment. It came at a Miami Beach rally staged by U.S. representative Dante Fascell of Miami. About two thousand people turned out; by Askew's estimate, they were predominantly middle-aged and elderly women of Jewish and Italian ethnicity. "Mr. Kirk," Askew told them, "called me a Momma's Boy. You know what? He's right. I love that Momma of mine." The ovation was tumultuous and prolonged. Askew looked to Fascell, who remarked that there was no need to say anything more. Askew was on his way to taking 70 percent of the Dade vote, second only to his 81 percent share of home-base Escambia. (When Kirk remarked years later that he had made Askew governor, Askew agreed. "I told him that he was right and that he was the quintessential opponent.") At the University of Florida's homecoming, a major political event in election years, Askew's impending victory was obvious not simply in the enthusiasm of his audiences but also in the conspicuous absence of the Kirk bumper stickers that had seemed to be on all the vehicles four years before. Askew was equally encouraged by the mood of some two thousand people at a chicken and smoked-mullet barbecue staged by the Union County sheriff; he had been too busy shaking hands to eat and returned to his Gainesville hotel with his trademark late-night snack of buttermilk and cookies. In the next day's *Miami Herald* he read the predictions of John McDermott, a columnist who nicknamed himself "Fearless" for being unafraid to guess wrong. "We're in trouble," he told Donna Lou. "'Fearless' says we're going to win."[24]

"Fearless" would be right this time. It was obvious also that Chiles would defeat Republican nominee William Cramer despite the Nixon administration's strenuous efforts on Cramer's behalf. The president visited Florida. So did his wife, Pat, Vice-President Spiro Agnew, Attorney General John Mitchell, and others. On a night when Republicans paid a thousand dollars a plate to attend a closed-door black-tie dinner for Cramer at Miami, Chiles staged nearby an outdoor fried chicken rally, open to the public. Television got the message. So did the voters. Nixon's efforts were futile, largely because he was not on the ballot when Askew and Chiles were running. The Democratic legislature's decision to move gubernatorial elections to nonpresidential cycles was the reason; Askew believed that he could not have been elected governor against a Nixon-led ticket in either 1968 or 1972. The 1970 campaign concluded with a televised debate in which Kirk boasted of his own "courage"—the one-word theme of most of his advertising—as if to say that Askew lacked it. But Kirk refused to take a stand on a pending constitutional amendment to allow eighteen-year-olds to vote in Florida. His own vote, Kirk said, was "a private matter." Askew pounced. "I think this demonstrates the 'courage' of the governor when he fails to take a stand or position," he said. As for himself, Askew said, he agreed with Nixon "when he said we should give the privilege of voting to eighteen-year-olds." Kirk had no retort; it was obvious that he had lost the debate. "The game plan," Gene Stearns exulted afterward, "was to take 'courage' away from Kirk." Florida voters rejected voting and majority rights for eighteen-year-olds, but they did not hold the issue against Askew.[25]

The only good news for Kirk that last weekend was an endorsement by the Florida League of Conservation Voters, which also recommended Chiles over Cramer. That mirrored a sharp division among Republicans themselves; many who supported Kirk opposed Cramer even if meant leaving the Senate seat in Democratic hands. Many Cramer loyalists were hostile to Kirk even though it could cost their party the governor's mansion. Nowhere was the split more evident than in Pinellas, Florida's first Republican county and Cramer's home, where Askew not only led Kirk but received more votes than Cramer. Republican voters in Broward, Collier, and Pasco counties split their tickets the same way. Askew carried fifty-seven counties to defeat Kirk 984,305 votes to 746,243, a 56.8 percent share. Of the ten largest counties, Kirk won only Orange, home of the *Orlando Sentinel*, which had incited him to veto the pay raise.[26]

Kirk conceded barely an hour after the last polls closed. Posted returns still showed him ahead, but the computer projections told a different story. At Pensacola, some two thousand of Askew's friends celebrated with soft drinks and cheered thunderously when he acknowledged Kirk's "very gracious" telephone call. "They said we couldn't do it, didn't they?" declared the man who not so long ago had been mocked as "Reubin who?" As Askew was about to learn, however, preparing to assume the office of governor could be as challenging and stressful as the ordeal of winning it.[27]

6

BAPTISM BY FIRE (1970–1971)

Reubin Askew ended the campaign thirty pounds lighter, physically and emotionally spent, and feeling the intense pressure of having to assemble a staff and program in less than two months. "The roof fell in," he said. Troubles arose even while the Askew family was taking a much-needed vacation in the Virgin Islands. Tom Adams arrived with an organizational chart that would make him in effect a deputy governor; it showed the entire staff under the lieutenant governor's direct control. Askew rejected it and began to reconsider assigning Adams to run the Department of Commerce, an option he had said he would not choose. As Adams's deputy, Jim Smith, saw it, Adams "almost from the get-go wasn't a full partner like he thought he was going to be." To Ed H. Price Jr., a former Senate colleague from Bradenton, Askew was like a man who had caught a tiger and did not know what to do with it. The transition pressures were so fierce that it was difficult for Askew to keep food down. "I was eating an awful lot of French toast with a lot of syrup," he said. He hid out from job seekers by working in his motel room instead of the transition office across the street from the capitol building. He appointed a committee to screen applicants but soon sensed that it had an agenda of its own and simply ignored it. He scrapped a plan to mail some five thousand thank-you letters when he saw that a close friend's name had been misspelled on one and realized that he would have to check all of them. In addition, he needed to prepare for an inaugural speech and a special legislative session and had to develop a budget. "I got into some deep prayer and I said, 'Lord, I thought this was maybe something you wanted me to do.'" As staff members soon learned, Askew was serious about everything. "He worried more than anyone I've ever seen in my life," Smith said.[1]

Askew was determined to draw a line between campaigning and governing. He selected no one from the campaign staff for his most critical appointments: chief of staff, press secretary, and general counsel. The press secretary position went to Don Pride, the *Palm Beach Post*'s capital bureau chief, who had exposed Kirk's honeymoon expenses and the Safire contract while writing for the *St. Petersburg Times* (see chapter 2). Pride had turned down an offer to be Askew's campaign press secretary because he doubted the candidate's prospects and commitment to reform. Speculating on the impending appointment, the Associated Press reported that Pride had cut his hair short for the first time in ten years. Askew valued Eugene Stearns's political advice "above anyone else's" and tried to recruit Stearns for the staff on the eve of the election. But Stearns was committed to serving Pettigrew in the Speaker's office, where he would become as valuable to Askew as if he had worked for him directly. The position of chief of staff, formally titled senior executive assistant, went to Jim Apthorp, who had been highly recommended by Ed Price. Apthorp was an Adams protégé whom Kirk and the Cabinet had appointed as director of the Internal Improvement Fund, the agency responsible for Florida's submerged land. Apthorp, who had not campaigned for Askew, was concerned that he would be resented by people who had. He accepted the offer when Askew made it clear that "he would let me do the job." It was understood, however, that Pride, the general counsel, and several other key staffers would have direct access to Askew. Unsure of a choice for general counsel, Askew pressed law partner David Levin into serving temporarily without pay or expenses for two months until Edgar M. Dunn Jr., a Daytona Beach lawyer and assistant state attorney, took the job.[2] Elmer Rounds, a former newspaperman who had been the campaign coordinator, was excluded from the new administration because of a predawn incident on election day. He had fired pistol shots to scare off two Kirk supporters who supposedly were tearing down Askew-Adams signs near Tallahassee. Askew was prepared to forgive Rounds for the offense but not for lying to him in denying that it had happened. When Rounds opened a public-relations office and attempted to trade on his perceived but nonexistent influence with the new governor, the staff ordered the Department of Transportation to shun any contractor "if Elmer shows up." Embittered, Rounds worked against Askew's reelection in 1974.[3]

Askew rounded out his inner circle with a quartet of elders: Harvey Cotton, a Pensacola businessman and member of his church, who was said to be Askew's ombudsman; Horry Hair, a former state senator, chosen to manage the office's budget and personnel affairs; deputy press secretary Maurice "Moose" Harling, a reporter for the *Pensacola News-Journal* who had stormed out of the office on learning it was endorsing Mathews; and Owen "Casey" Cason, a highway patrol veteran who had told him when Askew was a neophyte prosecuting attorney, "Now boy, if you ever get elected governor, I want to be your driver." Cason got his wish, which came with a captain's rank. Their special responsibility, Askew told them, was to warn him when they thought he was wrong. "If you do not come and see me once a month," he said, "then you are not doing your job because I am going to make mistakes." Other key staffers were Bernie Parrish, son of a former senator, who had been Askew's traveling aide during the campaign; Bill Owens, in charge of patronage; and Robert Hugli, for scheduling and appointments. A Cabinet liaison office nominally assigned to Adams included Jim Smith, Douglas Stowell, Jay Landers, and Greg Johnson. Askew intended to personally sign all correspondence drafted in his name but gave up when, on returning from a short trip, he found that secretaries Lorna Allen and Cappy Lamoreaux had covered his desk with stacks of letters two feet high.[4]

Askew's success as governor would depend in large part on the House of Representatives, where some conservative Democrats were still trying to fashion a coalition to keep Pettigrew from becoming Speaker. Miley Miers of Tallahassee was their candidate, but the actual leader was James M. Sweeney Jr. of Volusia County, the senior member of the House, who knew Pettigrew intended to replace him as chairman of the Committee on Finance and Taxation. For Sweeney to keep the chair would have killed Askew's tax reform program in its cradle. As Sweeney and Miers flew around the state, it was implied to other legislators that they had Askew's support. That notion evaporated when Representative Roy Hess of Pensacola, who had campaigned with Askew, withdrew his pledge to Miers and declared himself for Pettigrew. Sweeney had been instrumental in delaying Pettigrew's speakership by helping Schultz two years earlier. As it turned out, Pettigrew would accomplish a great deal more with Askew as governor than he could have achieved under Kirk. The Pettigrew alliance became vital to Askew, as he could not count on equivalent support from the new Senate president, Jerry Thomas. Pettigrew was an activist Speaker who promoted a broad program of liberal legislation that not only coincided largely with Askew's but supplied many proposals that the governor adopted as his own. Thomas, on the other hand, believed his role was simply to preside over the Senate rather than prescribe an agenda. For active support in the Senate, Askew would have to look to such friendly committee chairmen as Louis de la Parte and Kenneth Myers. Askew was helped considerably when Stearns became Pettigrew's staff director. Pettigrew had intended the role for Ted Phelps, who had led his reorganization staff. But Phelps resigned when Pettigrew, aware of Stearns's influence with Askew, insisted that Stearns be the Speaker's liaison with the governor's office.[5]

Still governor while Askew assembled his staff, Kirk invoked his authority to appoint eleven new circuit judges. He also had a supreme court vacancy to fill, following Justice Campbell Thornal's death on election night. Although Kirk had agreed to allow the Florida Bar to screen proposed judicial appointments on a confidential basis, he went his own way with the December appointments. The most questionable was of David McCain to succeed Thornal. Kirk disregarded a confidential Florida Bar report that was highly critical of McCain's ethics as a judge of the Fourth District Court of Appeal, to which Kirk had appointed him in 1967. Bar president Burton Young accused Kirk of delivering "a kick in the teeth to the competent and efficient administration of justice." Askew telephoned Young to congratulate him on the statement and to ask the Bar to recommend a nonpartisan method for choosing judges. That method would become one of the major accomplishments of the Golden Age.[6]

To make sure that Kirk could not fill an impending vacancy on the racing commission, Askew and Adams went to the secretary of state's office on New Year's Eve and signed their oaths of office postdated to inauguration day, January 5, 1971. Askew also designated Adams to be secretary of commerce. He said the assignment would be temporary but did not relieve Adams until his hand was forced two years later. For the moment, Askew decided to keep four Kirk appointees with whom he and the legislature were on good terms: Nathaniel Reed as chair of the Air and Water Pollution Control Board, Ed Mueller as secretary of transportation, James Bax as secretary of Health and Rehabilitative Services, and William Maloy as education adviser. The Maloy decision prompted a prickly letter from Floyd T. Christian, the education commissioner. He blamed Maloy for Kirk's attacks on him and complained that he had "done nothing in assisting you in being elected Governor." Presaging his intent to appoint minorities and women to many significant positions, Askew named M. Athalie Range, a businesswoman and Miami city commissioner, to be secretary of community affairs. She was the first African American to head any Florida department. As had most of his predecessors, Askew established patronage committees in each county to recommend candidates for various vacancies. He insisted that each committee include at least one woman and one African American. The committee in Bradford County was headed by one of Askew's unlikeliest supporters, Charley Johns, who had been a strong segregationist as a Pork Chop senator and as acting governor after the death of Dan McCarty in 1953. Johns named his wife and black yardman to the committee.[7]

Askew's election was accompanied by unprecedented turnover in the Cabinet. State senators Robert Shevin and Richard Stone, both of Miami, won the attorney general and secretary of state vacancies left by Earl Faircloth and Adams. Shevin and Stone were the first religious Jews to win popular election statewide.[8] A third Miamian, Metropolitan Dade commissioner Thomas D. O'Malley, became treasurer and insurance commissioner after upsetting incumbent Broward Williams in the Democratic primary. Williams became vulnerable when automobile insurance companies took advantage of a new law to raise premiums without prior approval. He was also faulted for not acting soon enough to conserve the assets of a failing insurance company. His successor was no improvement. O'Malley went to Tallahassee with a scheme in place to extort money from insurance companies through his former law partners.

Typically for Tallahassee, it was wet, windy, and chilly on the day of the inauguration. Neither the outgoing governor nor his successor seemed to mind. Kirk was actually jovial. He predicted history would give him a "good grade" and hinted at a comeback attempt with the words, "And for today, farewell." Kirk left Askew an overspent office budget and underfurnished quarters; he had taken some pieces from the capitol and even his bed from the mansion. His departing chief of staff wrote a personal check to reimburse the state.[9]

Askew used his inaugural address to come out fighting for the corporate profits tax. Unknown to the press or the public at the time, there was intense debate among his advisers not merely over how aggressive he should be on that subject but whether to fight at all. Some, including Adams, argued that it was unattainable and that Askew should drop it. Jim Smith and Pride sent an S.O.S. to Stearns, who recalls being "brutally candid, some might say disrespectful" in a confrontation with Askew. "I said, 'Are you out of your mind? You will be the laughing stock of this state. It doesn't hurt to lose as long as you're losing for a worthy cause. All we need to do is have the Supreme Court tell us the people have to decide.'" The inaugural address, which Stearns wrote, centered on the tax issue. Although Askew spoke strongly about protecting the environment, improving conditions in prisons and migrant labor camps, reforming education, and other progressive themes, his emphasis was on the budget and the necessity of a corporate tax to avoid drastic spending cuts. He said tax reform could not wait for the regular session of the legislature and that he was asking the Florida Supreme Court "today" for an advisory opinion on whether a corporate income tax would be constitutional. If not, the necessary amendment would be submitted to a special session already scheduled for late January on the auto insurance controversy. Askew warned the legislature and the lobbies against trying to substitute a sales tax increase for tax reform:

> We said several months ago that if we were honest with ourselves, we would have to admit that this is going to be one of those years in which the question would not be whether there will be new state taxes—but, rather, who will have to pay. . . . [F]or the Legislature to even consider increasing the sales tax in Florida to five

per cent, while our tax inequities still exist, would be a complete travesty of justice. Continually turning to higher consumer and property taxes to pay for needed public services without facing up to tax inequities is the answer for yesterday. It must not be, it will not be, the answer of today.[10]

Sitting beside Stearns in the audience was Arthur J. England Jr., a Miami tax lawyer newly appointed to advise the House committee that would introduce the corporate tax. He asked Stearns who was writing the supreme court request that Askew had just mentioned. You are, Stearns said; he had forgotten to tell him. England left without hearing the rest of Askew's speech and had the letter ready for Askew's signature and the court's consideration by day's end. Although the court was not obliged to rule on a law before it was passed, the justices accepted the responsibility in light of the state's fiscal plight. The projected deficit was $218 million, an immense amount for the time. Askew was particularly concerned over the prison system, which held 19 percent more inmates than its designed capacity. Later that month, Askew visited two of the prisons where officials as well as inmates complained of inadequate medical facilities and an unresponsive parole commission. Askew said he would request money for more parole examiners. The situation was explosive, and the fuse was shorter than he knew.[11]

A 1924 constitutional amendment, adopted to lure more people to Florida, forbade taxing the income and estates of "residents or citizens" of the state. The question before the court was whether corporations were "citizens" or whether the term applied only to natural persons. If it meant the latter, corporation income could be taxed immediately by majority votes in the legislature. If corporations were "citizens," the constitution would have to be amended before the tax could be enacted. A constitutional amendment must be approved by three-fifths of the membership of each house—at the time, 72 of the 119 representatives and 29 of the 48 senators—and by a referendum of the people. The referendum could not go on the ballot before the 1972 general election unless *three-fourths* of each house—90 representatives and 36 senators—approved an earlier special election. The court would decide whether the political advantage would be with Askew or with the special interests filing briefs against him. The opposing parties included the St. Regis Paper Company, the largest employer in Pensacola; the law firm of J. B. Hopkins, whom Askew had succeeded in the House; the Florida Bankers Association; and Associated Industries of Florida, the state's most aggressive business lobby, which retained Askew's erstwhile opponent John E. Mathews Jr. to argue its case. On Askew's side were the attorney general, the Florida Education Association, and England, nominally representing House Speaker Pettigrew. With the decision pending, Askew warned legislators in a luncheon speech that without a new tax there would be less money available to spend in fiscal 1972 than they had budgeted for 1971. Soon after, the court ruled six to one that corporations were indeed "citizens." It was never specified in 1924, said the court, that only people would benefit from the scheme "to create a climate favorable to capital investment." Although the opinion was unsigned, it was most likely the handiwork of B. K. Roberts, chief justice at the time and the court's dominant member. Years later, in retirement, Roberts let it be known that throughout his twenty-four years on the court he had continued to be the personal attorney for his close friend Edward Ball, Florida's most influential industrialist. As managing trustee of the Alfred I. duPont estate, Ball controlled the St. Joe Paper Company, which owned vast forests, the Florida East Coast Railroad, the Florida National Bank chain, and the St. Joseph Telephone Company. He was a principal opponent to Askew's tax reforms. Although the duPont estate subsidiaries were not parties to the tax case, the outcome was to their liking. Justice Richard Ervin, the most liberal justice and the most prolific dissenter, accused the majority of distorting the intent of the 1924 amendment and the meaning of the English language. "The words 'resident' and 'citizen' plainly bring to mind only natural persons," he wrote. Ervin observed also that "A poor tax base is the prelude to a poor state."[12]

Greg Johnson was making the same points at greater length in a white paper meant to persuade legislators that taxing corporate profits was not only necessary but fair. He described Florida's tax structure as one of nation's ten most "inelastic," in the sense that revenue growth failed to match increases in personal income, and as having one of the "three most regressive" systems in the United States, in that poor people paid a much higher percentage of their income in taxes than did the well-to-do. Corporate taxes nationwide averaged $6.51 for each $1,000 of a state's personal income, but Florida ranked forty-ninth, at a barely discernible 27 cents. Conversely, small businesses were taxed in Florida at three times the national average. A Senate report written for de la Parte, chairman of the Ways and Means Committee, asserted that a corporate tax could yield $175 million without putting Florida businesses at a competitive disadvantage. The state was one of only seven not taxing corporate income. Only seven had higher sales taxes than Florida's four cents on the dollar. It occurred to Ed Price, however, that to tax only corporate income would waste an opportunity. As president of the Florida Chamber of Commerce, he persuaded its executive board to endorse taxation of both corporate and personal income. Askew did not welcome the advice. He commended the chamber for a "good faith" effort but flatly rejected any talk of taxing personal income. He feared it would help special-interest lobbyists kill the corporate tax. The chamber membership was no happier; Price said that if the rules had allowed him to run for reelection he would have lost. There was dissension within the Askew administration as well; not everyone cared for taking a stand on the corporate tax. Adams, for one, reportedly argued that it was one campaign promise that did not need to be kept in the face of the supreme court opinion and the enmity of the business lobbies. So began a long-running rivalry between the liberals, led by Pride and Johnson, and the more numerous pragmatists and conservatives on Askew's staff. More than once Stearns was summoned to reinforce the liberals.[13]

The supreme court, meanwhile, made it somewhat harder for Askew to lobby the legislature. In an unrelated case arising from Miami Beach, the third in which the court broadly interpreted the 1967 "Government in the Sunshine" law, it ruled four to one that even "informal" meetings must be open to the public if the purpose is to discuss "foreseeable action." The case dealt with so-called work sessions, held to decide privately what would be discussed later in public. Shevin, an ardent supporter of the sunshine law, advised the press that reporters could attend any meeting in his office. When Askew inquired whether he had to admit reporters to his meetings with legislators, the attorney general answered yes. Askew, he said, was "none too happy." An Associated

Press reporter then gained admission to—and evidently broke up—a corporate tax strategy meeting in Askew's office. Ever since, governors have preferred to lobby legislators one at a time to keep the media from overhearing. Legislators whom Askew lobbied on the tax said he was gentler than Kirk but unmistakably firm in asking where in their districts they wanted to cut spending.[14]

As the special session convened, the corporate tax appeared to be in immediate trouble because the thirty-nine House Republicans took a caucus position against it. On February 2, however, the House approved the amendment by a vote of seventy-three to forty-five. There had been only one vote to spare. With Miers, Sweeny, and seven other Democrats voting no, the amendment would have failed without the support of two independent Republicans, William Fleece of Pinellas County and Jack Poorbaugh of Palm Beach County. The outcome shocked some anti-tax lobbyists, one of whom was heard to shout, "They lied to us!" Outside the chamber, Bernie Parrish encountered Glen Woodard, lobbyist for the Jacksonville-based Winn-Dixie grocery chain, an implacable opponent. Woodard shook his head, balled his fists, and complained, "This legislature is not like Texas. In Texas they stay bought." He was especially dismayed that six of Jacksonville's nine representatives had voted with Askew. One of them was Bill Birchfield, a lawyer serving his first term in the House, who had thought of himself as a "fairly conservative person" until he got to Tallahassee and saw that "our tax base wasn't growing as fast as our needs were growing." His conversion cost him "a tongue-lashing from Glen," he said. With the House seventeen votes short of the ninety needed to schedule a special referendum, the focus shifted to the Senate. Senators approved a May 11 referendum as well as the amendment itself. Six Republicans favored it, and only one Democrat voted no. The holdouts in the House were unimpressed, however, and refused to agree to the early election. So there would be no help for the 1971–72 budget year. Askew, conceding that "We knew from the beginning our work was cut out for us," chose to regard the outcome as more of a victory than a defeat. "I am looking for a four-year relationship. . . . The days of arm-twisting being effective are over. To win points with this legislature, you'd better do it with persuasion on the merits," he said. (Nonetheless, during the ensuing years more than a few legislators would complain of sore arms after leaving Askew's office.) The special session gave Askew nearly everything else he had asked for, including a law restoring the insurance commissioner's power to rule on proposed auto insurance rates, authority to replace the members of Kirk's Board of Business Regulation, and supplemental Medicaid funding. He appointed Richard Pallot, a Miami banker and early campaign supporter, to chair the board.[15]

Askew was one of four "New South" governors inaugurated in January 1971—along with John C. West of South Carolina, Dale Bumpers of Arkansas, and Jimmy Carter of Georgia—so named by the press because their elections seemingly put racial politics to rest. Although Askew's record on race was superior to Carter's, it was the Georgian who drew most of the national media attention for declaring in his address, "I say to you quite frankly that the time for racial discrimination is over." That Askew had already declared matter-of-factly a policy of "equal rights for all our people" was scarcely mentioned by *Time* or the *New York Times*, which took no note of the Athalie Range appointment. Carter's preemption of the January coverage demonstrated that location is as important in politics as in real estate; Atlanta was the regional headquarters for national media. Even so, it was a source of lingering resentment among Askew's staff, especially when it became Carter rather than Askew who ran for president in 1976.[16]

The special session had scarcely ended when Askew encountered his first crisis, an outbreak of violence at the sprawling Florida State Prison at Raiford. Inmates declared a strike over the parole commission's arbitrary decisions and other assorted grievances. Louie Wainwright, director of the division of corrections, met with their leaders and agreed to some of their requests. But some four hundred inmates refused to return to their cells from the recreation field where they had gathered. Shortly after nightfall, guards opened fire on them, injuring more than sixty. Superintendent Don Hassfurder disclaimed responsibility: "I didn't order the shooting, the major did," he told a reporter, referring to his chief of security. The official account, that the gunfire was provoked by inmates "charging the fence," was eventually refuted by a grand jury. Unrest persisted. Three days after the shooting, prison officers, state troopers, and wildlife agents staged what was called a "show of force" in another section of the prison, injuring more than twenty inmates with nightsticks and gun butts. Mistrusting what he was hearing from officials, Askew sent to Raiford two of his most liberal aides: Don Pride, his press secretary, and Hugh MacMillan, a young attorney. They reported that some nonresisting inmates had been attacked. Recognizing that serious overcrowding contributed to the disorder, Askew issued a five-page statement on steps the state would take to relieve the pressure. Because the prison complex was too large for one superintendent, Askew ordered it split into two institutions.

He and Wainwright disagreed seriously over discipline for certain staff members. Overruling what Wainwright had in mind, Askew ordered ten officers, including the chief of security and an assistant superintendent, suspended for up to thirty days. "Until the protection of rules and laws is provided inside prison walls, we will never adequately establish respect for law and order in our free society," Askew said. He contemplated replacing Wainwright but found that the director, who had risen from the ranks, was considered progressive by peers nationwide. "You've got the best in the country right now," one of them told Askew. If the director had a problem, it lay in his loyalty to subordinates who did not always deserve it.[17]

The Raiford disturbances had a significant influence on the new governor's first regular legislative session. In later years, Tallahassee would show no sympathy to prisoners, but the political climate in the early 1970s still preferred rehabilitation to retribution. Askew, Pettigrew, and like-minded legislators took the Raiford crisis as an opportunity to attempt to reform the parole system, build more halfway houses, expand probation, invest more money in prison education, build new facilities to relieve overcrowding, and ease some punishments that seemed excessively harsh. In July, a grand jury convened by Askew's special prosecutor, State Attorney T. Edward Austin of Jacksonville, reported that the inmates had committed no "significant, overt acts" before the gunfire, that there had been an "apparent bankruptcy" of leadership at the prison, and that some guards should be fired. But the grand jury sensed it would be a waste of time to put the guards on trial before sympathetic friends and neighbors and issued no indictments. No guards lost their jobs.[18]

7

"CURSE YOU, RED BARON"
(1971)

As matters stood, the people of Florida would vote in November 1972 on whether to authorize the legislature to enact a tax on corporate profits. Unwilling to wait half his term to begin collecting it, Askew kept pressure on the legislature for an early referendum. The budget he proposed to the 1971 session entailed $209.8 million in new taxes, including levies on corporate stocks, offset by $39.5 million in sales tax exemptions for renters and utility customers. To business leaders gathered at Tallahassee for the Florida Chamber of Commerce's annual pre-session briefing—an event intended to remind the legislature of its historic "true constituency"—Askew made thinly veiled threats to veto appropriations of interest to them. He mentioned a proposed new university at Jacksonville, a city that was a hotbed of opposition to the corporate tax. He criticized Associated Industries of Florida, the loudest anti-tax lobby, for refusing to identify its members. Simultaneously, Senate leaders vowed to appropriate only existing revenue, undercutting Askew's case for an early referendum. Representative Marshall Harris countered that the House would insist on spending even more than Askew was requesting. "All we're seeking is to impose the taxes we should have had the guts to propose years ago," said Harris, who chaired the appropriations committee. He pointed out that he needed only a simple majority to lay a heavy hand on corporations by removing the $2,000-a-year ceiling on stock tax liability. Speaker Richard Pettigrew was negotiating for more Republican votes for the early referendum, but there were still not ninety, dashing Askew's hope to call another special session in March.[1]

"The people cry out for action now," Askew declared to a joint session when the legislature convened on April 6.

> Let no one falsely raise the specter of big spending simply as a device to avoid tax reform. Let no one today give yesterday's answer for every fiscal crisis—further expansion or increases in consumer taxes without first requiring big business to pay its fair share. And let me make it very clear—this administration cannot, and will not, accept another penny increase in the sales tax to resolve our present fiscal dilemma. The time for tax reform is now, and I am asking you to take it up as your first order of business.[2]

Askew also laid out more than fifty major proposals, including comprehensive prison reform, creation of a bond finance agency to subsidize housing, rehabilitation rather than jail for alcoholics, a severance tax on phosphate mining, and a penny increase in the gasoline tax. He declared to state agencies that equal opportunity should become "a routine characteristic of the lives of all Floridians." No governor had asked as much of the legislature since LeRoy Collins's first address in 1955. Askew acknowledged that nearly every proposal had originated in the legislature itself. "He claimed everything we were going to do anyway," Pettigrew said. One such request was to reenact the nonpartisan judiciary legislation that Kirk had vetoed. The House passed it the first day by a vote of ninety-one to twenty-five, with sixteen of the thirty-eight Republicans in favor and only five Democrats opposed. Passage was more partisan in the Senate a month later; only three of the sixteen Republicans voted yes.[3]

Two weeks into the session, eight Republicans and five Democrats who had opposed an early tax referendum switched sides, leaving Askew and Pettigrew only four votes short in the House. Pettigrew was certain of the next attempt but wanted it to be a bipartisan victory, which would necessitate concessions to the Republicans. On a personal level, Pettigrew did not want to embarrass his friend, Minority Leader Don Reed. Politically, he needed Reed's Republicans for a united front against the Senate over the budget and many other issues on which the two chambers would likely disagree. It was in Reed's interest "not to go down jousting at windmills," his aide Pete Dunbar said. The compromise was set out in eleven pages consisting mostly of matters on which Reed and Pettigrew already agreed. Reed was able to tell his caucus that the Republicans had achieved "what we intended to do by squeezing them into close scrutiny of the budget." In the House that day, Pettigrew left the rostrum to speak from the floor for a bill setting a July 6 referendum, the earliest possible date. Exhausted and hoarse from the nonstop negotiations, he could barely manage the words "I continue to be very proud of the House" before he was overcome with emotion. His voice broke and he sat down. The House gave him a standing ovation lasting nearly half a minute and voted 102–16 in favor of the bill. Askew's polite but steady pressure and Pettigrew's bipartisan diplomacy had won over thirty opponents in barely two months.[4]

It was now the Senate's turn to balk. This was a new bill in a new session; its previous agreement to an early referendum was moot. When the House's July 6 bill came to the floor, Senator Dempsey Barron, a tall, redheaded attorney and cattle rancher from Panama City, was determined to stop it regardless of what Askew wanted. He made a dramatic speech, declaring that the moment was the first opportunity he had seen in fifteen years of lawmaking "to do something about cutting the cost of government." Sponsor Louis de la Parte, recognizing that no chance remained to win the vote, responded to Barron with the most memorable and certainly the shortest riposte anyone had heard. "Curse you, Red Baron," he said with a smile. The familiar phrase from the comic strip *Peanuts* convulsed the Senate. Barron laughed as heartily as the rest. It appeared to many, however, that there was more than ideology in Barron's objection to the early referendum: a jealousy, perhaps, of the former colleague, Askew, who had similar humble roots, had served a comparable constituency in the legislature, and had risen so much higher. Barron had become a legislator in 1956, two years before Askew, with whom he had some things in common. Both were self-made men; Barron, a stevedore's son, had quit school in the third grade because he was too poor to afford shoes. Like Askew, he had relied on the GI Bill to put himself through college and law school. He had voted bravely on race and reapportionment, positions that were as perilous in his district as in Askew's. Their similarities went no further. Barron drank and was as profane as Askew was puritanical. Barron distrusted government as much as Askew admired it. He was so disinterested in the details of legislation—most unlike Askew—that some thought he was lazy. His mission in the Senate was not to pass legislation for which he might be remembered but to control the process, and he succeeded. He became the most influential member—"Boss Barron," hostile editorials called him—for the last fourteen of his twenty-eight years in the Senate. Senate presidents invariably posed for their official portraits in suits and ties, often beside an American flag. Not Barron; his portrays him in an open cowboy shirt, astride his favorite palomino.[5]

Although a majority of senators had voted for the July referendum, there were still eight votes too few. Barron was one of four Democrats opposing it. Askew gave up hope for revenue from a corporate profits tax in the 1971–72 budget. When the Senate eventually approved a referendum for November 1971 he said it was "certainly a great deal better" than a year later. Barron and nine other opponents switched their votes on that occasion. That owed largely if not entirely to a strategic calculation by executives of the Winn-Dixie grocery chain that opponents would have a better chance of defeating the amendment in a special referendum, with likely low voter turnout, than in the presidential election a year later. One Jacksonville senator, Lew Brantley, had not gotten the instructions and started to object. He was called outside the chamber, where Winn-Dixie lobbyist Glen Woodard explained the deal in coarse language. The House, taking no chances on the Senate changing its mind yet again, quickly agreed to the November date. The budget, complicated by a school financing dispute that eluded compromise, remained unresolved until a difficult special session in June. The result was a penny-a-gallon gasoline tax increase for city and county roads, a two-cent-per-pack cigarette tax increase, and higher sales taxes on motor vehicles and industrial machinery. The legislature also enacted a $24 million corporate net-worth tax with a provision repealing it upon a profits tax becoming law. Reed switched his vote from no to yes to pass the net-worth tax. "When I pushed my button in the red, the devil made me do it," he said. The House also voted to tax advertising and other services, but the Senate would not hear of it.[6]

The special session kept Askew from addressing the Florida Bar's annual convention in Miami. Speaking for him, Bar president Burton Young announced that Askew would issue an executive order creating nominating councils to replace judges who died or resigned between elections. The method was known as "merit selection" or as the "Missouri Plan," for the state that had initiated it. Giving up part of his constitutional prerogative to fill midterm vacancies, Askew would bind himself to choosing only from nominees recommended by the councils. Most importantly, the nine-member panels would be beyond his control. He would appoint three lawyers to each. The Florida Bar would choose three more attorneys. Those six would select the final three, who could not be lawyers. No member could be a political party official. Askew said he meant to ensure that "only the most qualified, conscientious, and dedicated persons" would be appointed. Separately, he ordered his staff not to suggest candidates to the councils or interfere with them.[7]

Tom Adams's enthusiasm for the Cross-Florida Barge Canal became a problem for Askew early in 1971. The governor had yet to establish his own position when Adams spoke out against a federal judge's temporary injunction and denounced President Nixon's order to halt all work. Adams accused Nixon of an "unwanted and arrogated assumption of authority." Askew disagreed; he considered the president's action "unorthodox" but within his power. (A federal court eventually ruled Nixon's decision to be illegal.) Soon after, Adams declared that Nixon "threw the canal to the phony ecologists as he would a bone to a pack of hungry dogs." Askew told indignant environmentalists that he, not Adams, would make the administration's policy. He soon signaled what that policy would be by joining Shevin in a Cabinet resolution requesting the Corps of Engineers to restore the free flow of the Ocklawaha River, which had been dammed to create part of the canal route. It was a short-lived victory; canal supporters prevailed on Secretary of State Richard Stone to get the vote overturned. Privately, Askew and Stearns became concerned that Adams could be hurting the governor's image. With Florida's posture still unresolved, Nixon chose Nathaniel Reed to be assistant secretary of the interior for fish, wildlife, and parks. Reed told Askew, who tried to persuade him to stay in Florida, that he was accepting the promotion with "great regret." Askew took Reed's parting advice to appoint a conservation adviser on his personal staff. The post went to Ken Woodburn, an ecologist at the Florida Department of Natural Resources, whom Askew knew to be a valuable source for capital reporters. Askew appointed David Levin to Reed's official position as chair of the Air and Water Pollution Control Board. Another water project provided Askew with an anecdote he loved to retell. At the groundbreaking for the Tennessee-Tombigbee Waterway, Askew sat next to Alabama governor George Wallace while Nixon gave the main address. Wallace, who was partly deaf, kept asking Askew to repeat what the president had said. "Can you imagine the assignment I had that day," Askew joked, "interpreting Richard Nixon's remarks for George Wallace?"[8]

Adams continued to act as if it was his job to make trouble. In a dispute over workers' compensation legislation, he sent an insulting letter to Senator Mallory Horne, the Senate president-designate, threatening an Askew veto. In the letter, Adams renounced a country club membership that Horne had given him. "Tear the thing up," Horne replied, "for it was intended as a courtesy to a friend and it no longer discharges that function."[9]

Askew was soon thrust into a highly emotional public controversy. In Florida as elsewhere there was an outburst of sympathy for U.S. Army lieutenant William Calley, who had been convicted of murdering Vietnamese civilians in what came to be known as the My Lai massacre. Several hundred people confronted Askew at a shopping mall, where he was delivering a speech, to demand that he sign a clemency petition for Calley. Askew refused. "I was a proud soldier," he declared, "and our government has never condoned killing innocent people." In a statement refusing requests that he declare a day of mourning for Calley, Askew implied that some degree of mercy might be appropriate because the nation sent him to a dubious war. "While we cannot condone his actions, neither can we escape our share of the responsibility for them," he said. In the legislature, the Calley affair became one of the rare occasions when debate calmed tempers and changed minds. Freshman Republican Bob Johnson of Sarasota, making his first speech to the House, denied that Calley was a hero. The heroes of Vietnam, he said, were honorable soldiers who had died in action—among them the Army warrant officer whose widow Johnson had married. The House then shelved a resolution demanding a presidential pardon in favor of one asking in general terms for "fairness and justice" in the case. Speaker Pettigrew sent a transcript of Johnson's speech to each senator. The watered-down resolution died in the Senate after Senator Fred Karl of Daytona Beach, a respected lawyer who would later be elected to the state supreme court, recounted his experience in the Battle of the Bulge. He pulled his pistol on a captured German who had killed four of his friends, but put the weapon away "because it would have been murder." That, Karl said, "is when I cast my vote on Lieutenant Calley." Calley ultimately served a mere three and a half years under house arrest.[10]

Askew faced yet another intense controversy when the Senate lost its collective temper over the perceived morals and left-wing politics of some university students. A series of non-credit courses organized, taught, and financed entirely by students at Florida State University included one titled "How to Make a Revolution in the U.S.A." The lecturer was a student known as "Radical Jack" Lieberman. Another irritant was the Board of Regents' decision to allow male and female university students to visit in each others' dormitories. The Senate voted to abolish the Board of Regents, which would have put the governor and Cabinet in direct charge of the system. The bill went nowhere in the House. Meanwhile, a committee chaired by Senator Robert Haverfield of Miami investigated Lieberman, whose enrollment promptly surged from twelve students to eighty. His success was short-lived; FSU eventually expelled him. Elizabeth Kovachevich, a dissident regent, inflamed the situation by denouncing open dormitories as "taxpayers' whorehouses," a phrase she attributed to a parent. Askew reportedly asked in private, "How would she know?" Publicly, he called her allegations "exaggerated." In a speech at the University of Florida he declared, "We cannot hope nor attempt to enforce the rules of a kindergarten on a university community. In attempting to do so, it would ruin the atmosphere of freedom of learning." The regents ultimately adopted a visitation policy essentially limited to students over twenty-one. The publicity helped Kovachevich win appointment as a federal district judge. Another lasting consequence was enactment of a Haverfield bill requiring faculty members to teach at least twelve semester hours at universities and fifteen hours at junior colleges. Professors engaged in research often spent less time in classrooms. The House weakened the legislation by allowing committee work and other university service to count against the hours. Because Senate president Jerry Thomas had been particularly outspoken against the regents, it seemed to some that he was preparing to run for governor. He denied that he would, but in 1974 he did. As for Haverfield, who had served on Askew's Dade patronage committee, the governor in 1972 appointed him to a district court of appeal.[11]

Squabbling between the House and Senate is inherent in every bicameral legislature. During the 1971 and 1972 sessions it was accentuated by the contrasting personalities and philosophies of the two presiding officers, Pettigrew and Thomas. Even so, the two chambers agreed in 1971 on some of the most important legislation of the twentieth century. The Baker Act was a comprehensive reform, the first in ninety-seven years, of Florida's mental health practices. Named for its sponsor, Representative Maxine Baker of Miami, the law guaranteed civil rights and due process to psychiatric patients. It said they could be held against their will only if found to be dangerous to themselves or others, and then only so long as necessary. "In the name of mental health, we deprive them of their most precious possession—liberty," Baker told the House shortly before it approved her bill 101–6. The Myers Act, named for Senator Kenneth Myers of Miami, was a landmark in the treatment of alcoholics. It prohibited jailing people for simply being drunk and provided for detoxification centers to care for them. Myers was supported strongly by legislators with police experience. "Week in, week out, I took the same people to jail, alcoholics who were not really bothering anybody, not really committing any crime," said Representative Jim Tillman, a Sarasota Republican who had been a deputy sheriff. The House agreed to the Myers Act on the same day the Senate passed Myers's bill to establish state-run probation services to support juvenile courts. Tillman helped also to reduce to a misdemeanor the felony penalty for possessing five grams or less of marijuana. He had opposed a similar bill in 1970 but changed his mind after a subcommittee's visit to the prison at Lowell. It heard from three young women whom the legislators thought should have been in college rather than serving felony sentences. One had been caught with five marijuana plants. The others had been talked into buying the drug from narcotics agents. Askew also signed into law six other prison reform bills. He said they represented "a start in the right direction . . . toward not just warehousing bodies but rebuilding wasted lives." The principal measures authorized family furloughs, expanded work-release, ordered the parole commission to interview most inmates annually, and authorized government agencies to employ ex-felons. The parole commissioners, who owed their appointments to the Cabinet, lobbied successfully against Askew's proposal to reassign their professional staff to the division of corrections.[12]

A twenty-year fight to tax the phosphate mines that had made moonscapes of much central Florida terrain ended in a lopsided victory in the House, ninety-three votes yes to fifteen no. The Pork Choppers had stoutly opposed the severance tax, never allowing it to clear any committee. As enacted, it allowed mining companies to write off as much as half the tax for land reclamation. Sponsor A. S. "Jim" Robinson, a St. Petersburg Republican, said it was an acceptable amendment because "I am interested primarily in conservation." Some of the proceeds were dedicated later to the purchase of land for conservation and recreation. Another Pork Chop bastion fell when the legislature voted to cap each county's annual share of racetrack revenue at $412,000, the yield for 1970, so that the state budget would reap the benefit from future growth. Rural legislators said it betrayed a deal made to get their predecessors' votes to override Governor Doyle E. Carlton's veto of the 1931 bill legalizing pari-mutuel gambling. Yet another anachronism was overcome when Askew signed legislation to put the profit-making properties of nonprofit entities, such as the bars maintained by veterans' and fraternal organizations, on the real estate tax rolls. To control auto insurance premiums, the 1971 session enacted one of the nation's first "no-fault" laws obliging motorists to insure themselves against injury. Serious injuries and death remained subject to lawsuits. Its passage was the first of many significant accomplishments for Kenneth A. "Buddy" MacKay Jr., a second-term House member from Ocala who was said to be the only legislator who could explain the bill. It did not endear him to his fellow attorneys.[13]

Askew had recommended no-fault auto insurance but not no-fault divorce, an issue important to Pettigrew, Sandy D'Alemberte, Majority Leader Don Nichols of Jacksonville, and many others. The governor took no position during the intense debate over replacing adultery, cruelty, and other traditional grounds with a single cause: that the marriage was "irretrievably" broken. "You won't have it stated in a public record for little children to read that their mother goes out and commits adultery with everyone in town, if that's what she does, or that their father is a dope addict or has an ungovernable temper," said Representative Don Tucker, a Democrat from Tallahassee. Sponsors contended that such evidence was often manufactured to obtain divorces both spouses wanted. D'Alemberte and his judiciary committee staff director, Janet Reno—a future U.S. attorney general—were stunned to hear late one night that Askew was about to veto the legislation. When they tried to talk him out of it, he told them about his parents' divorce and the fact that he had never known his father. "Askew is a wonderful guy, but he is stubborn. . . . Once he makes up his mind, you're not likely to change him," said D'Alemberte. Not even Eugene Stearns could change the governor's mind; Stearns said it was the only time he lost an argument with Askew. His veto message contended that the bill would make dissolution too easy and turn Florida into a divorce mill. Askew's former law partner David Levin, who had been an outspoken opponent of the bill, denied insinuations that he had influenced Askew. "The people who attack Reubin Askew don't know him very well if they think I talked him into anything. This man prays about things," Levin said. The surprise veto interrupted Askew's honeymoon with Florida's liberals. Pettigrew told the House the governor had handled it "poorly" and should not wait until the "eleventh hour" to voice his concerns over major legislation. Senator Gerald Lewis of Miami, who had recently experienced a bitter divorce, accused Askew of having "satisfied the divorce lawyers at the expense of the average citizen." But the sixty-two members who voted to override the veto were nine short of the two-thirds necessary. Askew then agreed to a compromise negotiated by Reno and David Levin, and it was enacted during the special session. It satisfied Askew's objections by empowering judges to order marriage counseling and by allowing one spouse to contest the other's claim that a marriage was beyond repair.[14]

Askew also vetoed a $600,000 limit on the cost of any airplane purchased for his use along with bills to shift control of the Jacksonville Port Authority from the governor to the mayor, to loosen liquor laws in Nassau County, to give horse breeders a larger share of racetrack revenue, and to forbid urban renewal in Pinellas County without a vote of property owners. No Askew veto would be overridden until 1976.[15]

Historically, Florida's May presidential primary had accomplished nothing more than publicizing favorite-son candidates. At Pettigrew's insistence, the legislature moved it to mid-March, with provisions intended to ensure that Florida would have an early and dramatic influence on future nominations. The law required all known candidates in both parties to be listed on the primary ballots even if they preferred not to campaign in Florida. They could remove their names only by formally disavowing interest in the presidency. The motive was political. Pettigrew presumed that Florida Democrats would give a decisive early boost to a centrist candidate rather than a liberal. He favored Senator Edmund Muskie of Maine, the 1968 vice-presidential nominee. The Speaker was thinking ahead to November, when he feared that down-ballot Democratic candidates would suffer if the ticket was led by a liberal like Senator George McGovern of South Dakota, who was already campaigning. The ink was barely dry on Askew's signature when the law of unintended consequences came into play. Martin Waldron of the *New York Times* foresaw that Wallace "could sweep virtually the entire state of Florida."[16]

Through the special session in June 1971, the House members elected the previous November compiled a remarkable voting record. Of the 372 roll-call votes on significant controversies, only 161—fewer than half—were partisan. There were none in which all the Democrats voted together, and only four in which Republican ranks were solid. Despite the imbalance in numbers, the Republicans won thirty-nine of the partisan roll calls. They owed it to support from significant minorities of the Democrats. These were not always the conservatives; Democratic liberals were often their allies on the environment, education, and issues affecting the Cabinet. "On many of those votes, Democrats could not assemble a majority of the Democrats," D'Alemberte said. In thirty-seven of the partisan votes, Reed and Pettigrew were on the same side; one or the other was bucking his own rank and file. Some Republicans even tried to force Reed to step down as minority leader before the end of his term in November 1972. Jerry Thomas remarked that the Senate had replaced the House Republicans as "the loyal opposition party." When Schultz and Pettigrew were the Speakers, they and their staffs regularly consulted Reed and his aides to work out differences. "There really wasn't that much to fight about by the time the stuff got to the floor," Reed said. In 1974, Reed—no longer a legislator—broke party ranks to endorse Pettigrew for the U.S. Senate. Reed blamed incumbent Republican Ed Gurney for blocking his appointment to a federal judgeship. (Gurney withdrew from the race; Pettigrew lost in the primary.)[17]

With relatively little notice, the 1971 session also enacted "education accountability" legislation that led to routine testing of public school students. Controversy persists over how Florida eventually applied the results to punish or reward individual schools. The session failed to continue increasing the public school financing formula that Marshall Harris had created the year before. Its goal was to equalize per-pupil spending between wealthy and poor counties. The impasse particularly disappointed T. Terrell Sessums, the Tampa Democrat who was in line to succeed Pettigrew as Speaker. Acting on an earlier suggestion by Fred Schultz, Askew signed an executive order creating a blue-ribbon committee on education to make recommendations for the 1972 and 1973 sessions. He offered the chairmanship to Schultz, but there was a catch. Askew insisted Schultz interrupt a long-delayed family vacation in Europe and start work immediately. To make sure Schultz could not refuse, the governor said he could handpick most of the committee members. Mrs. Schultz was not pleased.[18]

8

"AND RIGHTLY SO" (1971)

Like many other journalists—the author included—Don Pride occasionally took a deadline to mean "no sooner" rather than "no later." Askew told him of a recurring nightmare in which he would be reading a speech to an audience while his press secretary sat at a typewriter behind a curtain, passing him the pages one by one. Another man's misfortune resolved their mutual problem with speeches. Roland Page, a young editorial writer for the *St. Petersburg Times*, had been fired for protesting that a new colleague with lesser responsibilities was being paid a higher salary. Pride seized the opportunity to hire a speechwriter and add another strongly liberal voice to Askew's mostly conservative staff. Chicago-born, Page had majored in history at Georgia Southern University and had earned a master's degree in political science at Florida State. Before writing editorials, he had won the admiration of black citizens in St. Petersburg who were surprised that a white reporter had fairly covered their grievances with the police. Soon after moving his family to Tallahassee, Page drafted the most significant speech of Askew's career.[1]

In April 1971 the U.S. Supreme Court held unanimously that North Carolina's Charlotte-Mecklenburg Board of Education should transfer black students from the inner city to suburban all-white schools. The ruling definitively upheld busing for racial balance as ordered by Ben Krentzman and other federal judges in the South. Claude Kirk, George Wallace, and many other southern politicians now had new fuel for demagoguery. In Congress, four Florida representatives proposed a constitutional amendment to supersede the decision. At first, President

Richard Nixon called for the law to be obeyed. Then, remembering his "Southern Strategy," he announced a policy to restrict busing "to the minimum required by law." He also maneuvered to withhold federal funds from busing. In so doing, he undermined his own Department of Health, Education and Welfare, which had been helping southern districts comply.[2]

During the 1970 campaign, Askew was skeptical of busing; unlike Kirk, he did not make an issue of it. He said that the effects of segregation would be remedied better by improving schools and faculties, because "massive busing has not proved to be the solution." He responded to the Charlotte decision with a very brief statement: "The court has spoken in a unanimous decision, and it is up to the states in good faith to try to comply with the least disruption possible in our school systems." That did not calm rising tempers in Florida. During the 1970–71 term, sixteen years after *Brown v. Board of Education*, nearly half of Florida's school boards were in litigation; fifty-two schools were still entirely black. Significant court-ordered desegregation was about to occur throughout the state, including the large counties of Pinellas, Broward, Orange, and Duval. Thomas Todd, executive director of the Florida School Boards Association, told Askew he feared violence; he had heard unconfirmed reports of plots to blow up school buses. Askew realized that "a strong statement had to be made." Simultaneously, Page was pleading to Pride that the governor should take a stand in support of busing. Pride agreed. A speech already scheduled at the University of Florida's summer commencement on August 28 seemed to be the right occasion. "We need very much to get off the defense and on the offense," Pride wrote in a memorandum to Askew. "This is a time when Reubin Askew needs to be heard. You stand for integrity in government, and people, particularly the students, will be asking you to speak out on the issue of our time." Privately, the young staffers were pessimistic. As Page wrote in a newspaper column seven years later, "The racial fever was so hot that Askew's continued failure to demagogue it threatened to alienate his more conservative supporters, kill his campaign for tax reform, and paralyze his administration for good." To their amazement, Askew told them to write the speech. They took a twenty-page draft to him while he was playing tennis at the home of FSU president J. Stanley

Marshall. Askew read it between sets, handed it back, and said "okay." Disbelieving their success, Pride and Page asked him to look again at the busing passage, which they had placed in the middle of an otherwise typical commencement speech. Had he read it? Yes, Askew said, "I didn't think it was strong enough." They made changes.[3]

"Perhaps the most crucial September in the long and remarkable history of our public schools will be upon us in a matter of days," Askew said to the graduates and their families. "How sad it will be if the emotions of the hour become the legacy of a generation. Our schools must be maintained. Our children must be allowed to learn. And our laws must be respected and observed."[4] Remarking that virtually every county in Florida was represented at the graduation, Askew appealed to the students and parents "to encourage reason and calm in your own communities in the days ahead" and to work toward "the broad community desegregation and cooperation which ultimately will make busing unnecessary." The words that followed went boldly where no other southern politician dared to go:

> For busing certainly is an artificial and inadequate instrument of change. Nobody really wants it—not you, not me, not the people, not the school boards—not even the courts.
>
> Yet the law demands, *and rightly so*, that we put an end to segregation in our society.
>
> We must demonstrate good faith in doing just that. . . . We must stop inviting, by our own intransigence, devices which are repugnant to us.
>
> In this way and in this way only, will we stop massive busing once and for all. Only in this way will we put the divisive and self-defeating issue of race behind us once and for all.
>
> And only in this way can we redirect our energies to our real quest, that of providing an equal opportunity for quality education to all of our children. If there is another answer, I have yet to hear it. Tolerance is the key. I hope that all citizens will use it in the days ahead.[5]

The phrase "and rightly so" appears to have been Askew's own addition to the draft. "I didn't want to hide behind a court opinion," Askew said many years later. He had second thoughts as he was about to speak but put them aside. What Askew had done, Page wrote in the column, moved "from merely accepting measures the South had resisted for more than a hundred years to actually endorsing them." Although Askew was exhilarated afterward, Page thought the speech had flopped. He wrote that the few in the audience who stood and applauded were like "occasional stalks of rattling corn among the acres of sodden silence."[6]

While Askew was speaking at Gainesville, Kirk was haranguing an estimated seven thousand cheering people at an anti-busing rally at a baseball stadium in St. Petersburg, where he vowed to lead a national campaign against busing. (Nothing ever came of it.) Wallace was provoking a similar frenzy in Jacksonville. The Orange County School Board was threatening to defy a judge's order. In most newspapers the next morning, those staff-written articles were displayed much more prominently than the wire-service account of Askew's commencement speech. The *Miami Herald* and *St. Petersburg Times* versions omitted the pregnant phrase "and rightly so." To Pride and Page, it was as if a tree had fallen and nobody had heard it. That was at first; their office had tipped CBS News, which had aired a portion that night. Over the next few days, national interest developed. Pride sent a copy to Tom Wicker, a prominent columnist at the *New York Times*, who wrote favorably about Askew and the speech. To Askew's irritation, various reporters began to speculate on his running for vice-president.[7]

The press office had kept to itself what Askew would say at Gainesville. Askew advisers including Jim Apthorp, Jim Smith, Ed Dunn, and even Eugene Stearns were astonished that they and others had not been consulted. Apthorp, for one, said later that he "agreed entirely" with the speech. Not for the last time, however, the conservatives in the administration feared that Pride and Page were leading Askew toward political oblivion.[8]

Schools opened relatively peacefully across Florida within days after Askew spoke. Busing was not a significant factor in the ensuing campaign for ratification of the corporate profits tax amendment. Yet it remained an intensely divisive issue, and as the school year wore on there were occasional battles between black and white students. A deputy was stabbed during one outbreak at Dixie Hollins High School near St. Petersburg, and all black students were sent home. While attending an Atlanta meeting of the Southern Governors Conference in November, Askew held an impromptu news conference to voice his distaste over anti-government remarks by Wallace, Georgia governor Jimmy Carter, and Mississippi's John Bell Williams. He called on them to abandon their "endless and useless rhetoric" and accept busing as a "temporary expedient to provide opportunity for all." Some governors, he complained, seemed to think that Washington was "a foreign power." Ten days later, speaking to the Florida PTA Congress, he deplored white flight to private schools, which he said often involved more busing than the courts had ordered. He foresaw a death spiral of declining enrollment and tax support "until only the very poor, both black and white, are left . . . and the great American system of public education is reduced to a baby-sitting service run on federal welfare." He was vehement over the convention's vote the day before to ask Congress for an anti-busing amendment to the Constitution. Even though a majority of the delegates had attempted to rescind the resolution, Askew warned that the damage was irreparable. "The way to end busing is to seek the broader community desegregation which will make it unnecessary," he said. "We must decide which is worse—temporary hardship and inconvenience, or continuing inequality and injustice. We must decide whether apartheid is what we really want in this country, be it *de facto* or *de jure*."[9]

Page would have many more busing speeches to write in 1972.

9

"SOME NUT WITH A
HUEY LONG OUTLOOK" (1971)

Barely two months before the public vote on the corporate profits tax amendment, Askew had yet to decide on a campaign strategy. Remembering the road bond debacle that had brought down Haydon Burns, some friends and advisers were warning Askew not to risk his own future on a referendum. Jim Smith disagreed strongly and contended that Askew should make a fight of it. Unlike Burns, Smith wrote in a memorandum, Askew "is immensely popular with the people and I think they will respond to his involvement." Smith also registered a complaint: Askew seemed no longer to be consulting "a number of people" who had helped elect him, among them David Kennedy, Elmer Rounds, Tom Adams, Smith himself, and even Gene Stearns. Smith said Askew needed to meet—"and very soon"—with his core supporters. Greg Johnson had already proposed a campaign that would rely on free media, personal appearances, and support from Ed Price and other sympathetic business leaders. Johnson cautioned that a "high-powered media campaign" would be a "tactical mistake." As Askew himself saw the situation, the people had not elected him simply to repudiate Claude Kirk, but neither was his victory a clear mandate for tax reform. He heard from his pollster, William Hamilton, that many voters would not understand the referendum and that he would have to frame it as a vote of confidence in him. "Stearns just hit me squarely," Askew recalled. "He said, 'If you want this thing to pass, Governor, you are going to have to do it.' So we ran it almost as a postscript to the general election."[1]

Once the busing speech was behind him, Askew devoted himself to the referendum. On September 8, 1971, he announced a campaign committee, Citizens for Tax Reform, chaired by Ben Hill Griffin Jr., the former Democratic senator and millionaire citrus grower who had advocated a corporate income tax when Askew was against it. Smith took leave as Adams's deputy commerce secretary to manage the campaign. It did not start auspiciously. Only four days later, Florida's principal labor leader, Charlie Harris, quit the committee in a huff. Harris, president of the state AFL-CIO, objected in a letter that Askew and the Cabinet had hired a non-union contractor to build a new capitol complex. (The lowest bidder, a union firm, had been disqualified on a technicality.) The successful bidder was from Pensacola, Askew's hometown. Harris also had grievances with Adams's staffing decisions at the Department of Commerce. Even so, most unions supported Askew in the referendum, and several published a full-page ad endorsing the amendment.[2]

Askew also lost a prominent business supporter. Prime F. Osborne III, president of the Seaboard Coast Line Railroad, telephoned the governor one night to explain why he had to quit the committee. Winn-Dixie, the grocery chain that had lobbied the legislature against the tax, had threatened to "not ship another pound" on Osborne's railroad. When that story eventually broke, just before the referendum, Winn-Dixie lobbyist Glen Woodard denied it. Osborne himself tacitly confirmed it by refusing to comment. His resignation was more than merely symbolic; his railroad owned a controlling interest in the *Florida Times-Union* and the *Jacksonville Journal*, the city's only mass-circulation newspapers, which took strong editorial positions against the corporate tax. Winn-Dixie was also thought to be a principal influence in Associated Industries, the umbrella lobby for commercial interests which refused to disclose its membership. Askew suspected Ed Ball of using the immense influence of the duPont estate to organize opposition to the tax. Ball retorted that Askew was "a damn liar" if he said that Ball was financing the opponents. He was denying what Askew had not said.[3]

Unlike Ball, Winn-Dixie was not publicity-shy. Customers went home with grocery bags imprinted with anti-tax propaganda. A form letter told stockholders that the tax would cost them up to $3 million over the ensuing three years. Other lobbies were equally vociferous. At the urging of the Florida Bankers Association, many banks stuffed their monthly statements with "Ax the Tax" leaflets. A Quincy tobacco dealer who had been a longtime customer of the duPont estate's Florida National Bank at Jacksonville wrote Askew that he had been turned down under curious circumstances for a routine, fully collateralized loan. That happened after a meeting in which Ball objected to the man's support for the tax. Askew took particular offense at the banks. Speaking to the Dade County Bankers Association in September, he charged that of all Florida businesses, "the banks have been among the first when it comes to winning government protection and assistance . . . but among the last when it comes to paying for the government." Several telephone and power companies stuffed "Ax the Tax" in their billing envelopes; at Askew's urging, the Public Service Commission (PSC) warned them against incorporating political expenses into their rate structures. Askew also wanted to compel the utilities to mail pro-tax pamphlets to their customers, but the PSC said it lacked the authority. Jack Eckerd wrote to the thousands of employees in his Florida drugstores, claiming that a yes vote would result in "a personal income tax somewhere down the road." Anticipating that red herring, Askew had sought the opinion of a blue-ribbon Florida Bar committee. The lawyers concluded that there was no "reasonable construction" of the amendment that would allow personal income to be taxed. Throughout the campaign, opponents sought to confuse the one tax with the other. Republicans in Orange County sold bumper stickers saying "Don't let A$skew tax you/Vote NO corporate tax." Askew won a significant tactical victory after challenging twenty-four television stations to give him free time equal to what they were selling to "well-funded opponents." The Federal Communications Commission ruled that Askew was entitled to the time under the agency's Fairness Doctrine. That success prompted a tongue-in-cheek demand from Don Reed for use of state staff and facilities to "give me equal opportunity, at taxpayers' expense, to discuss the other side of the corporate income tax issue." Askew did not reply.[4]

Askew's most effective selling point was a campaign parable, "The Rising of Joe Florida," which described the activities of an average citizen between waking in the morning and leaving for work. In that short time he used twenty-two national brand-name products. Their manufacturers paid taxes to other states; why not to Florida? In a speech to Associated Industries—perhaps the most hostile audience of the entire campaign—Askew warned that there would be no limit to increases in the new capital stock tax if the income tax failed. "It won't be repealed as claimed by your representatives," he said, "or else it will be repealed over my veto."[5]

The Cabinet gratified Askew with a resolution endorsing the tax. In winning it, Askew exposed the banking lobby's influence over Comptroller Fred O. "Bud" Dickinson Jr., who had abstained on the dubious ground that his capacity as state banking commissioner required his "neutrality." Dickinson did not explain how it would be improper for him to disagree with the banks on a political issue. Askew asked rhetorically whether he was also neutral as a member of the state Board of Education. It was too much heat for Dickinson, who left the meeting early. Subsequently, Askew charged that Dickinson's neutrality was false. He cited a sudden stream of press releases in which the comptroller appeared to imply that existing tax revenue was sufficient. In contrast to Dickinson, Education Commissioner Floyd Christian supported the referendum passionately. When a Tallahassee merchant mailed him an anti-tax pamphlet, Christian wrote back that "Neither my wife nor I, our daughter, our sons, our grandchildren, nor any other member of my family will ever put a foot in your store again!" He sent a copy of his letter to Askew with a handwritten note, "Rube I meant it!"[6]

In the final month, Askew campaigned as hard for the tax amendment as he had for his election a year before. When a reporter asked whether he intended to intensify the campaign, Donna Lou Askew replied, "There's no room to intensify it." Apthorp and Smith worried that Askew was becoming too confrontational and tried to send word through Pride, who was traveling with him, to tone it down. "And that's as far as it would go," said Pride, who kept the messages to himself. Askew repeatedly mocked William Dean Barrow, a garrulous state senator from Crestview, for supporting corporations that did not want to pay taxes. He cited Barrow's sponsorship of a 1970 law that required people who fished with cane poles to buy the same three-dollar license as those who used expensive tackle. On election day, Barrow filed a bill to exempt cane poles once again, but the 1972 session did not pass it.

Stumping at home during the last week of the campaign, Askew ripped into the *Pensacola News Journal* for its opposition to the tax, saying that the newspaper "has never forgiven us for winning." He accused the paper's political editor, who was sitting red-faced in the front row, of bearing a grudge after having had to wait for an appointment with him. "Nothing this administration does is right in his eyes," Askew said. He claimed that the journalist identified only the liberal groups backing the tax, never mentioning the business interests that supported it also. Having battled bronchitis for five weeks, Askew came down with fever, stomach pains, and dizziness on the last weekend but returned to the campaign against his doctor's advice.[7]

Askew also let it be known that he and his family no longer bought groceries from Winn-Dixie. On reading that, the company's board chairman, J. E. Davis, and Glen Woodard, its lobbyist, sent Askew what they intended to be a peace offering. There were two boxes of Crenshaw melons and a note saying, "We do want you folks back as customers." That same week, however, the *Wall Street Journal* had quoted Davis as referring to Askew as "some nut with a Huey Long outlook." Askew took the melons to a day nursery for poor children, where he remarked to the press that their parents were "paying Winn-Dixie's share of the state tax load." The story and picture were on the front pages of many Florida newspapers. That provoked an intemperate letter to Askew from Davis's brother Robert L. Davis, a Winn-Dixie vice-president, who concluded, "Why don't you consider spelling your name with two s'es?" Askew had that letter in his pocket on election day and made it public after the polls had closed, when he said it "reflect[ed] more clearly than anything else the quality of the opposition."[8]

Whatever the quality of the opposition, it was notably unsuccessful. Askew won the referendum with 70 percent of the 1.1 million votes cast. The turnout, better than two-thirds of the total that had decided his race with Kirk, was surprisingly high for a special, one-issue election. He carried fifty-nine counties, losing only Orange and Osceola, where the *Orlando Sentinel* prevailed, along with Jefferson, Lafayette, Lake, Madison, Nassau, and St. Johns. Dade voted 80 percent in favor, Duval with an emphatic 60 percent despite the *Times-Union* and *Journal*. Sarasota County, a Republican stronghold that Kirk had carried with 57 percent against Askew, voted 75 percent in favor of the tax. Escambia approved nearly three to one. William Mansfield, the *Miami Herald* capital bureau chief, wrote that Askew was now "the strongest chief executive in the state's history." Upon hearing victory was assured, the first telephone call he placed was to his mother. Then he met the press. "We have brought the shadow government into the sunshine," Askew said, "and it may have blinded their eyes." From the managing editor of *Cocoa Today*, Bob Bentley, came a personal telegram Askew enjoyed hugely: "CONGRATS ON THE BIGGEST WINN IN DIXIE. WE ARE BANKING ON YOU HAVING A BALL IN CELEBRATION." Ed Ball's only reported comment was a succinct, "Well!"[9]

There were recriminations. George Firestone, a pro-tax Democratic state senator from Miami, lost his job as an executive of Gray Security Services, a company he had founded. He had sold it to the Eckerd Corporation, which he said asked for his resignation the day after the referendum. Winn-Dixie withdrew its sizable deposits from a Boca Raton bank whose chairman, Thomas Fleming, had supported Askew. As Askew's side saw it, however, the special interests that opposed the tax had been their own worst enemies. Their aggressive fight helped capture and hold the public's attention. As Askew had hoped and Greg Johnson had planned, the foes had overplayed their hand. "They made a mistake in spending the money," said Johnson. "I thought it would be terribly close," said Louis de la Parte. "If these guys had not been involved, we would have had a hard time. You can't pass an issue without an opponent." I wrote at the time that Askew had been "playing bait the bear with an obliging bear."[10]

"It was like running for re-election in my first year of office," Askew said. The national media mentioned him as a possible and perhaps likely choice for the Democratic vice-presidential nomination in 1972. Askew did not want it and tried unsuccessfully to quash the speculation. He was troubled that the campaign had resulted in a perception that he and Florida were "anti-business." Alluding to that in a letter to Askew, *Miami Herald* chief executive Alvah H. Chapman Jr., whose paper had endorsed the amendment, suggested that the tax be phased in over three or four years. Askew replied that the state needed the money immediately but added, "The matter concerns me and I would like to pursue it further."

Chapman may have had in mind Askew's strong remarks at the annual fall banquet at Palm Beach of the Council of 100, a who's who of Florida business leaders.[11]

It was customary to invite the governor to address the banquet, which in 1971 was scheduled two days after the election. Askew initially declined, intending to rest after the campaign, but en route to a short vacation at Key Largo he decided at nearly the last moment to attend after all. The ballroom of the luxurious Breakers resort was filled with men in tuxedos and women resplendent in gowns and jewels. They were powerful, prosperous people unaccustomed to the sort of tongue-lashing that Askew, speaking without a script, was about to give them. "We don't have too many poor people in this room tonight," he said, contrasting the glittering scene with the poverty of migrant labor shacks at nearby Pahokee. Florida "isn't so beautiful for a lot of other people, and there's no reason for it, Florida being so affluent as it is," he declared. "This is not the end of tax reform," he told them, "but the beginning— the beginning of a new day." Accusing Associated Industries of having "shot us when we were on the ground," he said he had been thinking of asking those in the room who were members of the lobby to stand up and reveal themselves, "but my wife says I shouldn't do it, so I'm not." Acknowledging that some in the room had supported the referendum, he said he needed the help of all of them "because the last thing I would ever want my administration to be called is anti-business. I want it to be called a people administration, because it is. . . . And there's no reason why this group, whether you choose to or not, cannot come forward and join us, because I'll tell you something, friends, I plan on going anyway."[12]

Askew also commented pointedly that he saw only white faces before him. "There's no more serious problem facing this nation right now than our unwillingness to accept each other and live together," he said. Don Pride remembered the audience as "more stunned than receptive." Some people walked out. Because Askew had not been expected, only one journalist was present—editor Gregory Favre of the *Palm Beach Post*. There was no coverage elsewhere of what was probably the toughest speech of Askew's career.[13]

Governor Farris Bryant had created the Council of 100 in 1961 to advise him on issues of concern to the business community. New members were chosen by a secret committee of the organization and formally appointed by the governors. Askew did not intend to wield a rubber stamp. Commenting on a proposed form letter to new members, Askew wrote on the draft, "I want to *personally* sign any such letter because I want to make sure I *personally* approve of any new appointment." In August, he and the council's chairman, P. Scott Linder, had jointly announced the appointments of two new members representing ex officio the clergy and academe. They were the Reverend Canon Theodore Gibson of Miami and Dr. Richard Moore, president of Bethune-Cookman College at Daytona Beach. They were the council's first black members.[14]

10

PROMISES FULFILLED (1971)

Askew was still in a fighting mood as he prepared for a special session in December 1971 to enact the newly authorized corporate profits tax. He wanted also to repeal the allowances, generally 3 percent, that the state gave merchants for collecting sales, cigarette, beverage, and motor fuel taxes from their customers. "A lot of money is being made . . . by large dealers," Askew wrote in reply to a legislator who objected that it would seem vindictive. When Governor Fuller Warren signed the first sales tax into law in 1949, shopkeepers had kept track by dropping coins into jars and cigar boxes marked "Pennies for Fuller." Twenty-two years later, modern cash registers made the accounting effortless. Askew knew that Winn-Dixie and other large merchants were likely making money off the tax, but this would be a fight he could not win.[1]

He wanted judicial reform as well as tax reform from the special session. Because of an unusual coincidence, it would be a unique opportunity to finish what had been left undone during the 1968 constitutional revision. By chance, every six-year circuit judgeship was up for election in 1972. The circuit judges had been largely responsible for defeating Askew's court reform amendment in 1970. It would be easier to outmaneuver them if a new judicial system could be put before the voters in a special referendum before the 1972 general election. It would also simplify the job of doing away with a number of other judgeships that could be abolished or converted into circuit court positions. The timing depended on adding a revised Article V to the already scheduled March 14 presidential primary ballot. Once again, three-fourths of each chamber would have to agree.[2]

Askew had favored court reform since he was a young legislator. In 1961 he had watched Florida Supreme Court justice Stephen O'Connell try to persuade Senate president Dewey Johnson that the judiciary needed a modern overhaul. Johnson heard O'Connell out. Then he turned to Hugh Taylor, the preeminent circuit judge in the county where Johnson practiced law. Taylor simply shook his head to signify no, and that was the end of it. The revision that Senate president John E. Mathews Jr. had entrusted to Askew had fallen just short at 49 percent of the vote in November 1970. There would still be enormous resistance to the next attempt: circuit judges who did not want more responsibility or who feared loss of prestige on an expanded bench, juvenile court judges who did not want to shoulder broader responsibilities, dozens of judges of localized courts who might not be given places in the new system, and justices of the peace and municipal court judges whose offices would be abolished. Success in the special session depended on an all-out effort by the legislative leadership, especially the judiciary committee chairs, Sandy D'Alemberte in the House and Dempsey Barron in the Senate. D'Alemberte was enthusiastic but advised Askew that Barron needed some persuasion. Hearing that Barron and his wife happened to be in Tallahassee, Askew invited them to lodge at the governor's mansion that weekend so that he and Barron could discuss court reform at leisure. Barron accepted, but it was not long before he telephoned D'Alemberte to complain that he was not a guest but a "political prisoner." There was not a drop of alcohol in Askew's mansion, and Barron said the governor would not let him leave without a deal. Barron extracted just one concession: the legislation, though developed by a special joint committee, would have to bear a Senate number. Even so, the House staff did most of the work. The Senate was pinching pennies so tightly that D'Alemberte's staff director, Janet Reno, became Barron's as well. The future attorney general of the United States was as tall as Barron and, despite her youth, just as blunt and forceful. Barron respected her, and that had a lot to with passing the bill.[3]

The House had intended for the circuit courts to be the sole remaining trial bench. The Senate insisted on retaining county judges, at least one for each county, to conduct arraignments, set bail, try misdemeanors, and dispose of smaller lawsuits. That meant allowing some non-lawyer county judges to keep their jobs as long as the voters would continue to reelect them. Barron and D'Alemberte were of like mind on the boldest and most controversial idea: to phase out municipal courts by 1977 and do away with justices of the peace. The county courts would take over their cases. It was not just for efficiency's sake; there were serious doubts as to the quality of justice in some of those courts. Justices of the peace were not required to be lawyers. To some, their most important constituents were the merchants whose bills they collected from customers facing jail for worthless checks. D'Alemberte argued that the municipal courts epitomized cash-register justice and questionable ethics. He said their part-time judges frequently tried people whose attorneys were part-time judges in nearby cities and who "strangely seemed to never lose a case." City councils commonly regarded the municipal courts primarily as revenue sources. Representative John Santora, who had been a Jacksonville municipal judge for fourteen years, told a colleague that he quit the job to run for the legislature because it "wasn't a very pretty sight" to dispose of more than seventy thousand cases a year. "Nobody left my court with any great respect for the law, and many of them left the court with very little respect for me," he said. When the reform amendment became bogged down in the House, sponsors suspected the influence of a Miami Beach justice of the peace who was a law partner of Representative Murray Dubbin, Speaker Richard Pettigrew's influential rules chairman. Eugene Stearns, the Speaker's chief of staff, put Dubbin on the spot by tipping a reporter to the situation. Dubbin voted for the bill. "I must say that had Pettigrew not been strong as hell, Murray could have caused us a lot of problems," D'Alemberte said.[4]

After one nerve-wracking defeat, there were seventy-six votes, four to spare, when a conference committee's final compromise reached the House floor late on the eleventh day of what was supposed to have been a ten-day session. That set up a crisis in the Senate, where Barron was sulking away from the floor because he thought the conference committee had given up too much. It had allowed fifty new circuit court seats as campaign opportunities for displaced judges of lesser courts. Askew rushed upstairs to lobby Barron. After a half hour of pleading from Askew and others, Barron agreed to return to the chamber, but his own vote was in doubt until Senator Fred Karl of Daytona Beach plied him with flattery. The vote was thirty-four to ten. All but two of the dissenters then agreed to the special election. That set up an intense final drama in the House, where the whole plan would collapse without fourteen more votes for the special referendum. Pettigrew, D'Alemberte, Minority Leader Don Reed, and Askew's lobbyists begged opponents to let the voters decide. The vote would be perilously close. In one of the last speeches, Representative Ed Blackburn Jr., a former sheriff from Hillsborough County, said that although he still disliked the revision, he would vote for it. His wife, Frances, had told him it was time to stop fighting and go home. The twin electronic boards beside the Speaker's rostrum began to display the results as members pressed their buttons: green lights for yes, red lights for no. When the count stopped, there were precisely the necessary ninety yes votes. Cheers rang through the chamber. An ebullient Askew sought out the Blackburns. He was not there to shake the legislator's hand; rather, he said, "I want to kiss Frances." Chesterfield Smith, who had chaired the Constitution Revision Commission of 1965–66, wrote Askew that this Article V was better than anything they had attempted earlier. "This is your greatest achievement as governor," he said.[5]

The amendment meant—if voters approved—that Florida would have a unified judicial system supervised by the state's supreme court. Jurisdictions would be the same throughout the state. All judges, prosecutors, and public defenders would be state-salaried, although it would take another three decades for the state to assume the cost of support staffs and facilities. The amendment also incorporated Askew's nominating councils, which would now be called commissions, to fill judicial vacancies between elections. It did so with a critical fault that allowed the 1991 legislature to change the manner of selection. All nine members of each commission are now appointed by the governor, forfeiting the independence that was so important to Askew. D'Alemberte thought it too risky to try to make the selection method immutable. Thirty-five House members, all but eight of them Republicans, had already voted for an unsuccessful motion to eliminate the commissions. Reed saw to it that a majority of Republicans supported the final compromise. Askew made a point of publicly praising the minority leader; Reed wrote to him that it was "one of the highest compliments ever paid me."[6]

The session gave Askew virtually everything he wanted in the corporate tax: a 5 percent rate with only a $5,000 exemption. Although there were few significant loopholes, one was large: it exempted companies that chose to have their stockholders pay federal taxes on the profits. Lawmakers also fulfilled Askew's campaign promise to repeal the sales taxes on rented residences and household utilities. But the merchants' lobby foiled his attempt to end the tax collection rebates. On the session's opening day, Askew had devoted half his speech, containing the toughest language, to that issue. Mocking the argument that repeal would hurt small businesses, he noted that for most merchants the rebates averaged only 86 cents a month. The ten largest, on the other hand, averaged $226,000 a year. For small businesses, Askew proposed to replace the rebates with repeal of the state occupational license tax. "Virtually every tax proposal now before you was either implied or spelled out in the recent referendum campaign . . . [and] endorsed by more than 70 percent of the voters," he declared. "We cannot subvert it. We cannot, and we should not, attempt to diminish it in the eyes of the people who delivered it to us." Legislators could, and they did. This was one partisan vote the Republicans would win. The House voted sixty-five to forty-six for Reed's motion against reducing the sales tax allowances. (Years later, the sales tax rebate was capped at thirty dollars a month.) The legislature also defeated Askew's requests to repeal the occupational tax, postpone local tax reductions required by the 1968 constitution, establish a fund to supplement police officer salaries, and exempt cane poles from the fishing tax. Even so, Louis de la Parte, who managed Askew's bills in the Senate, said it had been "one of the most significant special sessions in the history of Florida." No one could foresee just how significant it was; it remains the only time that Florida successfully reformed its tax structure, which depends almost entirely on consumers, to make it less regressive.[7]

Impressed by Askew's two significant election victories only a year apart, more of the national media began speculating on him as a vice-presidential candidate. Although he replied that he "flatly would not accept it," journalists continued to find him an attractive subject. In a profile on the forthcoming Florida presidential primary, *Newsweek* wrote that the corporate tax campaign had rid southern populism of the race issue and revived it "as a working euphemism for liberalism, still all too suspect." The article described Askew as "graced with a face that could sell Bibles door to door."[8]

Greg Johnson's staff analysis of key votes in the special session showed Askew that House members had backed him 55 percent of the time, with Democrats averaging a respectable 65 percent. He wrote Askew that he was now the "strongest chief executive in the state's history." If so, the Cabinet was unimpressed, giving Askew reasons to regret his defense of it during the 1969 reorganization. In November 1971, four Cabinet members defeated his request to authorize more right-of-way appraisers so that the Department of Transportation could accelerate construction of Interstate 75 south of Tampa. Roads were the governor's exclusive responsibility, but the Cabinet could still hobble him over certain fiscal issues such as budget transfers and new positions. Ahead lay a power struggle between Askew and the Cabinet over a successor to the director of the Department of Natural Resources, Randolph Hodges. Askew saw it developing; he had bought some time by persuading Hodges to postpone his retirement.[9]

Reprising the reorganization debate of 1969, Schultz's Citizens Committee on Education riled most of the Cabinet and much of academe by voting that Florida should do away with both the Cabinet Board of Education and the Board of Regents. In their place, it recommended a fifteen-member appointed board of laypersons, nominated by the governor and confirmed by the Senate. The arguments were familiar: Cabinet members did not have enough time to devote to education, and the regents were micromanaging issues that should be left to the university system chancellor. Ed Price, the former senator whose legislation had established the Board of Regents, cast the sole dissenting vote to the Schultz panel recommendations. Few of those who did vote for them had any illusions that the legislature would agree. "Let us now proceed with the perpetration of our latest heresies," remarked Buddy MacKay, one of the three House members on the committee. Attorney General Robert Shevin, who hoped to be Askew's successor, expressed support for the commission's proposal. Surprising some, so did Floyd Christian, who had already said he would not run for reelection as commissioner of education. There was a caveat: Christian recommended there be an elected nonpartisan education commissioner to execute the appointed board's policies. Askew strongly endorsed the commission's recommendations to eliminate the Cabinet from education governance and appoint a commissioner. This plan would come to pass, but in 1998, not 1972.[10]

Reubin O'D. Askew's official state photograph. (Courtesy of the State
Archives of Florida.)

While governor of Florida, Reubin Askew visits one of his boyhood homes in Muskogee, Oklahoma, along with his mother, Alberta. It was not air-conditioned when they lived there. (Courtesy of Don Pride.)

Florida's first family: Kevin, Angela, Donna Lou, and Reubin Askew at the governor's mansion during his first term. (Courtesy of the State Archives of Florida.)

Where policy often was made: Governor Reubin Askew at the governor's mansion in conference with his press secretary, Don Pride (*center*), and speechwriter Roland Page. They were his most liberal advisers during his first term. (Photo by Guy Ferrell. Courtesy of the *Palm Beach Post*.)

Friendly foes: When former House Speaker Fred Schultz returned in 1971 for the unveiling of his official portrait, Minority Leader Don Reed (*right*) stealthily substituted the portrait of 1893 Speaker John B. Johnson. Photographer Donn Dughi captured Schultz's surprise when the cloth was removed. (Courtesy of the State Archives of Florida.)

A moment of triumph: Governor Reubin Askew signs the hard-won 1971 legislation setting a special referendum to authorize a corporate income tax. Senate president Jerry Thomas (*left*) and House Speaker Richard Pettigrew enjoy the moment. (Courtesy of the State Archives of Florida.)

Speaker Richard Pettigrew (*left*), appropriations chairman Marshall Harris (*center*), and rules committee chairman Murray Dubbin discuss a question of procedure during the 1971 session of the Florida House of Representatives. (Courtesy of the State Archives of Florida.)

Governor Reubin Askew is pictured at his first meeting with the elected Cabinet in 1971 (*from left*): Attorney General Robert Shevin, Commissioner of Education Floyd T. Christian, Agriculture Commissioner Doyle Conner, Askew, Comptroller Fred O. Dickinson, Secretary of State Richard Stone, and Treasurer Tom O'Malley. (UPI photo. Courtesy of the State Archives of Florida.)

Stars of the Golden Age: T. Terrell Sessums, the new House Speaker (*left*), and Senator Louis de la Parte are pictured with Governor Reubin Askew in December 1972. (UPI photo. Courtesy of the State Archives of Florida.)

Senator Verle Pope of St. Augustine was known as the "Lion of St. Johns" for his courage in opposing special-interest legislation and fighting for fair apportionment of the legislature. He presided over the Senate in 1967 and 1968, following court decisions and elections that overthrew the rural clique known as the Pork Chop Gang. (Courtesy of the State Archives of Florida.)

Ken Myers of Miami, who served two years in the Florida House of Representatives and twelve in the Senate, was the author or a principal co-sponsor of more than 150 progressive laws, including landmark legislation providing for the treatment rather than the incarceration of alcoholics. (Courtesy of the State Archives of Florida.)

Grim news: Governor Reubin Askew's face reflects the election returns he is hearing in March 1972. George Wallace of Alabama, whose racial policies Askew detested, is winning the Florida presidential primary, and voters are overwhelmingly approving a straw ballot against busing. Also pictured are aide Bernie Parrish (*standing*) and press secretary Don Pride. (Photographer unknown. Photo courtesy of Don Pride.)

Lieutenant Governor Tom Adams, who helped elect Reubin Askew governor in 1970, announces in 1974 that he is opposing Askew for reelection. Adams, pictured with his wife, Fran, ran third in the Democratic primary, and Askew won without a runoff. (UPI photo. Courtesy of the State Archives of Florida.)

The victors: Governor Reubin Askew and his new lieutenant governor, Jim Williams, are shown moments after they are declared the winners over Republicans Jerry Thomas and Mike Thompson in November 1974. (AP photo. Courtesy of the State Archives of Florida.)

Governor Reubin Askew and the elected Cabinet in 1975 (*from left*): Agriculture Commissioner Doyle Conner, Comptroller Gerald Lewis, Secretary of
State Bruce Smathers, Askew, Attorney General Robert Shevin, Treasurer
Tom O'Malley, and Education Commissioner Ralph Turlington. O'Malley
was impeached and resigned not long after this photograph was taken,
leaving Conner and Shevin as the only Cabinet members who had served
with Askew since 1971. (Courtesy of the State Archives of Florida.)

Above: Rivals relish a victory: Senator Dempsey Barron (*center*) and Governor Reubin Askew, who is shown shaking hands with Senate president Lew Brantley, shelved their differences to enact major legislation in 1978, including the bill to appoint rather than elect Florida's Public Service Commission. Others (*from left*) are Senators Pat Thomas and W. D. Childers. (Photo by Donn Dughi. Courtesy of the State Archives of Florida.)

Left: In quest of the presidency, former Florida governor Reubin Askew addresses a Massachusetts state Democratic convention in 1983. (Photo by Bob Laramie.)

Hatless in the snow: Former governor Reubin Askew braves a spring blizzard in Portsmouth, New Hampshire, as he campaigns in 1982 for the 1984 Democratic presidential nomination. He is accompanied by his law partner Jim Bacchus, who later served in Congress and on the highest court of the World Trade Organization. (Used with permission of the *Orlando Sentinel* [2009]).

Left: The lost cause: Governor-elect Bob Graham addresses a rally in support of the Equal Rights Amendment in December 1978. (Photo by Donn Dughi. Courtesy of the State Archives of Florida.)

Below: Last of a "Long Generation": Lawton Chiles (*left*) and Buddy MacKay, shown during their successful 1990 campaign. Chiles died in December 1998, during his last month in office, and MacKay, his lieutenant governor, succeeded him. (Photo by Phil Pollack. Courtesy of the State Archives of Florida.)

11

BUS WRECK
(FEBRUARY–APRIL 1972)

As the Florida legislature was about to begin its 1972 regular session, Democratic National Committee chairman Lawrence O'Brien announced that Reubin Askew would deliver the keynote address at the party's convention at Miami Beach in July. The keynote address is one of the most conspicuous and coveted assignments in politics. In Tallahassee, some Republican legislators quickly seized an opportunity to embarrass Askew and his party. A new rule entitled each senator to early session floor consideration of two "pet" bills that otherwise might have been stalled or killed by committees. Ultraconservatives Richard Deeb of St. Petersburg and Charles Weber of Ft. Lauderdale took advantage of the rule to pass legislation calling for an anti-busing straw vote on the March 14 presidential primary ballot. The question: Did voters favor a constitutional amendment to prohibit "forced busing"? Democratic legislators suspected that the Nixon administration had something to do with it. Harry S. Dent, a deputy assistant to the president, denied having instigated the legislation but admitted that Deeb and Weber had asked his opinion of what they had in mind, and he had encouraged them to pursue it. The importance to the White House would be demonstrated when George Wallace capitalized on the issue to win 42 percent of the Democratic primary votes and seventy-five of Florida's eighty-one convention delegates. Edmund Muskie, who was presumed to be Nixon's strongest potential opponent, came in not even second but fourth. His campaign never recovered; George McGovern, perceived as Nixon's most liberal and potentially weakest opponent, would win the nomination and lose overwhelmingly in November. The straw ballot "was a great idea and it worked to our benefit—on the GOP side and the Democratic side of the primary," Dent exulted. It was one of the most transparent of assorted Republican tactics intended to sabotage the Democrats in what became known as the year of Watergate, named for the site of a burglary of the Democratic National Committee offices that led to Nixon's resignation in 1974.[1]

Askew detested the straw ballot. But he calculated that at least two-thirds of each house would vote to override a veto. To muddle the message Florida would send, he persuaded the legislature to agree to a second ballot question. This one would ask voters whether they favored "equal opportunity for all children regardless of race" and opposed "a return to a dual system of public schools." It meant that they could vote simultaneously for and against segregation, which is what they did on March 14. Although the straw ballot was legally meaningless, Askew took it as a moral issue he could not leave to chance, and he found himself conducting his third statewide campaign in less than two years.

It was a major distraction from the ambitious and controversial agenda he presented to the 1972 session. Askew proposed landmark water- and growth-management legislation and asked the legislature to strip the Cabinet of its roles in education and the management of natural resource agencies. He also sought an affordable housing program, reforms to make the Public Service Commission more responsive to consumers, a moratorium on the death penalty, and creation of a consumer adviser position in the governor's office. Of those major goals, only water and growth management would be achieved. Saying that he considered the Schultz recommendations his top priority, Askew maintained that Florida did not need an elected Cabinet to oversee the governor. "The Legislature is the check on the governor, and it has performed that function quite effectively in recent history," he said. "Nor should it be forgotten that the people of Florida have demonstrated their ability to reject for re-election governors who do not live up to their expectations." When they do elect a new governor, Askew argued, "He hasn't the tools, or the authority, in many critical areas, to make a difference, to change things, to make the system respond." Turning to the environment, he warned that Florida was in danger of becoming a "paradise lost." He recommended legislation to define and protect "areas of critical state concern," such as the Everglades; to plan and regulate "developments of regional impact"; to freeze construction in areas where schools, water supplies, and other infrastructure were "on the brink of collapse"; and to manage all of Florida's surface water and groundwater sources. Many of these recommendations owed to a conference Askew had convened the previous September when Florida was in the second year of a drought so serious—the worst since the 1930s—that half a million acres of the Everglades burned. To better manage the environment, he wanted the Cabinet's Internal Improvement Fund and the Department of Natural Resources merged with his Department of Pollution Control into a single department of environmental protection responsible only to him. Because "no single person should have the power to sell, purchase or lease the public's land," he agreed that the Cabinet should retain that one collegial function.[2]

Askew also chose this moment to begin a campaign to make the Public Service Commission more sensitive to customers of the state's electric, telephone, transportation, and natural gas companies. Attorney General Robert Shevin had appealed successfully to the Florida Supreme Court to make the PSC hear his opposition to a 1971 Florida Power Corporation rate increase, but it was only a partial victory. The court refused to order the PSC to pay for Shevin's expert witnesses. To Askew, the regulatory regime remained one-sided. "The [PSC] staff seldom takes the stand in a rate hearing, and its findings and recommendations to the commission are kept secret," he told the legislature. Askew proposed a new professional department to analyze data and speak for the public; the three commissioners would be restricted to the role of judges.[3]

The legislature went into session in February, two months earlier than usual, to leave time at the end for the required decennial reapportionment. This unusual timing made it possible for the Republicans to make mischief with the March 14 primary. They had gauged correctly that few Democrats would have the courage to oppose the straw-ballot bill. Only seven senators voted against it; among them was Senate president Jerry Thomas, who called it a "hoax on the public." In the House,

Speaker Richard Pettigrew tried to dispose of the Senate bill by sending it to a committee that would kill it, but the House voted seventy-nine to thirty-two to act on it immediately. William Fleece of St. Petersburg was the only Republican who voted no. Pettigrew next attempted to keep the bill from going to the governor until after February 14, which the secretary of state had said was the practical deadline to expand the March 14 ballot. The delaying tactic involved adding a straw-ballot question favoring prayer in the public schools, which meant sending the bill back to the Senate for another vote. That did buy time, but not enough; the Senate approved it as amended with only thirteen liberal Democrats voting no.[4]

Askew's options were limited. He could keep the bill on his desk for several days beyond March 14 before deciding whether to sign or veto it, but he could not be confident that Secretary of State Richard Stone, who was ambitious for higher office, would enforce the deadline. Askew promised to sign the bill if the legislature would add the "equal opportunity" question to the straw ballot. The legislature did so promptly. Askew kept his word even though he was warned that the straw ballot would help Wallace campaign in the Florida presidential primary. When Deeb asked when Askew would sign the bill into law, the governor refused to tell him, and did not invite him to witness the signature. Askew said at first that he would not campaign against the straw vote. But a week later, after what press secretary Don Pride described as some "soul-searching," Askew announced that he would campaign "as frequently as time permits and as forcefully as I know how" against the anti-busing question and for a yes vote on equal opportunity. According to Jim Smith, one of Askew's more conservative aides, there had been "a hell of a staff fight." Some suspected others—meaning Pride and speechwriter Roland Page—of "trying to posture him for the presidency," Smith said. In 1972, Smith thought that Askew's reelection was more important for Florida than the outcome of a nonbinding straw vote. In 1978, however, he conceded that Askew had done the right thing. "I've never quite had the odds against me such as this," Askew told a *Time* magazine reporter, "but I feel very strongly that this issue should not go by default. . . . I perceive it as potentially one of the most dangerous and divisive issues since I've been old enough to know anything about government."[5]

Askew began campaigning in Orlando, where 90 percent of the voters had opposed busing in a local straw vote in November. His speech echoed what he had said at the University of Florida, condemned the idea of amending the U.S. Constitution to restrict civil rights, appealed for harmony, and warned that, once again, racial issues were distracting Floridians from "the real economic and environmental problems of the people, both black and white."

> For if the people remain divided against themselves on the race issue, they'll have no time to demand a fair share on taxes, on utility bills, on consumer protection, on government services, on environmental preservation, and other problems.

> In this session of the Florida Legislature alone, we've seen our proposals for reform of education, environmental controls, and utility regulation take a back seat to a straw vote on busing which, in the final analysis, doesn't really accomplish anything.

> Believe me, you can be sure that while the Legislature and the news media were focusing your attention on the busing debate, the lobbyists and special interests were hard at work undermining those programs which would put money into the pockets of the people and which would help us protect the people and the other living things which make Florida a worthwhile place in which to live.[6]

In Washington, Senate majority leader Mike Mansfield, who had already recommended Askew for the vice-presidency, did so again and placed an editorial praising him into the *Congressional Record*. R. W. Apple Jr. wrote in the *New York Times* that Askew was the only "New South" governor who was not silent in the face of the busing uproar. Apple also noted that Askew was staying out of the presidential primary, refusing to attack Wallace or endorse another candidate. "It might help Wallace. It might turn out to be counterproductive," Askew told Apple. Privately, Askew preferred Senator Henry Jackson of Washington, who committed himself during the Florida campaign to support federal funding for preserving Florida's Big Cypress Swamp. Sparring with the conservative newspaper columnist James J. Kilpatrick on NBC's *Meet the Press*, Askew said that busing "may be a least-desirable instrument, but it . . .

has been the most effective instrument we've had to try to break down segregation and to try to provide equal opportunity." Senator Barry Goldwater of Arizona, the 1964 Republican presidential candidate, saw the program. "I do not agree with your feelings about busing," he wrote to Askew, "but I must tell you I have great admiration for you, not only for the courage it takes to maintain your position, but for the forthright, understandable way in which you discussed it. As a Republican I see a long, successful career ahead of you." Askew replied that he was honored to receive such praise from Goldwater, whom he had long admired for his "honesty, candor, and courage." Campaigning at Sarasota, Muskie said that he too admired Askew's courage, but he was unwilling to take a stand on the straw vote.[7]

Askew organized a Committee for Equal Education to raise campaign money. It received $53,517 in contributions, including $500 from Lloyd C. Hagaman, who, as Claude Kirk's chief of staff, had been on the front line of the busing confrontation at the Manatee County School Board headquarters in 1970. "Every governor has a right to get his point across," Hagaman said. Duke University president Terry Sanford, a former North Carolina governor and future U.S. senator, contributed $2,000. Askew enlisted an ecumenical group of eleven religious leaders to appear with him on television. Most Florida politicians ran for cover. Notable exceptions included Education Commissioner Floyd Christian and state senator Fred Karl. Christian wrote a newspaper column supporting Askew and joined him at a press conference to announce that many districts were busing fewer students than when schools were segregated. Karl wrote in the *St. Petersburg Times* that he was a "little ashamed" of having said nothing during the Senate debate, which reminded him of the segregationists he had opposed as a freshman House member in 1957. In the closing days of the campaign, sign-waving hecklers dogged Askew at appearances at Clearwater and Bradenton. To a woman who screamed at him, "You're taking our children from us, give us back our children," Askew snapped a reply: "I hope you haven't already lost them, lady." Speaking of the campaign nearly thirty years later, he was still haunted by "the hate in people's faces." At Sarasota, a woman spat at him. (She missed.) Admitting that he expected to lose the straw vote, Askew said he hoped only to keep the anti-busing percentage under 70.[8]

He was disappointed. Of the 1.5 million votes cast, 74 percent opposed busing. The straw vote swept every county; only in Alachua was it even close. Askew took comfort in the fact that the separate "equal opportunity" question (on which fewer people voted) drew nearly 79 percent support. The prayer-in-schools question, scarcely mentioned amidst the busing hubbub, carried by the same margin. Askew was in Miami as the returns came in. A reporter in an adjoining room heard an unmistakable tone of shock in the governor's voice. He sounded troubled not so much by the anti-busing vote as by the magnitude of Wallace's victory. Wallace, who had harped on busing during every appearance in Florida, led the Democratic ticket in every county. He carried every congressional district except for one in Dade County that Hubert Humphrey won. Putting the best face on the day's events, Askew said that it was the first time "any Southern state has by referendum expressed an overwhelming commitment to equal education opportunity." The point was lost on some opponents. The morning after the straw vote, the House of Representatives gave a four-vote margin to a Republican motion to take up a bill barring the use of state funds to comply with busing orders, but it fell short of the two-thirds needed. The bill remained in a committee where Pettigrew had sent it to die. In Pinellas County, Parents Against Forced Busing, a group that had urged voters to boycott the equal opportunity question, sent Askew a mocking telegram thanking him for the large turnout. "By the way," the telegram said, "how does it feel to be a one-time governor?" The only undiluted good news for Askew that election night concerned the judicial reform amendment, almost unnoticed amidst the busing furor, which was ratified with more than two-thirds of the vote.[9]

Askew had campaigned extensively. Back in Tallahassee, his 1972 legislative program was in disarray. As citizens voted on March 14, Jerry Thomas, a likely opponent to Askew in 1974, was persuading senators to undermine Askew's affordable housing program. According to tradition, Senate presidents did not personally sponsor amendments to legislation, but Thomas put his name to one that deleted bonding authority from Senator Kenneth Myers's housing agency bill. The press reported that eleven of the senators who evidently agreed with Thomas that bonds for housing would be "socialistic" had voted to approve industrial development revenue bonds in 1969. Askew's reorganization plans for education and environmental agencies were already dead or dying. Two days after the busing referendum, a Senate committee wrote off the environmental reorganization without giving its House sponsor a chance to speak. In the House, despite intensive efforts by Pettigrew and Minority Leader Don Reed, two attempts failed to muster the necessary three-fifths vote to end the Cabinet's oversight of education. Pettigrew remarked that the corporate profits tax had been easy compared to fighting the Cabinet.[10]

Pettigrew had been having other problems with the House, which he thought was too large for efficiency. His top priority for reapportionment was to reduce the membership from 119 to 100, which he said would save $10 million to $15 million a year. He was defeated, sixty-nine votes to forty-six. Members then opted for the constitutional maximum of 120 seats. Reed and twelve other Republicans supported Pettigrew, but for the most part, other urban legislators were as jealous of their offices as the Pork Choppers had been. Among the large delegations, only Duval and Dade were willing to relinquish seats. "When you get too small, you become too cozy," said Representative Ralph Turlington, referring to the lobbyists. Pettigrew countered that Turlington had once advocated a one-house legislature of only ninety members.[11]

A week later, the House overruled Pettigrew's decision to have the *Journal* omit a visiting clergyman's opening prayer, which had offended some members with its extreme political conservatism. One member had walked out, and others had complained to Pettigrew. The House's only African American members, Gwendolyn Cherry and Joe Lang Kershaw of Miami, took particular offense at the preacher's remark that "free men are not equal and equal men are not free." Representative Harvey Matthews of Orlando, the Republican member who had sponsored the clergyman of the day, persuaded the House to "correct" the *Journal* by printing the prayer in the next day's edition. The House voted seventy-one to thirty-four for his motion. Although no one but Matthews defended the prayer, several of Pettigrew's usual allies decried his censorship. Former vice-president Hubert Humphrey, who was campaigning in the Florida presidential primary, waited to address the House as the prayer debate went on for twenty minutes.[12]

In every session since reapportionment, legislators had tried in vain to rewrite a century-old law that allowed abortion only to save a woman's life. In 1972 the Florida Supreme Court forced the issue by declaring the law unconstitutional. The debate erased the legislature's usual political divisions; conservative Republicans joined liberals like Myers in support of therapeutic abortions. The much-amended bill, which required a married woman to obtain her husband's consent, was scarcely on the books when the U.S. Supreme Court's decision in *Roe v. Wade* superseded it. Legislators had less heart for taking on capital punishment before the Court's anticipated ruling on that issue. Florida had executed no one since 1964, and there were now ninety men and one woman on death row, second only to California. When he could not get action on a death penalty moratorium, Askew imposed one by executive order. Lawmakers did agree with Askew to separate the guilt and penalty phases of a capital trial. They would have to do it over again after the Court finally acted.[13]

In one of the few times the legislature ever ceded power to the people, the 1972 session agreed to a constitutional amendment expanding the initiative process to cover "one subject and matter directly connected therewith." That responded to a Florida Supreme Court decision against a petition for a single-house legislature, an idea promoted by Sandy D'Alemberte, Bill Gunter, and others. The court held that the 1968 constitution limited each initiative to changing only one section of the constitution, which made the method impractical to use. The 1972 amendment had many far-reaching consequences, but unicameralism was not one of them.[14]

Askew had to contend with a virtual civil war within his office. The liberals and conservatives continued to clash over philosophy and strategy. One tactic was to preempt seats on Askew's airplane, the better to lobby him without rebuttals from the other side. At one point, Pride wrote a confidential memorandum urging Askew to be more activist and aggressive. "I'm convinced that your success, both past and future, is primarily based with the people, not with political supporters," he said. The strife came to a head over Askew's desire to have Eugene Stearns, Pettigrew's chief of staff, join the governor's office after the 1972 session. Other staffers were already bridling at Stearns's direct access to Askew. Pride and Page sent for Stearns whenever they thought they needed reinforcement. "He had a mesmerizing effect on Askew," Page explained. According to Askew aide Bernie Parrish, "a lot of us were jealous of Gene because he was so bright and had so much more talent." It proved impossible to create a position for Stearns that would suit both him and Jim Apthorp, the senior executive assistant who was de facto chief of staff. As Stearns described the conflict, "My deal with Askew was that I would report only to him. Apthorp told me not so. He said that I reported to him; he would tell the governor that which he thought the governor needed to hear; and that my direct access was over. Although I probably would have won that argument, I was tired of the fight and simply moved on to make a living and support my family." The day before he was to officially join the staff, Stearns quit without telling Askew of his showdown with Apthorp. In a parting note to Askew, he urged him to "begin bringing people to Florida government who measure up in competence and character to the standards that you set for yourself." Jim Smith, weary of the infighting, resigned soon after, leaving Askew with only one of the advisers—Greg Johnson—who had inspired the corporate profits tax campaign. Stearns became a highly successful trial lawyer at Miami, but there would be no more service as an adviser to Askew.[15]

There was unusual friction within the legislature as well. One issue was frivolous, or so it seemed to the House. Senate president Jerry Thomas wanted to enact a law establishing a distinctive official seal for the Senate. The House, which considered the existing state seal adequate for all documents, refused to act on the Senate's bill until it became obvious that its own bills were going nowhere in the Senate. When Pettigrew finally agreed to take up the seal legislation, senators lined the rear wall of the House chamber to observe its passage. They were not amused when Don Reed proposed to replace the seal with a cartoon of an ostrich with its head in the sand. After House members had their laugh, Reed withdrew his "amendment" and the Senate had its seal. What Senator Fred Karl called the "bicameral syndrome" seemed to apply to most of the significant legislation as well. Former Senate president Verle Pope, serving the last of his sixteen sessions, said it was the worst dissension he had seen. Without naming names, Pope blamed it on "jealousy." Thomas would not have admitted envying Askew, but he was outspokenly critical of the cordial relationship between the House leadership and the governor's office. "Philosophically, the governor and the speaker are together," he told reporter Barbara Frye of United Press International. "If the president were with them, where's the check and balance for the public? If ever the House and Senate and governor are in complete concert, the public is in profound trouble."[16]

House-Senate relations hit bottom in the session's last week over Thomas's refusal to let the Senate vote on ratifying the proposed Equal Rights Amendment to the U.S. Constitution. The House approved it eighty-one to three the day after Congress completed action on the ERA, which would have forbidden gender-based discrimination. Thomas invoked a provision in the Florida Constitution that said the legislature could not ratify a federal amendment until after the next election. The restriction had been adopted in reaction to the post–Civil War amendments that ended slavery and established the rights of African Americans. Aware of the racist history, the U.S. Supreme Court had long since ruled in a case involving the female suffrage amendment that state constitutions could not impede legislative consideration of proposed federal amendments. Pettigrew and six other House members sued Thomas and eventually won a federal court ruling that he should have allowed the Senate to vote. But the ruling came too late; the legislature was long out of session, and the moment was lost forever. In 1972 the Florida Senate most likely would have voted to ratify the ERA; there was not yet the concerted nationwide opposition that ultimately defeated it. Thereafter, the Senate was hostile to the amendment, Florida never ratified it, and it was three states short of the necessary thirty-eight when the final deadline expired in 1982.[17]

The Senate was also a killing field for Askew's legislation to establish a consumer advocate at the Public Service Commission. Representative Buddy MacKay steered it through the House, but the Senate rules chairman, George Hollahan, refused to call it up for debate. In their preoccupation with that bill, the utility lobbyists failed to notice money that Fred Karl put into the budget for a consumer adviser on the governor's staff. The job would go to Arthur England, who had written the corporate tax bill.[18]

After defeating Republican-sponsored amendments calling for single-member districts, both houses approved legislative and congressional redistricting schemes that were close to mathematically precise. At last, there was nothing for the federal courts to undo. The plans broke up the largest urban districts, limiting those in the House to no more than six members and those in the Senate to three. Large counties would be split into two or more districts for the first time. In the House, Pettigrew's staff manipulated the dividing lines in Duval, Broward, Hillsborough, Pinellas, and several other counties to elect relatively liberal candidates who could not have won countywide. The object, said aide Jim Minter, a former newspaper reporter, was that "as many good guys as possible would emerge from a stronger Legislature." In later years, computers would gerrymander with exquisite precision, but in 1972 colored pencils, crayons, blank maps, and adding machines were the tools of the game. Both houses attempted to protect incumbents of both parties, but the Senate had to sacrifice some to the new constitution's limit of forty seats. That marked the end of Verle Pope's luminous career. The longest-serving senator consented to a plan that put him in the same district as Senator Welborn Daniel, a Democrat from Lake County who was twenty-three years younger. "I would have preferred a different district," Pope said, "but when you reduce the Senate by eight seats it's difficult." In failing health, Pope decided to retire. When he died in July 1973, the "Lion of St. Johns" was mourned as few other Florida politicians ever were.[19]

By far the most significant achievements of the 1972 session concerned the environment. All of Askew's major goals were enacted, setting examples for the nation. The legislation provided for "areas of critical state concern," initially the Keys and the Green Swamp in central Florida, where development would be restricted. It authorized the state to oversee "developments of regional interest," projects of such size that approval by the jurisdictions where they were situated might adversely affect neighboring cities or counties. Lawmakers approved, subject to referendum, a $200 million bond issue to begin buying environmentally sensitive land for conservation and parks. Another bill established five water-management districts to conserve groundwater and regulate consumption, rationing it if necessary. The session established a division of state planning, repealed exemptions that had made it easier to develop submerged land in the Keys than elsewhere in Florida, and strengthened judicial remedies against pollution. Two House freshmen, Democrat Jack Shreve of Merritt Island and Republican Donald R. Crane Jr. of St. Petersburg, rose to stardom in helping to pass those bills. So did Bob Graham, in his first term as a senator; environmentalists credited him with rescuing the water-management bill at a critical juncture. "We had a hell of a time getting some of these things through the legislature," recalled John DeGrove, a professor who had co-chaired the 1971 governor's conference that inspired the legislation. The pro-environment attitudes of many Golden Age legislators owed to the campaign spending limits in force during the early 1970s, which limited the influence of development lobbyists. The U.S. Supreme Court in 1976 ruled such campaign limits to be unconstitutional, and within a generation Florida's land developers once again controlled the legislature.[20]

Greg Johnson's analysis of House votes on Askew's issues during the 1972 regular session established that the Republicans were more supportive of the Democratic governor than was the conservative wing of Askew's own party. Johnson identified thirty Democrats who had supported Askew less than half the time, averaging 32 percent. The other fifty Democrats had averaged 81 percent support for Askew. The Republicans collectively had given the Democratic governor 47 percent of their votes. On the west coast, Republicans from Sarasota and Pinellas were more favorable to Askew than were the Democrats from Manatee, Lee, and Collier. "There are three voting blocs in the House: supportive Democrats, non-supportive Democrats, and Republicans," Johnson concluded. The "non-supportive" Democrats included Don Tucker of Tallahassee, who was well on his way to nailing down the House speakership for the 1975 and 1976 sessions.[21]

Even more significant, however, were the results of a statewide poll showing that Askew's courage on the busing issue had not hurt him politically. In fact, he appeared to have improved his standing among his most important constituents. His approval rating in June 1972 was 64.5, compared with 61.8 in September 1971. His unfavorable rating increased equivalently, from 26.7 to 29.3, owing to a slippage among white-collar workers. But by then he was a familiar figure to nearly every Floridian;

only 6.2 percent had no opinion of him. Despite busing, only 12.2 percent rated his performance poor. The proportion rating him excellent—his "hardcore supporters," Johnson noted—had nearly doubled; among lower-income groups it had tripled. Johnson attributed that to the corporate tax issue, in which the public saw Askew as "the little man's leader fighting the big special interests," and to his courage on the busing issue. With such numbers, Askew could be confident of winning re-election in 1974. But he was not at all sure he wanted to run.[22]

12

THE POLITICS OF 1972

Reelection was far from Askew's mind in 1972. His immediate concern was to avoid being on that year's Democratic national ticket. The vice-presidential nomination could have been his for the asking, but he remembered his difficult transition after the 1970 election and felt utterly unready for the national stage. "Two years ago," he said, "I was just a state senator. . . . I'm still in the learning process of being governor." In the eyes of the national media, he was already an uncommonly accomplished and courageous governor. Nine days before the busing referendum, the *New York Times Magazine* featured him in an article titled "Florida's 'Supersquare'—A Man to Watch." The complimentary coverage included a photo caption saying Askew was "liberal, telegenic—and may be after [Spiro] Agnew's job." He denied that he was, but in a *Meet the Press* interview he stopped somewhat short of echoing General William T. Sherman's famous remark that if he were nominated he would not run and if elected he would not serve.

> Haynes Johnson [panelist]: Would you like to be vice president?
> Askew: No, sir, I have no national aspirations at all. . . .
> Johnson: None whatever. You wouldn't take it?
> Askew: I would couch it this way. . . . I don't know that you can
> say what you would do under a given set of circumstances, but
> I think my very strong inclination would be to remain governor
> of Florida.[1]

Those words were not nearly strong enough to discourage Senator George McGovern. Campaigning in the Pennsylvania primary, he was asked about a running mate. "If I had to pick one this afternoon, I'd pick Governor Askew of Florida," he said. McGovern had been talking about Askew in private since early in the Florida primary campaign, and he never spoke anyone else's name in public until he was out of time to make his selection at the convention. Although major policy differences would have kept Askew from accepting McGovern's invitation in any event, Askew was also receiving discreet inquiries from the campaigns of former vice-president Hubert Humphrey and Senator Henry M. Jackson. One Saturday in April, Askew held an unannounced conference to seek advice. It took place at The Grove, the antebellum home of former governor LeRoy Collins, which is situated across a shaded side street from the governor's mansion. Joining Askew there were Collins, who had chaired the 1960 Democratic National Convention; a few Askew staffers; and some carefully selected friends, among them Ed Price, the former senator who was also a confidante of Collins, and David and Fred Levin, Askew's former law partners. Everyone except Don Pride and Collins agreed that Askew should not accept anyone's invitation to run for vice-president. "It was not really a very difficult decision," Askew said. Pride was bitterly disappointed; he persisted to the end in trying to change Askew's mind. As McGovern's nomination looked more and more certain and Askew was deciding whether he needed to issue a categorical disclaimer of interest, Pride wrote a three-page memorandum begging him to reconsider. "I don't think a populist, national campaign of only a few months' duration would hurt you in Florida; and even if it did, there would be more than half of your term to recoup any losses," he wrote. That was the opposite of what Askew was hearing from advisers who feared that *any* support on his part for McGovern would damage his administration and jeopardize his chances for reelection.[2]

Askew had not participated in any Democratic national politics and was unaccustomed to high-level protocol. In mid-April, he was invited to the launching of *Apollo 16* at Cape Kennedy. Another guest was King Hussein of Jordan. Upon being introduced to the monarch, Askew completely forgot his briefing, extended his hand and said, "Hi, King." He relished telling the story on himself.[3]

Askew tried to refuse the assignment to deliver the keynote address at the Democratic National Convention at Miami Beach, but Lawrence O'Brien, the party's national chairman, insisted that he accept it. O'Brien did not want to select someone else who might use the opportunity to promote his own candidacy. Askew already thought he had his hands full with the convention's security arrangements. Then, with only three months' notice, the Republicans moved their convention to Miami Beach, ostensibly because an intended site in San Diego would not be ready. Askew now had to worry about security for two major conventions while preparing for "the most difficult speech I have ever given." In May, Roland Page began the first of nine drafts. Only a fifth of that draft survived editing by Askew, Pride, and Jim Apthorp, the governor's chief of staff. Askew and the three aides took the second draft to LeRoy Collins's beach house on isolated Dog Island, a Gulf of Mexico sanctuary accessible only by boat, where they worked on it for two days. Page continued typing and retyping by the light of a kerosene lamp when the power went out.[4]

The keynote assignment gave Askew an excuse for not serving as a Florida delegate, in which event state law would have required him to support George Wallace in early balloting. Although the Alabama governor had been shot and paralyzed by a would-be assassin in Maryland in May, he was still campaigning for the nomination. His convention delegates joined Muskie's and Humphrey's in an unsuccessful anyone-but-McGovern movement. By that time, Askew had renounced national ambitions as firmly as he thought he could; he said on ABC's *Issues and Answers* that he would not accept a nomination under "any circumstances." Some refused to take his no for a final answer. Lawrence Spivak, moderator of *Meet the Press*, told Askew that he had known all the presidents for four decades and considered him "as ready as anyone I have seen to be president." Robert L. F. Sikes, Florida's senior congressman, told Askew that Senator Henry Jackson might propose Askew as a compromise candidate for *president* in the event of a deadlock. "Bob, please, if you're my friend don't do this to me," Askew replied. There would be no such occasion; McGovern ensured his nomination by winning a crucial convention fight over seating his California delegation. To spare him the embarrassment of a publicized rejection, Askew sent word through state representative Sandy D'Alemberte, McGovern's Florida campaign manager, that McGovern should not offer him the second spot.[5]

Meanwhile, Askew had allowed only O'Brien and party treasurer Robert Strauss to see the finished speech—a seventh draft—before the delegates would hear it. On the night of July 11, Askew waited nervously backstage as proceedings droned on for two hours past his scheduled hour of 7:30 P.M. eastern time. The convention hall was darkened to try to focus the delegates' attention on him and to prevent television crews from conducting distracting interviews on the floor while he spoke. The goal for the speech was to "find a common denominator" for a party that had George Wallace on one extreme and George McGovern on the other. Askew wanted to be an "apostle of hope" and so there would be no slashing attacks on incumbent president Richard Nixon or other Republicans. Floridians heard familiar themes from the corporate tax and busing campaigns. Though some members of the media were unimpressed, the speech was a success with his primary audience, the delegates in the hall, who interrupted him forty-six times with applause. "There is a feeling in the land," Askew said,

> that politics are dictated not by how they will help the people but by how they will help the re-election of a president, the profit margin of a utility, the power of a union leader, the bankroll of a multimillionaire, the welfare of an agriculture giant or the budget of a big bureaucracy.
>
> The people seem convinced that such a system has forgotten the average man or woman in America today.
>
> And it's no wonder they feel that way.
>
> What can we expect them to think?
>
> When the business lunch of steak and martinis is tax-deductible, but the working man's lunch of salami and cheese is not.[6]

The "steak and martinis" reference, originally suggested by Askew's tax expert, Greg Johnson, appealed to McGovern, who incorporated it into his standard stump speech for the fall campaign. To Askew himself, however, the most memorable passage was his opening: "More than a hundred years ago, near the mountains of southeastern Arizona, a great

American leader sat down in council with officers of the United States government. His name was Cochise, and he was chief of the Chiricahua Apache. He knew that there can be no trust among people unless there is understanding as well. So Cochise on that day made one request that transcended all others. 'Speak straight,' he said, 'so that your words may go as sunlight to our hearts.'" Following his journalist's instinct to close the circle on a theme, Page reprised the opening at the conclusion of the speech: "Let us create a new America that listens to the dreams of mankind and goes as sunlight to the heart of the world."[7]

As Askew spoke, the convention's Native American delegates, some in ceremonial dress, gathered at the foot of the speakers' platform a long flight of stairs below. Touched by his reference to Cochise, they stood in a silent tribute to Askew throughout his speech. Afterward, they thanked him in person.[8]

Although Askew thought he had nearly memorized the speech and had followed the teleprompter word for word, an academic analysis counted sixty-seven deviations from the text that had been issued to the media. No such detail mattered to the public, whose reaction was favorable. "The Bonifay Nursing Home virtually stood at attention through the entire address," one fan letter said. Bobby Bowden, who had been an assistant football coach at Florida State University, wrote from West Virginia that he was proud to have known Askew, and "I get the opinion, hearing you again for the first time in seven years, that you are still committed to Christian doctrine."[9]

On the day after his nomination, McGovern still had no running mate. Humphrey and Muskie had turned him down. Askew had warned McGovern's staff that if McGovern asked him, he would refuse. That morning, McGovern asked Senator Edward M. Kennedy, who declined (as McGovern knew he would) and suggested Senator Tom Eagleton of Missouri. Eagleton wanted to be chosen, but McGovern was reluctant because he did not know him well. Senators Abraham Ribicoff of Connecticut, Walter Mondale of Minnesota, and Gaylord Nelson of Wisconsin turned McGovern down also. Boston mayor Kevin White was receptive, but the Massachusetts delegation objected to him. McGovern even considered asking Walter Cronkite, the CBS News anchor. He also made a direct attempt to persuade Askew, who interrupted a tennis game to take McGovern's call in his suite at the Fontainbleau Hotel. Again, Askew said no, and he recommended Senator Ernest Hollings of South Carolina. Even as they spoke, Pride was arguing passionately to Apthorp and Bernie Parrish that the governor should accept McGovern's offer. With only fifteen minutes remaining before a 4 P.M. deadline to declare his choice, McGovern finally telephoned Eagleton, who said he had been "hoping and praying" for the call all day. He told McGovern's political director there was nothing troublesome in his background. "History," McGovern wrote in 2008, "would render a different judgment."[10]

Less than two weeks later, Eagleton acknowledged that he had been hospitalized three times during the 1960s for psychiatric problems and had undergone electric shock treatment twice. McGovern said initially that he had a "thousand percent" confidence in Eagleton and refused his offer to withdraw from the ticket, but the political pressure became inexorable. Eagleton was gone five days later. McGovern telephoned Askew at Asheville, where he was vacationing at the North Carolina governor's western residence. Askew reiterated what he had already told the press: he would not substitute for Eagleton. Sargent Shriver, a Kennedy in-law and former director of the Peace Corps, became the vice-presidential nominee. Pride, who had urged Askew to take Eagleton's place, flirted with an offer to be Shriver's press secretary but decided to stay with Askew.[11]

The liberal ranks on Askew's staff were becoming even thinner. Greg Johnson had left to manage state senator Gerald Lewis's campaign for the Public Service Commission. Page was scouting for a way to resume his newspaper career. The staff strife and the long hours expected of all Askew staffers (and of the press section in particular) were wearing Page down and straining his marriage; one night when he was working late at home, his exasperated wife, Hallie, threw his portable typewriter across the room. The Associated Press, citing the McGovern debate, reported that "aides who counsel pragmatic caution have outlasted a progressive, reformist faction in a rancorous conflict over who will influence Reubin Askew's mind." The appointment of Transportation Secretary Walter Revell, a Jim Smith protégé, was another defeat for the liberals.[12]

The Eagleton affair had damaged McGovern's campaign beyond repair; in November he would win only Massachusetts and the District of

Columbia. It had also distracted most of the media from the unfolding story of a June 17 burglary of the Democratic National Committee headquarters at Washington's Watergate complex. The crime precipitated a series of investigations that resulted in President Nixon's resignation two years later. Had Askew accepted his offer at Miami Beach, McGovern remarked in a 2008 interview, "It would have saved us a lot of grief later on."[13]

Problems in Tallahassee had not been put on a shelf for the convention. In May, Askew was taken by surprise at a Cabinet meeting when Agriculture Commissioner Doyle Conner, Treasurer Tom O'Malley, Comptroller Fred O. "Bud" Dickinson Jr., and Secretary of State Richard Stone voted to ask natural resources director Randolph Hodges to postpone his retirement yet again. Askew, Attorney General Robert Shevin, and Education Commissioner Floyd T. Christian, supported by the Audubon Society and other environmentalists, wanted to replace Hodges with someone considered more of a conservationist. "Obviously, everyone but you, Christian, and Shevin knew what was going on," Apthorp wrote to Askew, adding that "out of common courtesy, Hodges should have informed you." Askew told the press that although he still supported the Cabinet conceptually, he now had a different opinion of it in practice. The same four-three split would select one of Hodges's assistants to succeed him a year and a half later.[14]

In 1970 there had been a radio campaign jingle with the words, "From out of the west rode a tall, lean man—Reubin Askew to the rescue." After digging through many documents a year and a half later, Bill Mansfield reported in the *Miami Herald* that "the white horse has stumbled." Many of Askew's campaign contributors had received major appointments; others did business with the state. Jane Love, the aide who managed Askew's patronage, advised him privately that seventy-two members of his patronage committees held state appointments, mostly to judicial nominating councils and junior college boards. Ed Price, who chaired the Citrus Commission, was the most prominent. Some of what Mansfield wrote had been reported previously, but the most damaging finding was new: of every ten dollars his Department of Transportation spent for tires, eight went to Askew contributors. One of them was Bernie W. Simpkins Jr., a member of the Board of Business

Regulation. Another was a cousin of the board's chairman, Richard Pallot. Simpkins and another member had also switched deposits to banks of their choice. Askew aides admitted that lists of "friendly" sources had been sent to his agencies. The story also reported that Askew was accepting free hotel rooms in his travels around the state; Pride and Page had argued unsuccessfully that he should not. Askew acknowledged the criticism, ordered all of his agencies to seek bids for tires, and said that one of Arthur England's duties as his new consumer adviser would be to monitor the awarding of state business and maximize competitive bidding. "I think that we are finding out how difficult it is to run a tight ship. It was naïve to think that because the governor made no commitments, everybody who donated money felt the same way and didn't expect something in return," Pride said. (Checking again the next year, Mansfield wrote that the administration's tire and insurance purchases were in fact being put out to bid as Askew had promised.) Soon after his first story, the *St. Petersburg Times* wrote extensively on what it called "mismanagement, frustration, inertia and impotence" in the Department of Community Affairs. The article attributed the problems in large part to Secretary Athalie Range, who was spending much time back in Miami tending to her family's funeral home. Askew strongly defended his first black department head, who said she had declined a similar appointment from Kirk; but she resigned six months later.[15]

In May, the governor's general counsel, Edgar M. Dunn Jr., briefed Askew on what would become a historic confrontation with Lake County sheriff Willis McCall, an outspoken racist who had been one of Florida's most feared politicians for twenty-eight years. The FBI and the Florida Department of Law Enforcement were investigating allegations that McCall had killed a black prisoner, Tommie Lee Vickers, by kicking him in the side and stomach with a pointed-toe cowboy boot. A coroner's jury had absolved McCall in the fatal shooting of a black prisoner in 1951, but this incident would have a different ending. On Dunn's advice, Askew appointed a special prosecutor to take the case before a grand jury in neighboring Orange County. Lake County was out of the question because "McCall is reputed to be able to 'pick' the grand jurors," Dunn said. He warned also that the resident state attorney, Gordon Oldham, had "a history of whitewashing the atrocities perpetrated by Sheriff McCall." When a grand jury in Orange County charged McCall with second-degree murder, Askew immediately suspended him. Dunn worded the order carefully so that Askew would not have to reinstate McCall if he was acquitted. LeRoy Collins telephoned to congratulate Askew, saying he wished he had been able to suspend McCall when he was governor. The inmate's death was one instance among many in Dunn's file on McCall. A federal court had established that McCall deputies fabricated plaster tire track casts to convict two black men of rape and send them to death row. With Oldham's help, McCall had closed a rape case by framing a nineteen-year-old retarded man, Jesse Daniels. Daniels was then rushed off to a psychiatric hospital—an improper place for his disability—to avoid a trial that would have exposed the wrongdoing. Daniels remained in custody nearly fourteen years before the Second District Court of Appeal effectively ordered his release. The Department of Law Enforcement told Askew there was evidence of "a continuing and ongoing criminal conspiracy between Gordon Oldham, Willis McCall and others" to rob Daniels of his liberty and block legislation to compensate him and his mother. In August, McCall was acquitted of the prisoner's death—the jury was out only seventy minutes— but Askew refused to reinstate him. He said the suspension should be considered in the Senate, where "the standards of proof would be different than in a court." The Senate had not had a chance to act when McCall was defeated for reelection. That was a relief to Askew, who doubted that he could have successfully suspended McCall again. (McCall's son Malcolm won the office four years later but served without his father's notoriety.) The Florida Department of Law Enforcement took the Daniels case to a federal grand jury but could not obtain an indictment. The U.S. Justice Department advised that there was "no corroborating evidence to support a conspiracy theory." All the same, Askew had succeeded in liberating Lake County from Willis McCall's rule.[16]

On June 28, two weeks before the Democratic National Convention, the U.S. Supreme Court ruled five to four that the death penalty as then practiced throughout the United States violated the Eighth Amendment's prohibition against cruel and unusual punishment. The five justices in the majority wrote six separate opinions; nothing was made clear except the point that too much discretion had been left to juries or judges. It appeared that the Court would approve new laws that allowed less latitude. The decision spared ninety-seven inmates in Florida alone. Although Askew had expected it, it could not have come at a worse time. Every seat in the legislature was up for election in the next several months. Some incumbents began clamoring for a special session in which they could prove themselves tough on crime by reenacting capital punishment. Askew refused to consider calling one; Pride said the governor thought there would be too much "political posturing." A special session after the November election was more likely. Askew appointed a blue-ribbon commission to consider whether Florida should reinstate the death penalty, and if so, how. He chose a widely respected retired Supreme Court justice, E. Harris Drew, as chairman and named LeRoy Collins as one of the members. Both opposed the death penalty, but the commission majority eventually sided with Attorney General Robert Shevin, who passionately favored capital punishment. Shevin's father, a Miami merchant, had been fatally injured during a robbery at his store.[17]

In October, Askew took time out to visit his Oklahoma birthplace and speak at Muskogee's Founders Day banquet. He joked that it was a town "where even squares can have a ball," and reminisced on his boyhood. "The one thing I remember most about this town," he said, "was a spirit of patriotism, a love of country. . . . It seemed we were always breaking out the red, white and blue for one reason or another. There seemed to be an immense sense of pride not only in being 'Okies from Muskogee' but in being Americans as well."[18]

The Florida Public Service Commission, in a decision that would help to end Chairman Jess Yarborough's career, ruled that regulated utilities could charge their consumers dollar-for-dollar for the cost of the new corporate profits tax. Askew accused the PSC of violating "the spirit of tax reform and the basic understanding of fairness." He petitioned for reconsideration and threatened to seek legislation if necessary. Arthur England represented him, arguing that the PSC had heard from no consumer advocate before it ruled, that none of the major policy questions "was fully argued or briefed," and that the result was "unjust, unreasonable, and unjustly discriminatory." The PSC eventually agreed to modify the impact. The utilities appealed to the Florida Supreme Court, where improper contact between two justices and one of the company lawyers led to an impeachment investigation, and to the resignation of one of the justices (see chapter 15). Yarborough, a former high school football coach who had served six years in the Florida House of Representatives, lost the Democratic primary to Senator Gerald Lewis, who ran a pro-consumer-reform campaign. In November, when Lewis shared the Democratic ballot line with McGovern, he had the dubious distinction of becoming the first Floridian to poll more than a million votes and lose. Paula Hawkins, a member of the Republican National Committee and a future U.S. senator, received 32,059 votes more than Lewis, a margin of less than 1.5 percent of the turnout. Hawkins, the first woman to win a statewide office in Florida, had not known what the job entailed when U.S. representative C. W. Bill Young and other Republican leaders recruited her to run. They had asked her husband for permission before approaching her.[19]

In the Democratic primary, Pettigrew had won a closely watched, hard-fought, and narrow victory over state senator George L. Hollahan Jr. of Miami, who claimed sufficient pledges for a subsequent Senate presidency. Hollahan had been an urban ally of the Pork Chop Gang early in his sixteen-year career. It was an extremely conservative district, comprising agricultural south Dade and the Florida Keys, where Hollahan supposedly had an advantage. Pettigrew won it by attacking Hollahan's record and integrity. He made an issue of Hollahan legislation that had once exempted the Keys from dredge-and-fill controls. He forced the incumbent to disclose income tax returns that implied he was taking legal fees for doing no work. In November, Pettigrew faced an even tougher opponent in Republican Mike Thompson, whose billboards defined the race as "McGovern-Pettigrew vs. Nixon-Thompson." Pettigrew managed to win by two percentage points even as Nixon carried the district in a landslide. Pettigrew's protégé Janet Reno had spent so much time and effort on his campaign (and on McGovern's) that she neglected her own and became the first Dade Democrat to lose a state House race to a Republican. Hollahan's defeat had long-term consequences: it cleared the deck for Dempsey Barron to become Senate president two years later. For most of the ensuing sixteen years, Barron would be the de facto boss of the Senate. "He's so independent it scares me," said Senate president Mallory Horne as he gave Barron the rules chairmanship that Hollahan would have had. The Republicans also picked up their first Senate seat from Dade. Although they sustained a one-seat net loss in the Senate, they were now stronger, numbering fourteen of forty rather than fifteen of forty-eight. In their most significant victory, Representative Jim Glisson of Eustis defeated Democratic senator Welborn Daniel, for whom Verle Pope had been forced to step aside. Ed Price said that when he told Pope what had happened to Daniel, "He gave that great big belly laugh he always had and said, 'It couldn't happen to a nicer guy.'"[20]

The 1972 campaign had dire consequences for one of Askew's earliest and strongest supporters in the Florida media. *Palm Beach Post* editor Gregory Favre resigned after Cox Newspapers, the parent corporation, insisted its editors endorse Nixon in violation of a pledge of local editorial autonomy. Refusing to delegate the odious chore, Favre wrote the editorial himself, stressing Nixon's foreign-policy expertise, before cleaning out his desk. Favre became executive editor of the *Sacramento Bee* and eventually president of the American Society of Newspaper Editors. He regards the Nixon editorial as "the only piece of fiction I ever wrote."[21]

Askew had been contemplating another crusade, this one to require financial disclosure by public officials. He began to organize it after the 1972 general election. "The issue that encompasses all other issues is that of confidence," he told a Democratic convention at Orlando as he announced the formation of a bipartisan nonprofit corporation to promote the cause. His friend Jon Moyle, the state party's chairman, was one of the organizers. Don Reed, freshly retired as a legislator and House Republican leader, was another.[22]

Askew's blue-ribbon commission recommended legislation to restore capital punishment, with Collins and Drew dissenting. In late November, Askew called the legislature into special session to act on the proposal. Askew particularly approved of the commission's recommendation of a two-trial process, the first to determine guilt and the second to determine whether a defendant convicted of a capital crime should serve life in prison or be executed. He strongly disagreed with the attorney general, who proposed mandatory death sentences for certain types of murder. If juries knew that death sentences would be automatic, Askew warned, they would be likely to return convictions of lesser charges, perpetuating abuses of discretion. As a safeguard against discrimination, Askew said, panels of senior circuit judges should determine sentences. The lawmakers needed only four days to make Florida the first state to adopt a new death penalty statute that might satisfy the U.S. Supreme Court. The law provided for split—or "bifurcated"—trials by the same jury; one on guilt or innocence and a second, if necessary, for punishment. The proposal for sentencing by judicial panels vanished during a late-night conference committee meeting that decided on a novel process: the jury would recommend life or death, but the trial judge alone would make the decision. Rape of an adult would no longer be a capital offense. Death-sentence convictions would be appealed automatically to the Florida Supreme Court. The only alternative to a death sentence for first-degree murder would be life in prison without parole eligibility for twenty-five years. On final passage, only one senator and two representatives voted against reinstating the death penalty. Although he still opposed capital punishment, Drew advised Askew that the legislature had reflected overwhelming public opinion "and your signature is clearly required." Askew signed the bill in private, considering a ceremony inappropriate to the subject. "It was a hard decision for me, and I am deeply grateful for your understanding," he wrote Drew. Askew had also urged the special session to ratify the Equal Rights Amendment, but legislators became flustered by intense, unanticipated public opposition and neither house took it up.[23]

The Florida and U.S. Supreme Courts upheld the capital punishment law in opinions that did not describe it accurately. "Review by this Court guarantees that the reasons present in one case will reach a similar result to . . . another case. . . . [T]he sentencing process becomes a matter of reasoned judgment rather than an exercise in discretion at all," wrote Florida justice James C. Adkins Jr. The U.S. Supreme Court took Adkins's words as true, opining that "the Florida court has undertaken responsibility to perform its function of death sentence review with a maximum of rationality and consistency." The reality was—and remains—otherwise; a law review article characterized Adkins's analysis as "a pleasant fiction." Because the Florida Supreme Court routinely sees only death-sentence cases, it is unable to compare them to the much greater number of homicide convictions in which the defendants are originally sentenced to life. Those cases rarely progress beyond the district courts of appeal.[24]

Upon signing the bill, Askew flew to Washington to help unseat Jean Westwood, whom McGovern had installed as chair of the Democratic National Committee, and elect an Askew friend, party treasurer Robert Strauss, in her place. "I say to you without reservations he is a good man," Askew told delegates in support of Strauss. Some Democrats objected that Strauss was too close to fellow Texan John Connally, a Nixon supporter, and too friendly with labor leaders who had opposed the party's delegate selection reforms.[25]

13

DOWN ON THE FARM
(SPRING 1973)

Reubin and Donna Lou Askew tried to maintain a normal family life for their children, Angela and Kevin, under the unusual circumstances of living in a government building that served as a home, an office, a public gathering place, and a museum. The move from Pensacola was hardest on their dachshund, Fritz. The many doors to the mansion confused the dog when he needed to be let out. Fritz was given to a security agent who lived nearby. For the children, being guarded around the clock was the hardest part—no sleepovers at friends' homes, no hanging out at malls. When the governor and his wife were out of town one weekend, the mansion security office telephoned to report that Angela was missing. The agents called again soon after; they had found her climbing the back fence on her way back home. She confessed to her father that it was not the first time she had escaped to be with her friends. (There had been no fence when they moved in; it was built after the U.S. Secret Service said the mansion was too insecure for Vice-President Spiro Agnew to stay overnight.) The children lived normally in other respects, attending public schools, church, and youth organizations. Like many other fathers, the governor stayed up late one night, in February 1973, to finish Kevin's Cub Scout project, a wooden model of Dr. John Gorrie's historic Apalachicola ice machine. Askew was still tinkering with it after midnight, his son long since in bed, when he decided to send education aide Claud Anderson to deliver his scheduled speech at a teachers' convention in Tampa that morning. Reporters expecting to ambush Askew outside the convention hall were sorely disappointed to encounter Anderson instead.[1]

The journalists wanted the governor's comments on what was about to become the worst crisis of his first term: the news that Lieutenant Governor Tom Adams had been using a Commerce Department employee to run a private farm in Gadsden County, just west of Tallahassee. Adams knew the exposé was coming; he had been interviewed by investigative reporters Bill Cox of the *Ft. Lauderdale News* and John Hayes of Tampa television station WTVT. But Adams had not warned the governor, who would learn about it in the same way the public did—from Cox and Hayes. The journalists waiting at Tampa, unaware of Kevin's Cub Scout project, thought that Askew had deliberately avoided them.[2]

Roger A. Getford Jr., a Commerce Department storekeeper paid with federal funds, was conducting much of Adams's farm business on the state's time. The state had paid for his travel. He had signed documents identifying himself as the farm manager. Adams rationalized to Cox and Hayes that it was economical to send his low-paid "Man Friday" on private errands that would otherwise take Adams himself away from the office. Among the questions left unanswered: How did Adams, who still admitted owing as much as $10,000 on a thirteen-year-old campaign debt, and whose only claimed income was his state salary of $36,000, finance a thousand-acre farm?[3]

The scandal quickly covered front pages statewide. Journalists and politicians who respected Askew did not necessarily esteem his lieutenant governor. The new Senate president, Mallory Horne—perhaps remembering the vituperative letter from Adams two years before—implied that the House should consider impeaching Adams. Terrell Sessums, the House's new Speaker, ordered an investigation by the legislature's joint auditing committee. Askew's enemies exulted in his embarrassment. On February 13, a day before the Adams story broke, Askew had made yet another appeal for a financial disclosure law. "We must meet every legitimate challenge to the faith of the people in their government with a response that not only restores but enhances that faith," he had said.[4]

This was not the first time Askew felt betrayed by Adams. He had learned that the old campaign debt (see chapter 5) was much larger than Adams had let on. Askew thought also that he had been served poorly by Bernie Parrish and several other aides who knew about the farm but had not told him. When Parrish admitted to that, the governor told him bluntly, "You're fired." By the next morning, he had cooled off and told Parrish to stay. "Don't ever keep things from me again," he said.[5]

The state personnel director, Conley M. Kennison, concluded in a preliminary report to Askew that the allegations were substantially true. Askew then called Adams to the mansion on February 23 for a meeting that lasted more than two hours. "This whole thing has been blown out of context," Adams told reporters as he left. When Askew himself finally met the press that evening, more than a week after the first news of the scandal, it was at the unusual hour of 8 P.M. on a Friday, a particularly inconvenient time for weekend news coverage. Askew said he could not condone Adams's conduct. Even so, Adams would stay on as commerce secretary—but only through 1974. Saving the biggest news for last, Askew announced that Adams would not be his running mate again. He said that the decision had been made, "for all practical purposes, the last of December." Askew conceded that Adams had been unhappy "to play second fiddle."[6]

Kennison concluded that Adams owed the state $1,736 for Getford's farm-related time, travel, and expenses. Although the sum was not great, Askew underestimated how it would appear to the public. His problem was that there were few options for disciplining Adams. The voters had elected the lieutenant governor; the only way he could be removed during his term was by impeachment. If Askew sacked him as commerce secretary, Adams would continue to draw his salary as lieutenant governor while doing no work. But the editorial writers were impatient and unforgiving. The *Miami Herald* charged that "the Askew-Adams administration has widened the breach of believability in Tallahassee even as it has accepted a black mark in default of duty to the trusting people of Florida." The *Orlando Sentinel* implied that Askew applied double standards. The paper cited the unsuccessful criminal prosecution of a Citrus Commission chairman for the comparatively trivial matter of purchasing promotional Christmas gifts. Bill Cox wrote in a weekend column that Adams "was not punished at all, simply asked to make restitution." Editorials in the *Tampa Tribune* and *Pensacola News-Journal* called for abolishing the office of lieutenant governor.[7]

Adams expressed no gratitude for Askew's indulgence. His scorn surfaced at a Jaycee convention which serenaded him with a chorus of "Old Tom Adams had a Farm." Adams said he had decided on his own "some time ago" that he would not again be the governor's running mate. He claimed that his troubles with Askew were rooted in the governor's stand on "forced busing . . . in direct opposition to my philosophy." Replying for Askew, press secretary Don Pride said the breach was "not a matter of philosophy as much as it was a matter of ethics."[8]

Supporters of Adams sought to ward off impeachment proceedings by tipping the *St. Petersburg Times* to a similar story about Agriculture Commissioner Doyle Conner's private farm in Jefferson County, seventeen miles east of Tallahassee. A state employee spent time there too. Conner conceded that but insisted that the man's duties were relevant to Conner's official business. Kennison reported that he had found no violations in the agriculture department's records; the legislature had no interest in probing any deeper. Legislators would question Adams, his employee, and others under oath. None cared to question Conner.[9]

As that was happening, Askew appeared voluntarily before a Leon County grand jury that was investigating $25,000 in unreported Democratic Party expenditures for his 1970 campaign. "I don't think chief executives should hide behind executive immunity," Askew said. Both the money and the tip to the grand jury had originated with Elmer Rounds, who was bent on revenge after having been shut out of Askew's patronage. He claimed he had collected the money from labor organizations to be laundered through the party for Askew's benefit. The grand jury issued a report that exonerated the governor and called for stricter provisions in the election law.[10]

Adams's impeachment was becoming a serious possibility. Since he and Adams were barely on speaking terms, Askew sent for a mutual friend, Ed Price, the Citrus Commission chairman, and asked him to negotiate something that might calm the storm. A security guard smuggled Price through the back door of the mansion, where he met secretly with Adams over a three-day period to obtain his resignation as commerce secretary. To avoid discovery by the media, Price met at midnight with Sessums at the capitol. He wanted the Speaker to either squelch the impeachment move or convert it to a resolution of censure. Price worried that impeachment would hurt Askew's chances for reelection. He persuaded Adams to resign as commerce secretary and to agree to a statement Askew would make that Kennison's investigation was more damaging than had appeared at first light. Getford had worked the equivalent of two and a half months on Adams's private business during sixteen months on the state payroll. Adams was left with nothing to do but chair the Florida Bicentennial Commission. Don Spicer, a former St. Petersburg mayor already working for Askew in another capacity, succeeded Adams at the Commerce Department. "It's worth $3,000 a month to keep Tom Adams idle," said the *Miami Herald*'s editorial.[11]

When the auditing committee heard fifteen hours of testimony on March 19, the Senate members withdrew so that they would be untainted jurors in the event of impeachment. Adams, Getford, and thirty other witnesses testified, but Adams was not cross-examined on his prepared statement. The evidence showed that Commerce Department employees had kept the farm's books, written its checks, cleaned Adams's bachelor apartment, and washed his clothes. Adams had also isolated his personnel director, giving him only meaningless tasks, while illegally paying other people to do the work.[12]

The Adams affair was a major distraction as Askew and the legislature prepared for a full and daunting 1973 agenda. In the week before opening day, the *Miami Herald*'s Bill Mansfield and Bruce Giles turned up the pressure for campaign reform with a six-part series, "The Greening of the Legislature." They documented how lobbyists and four major interest groups—builders, attorneys, financial institutions, and the insurance industry—accounted for at least half of the money contributed to legislative candidates in 1972. A campaign finance disclosure law that had been enacted in 1949 had turned out to be ineffective. To document the "greening," the reporters and their research assistants had spent six months poring over city directories and other data sources to determine the donors' occupations and business interests. They recorded the data on sixty thousand color-coded index cards that they used to connect the contributions to specific votes by legislative committees. It was timely for Askew, who used his session-opening address to lecture the legislature on ethics. "The faith of the people, like the love of a child, cannot be demanded. It must be earned, and earned, and earned again," he said. He called for a law requiring all elected officials, candidates, and major appointees to disclose "all of their financial interests," including their income tax returns; for campaign reforms to include the disclosure of contributors' occupations; and for an experimental program to finance campaigns with public money. The Adams affair itself exemplified the case for mandatory financial disclosure.[13]

Askew also wanted the legislature to establish a "consumer anti-bureaucracy" in his office. A study by his consumer adviser, Arthur England, found that 70 percent of Floridians wanted better protection and did not know which state agency (if any) could help them. "Our regulatory agencies seldom are motivated to protect the consumer as opposed to the regulated," Askew said. England's report and Askew's recommendations drew bitter opposition from the offices of Conner and Comptroller Fred O. Dickinson Jr. Askew renewed his request for a consumer advocate at the Public Service Commission. He challenged the twenty elected state attorneys, who comprised a powerful political force, with a proposal to establish a statewide grand jury to investigate organized crime. And he said lawmakers should require architects, engineers, and other professionals to be awarded state contracts through bids rather than negotiations. He also made a strong pitch for the Equal Rights Amendment, which had already been blocked by a pre-session tie vote in a Senate committee. Three weeks later, the House voted sixty-four to fifty-four against the ERA. Barely a year had passed since only three representatives had voted no.[14]

Most legislators still had no interest in the Schultz commission's proposal for an appointed board of education. In the second phase of its work, the commission undertook to overhaul the school finance formula. There was strong support from Sessums and other legislative leaders. The commission also proposed the establishment of school advisory councils comprising teachers, parents, and students. Askew strongly endorsed the idea, which he thought would strengthen public support for education and help renew faith in government.[15] A House subcommittee chaired by Buddy MacKay took on the financing task in the face of strong skepticism in the Department of Education. Education Commissioner Floyd T. Christian and some of his experts claimed the issue was too complex for the legislature. MacKay and Bob Graham, who chaired the Senate education committee, thought otherwise. Their staffs labored nights in the education department's basement offices, copying data to be analyzed at the University of Florida at Gainesville.[16]

A legal crisis disrupted everything when the session was only three days old. A split decision of the Florida Supreme Court overturned an essential provision of the existing school finance formula. Adopted in 1971, it reduced state aid to counties whose tax rolls were found to be undervalued, making more money available to the others. Although the court acknowledged the problem of under-assessments, it threw out the legislature's remedy of tax ratio studies commissioned by the auditor general. The majority opinion said it was unconstitutional for the auditor general, a legislative employee, to "usurp" the judgments of the elected county tax assessors. The court's reasoning was disingenuous at best. The auditor general's findings affected only the level of state support and did not alter anyone's local tax assessment. Without some adjustment mechanism, legislators were powerless to equalize spending between rich and poor counties. This was a particular concern to Sessums, whose county of Hillsborough was considered "pupil-rich, property-poor." Sessums denounced the decision as "tragic" and temporarily shut down the legislative process to focus on finding a way around the ruling. The solution, developed by Representative Carl Ogden of Jacksonville, gave the power to review tax rolls to constitutional officers: the governor and Cabinet, acting as the Department of Revenue. The legislature also committed the state to paying for all school construction. The new formula recalculated the state's classroom dollars on the basis of the number of students rather than by an arbitrary "classroom unit" standard dating to 1949. "No one in the United States thought a state could pull off what Florida did," said Charles B. Reed, who represented the Department of Education on Schultz's commission and later became chancellor of the state university system.[17]

The reform nearly fell apart at session's end. Sessums understood that the House-Senate conference committee had specified a fixed tax millage rate for the counties' contributions to their schools. Speaking for the Senate, Graham wanted to specify a dollar amount, which Sessums objected to on the basis that it would lead to a "political tug-of-war every year." After the session had adjourned, Sessums discovered that the bill both houses supposedly had approved was actually pasted together after lawmakers had gone home—and it contained the Senate's formula. For several weeks the Speaker refused to sign the bill and send it on to Askew. Askew eventually persuaded Sessums that if he did not sign it, there would have to be a special session and "it's only going to get worse." Although the *Miami Herald* hailed the new formula as "certain to be the envy of every other state," the circumstances were hardly praiseworthy. "It was really written Saturday and Sunday after it 'passed' Friday night," Reed said. The rest of the budget occasioned relatively little controversy. Marshall Harris and the appropriations chair in the Senate, James H. Williams of Ocala, eventually agreed with Askew's budget director, Joe Cresse, that an anticipated surplus should be spent on infrastructure such as bridge repair and accelerated interstate highway construction, which could be omitted from subsequent budgets in the event of the recession they anticipated. Sessums thought too much went to south Florida.[18]

The legislature had yet another problem at the Florida Supreme Court. A vending machine company was litigating for the return of sales taxes it had paid on food and drink items; many millions of dollars were at stake. The case had just been filed when Justice B. K. Roberts sent word to a meeting of Senate committee chairmen that the court would not order the state to refund any money. The messenger, a former legislator, also conveyed Roberts's delight that a bill had been filed to name the Florida State University College of Law building for him. The bill passed both houses in May and became law. In October, the court unanimously ruled as Roberts predicted it would. The tip to the legislature implied several grave ethical violations, but no investigation ensued.[19]

Meanwhile, the committee investigating Adams voted three to two to impeach him. "I strongly disagree," Askew said in a terse prepared statement. Two of Askew's strongest allies, Representatives MacKay and Harris, took opposing sides. MacKay voted to impeach. So did committee chairman James L. Redman, a Plant City attorney who had been

MacKay's high school classmate and college roommate, and House minority leader Jim Tillman. Harris and Representative Ralph Turlington argued that a censure resolution would be sufficient punishment for Adams, whose political future already seemed to be in ruins. "My confidence in the man and in the office is gone. This is so far out of bounds, over twenty-five incidents," Redman replied. The twenty-two formal articles of impeachment charged that a total of $214,057 had been misspent on personal errands for Adams by Getford and other employees and on salaries and travel for fifty-seven Commerce Department employees who had served in unauthorized positions, sometimes with no work to do. But impeachment lost momentum when Sessums announced that he would oppose it and that he would rule that Adams could be censured by a mere majority vote. That gave a tactical advantage to Askew and Adams. Adams did not lack for friends; he still had his state-paid publicist and lobbied aggressively. Unsigned memoranda sent to House members maintained that Adams had been "singled out for practices which have been standard practices in state government for many, many years." They mentioned Askew's own beverage director, Winston Wynne, who had been required to repay $794 for frequent trips to Miami, his hometown. Askew's lobbying was less obvious, but he had a tense meeting in his office with Redman; the committee's staff director, Michael Rose; and Auditor General Ernest Ellison. "I couldn't believe the way Askew talked to Jim Redman," Rose said. "He talked to him like he was a serf." Redman, a deeply religious man, once said, "I think the Lord gave me a gift of not getting mad at people who disagree." Typically, he said nothing of the encounter with Askew other than to describe it as a "disappointment" and to remark years later that "I think I was very unpopular with Reubin."[20]

In the debate on May 17, Redman argued to the House that it should function like a grand jury, finding "probable cause" to send Adams to the Senate for a trial where he would have "an opportunity to defend himself, protected by all constitutional safeguards." Censure, MacKay said, "would either be meaningless—which I think it would be—or else it would be unconstitutional." But as everyone in the chamber knew, Adams greatly preferred censure. It would avoid a Senate trial that might not only remove him from one office but also bar him from ever holding another. His defense was a version of "everybody does it." Representative Donald L. Tucker, a Democrat from Tallahassee, objected that impeachment would "create crimes and inflict the most serious penalties on acts never before suspected to have been criminal." Redman's retort, spoken with his right hand resting on a volume of the *Florida Statutes*: "We aren't setting standards. The standards are *here*." The vote to impeach was sixty-one to fifty-five, seventeen votes shy of the necessary two-thirds. The vote to censure was eighty-eight to twenty-six; all but three of those who voted against censure had voted to impeach. Afterward, Adams sounded curiously unrepentant: "*If* any mistakes were made by me, they were mistakes of the head and not the heart," he said (emphasis added). Askew issued a carefully worded statement that praised Adams's cooperation, extolled the legislative process, and concluded that "Hopefully, the standards of ethical conduct among public officials have been strengthened as a result." Redman asked Harry Morrison, the state attorney at Tallahassee, to consider criminal charges against Adams. Morrison declined. "The law has been violated," Redman complained. "If he can't see that, he can't see anything."[21]

The 1973 session settled a hard-fought contest for the 1975–76 House speakership when MacKay conceded to Tucker. MacKay had been unable to persuade freshman members to withhold their pledges until they knew the candidates better. He warned them they also needed to reform House rules "or the lobbyists are going to run the place." The lobbyists were running it soon enough; some who represented racetracks were instrumental in delivering most of the Dade delegation to Tucker. "We lost the thing in one night," MacKay said. Tucker's victory meant that MacKay would take the next opportunity to run for the state Senate and that Harris, who had supported MacKay strongly, had no future in the House.[22]

When the session ended, Askew had achieved eleven of some thirty major goals. Some, such as ratification of the ERA, would have failed in any event, but it was obvious that the Adams affair had handicapped his lobbying on other issues. His major successes included the new school financing formula, a $150 million interstate highway construction advance which the federal government would repay, the statewide grand jury, authority to acquire the Big Cypress Swamp for conservation purposes, creation of the Florida Elections Commission as part of the *Miami Herald*–inspired reforms, a resolution implementing the developments of regional impact legislation of 1972, and a law empowering the attorney general to propose regulations and file lawsuits against unfair and deceptive trade practices. The so-called Little FTC act, named after the Federal Trade Commission, left Conner with a hollow victory. The agriculture commissioner's office would still be the clearinghouse for consumer complaints, but Attorney General Shevin, an Askew ally, would have the power that mattered. Conner's friends retaliated by eliminating the budget for Askew's consumer office, and with it, Arthur England's job. Soon after, Askew vetoed legislation giving Conner exclusive public health jurisdiction over milk and milk products. Prison reform was a failure; there was money for new, smaller prison facilities but not nearly enough to cope with a federal judge's recent order to increase capacity or release twenty-five hundred inmates within twelve months. The parole commission's aggressive lobbying squelched any broad reform of corrections. The session rejected PSC reform, financial disclosure, environmental reorganization, collective bargaining for public employees, and bail bond reform. A comprehensive criminal code revision passed the House but died on the Senate calendar.[23]

Askew had been virtually silent—ominously so, some thought—on legislation lowering the age of legal majority from twenty-one to eighteen. The bill involved every legal right, including the powers to incur debt and sign contracts. (The voting age had been lowered to eighteen several years before.) "This is disturbing a lot of church people, including the church person on the second floor," argued Senator Bill Gillespie, a Democrat from New Smyrna Beach, in an unsuccessful attempt to exclude alcohol and gambling. He was referring to Askew, but to widespread surprise Askew signed the bill into law within hours after receiving it. "While this was one of the most difficult decisions I have ever had to make," he said, "it also represents my own belief that our young people will continue to live up to the confidence and trust that we have placed in them." An editorial in the *Florida Baptist Witness* accused Askew of deliberately acting quickly so that religious conservatives could not lobby him for a veto. Askew had to draft a form letter to respond to the protest mail. He did veto legislation that would have allowed children as young as twelve to attend horse races with their parents, along with another allowing persons under seventeen to be actors or musicians at dinner theaters that served alcohol.[24]

Roland Page resigned after the session to return to journalism as Washington correspondent for the *New York Times* subsidiaries in Florida. Paul Schnitt, a *St. Petersburg Times* assistant city editor, filled Page's slot as deputy press secretary. It was an awkward development for the *Times*, since Schnitt was dating former colleague Virginia Ellis, who had transferred to the paper's bureau in Tallahassee. Askew cared only for the fact that they were not married, and kept after Schnitt until they wed.

14

SCANDALS IN THE CAPITOL
(1972–1975)

Capitalizing on President Richard Nixon's 72 percent landslide in the state in November 1972, Florida Republicans began intensively recruiting Democrats to change parties. Jerry Thomas was the prize catch in their "Operation Switchover." Vice-President Spiro Agnew flew down to personally welcome the former Florida Senate president into the GOP. Although Askew assumed Thomas would run for governor in 1974, he was privately uncertain that he wanted a second term for himself. Among other reasons, he said, he feared "drifting into the national picture, and I just don't feel prepared. . . . I don't have that much ambition." He delayed his reelection commitment until April 1974, four months before the primary, when Jim Apthorp, his chief of staff, forced his hand. Apthorp warned that it was already too late for any acceptable Democrat to take his place.[1]

In August 1973, Askew had invited Richard Pallot, Jon Moyle, David and Fred Levin, Apthorp, Don Pride, Jim Smith, and thirty other old friends, campaign supporters, and staff members to a fishing lodge on the Ochlockonee River near Tallahassee. It would be remembered as the "Sopchoppy Summit." They feasted on a true southern dinner of shrimp, chicken, black-eyed peas, okra, and cornbread—"the best food I ever had," said Moyle. Then, they nearly choked on unexpected news. Askew said he had decided to accept no more than $300 from any contributor during the course of the campaign. The law would let him take up to $9,000, which in practice meant $18,000 from a husband and wife.

Askew's friends were dismayed at first by how much harder they would have to work to raise money. Their mood brightened as they realized how much less it would cost them personally. Conceding that only an incumbent could afford such a gesture, Askew said his motive was not to embarrass other candidates but to ease his own mind. "I was not looking for the high ground as much as I did not want anybody out there thinking they were going to get something by a series of $3,000 contributions," he said. Askew also said that Pallot, Price, and anyone else he had appointed to a regulatory agency would have to resign before campaigning for him.[2]

The absence of one old friend was conspicuous. Miami mayor David Kennedy, Askew's chief strategist in the 1970 primaries, had been indicted and suspended in a Dade County judicial bribery scandal. Askew lifted the suspension after Kennedy's indictment was dismissed, but there would be no more roles for Kennedy in Askew's political life. The Miami case fizzled with the acquittals of the two circuit court judges who were the principal targets, but other scandals soon ensued. Unethical conduct at the Florida Supreme Court resulted in the resignations of two justices. Half of the Cabinet members—Education Commissioner Floyd T. Christian, Treasurer Tom O'Malley, and Comptroller Fred O. Dickinson Jr.—were driven from office by criminal investigations. The corruption weighed on Askew as he thought about whether to seek a second term or return to his law practice. "I never really wanted to run for reelection," he said years later. But he doubted at the time that anyone else could clean up the state government, "which I felt I had to do." From early 1973 to mid-1975, few days passed without newspaper headlines referring to one or more of the investigations. Meanwhile, Agnew resigned the vice-presidency because of crimes he had committed as a county executive in Maryland. The Watergate probe resulted in President Nixon's resignation and imprisoned nearly a score of his people. Edward Gurney quit his campaign for reelection to the U.S. Senate to concentrate on his ultimately successful defense to federal bribery charges.[3]

While debating with himself whether to run again, Askew had to deal with the consequences of an Arab oil export embargo in 1973 and 1974. Federal gasoline allocations occasionally left Florida critically short of

fuel, threatening its tourist economy. The situation influenced his decision to accept legislation somewhat weakening Florida's model oil spill
law, which had been upheld recently by the U.S. Supreme Court.[4]

Askew faced increasing difficulties with the Cabinet and the legislature. Donald Tucker, the House Speaker-designate, had not been notably
supportive. Dempsey Barron, the Senate president-in-waiting, spelled
even bigger trouble. In late 1973, Barron, Tucker, and Senate president
Mallory Horne began pressuring the Cabinet to appoint a friend of
theirs to succeed Randolph Hodges. The natural resources director was
unwilling to delay his retirement any longer. The legislators' candidate
was Harmon Shields, a political ally from Panama City. He was chief of
the department's law enforcement arm, the Marine Patrol, and a friend
of the commercial fishing industry. He had been part owner of a laundry
when his political connections with Tom Adams led to his first state job
as the Department of Natural Resources' seafood marketing director.
The Marine Patrol had conducted fish fries for influential politicians and
civic clubs until the auditor general put a stop to it. Askew considered
Shields unqualified to head a conservation agency; he preferred Ney
Landrum, the state parks director, to succeed Hodges. Attorney General
Robert Shevin and Christian supported Askew. Dickinson, O'Malley,
and Agriculture Commissioner Doyle Conner were for Shields. O'Malley
told Askew that he feared for his budget if he did not vote as the powerful legislators demanded. The deciding vote would be cast by Secretary
of State Richard Stone, who intended to run for Gurney's Senate seat.
On Stone's orders, his representative on a nominating committee saw
to it that Shields would be recommended along with Landrum and two
other finalists. Florida's environmental activists were irate, but Shields
won on a four-to-three vote. Four years later, Askew's objections proved
prescient when the Cabinet had to remove Shields during an FBI investigation of the department's land-purchase practices. Shields was eventually sentenced to five years in a federal prison for conspiring to extort a
$235,000 bribe.[5]

Askew's worst defeat in a Cabinet conflict was also the beginning of
his extreme difficulties with Barron. The senator went to the mansion
to show his hand—four votes for Shields—and to urge Askew to give
up the fight. "What you're doing is wrong. It's a basic violation of the

whole separation of powers," Askew replied. Barron's face reddened. "You know, Governor, this means war," he said.[6]

Another clash with Barron was the eventual result of Askew's June 1973 decision to appoint O. J. Keller to head the Department of Health and Rehabilitative Services (HRS), Florida's largest agency. Keller replaced Emmett Roberts, who had once been a state legislator. Keller was a charismatic former disc jockey who became director of the Illinois youth corrections system and reformed it. Senator Louis de la Parte, the father of HRS, had arranged for him to become Florida's youth services director. Askew hoped that Keller's promotion would please de la Parte, Kenneth Myers, and other legislators who had expressed concerns over problems in the unwieldy department. But in one of his first acts, Keller antagonized some other lawmakers by firing Paul A. Skelton Jr., the director of administrative services, who complained that Keller had no reason. Skelton had worked twenty-five years for the state and had friends in the legislature. Louie Wainwright, the director of corrections, promptly hired Skelton for the prison system, which the legislature divorced from HRS a year later. In 1975, Barron would force Keller out of office on trumped-up accusations that he was a poor administrator.[7]

Floyd Christian's fall was painful for Askew because of the hearty support the commissioner had given him on every issue other than the structure of education governance. In 1972, *St. Petersburg Times* reporter Bette Orsini began to investigate state contracts Christian had awarded to a circle of friends that included Robert N. Bussey, a prominent St. Petersburg attorney and banker. During a critical interview, Orsini's tape recorder had malfunctioned; she had few useful notes. Christian did not know that when he was considering the newspaper's request for a copy of his secretary's transcript. "I think the transcript puts you in a good light," wrote Howard Friedman, Christian's press secretary, in a memorandum urging him to cooperate with *St. Petersburg Times* editor Eugene C. Patterson. The worst the newspaper could write, Friedman said, was that a friend of Christian's was involved in substantial business that the department was awarding without bids. But as bad as that might be, Friedman concluded, "that kind of story I think we can weather." Christian had not told him the full story, which was worse than Friedman could imagine. A month later, Christian rashly asked House Speaker Terrell Sessums for an investigation by Representative Jim Redman's auditing committee. He expressed confidence that it would refute the newspaper's "easily recognizable campaign of character assassination and personal harassment." Christian renewed the request in February 1973—just before the Adams scandal preoccupied the committee's time. Unfortunately for Christian, his case soon would be taken just as seriously by Redman, his staff, and Auditor General Ernest Ellison. Their break was the failure of a bank in the Bahamas that Bussey had helped to organize. Redman's staff director, Michael Rose, flew to Nassau and found a signature card in the name of "Zera R. Tom," relating to deposit certificates totaling more than $130,000. It was a fictitious name fashioned from the names of Christian's children. Redman and his cochairman, Senator George Firestone, were certain that they were dealing with a potential criminal case, but they did not want to entrust it to Harry Morrison, the state attorney at Tallahassee, who had declined to prosecute Tom Adams. Askew obliged the committee's unanimous request for a special prosecutor by appointing Edward Austin, the state attorney at Jacksonville, who had probed the 1971 clashes at the Raiford prison. Askew already had doubts about Morrison. He knew from conversations with Christian that there were affidavits which Christian should have turned over to Morrison. Christian had given nothing but news clippings to the uninquisitive prosecutor, who asked for nothing more.[8]

Christian could not have been candid with his attorneys, or they would not have allowed him to waive immunity and testify twice to Austin's grand jury. In mid-April 1974 the jury indicted him on nineteen counts of bribery, conspiracy, and perjury. He was accused of taking more than $70,000 in bribes and kickbacks on contracts that had cost the state $1.5 million. It made him the highest-ranking state official ever to be indicted for conduct in office. With less than nine months to go before his planned retirement, Christian declared he would fight the charges and refuse to resign. He changed his mind about resigning a week later, as a House committee was about to begin impeachment proceedings. Askew named Representative Ralph Turlington, already an announced candidate for the office and a strong favorite to win it in

November, to succeed him. Askew spoke of a "deep sense of sadness" in accepting Christian's resignation. With his eyes red as he bade farewell to the House of Representatives, where he had served since 1951, Turlington spoke fondly of Christian's leadership during the 1968 statewide teacher strike.[9]

Austin's work—and ordeal, as it turned out—had only begun. Supported by Ellison, Rose, and committee staff counsel Marvin Rudnick, the prosecutor and grand jury began looking into evidence that O'Malley was taking kickbacks from his former law partners for advising insurance companies to retain them. There were also reports of a $50,000 bribe fund that service station owners had collected to influence O'Malley, who was also the state fire marshal, against approving self-service gasoline sales. Another state attorney had tipped Morrison to the bribe rumor, but Morrison confessed to reporters that he had lost the file. Austin also issued subpoenas to several well-known lobbyists, striking fear in many legislators. His target was the former Senate rules chairman, George Hollahan, who had lost his seat to Richard Pettigrew. Some legislators and Cabinet members began to suspect that Askew was instigating a massive purge. They were particularly unhappy that the auditor general, a legislative employee, was involved. The investigations, Horne said, had "everybody seeing spooks." Askew insisted he did nothing but approve requests from Austin and the grand jury to follow leads unearthed during the Christian probe. "We did not go into what the evidence is," he said. Redman tried to persuade his colleagues that it had nothing to do with the political stresses between the governor and the Cabinet. "As long as I can pull a lever, I'll support the Cabinet," he said. Redman and George Firestone came under pressure from other legislators who opposed their cooperation with Austin and wanted to see the prosecutor sent back to Jacksonville. Austin, whom a feature writer described as having "an unhandsome, unugly, uncomplicated face that makes you think of saddles and pastures," said he understood the resentment. The problem, he said, was that people occasionally elect corrupt politicians and "keep them a long time because some prosecutor is sitting on his hands." The remark, unmistakably describing Morrison, could not have been well received by Morrison's most influential cousin, Florida Supreme Court justice B. K. Roberts.[10]

In July, acting entirely on his own whim—or so he said—Chief Justice James C. Adkins Jr. ordered the investigation shut down until after the November election. Citing no evidence, Adkins implied that the probe had been timed to defeat O'Malley's reelection campaign. The order came without prior notice to Austin, Attorney General Robert Shevin, or the supreme court itself. At the request of Ben F. Overton, the newest justice, the full court reviewed Adkins's decision a week later, but upheld it in modified form with Roberts casting the tie-breaking vote. Adkins voluntarily withdrew the decree after it had been in force twelve days. His change of mind closely followed three events: a unanimous plea from the grand jury, Shevin's decision to appeal to the U.S. Supreme Court, and publication of a *Miami Herald* article in which Hollahan admitted that he was one of Austin's targets. He was under investigation for taking "referral fees" from lobbyists to whom he had sent clients who had business before the legislature. The newspaper reported that a two-year statute of limitations would expire, preventing Hollahan's prosecution, if the grand jury had to remain idle until after the election. Askew said he was pleased that Adkins had avoided an "unnecessary constitutional crisis."[11]

The grand jury indicted Hollahan in August and O'Malley in October. The former senator was charged with three counts of receiving bribes totaling $19,000 to support small loan, cemetery, and liquor license bills. The treasurer was accused of taking more than $50,000 in kickbacks and perjuring himself to conceal it. Among other things, the O'Malley indictments said he had arranged with his former law partners for up to $239,000 over eight years for steering insurance clients their way. In a comic-opera twist, the grand jury accused the Florida Petroleum Marketers Association of attempting to bribe O'Malley with a bag full of cash that O'Malley's general counsel testified he kept under his bed for eight months before returning it. The grand jury said the money was delivered by Bernie W. Simpkins Jr., who was not indicted. Simpkins, a fuel dealer at Cocoa, was a member of the Board of Business Regulation at the time of the alleged bribe attempt. Askew had demanded his resignation when he learned of the investigation.[12]

The Florida judiciary had more unpleasant surprises in store for the prosecution. In November the First District Court of Appeal threw out the Christian indictments—and, in effect, the Hollahan and O'Malley cases as well. It ruled that Askew lacked the authority to assign Austin in Morrison's place, that Austin's assistants from Jacksonville should not have appeared before a grand jury in Tallahassee, and that only one prosecutor at a time could be in a grand jury room. Two of the three district court judges involved, John Rawls and Dewey Johnson, had served in the Senate with Hollahan. The decision left the governor's office virtually powerless to pursue official corruption. Askew called the legislature into special session; it rewrote the law to moot the court's objections. But the changes could not apply retroactively; the indictments would remain void unless the Florida Supreme Court accepted Austin's appeal and overturned the district court's decision. The supreme court, three of whose justices were facing possible impeachment themselves, did overrule the district court on most points but still managed to dispose of the indictments. They ruled four to two on a strikingly picayune technicality, holding that Austin's assistants from the Fourth Circuit should have been sworn in as assistants in the Second Circuit before working with the grand jury. Askew's new law had already mooted that issue for future prosecutions. Hollahan was now immune, however, because the state's time to charge him finally had expired. Christian and O'Malley were re-indicted, but the most serious charges—that Christian had perjured himself before the grand jury—were gone forever. Christian eventually pleaded no contest to three counts. They involved a $29,000 kickback from Bussey for a portable classroom contract and Christian's false testimony to the legislative auditing committee. The plea bargain with Austin preserved Christian's $25,000-a-year pension. Although Christian could have gone to prison for twenty-five years, Circuit Judge Ben Willis sentenced him only to probation for seven years and $43,000 in fines. A U.S. district judge was not quite so lenient when Christian stood before him for income tax evasion. He sentenced him to 135 days in a minimum security prison followed by a year of probation. "All I'm saying now is I'm at the bottom. I need to be given a chance to come up," Christian pleaded to the federal judge.[13]

Ninety-two people, including Askew, had written to Willis, most of them on Christian's behalf. Conceding that Christian deserved punishment, Askew refrained from recommending what it should be. He wrote that there was "much that was positive" in Christian's record of public service, including his "courageous and responsible leadership" when Florida schools were desegregating and his "determined stand" to keep the schools open during the 1968 teacher walkout. Although Askew was criticized for saying as much as he did, Christian failed to appreciate it. As he was preparing for prison, Christian went to the mansion. With tears in his eyes he told Askew he had done nothing wrong and asked a question that stunned the governor: "Why did you do this to me?" Askew told Christian that he had done it to himself. "If anything, Floyd, I didn't prosecute you vigorously enough," he said. They had not reconciled when Christian died in May 1998. "I always wished I could have sat down and talked with him about it," Askew said.[14]

Austin still had O'Malley on his hands. Having had his fill of Tallahassee justice, the prosecutor helped the House impeach O'Malley, who had been reelected despite the first indictment. Austin obtained O'Malley's resignation in a plea bargain and delivered his evidence, "with ribbons on it," to the U.S. Justice Department. After a dozen delays owing mainly to his ill health, O'Malley went to trial in a federal court in 1978. He was convicted of two counts of extortion and nineteen of mail fraud and eventually served two years in prison. Dickinson lost his office, though not his liberty, on account of a federal investigation into his role as state bank regulator. The media reported that he had invoked the Fifth Amendment during a five-minute appearance before a grand jury. He ran second in the Democratic primary and lost the runoff to former state senator Gerald Lewis, who won easily in November. Lewis was the first person to become comptroller by election since 1921; Dickinson, like several predecessors, had been appointed to fill a midterm vacancy. A former Dickinson law partner went to prison for lying to a grand jury about $25,000 in bank stock that Dickinson owned secretly. Dickinson himself was acquitted of extortion in one trial. In another, a jury acquitted him of one count of evading taxes on gifts from bankers and deadlocked on two others. He eventually plea-bargained to a misdemeanor charge, failure to fully pay his federal taxes in 1971, and was fined $3,000.[15]

15

SCANDALS IN THE COURT
(1973–1976)

Askew was walking to work one morning in December 1973, his mind occupied by the energy crisis and the Harmon Shields controversy, when he learned abruptly that he had a serious problem at the Florida Supreme Court. This author, making his way to the court, a block from the capitol, showed Askew a copy of a curious memorandum that Justice David McCain's secretary had written to McCain at the request of Justice Hal P. Dekle. It concerned a case styled *Gulf Power v. Bevis*:

> Judge Dekle asked me to write you this note.
> "HPD says that he thought you were with him on his 'dissent'; that Ed Mason spoke to him on it but missed seeing you."

As a lawyer, Askew instantly recognized the significance. Justices were not simply discussing the pending decision but were allowing themselves to be lobbied privately by a lawyer—Ed Mason—who represented two of the litigants. That was a flagrant violation of the codes of ethics for judges and attorneys. Askew was a party to the case; his corporate profits tax was the issue. The question was the extent to which public utility customers would bear the cost of the $6 million a year in corporate taxes that the electric, telephone, and gas companies were paying. Mason represented two telephone companies on the opposing side. Askew was a victim of whatever was going wrong at the court. "It looks," he said, "as if we're being *ex parted*."[1]

The utilities were appealing a compromise decision of the Public Service Commission to include the tax in the rate-making formula rather than allow it to passed on to customers dollar-for-dollar. The situation at the court was even seamier than it appeared that December morning. Dekle had taken his "dissent," which he intended to become the court's majority opinion, almost word for word from a document Mason had drafted for Justice Joseph A. Boyd Jr., an old friend from Miami. Mason and Boyd had discussed the *Gulf Power* case—another ethical transgression—during a golf outing that left the lawyer believing the justice needed help in writing an opinion that would express what the court wanted to say. Boyd destroyed his copy after belatedly realizing the ethical implications. He tore it into what he later testified were "seventeen equal" strips and flushed them down a toilet in the justices' lavatory. He then wrote a short opinion *against* the utilities. But by then two law clerks, Roger Schwartz and David La Croix, had seen Mason's document. They recognized it when Dekle used a copy, which Mason had given him, to draft his "dissent." La Croix alerted his boss, Chief Justice Vassar Carlton, who ordered Dekle to rewrite the opinion so as to cover up the improper influence. Under the Code of Judicial Conduct, every justice who knew about Mason and the colleagues who let him lobby them had a duty to inform the Florida Bar and the Judicial Qualifications Commission (JQC). None did. Dekle's original "dissent" vanished. So did the second copy of Mason's memorandum.[2]

At the cost of their jobs, it was the law clerks who blew the whistle. They had no hard evidence to prove who ghosted Dekle's opinion, but they did have a copy of the memorandum that referred to Mason's lobbying. They leaked the memo to the *St. Petersburg Times*. The exposé contributed to a final decision essentially sustaining the PSC's compromise, which took the tax into account in calculating a "reasonable" profit for the utilities.[3] The disclosure also triggered an investigation by the JQC, which recommended that the supreme court expel Dekle and Boyd. A substitute panel of judges voted only to reprimand them. Dissatisfied with that outcome, the 1975 House opened impeachment proceedings. Those resulted in the resignations of Dekle and McCain. Dekle was also accused of trying to influence a circuit court judge in a campaign supporter's civil case. McCain had tried to fix a bribery conviction appeal for a labor union leader who, according to the *St. Petersburg Times*, had also bribed him. Mason was suspended from the Bar for a year. The episode contributed to several constitutional amendments, including one of the most important of Askew's career, a 1976 revision providing for the appointment rather than the election of all judges of the supreme court and district courts of appeal.

Even before the *Gulf Power* scandal, Askew was aware of problems within the court. B. K. Roberts, the senior and most influential justice, had told him privately of justices who drank too much and talked out of court. On Roberts's advice, Askew obtained supplemental funds for the JQC, a panel of lawyers and judges created in 1965 as an alternative to impeachment. Roberts, though, was something of a double agent; he wanted the problems dealt with privately and in ways he could control. He did not alert Askew to the worst ethical offenses. He led the hunt for the clerks who had leaked the McCain memorandum. He wrote a February 1974 opinion that temporarily crippled the JQC by forbidding it to investigate a judge for any conduct predating his present term of office. That decision stalled a pending JQC investigation into McCain's earlier behavior on the Fourth District Court of Appeal.

That four-to-two decision, with Boyd and Richard Ervin dissenting, responded to a petition filed by Jack Turner, a Dade circuit judge who had been acquitted of bribery. Faced with a separate ethics investigation by the JQC, he retained an old friend of Roberts's to persuade the supreme court to thwart it. The outcome prompted a 1974 constitutional amendment empowering the JQC to look into any conduct in private or public life affecting a judge's "present unfitness to hold office." Reacting to the intense criticism, the court had already "clarified" the Turner decision so as to allow investigations into a judge's prior term.[4]

In January 1974, with the Turner decision still pending, Carlton announced he would retire with less than a year left in his term. His decision foreclosed a potential JQC investigation of a high-roller junket to Las Vegas, where Miami television station WPLG had filmed the incautious chief justice at a dice table. It was Askew's first opportunity to name a supreme court justice and the first such appointment under the merit selection process he had established. He told his legal staff not to interfere with the commission or tell him who might be applying. "He wanted it to be really straight . . . without pressure from the governor's office," said Arthur Canaday, his new general counsel. One of the applicants was former governor LeRoy Collins, Askew's acknowledged role model and his neighbor in Tallahassee. The nominating commission shelved Collins's application without an interview. Friends were rebuffed when they tried to lobby the governor's office. The nominee whom Askew eventually selected was Ben Overton, a forty-seven-year-old St. Petersburg circuit judge known as a stickler for ethics. Dixie Beggs, a Pensacola attorney who chaired the nominating commission, had called on Overton in 1973 to help him persuade the supreme court to stiffen the Code of Judicial Conduct. The Gulf Power exposé had made it clear to Askew that the court's own ethics sorely needed repair. Chesterfield Smith, president of the American Bar Association, sent him a letter saying that no current issue was as important as Carlton's replacement. In addition to legal qualifications, Smith wrote, the appointee "should be *young*, hard-nosed, and unyielding on ethical transgressions by others." Overton fit the description. His first opinion, for a unanimous court, turned away a legislator's lawsuit for access to all the JQC's files but held that they should be made available to the House of Representatives for any specific impeachment inquiry. That decision would be costly to McCain a year later.[5]

Collins, like most governors, had preferred to give judicial appointments to friends, staff members, and campaign supporters whom he knew and trusted. Askew scarcely knew Overton. They had been in different classes at the University of Florida law school, and their paths had rarely if ever crossed afterward. Askew relied on the nominating commissions to vouch for the reputations and abilities of his judges, but some characteristics of the commissions did concern him. At a meeting late in 1974 he told them that they seemed to prefer candidates from prestigious law firms. He admonished them to "guard against the danger of replacing patronage politics with Bar politics." He warned the nominating commissioners who were not lawyers against letting themselves be intimidated by the attorneys. He asked that more women and minorities be nominated.[6]

16

ONLY IN FLORIDA
(POLITICS OF 1974)

As he entered upon what he knew would be a difficult year—and possibly his last in office—Askew was comforted by a Democratic Party poll showing that Floridians respected him even more than Walter Cronkite. It turned out that even some of his troubles could be turned to advantage. With household utility bills soaring on account of the Arab oil embargo, the legislature was finally receptive to Askew's request to appoint a public counsel to represent consumers before the Public Service Commission. The Cabinet scandals underscored what Askew called his "absolute top priority," the issue of ethics in government. Laws were enacted to limit conflicts of interest, to require some financial disclosure by officials and candidates, and to establish a commission on ethics. Thanks to three years of conservative budgeting, including the 1973 decision to lend surplus funds to the interstate highway program, Florida was able to sustain a severe recession without extreme reductions in programs. The legislature even managed to end the 1974 session on time.[1]

Even so, Florida politics were frequently a theater of the absurd. Askew's strongest Democratic primary opponent turned out to be former senator Bill Hill Griffin Jr., a surprise candidate who waited until the last moment to decide to run for governor and drafted his wife as his running mate. Treasurer Tom O'Malley won reelection despite his having being indicted just before the November election. Republican primary voters had passed over Representative Eugene Tubbs, a competent but overconfident candidate who might have defeated O'Malley. Instead, they nominated Jeffrey Latham, a political unknown who then admitted seeking Ku Klux Klan support and said he would be "proud" of it. O'Malley owed his narrow victory to responsible voters who anticipated that his conviction or impeachment would allow the governor to appoint a suitable successor. Florida Supreme Court justice Joseph A. Boyd Jr. won reelection in a campaign made bizarre by the misdeeds in the *Gulf Power* case and Boyd's allegation that Justice B. K. Roberts had tricked him into going into a clinic for a physical examination so that it would appear his mental health was in question. The supreme court ordered an election in which it expected a friendly candidate would replace Justice Richard Ervin, who was retiring. Askew's former consumer adviser, Arthur England, won instead.[2]

In late January, with legislators coming to Tallahassee for committee meetings, Askew called a special session to try to exempt most of the state from the year-round daylight saving time that Congress had imposed as an emergency energy measure. Askew was reacting to reports that more children were dying in predawn traffic accidents. The House considered the data unconvincing and refused to act. It could not be determined whether the deaths owed to the extra hour of morning darkness or to unusually heavy fog. Some said that a corresponding hour of daylight in the afternoon might be saving children's lives.[3]

Askew had trouble with three of his high-profile appointees. Editorial writers and Senate investigators attacked Winston Wynne, the beverage director, over questionable management practices and an interview in which he referred to African Americans as "darkies." Askew merely admonished Wynne, who resigned seven months later. Don Spicer, Adams's successor as secretary of commerce, sacked a division director, Ben Patterson, who was popular with organized labor. Patterson's friends on Askew's staff retaliated by blocking Spicer's access to the governor. Askew fired Spicer after the election, appointing former legislator Edward Trombetta in his place. The media criticized Transportation Secretary Walter Revell for intervening in hiring the father of Jim Smith, Askew's campaign manager, for an unadvertised vacancy. Revell resigned after the election and was replaced by a career employee, Tom Webb.[4]

In his opening-day speech and supplemental messages to the 1974 legislature, Askew called for a broadened homestead tax exemption for the elderly and disabled; a $20,000 exemption from taxes on the value of stocks, bonds, and other intangible assets; and a 20 percent reduction in the ceiling on the local property tax rate for schools. The normally supportive *St. Petersburg Times* objected that Askew was inviting higher consumer taxes and said that the budget "seems to be addressed less to public needs than to the political realities of an election year." Askew was attempting to preempt more radical tax-cutting proposals, among them a Republican bill to repeal the entire intangibles tax, which was the state's only wealth-based revenue source. The legislature approved most of Askew's tax program but not his renewed attempt to stop cities from granting tax discounts to large utility users. Acknowledging that there was "no single 'right' answer" to financial disclosure, Askew signaled that he would accept what the legislature eventually enacted: disclosure of sources without dollar values attached to them. He asked the legislature to allow the Public Service Commission to require electric utilities to pool their generating and transmission facilities.[5]

Senator Louis de la Parte, who had announced that his twelfth year in the legislature would be his last, wanted to finish what he had started at the Department of Health and Rehabilitative Services. He intended to break up the eleven separate divisions of HRS; Representative Buddy MacKay, an ally, called them "petty fiefdoms." The plan was to decentralize authority. Regional secretaries would become responsible for delivering "one stop service" to needy people. HRS's secretary, O. J. Keller, conceded that clients were "falling through the cracks" but said that the legislation went too far. With Askew's backing, he opposed it. De la Parte spent more than one hundred hours negotiating Askew's agreement to a compromise version, but agency workers and professional interest groups continued to lobby against it. A House committee killed it in retaliation for Askew's opposition to a pro-Cabinet environmental reorganization bill. "You've made your point but you're picking on the wrong guy," de la Parte pleaded in frustration before leaving the meeting in tears. The failure led ultimately to what de la Parte was trying to prevent: the dismemberment of HRS.[6]

Most of Askew's energy legislation had strong bipartisan support in the House, which voted 102–9 for MacKay's energy grid bill and 107–8 for Republican Curt Kiser's public counsel bill. The legislature would appoint the public counsel through its joint auditing committee, which gave the job to former senator Fred Karl. He was widely respected for his intelligence and integrity, but he did not stay long in the position. The Senate passed the energy grid and public counsel legislation on the next-to-last day of the session; Senator Dempsey Barron, the rules chairman, had held them up in his committee. He was attempting to exempt Gulf Power Corporation, the major utility in his district, from having to share generating and transmission capacity with Florida utilities rather than with its corporate parent in Georgia. As Senate president Mallory Horne had feared, Barron was not waiting to be formally elected president before assuming the power. Horne, having promised Askew that the Senate would pass the energy grid bill, gave Barron an ultimatum: "I want that bill out or you're no longer rules chairman." In one of his last acts as Senate president, Horne yielded the gavel and took the Senate floor to personally manage passage of the bill. During a chance hallway encounter with three other senators who supported the bill, Barron seized Bob Graham and Dan Scarborough by their neckties and accused them of plotting against him. "If you lay your hand on me," warned the third senator, Jim Williams, "I'm going to invite you to go outside." From then on, Williams said, "We understood one another."[7]

Senator Bill Gillespie's last legislative act was a good deed for a powerless constituent. He forced the Senate to compensate Jesse Daniels, the mentally retarded young man whom Lake County sheriff Willis McCall and State Attorney Gordon Oldham had sent to a state psychiatric hospital to falsely clear a rape case. The House had already sharply reduced Daniels's award to $75,000, $100,000 less than recommended by its claims committee. Oldham was still in office; his friends in the Senate were unwilling to approve even the lesser sum. Late on the session's last night, the Senate was rushing through uncontroversial legislation that needed unanimous consent to be heard. "I'm going to object to every one of them if I don't get this bill passed," Gillespie declared. With Oldham watching from the gallery, the Daniels bill passed unanimously.

Although Gillespie and Askew were friends, Edgar M. Dunn Jr., Askew's former general counsel, was planning a campaign for Gillespie's seat. Gillespie retired from the Senate rather than undergo a costly and bruising Democratic primary campaign. Dunn succeeded him.[8]

The ethics package remained in doubt until the eleventh hour. Seldom had legislators debated so long and compromised so much as on a comprehensive bill to curb conflicts of interest and require thousands of state and local public officials to disclose their finances. The House considered 111 amendments over four days. As enacted, the bill required disclosure not of dollar amounts but only of the identity and sources of significant investments and income. Askew objected that the legislation did not require legislators and other constitutional officers to reveal their net-worth statements and income-tax returns. Marshall Harris and Buddy MacKay, who managed the bill in the House, had decided that it would be impossible to pass what Askew wanted. For most of the session it was doubtful that any disclosure bill could be enacted, let alone one acceptable to Askew. Representative Don Crane, a St. Petersburg Republican, thought he had enough votes to pass an amendment eliminating public disclosure; it provided for confidential reports to an ethics commission. House Speaker Terrell Sessums kept the voting board open while Harris, MacKay, and others worked the floor until Crane's amendment was defeated thirty-nine to seventy-seven. Many of the ninety-six representatives who voted to send the much-amended bill to the Senate hoped it would be weakened or killed there. After the Senate finally acted on the bill a month later, with only three days left in the session, Jim Williams complained that it left nothing subject to disclosure except an official's "name and phone number." Nearly half the House, including Speaker-designate Donald L. Tucker, voted to accept all the Senate's amendments. With Askew threatening a veto and a special session, the Senate restored some of what it had taken out. Harris damned the outcome with faint praise and boycotted the signing ceremony. Askew called it as a "fair compromise between conflicting views in a very sensitive and complex area," but on signing the bill he cautioned that it needed to be "substantially strengthened." As enacted, it gave candidates and major officeholders a choice. They could identify some of their income sources and assets, or they could provide the public with copies of income-tax returns and net-worth statements, as Askew himself was already doing. The law also required officials to regularly identify clients whom they or their partners represented before agencies at the same level of government. This applied, among others, to legislators who practiced before the PSC. Some thought the law too strong; twenty-two local officials immediately resigned rather than comply.[9]

The ethics commission bill passed with no opposition. When sponsor Paul Danahy Jr., a House member from Tampa, had first proposed it five years earlier, colleagues literally laughed it to death. Askew appointed to the commission, among others, LeRoy Collins; retired supreme court justice E. Harris Drew; and George Allen, the University of Florida law school's first African American graduate. The law provided also for members to be appointed by the legislature's presiding officers; Sessums chose Sandy D'Alemberte, who became the first chairman. The commission undertook with no success then (or ever) to persuade the legislature to correct the most significant weaknesses. The commission had no power to issue cease-and-desist orders or to investigate any suspected offense without a sworn complaint from the public.[10]

It was a bittersweet final session for Sessums. He had given decisive support to the ethics legislation but saw Barron defeat his environmental legislation. Sessums wanted to require comprehensive local planning, to restrict development according to the community's capacity to absorb it, and to inventory state resources. Speaker-designate Tucker used his emerging power to pass a collective bargaining act for public employees and increase compensation to injured workers. Most legislators opposed bargaining rights for public employees despite plain language in the 1968 constitution, but they knew that the Florida Supreme Court had threatened to establish them by judicial order. Because Tucker had displayed a heavy hand on several issues, Harris made a last-ditch attempt to contest the speakership. Tucker accused Harris of opposing him because he had been told he would not chair the appropriations committee again. "I just didn't like the way he did business. I didn't trust the man," Harris said, conceding that on civil liberties issues he and Tucker had voted together "the whole time."[11]

The session's other notable successes included a constitutional amendment overturning the Turner decision described in chapter 15. It also made the Judicial Qualifications Commission more independent of the supreme court. A new criminal code closed a bribery loophole the court had established in the case that would lead to Justice McCain's resignation and disbarment. An administrative procedure act provided for independent hearing examiners to consider agency rules and enforcement actions. A revised education finance plan cut the maximum local school tax rate by 20 percent, as Askew had requested. A statewide school construction code was enacted along with a $25 million portable classroom appropriation to end double sessions in many counties. A prison reform bill expanded the parole commission in an attempt to accelerate prison releases. Major defeats included environmental agency reorganization, blocked again by the Cabinet and Senate; the Equal Rights Amendment, rejected nineteen to twenty-one by the Senate; and an unsuccessful proposal to appoint judges.[12]

Askew signed Senator Kenneth Myers's prison reform bill despite his misgivings about a provision restoring civil rights to convicted felons upon completion of their sentences or paroles. He asked the supreme court for an advisory opinion; it held six to one that the constitution allowed only the governor and Cabinet to restore civil rights. Justice Richard Ervin dissented. He wrote that the legislature had the power and the duty to restore civil rights "speedily, automatically and routinely." (In 2007, Governor Charlie Crist won a split Cabinet vote to make restoration nearly automatic for ex-offenders whose crimes were nonviolent. By then, an estimated 950,000 people, more than in any other state, were barred from voting, serving on juries, or holding state-licensed jobs in health and service professions.)[13]

Askew established a privately financed committee of seventy-seven business leaders chaired by modular housing executive Jim Walter to propose cost-saving measures for the executive branch. It made 617 recommendations; they came out during the 1974 campaign, and Askew issued an executive order to agencies to adopt them. He said they could save the state $100 million a year, but that was extremely optimistic, considering that many of them dealt with sacred cows. For example, the committee's recommendation that Floridians be able to get driver's licenses and auto plates at the same place remains unfulfilled at this writing.[14]

Tom Adams had announced that he would run for secretary of state, his former office, but he still craved revenge against Askew. Elmer Rounds and David Kennedy, discarded advisers from the 1970 campaign, were encouraging Adams to run for governor. He obliged them by announcing his gubernatorial candidacy on April 22. He came up mostly empty-handed, however, when he tried to recruit the many former "Adams Army" members now working for Askew. "This is the first time Floridians have known BEFORE the election that a candidate was a certified cheater," said a *St. Petersburg Times* editorial. Adams hoped voters would overlook the farm scandal if he could arouse them over Askew's stands on busing and the Cabinet. He bid unabashedly for the support of George Wallace voters, saying that the Alabama governor "stands today, in many important ways, for so much of what is needed to put America back on the track." Askew's staff feared that his support was eroding in thirteen Panhandle counties where he had polled 77 percent of the vote against Kirk. The busing issue already had contributed to the 1972 reelection defeat of Tom Beasley, a circuit judge in the Panhandle, who was a former House Speaker and friend of Askew. It seemed clear that Askew could not rely upon his home turf in 1974 and would need to maximize turnout elsewhere.[15]

Adams, fifty-seven years old, made his announcement on April 22 with his bride of seven months by his side; his second wife was twenty-four, a Peace Corps volunteer he had met in South America on a state-financed trip. The *Tampa Tribune* alleged that he was paying two campaign aides through contracts with the Florida Bicentennial Commission, his only remaining official responsibility. Some Republicans talked gleefully of a "Tom and Jerry Show"; they assumed that Adams would lose the primary but weaken Askew for Jerry Thomas's benefit. The Republicans also hoped that voters loyal to Floyd Christian, Fred Dickinson, and Tom O'Malley would blame Askew for their difficulties.[16]

The governor still had not committed himself to running again. But he had to assume that if he did not, Adams might well be the Democratic nominee, and Thomas would be the next governor. Askew agonized for two more weeks before deciding and announcing that he would run for a second term. To his aides he remarked, "You will never know how difficult that was." The announcement, including his voluntary contribution ceiling of $100 at a time or $300 for the entire campaign, was nearly overshadowed by intensive media coverage of the Dickinson and O'Malley investigations. Reporters questioned him as much about the Cabinet scandals and the ethics legislation as about his own campaign. Adams immediately began issuing a series of sarcastic "Dear Reubin" letters, ghost-written by Rounds, that accused Askew of mismanagement, hypocrisy, liberal spending and taxation, betraying old friends, and being sanctimonious in his opposition to legalized gambling, which Adams favored. One letter claimed that Askew was responsible for the unreported Democratic Party campaign funds in 1970. Another said Askew had instructed the transportation department, over Adams's objections, to purchase costly highway material from a campaign supporter. Askew issued denials through his press office but generally refused to respond in person. "I wouldn't be getting any 'Dear Reubin' letters if I hadn't sent him a 'Dear John' letter last year, and I think that's what this campaign is all about," he said. The avoidance tactic made it appear that he was unworried by Adams and took only Thomas's opposition seriously. Adams scored a point in an attorney general's opinion that Askew should have been reporting the free hotel rooms customarily offered to the governor when he traveled around Florida. "Practice what you preach," Adams said.[17]

Thomas chose the Senate chamber as the venue for his own long-expected announcement. He said he was running to "rekindle some plain old common sense and fiscal sanity." Thomas promised to reveal his financial holdings and income sources, but not his tax returns. He claimed to have paid more in taxes than the governor's salary of $40,000. Askew, meanwhile, reported his net worth at $82,433, and Adams said his was merely $14,878.[18]

Speaking to campaign workers at Tampa, Askew said that public integrity "above all else . . . is the challenge to which this campaign will be dedicated, and to which, if we are successful, the next four years will be dedicated." He would not allow the legislature to rest on what it had just done. In an interview, he said that there might not be as many new programs in a second term as in the first "because, frankly, we just won't need to do as much as we did before." He acknowledged that progress would be more difficult with many supportive legislators leaving and Barron and Tucker coming into power.[19]

Unlike the situation in 1970, Askew had his pick of a large field of politicians for his running mate. Senator Bob Graham all but begged to be chosen. Attorney General Robert Shevin, anticipating Graham to be his major opponent for governor in 1978, pleaded with Askew to pick anyone but Graham. State senator Lori Wilson, the wife of an influential newspaper publisher, was another contender. Askew seriously considered Graham and Terrell Sessums, but from the beginning he leaned toward Jim Williams. Williams, a real estate broker and citrus grower from Ocala, was respected by colleagues and the media as a budget expert and as the workhorse of the Senate, where he had chaired the committee that handled the ethics and utilities legislation as well as four of the 1974 session's five conference committees. Williams's reserved manner and laconic speaking style kept him from being quoted in the media as frequently as some others, but that was just fine with Askew. He chose Williams for dependability and competence and said that his working assignment would be secretary of administration, in charge of budgeting and personnel. Theirs would become a singularly successful partnership. Adams's running mate was Burl McCormick, mayor of a small municipality, Hialeah Gardens, who was an independently wealthy developer. He brought no political strengths to the ticket.[20]

Griffin's surprise candidacy was not the only shock for Askew on filing-deadline day, or even the worst. He was shaken when Don Pride resigned as his press secretary to run for secretary of state. Pride worried that none of the other Democratic primary candidates could defeat state senator Bruce Smathers, son of former U.S. senator George Smathers. Pride said he did not think Smathers cared enough about election reform and enforcement. When Pride confided the week before what was on his mind, the governor held his head in his hands and said, "Oh, no, Donald," but thought he had talked him out of it. Half an hour before the noon filing deadline, Pride decided to go through with it. Askew was not concerned simply about losing Pride as press secretary and adviser. Some members of the media and the Cabinet thought it meant that Askew was scheming to control the Cabinet. Askew and Pride emphatically denied that, but Adams and Griffin refused to take them at their word and made a campaign issue of Pride's candidacy. Pride's campaign was thinly financed and run by volunteers working out of his living room. The former press secretary ran remarkably well nonetheless but finished third in the primary, 6,042 votes behind Beverly Dozier of Tallahassee. Smathers won both the runoff and general election despite his admission that he had telephoned the Ku Klux Klan's Florida grand dragon to advise him that "I was running for office."[21]

Pride's deputy, Paul Schnitt, succeeded him as the governor's office press secretary. Jim Bacchus, a twenty-five-year-old doctoral student in history and an occasional reporter for his hometown *Orlando Sentinel-Star*, became campaign press secretary only three weeks after Pride had hired him to write speeches. Overnight, he found himself the middleman between Askew on the campaign trail and the state government back in Tallahassee. Bacchus's intensive on-the-job training was the start of a career that took him to Congress and to the highest court of the World Trade Organization. As a bachelor in 1974, though, he "had no other life," a situation ideally suited to Askew's unconventional work habits.

The governor typically spent most of the morning reading newspapers at the mansion. He would arrive at the capitol around 11 A.M., lunch in his office, and return to the mansion to work after supper until midnight or later. Askew preferred to make or return telephone calls in the evening. "People who called me at their convenience, I figured could be called back at my convenience. My convenience was up to 11 P.M.," he said. He was oblivious at first to the toll on his staff. "It was not unusual for him to call at midnight," said Apthorp, who eventually reminded Askew that his employees were expected to be at work and alert at 8 A.M. Askew once dispatched two aides at 3 A.M. to rouse a legislator who had no telephone.[22]

While Askew was keeping an outwardly aggressive stump schedule, aide Bernie Parrish, who remained in Tallahassee to raise money, found it increasingly difficult to focus Askew's attention on fund-raising, a chore the governor hated. "Bacchus would get on that plane and all they would want to talk about was issues and policy. It drove me nuts,"

Parrish said. Even so, Askew's campaign received more than five thousand individual contributions during the first primary alone. Griffin managed to outspend him, but only by tapping his own wealth. It was the only primary race in which the biggest spender did not win. Griffin's candidacy affected Adams more than Askew; Griffin took more of the rural and conservative votes that were critical to Adams's chances. Adams won only one county (Holmes), ran a weak second to Askew in six counties, came in third behind Griffin in fifty-eight, and was last in two. Askew was never seriously threatened and won renomination with a stunning 68 percent of the vote, the most ever in a gubernatorial primary, to 16.3 percent for Griffin, and 10.2 percent for Adams. Norman Bie, a Clearwater attorney and George Wallace activist who had selected the first woman running mate, Florence Keen, ran last. Askew's sweep placed him first in sixty-four of the sixty-seven counties but with only a plurality in twenty-three small ones. He was obviously weakest in the Panhandle. The public there had reacted unfavorably to one of the few significant news breaks of the primary campaign. The story was that Askew was considering pardoning Freddie Pitts and Wilbert Lee, black men who had been twice convicted of a double murder at Port St. Joe to which another man had reportedly confessed. Although he knew he was far ahead in the preelection polls, Askew feared voter apathy and campaigned in twelve cities during the last weekend of the primary campaign.[23]

A campaign Askew said he considered as important as his own, although far fewer voters paid attention to it, was the supreme court race between Arthur England and Sam Spector. Justice Richard Ervin, who was facing mandatory retirement on his seventieth birthday in January 1975, disliked Askew's appointment system because he thought it was dominated by silk-stocking lawyers. Ervin submitted a prospective resignation intended to force an election for the seat. Askew refused to accept the resignation and obtained an opinion from Shevin that an election would be legal only if Ervin left at the end of a term. Askew had appointed Dorothy Glisson, a career employee, to finish the term of Secretary of State Richard Stone, who had resigned to run for the Senate. (She was the first female Cabinet officer.) Relying on Shevin's opinion, Glisson refused Spector's attempt to qualify as a candidate for

Ervin's seat. Spector, a judge of the First District Court of Appeal, asked the Florida Supreme Court to order an election. England, suspecting that a fix was in, attempted to qualify and intervened in Spector's case, arguing that the seat should be filled by appointment instead. As England had anticipated, the court ordered an election limited to the two candidates who had qualified before the filing deadline. Had England not filed, Spector would have won by default. Their nonpartisan race was decided in the September primary, which England won with 58 percent of a paltry turnout. Ben Overton, Askew's appointee, also won that day. "Newspaper endorsements carried it," said Sandy D'Alemberte. The Overton and England victories presaged the end of B. K. Roberts's control of the court.[24]

The 1974 Democratic primary disappointed Richard Pettigrew and Mallory Horne, who finished third and fourth, respectively, in the U.S. Senate race. Stone, coming from behind, upset U.S. representative Bill Gunter in the runoff and went on to defeat Jack Eckerd, who had won a Republican primary against Public Service Commissioner Paula Hawkins.[25]

Askew celebrated his victory and his forty-sixth birthday the next day in Austin, Texas, where he was installed as chairman of the Southern Governors Conference. He cautioned the other governors against the prevalent practice of luring industry with promises of low wages and exemptions from taxes and pollution controls. "Yes, we want industry to come to the South but we want it on our terms," he said.[26]

Thomas had won the Republican nomination without opposition. Opening his general election campaign, Askew said he considered the election "a referendum on the future . . . in which the people of Florida are being asked whether they want to continue our programs of practical and progressive reform, or, instead, reject those reforms and return to the crisis-by-crisis, special interest, shadow government of the past." Thomas's running mate was Mike Thompson, an acerbic public-relations man who had lost narrowly to Pettigrew in the 1972 state senate race. Tacitly conceding a point to Askew, Thomas said that he, too, would ask Jim Williams to serve as secretary of administration. He did not say whether he expected Williams to accept the offer. In what would become recurring themes of his uphill campaign, Thomas attacked Askew over busing, tax increases, the "open bedroom policy" at colleges and universities, and the legislation "for 18-year-olds to go to pornographic places and whiskey parlors." In an openly political speech from the pulpit of a St. Petersburg Baptist church, Thomas said the dormitory visitation issue, "more than anything," had inspired him to run for governor. Meanwhile, an obscure third-party candidate withdrew from the governor's race, saying he did not want to split the conservative vote against Askew. Thomas launched a blitz of paid half-hour television commercials that attacked the media and accused Askew of "forced busing," waste and mismanagement, and "ultra-liberalism."[27]

In a development embarrassing to Askew, corrections director Louie Wainwright ordered his overcrowded prisons shut to new inmates for the third time in a year. Askew convened a task force to propose emergency solutions. The legislature had voted $66 million for new prisons, but they could not be built fast enough. The emergency response called for hiring more caseworkers in order to accelerate parole releases from 225 a month to 1,000. The hastily made arrangements included boarding state prisoners in county jails and housing some at the mental hospital in Chattahoochee. Soon after announcing the plan, Askew held his first press conference in a month; capitol journalists were complaining that he was rarely available to them. He was answering questions almost daily from local reporters on the campaign trail, but that did not satisfy the Tallahassee-based journalists.[28]

Until near the end of the campaign, Askew also avoided face-to-face confrontations with Thomas, although they appeared on the same stage at different times at several events. When a poll showed that Thomas was making modest gains, Askew went on the attack, accusing Thomas of trying to "drown the facts in a storm of political rhetoric and storm of distortion." He challenged the prosperous banker to release his income-tax returns and net-worth statements. Thomas's election, he said, would restore "shadow government" under the influence of special-interest groups. Thomas retorted that Askew should compel his campaign manager (Jim Smith), his former law partner (David Levin), and Democratic Party chair Jon Moyle to disclose their finances. Although Thomas said

Askew's counterattacks meant it had become "a real governor's race," his own rhetoric became increasingly shrill. He joked to the press that he was beginning to sound "a little like George Wallace."[29]

Newspaper endorsements favored Askew heavily. The *Miami Herald*'s said Thomas "has hammered at the old Agnewisms of teenage permissiveness, pornography and soft-on-crime in an attempt to make a dirty old man of Reubin Askew, whose strongest cussword is 'golly' and who would have made a good Puritan Father." The *Orlando Sentinel-Star*, a newspaper thought likely to endorse Thomas, recommended Askew instead, saying his opponents "have had real trouble trying to find valid criticism of his administration." In an attack that made him sound desperate, Thomas tried to compare Smith, Moyle, and Levin to three high-ranking Richard Nixon aides who were on trial in the Watergate scandal. Goaded by Askew in a climactic television debate, Thomas responded by disclosing a gross income of $145,638 and a net worth of nearly $700,000—more than eight times Askew's. As Askew served mulligan stew, crackers, and orange drink on election eve to an estimated 5,400 people at a Tallahassee baseball park, Thomas campaign workers passed out leaflets to the crowd, only to see most of them thrown in the trash. "Can't we stop them?" one of Askew's staffers asked Bacchus. "We'd be doing the same thing if he had an event like this and we were losing," he replied.[30]

"I said four years ago the thing I wanted to do above all else was to set a new tone in the governor's office. I hope I've done this," Askew said. Voters evidently agreed; they reelected him with 61.2 percent of the vote. He carried forty-four of the sixty-seven counties, including the sixteen largest. It was obvious, however, that Thomas had gained substantial ground since the third week in October, when Askew's own poll put him at 81 percent. The Republican had won the battle for late-deciding voters. The data also reflected once again that there were two Floridas. All but one of the twenty-three counties Askew lost were north of the Suwannee River. He carried only two of those west of Tallahassee. Escambia, his home, barely matched his statewide average; it had given him 81 percent against Kirk. The north Florida losses were more than offset by large gains in Broward, Dade, Hillsborough, and especially Pinellas, a Republican county. Even so, what happened north of the Suwannee foretold that the Democrats would eventually lose the balance of power in the legislature. But for the moment, capitalizing on the nationwide backlash from Watergate, the Democrats had enlarged their majorities by nine seats in the House, where the Republicans now held only thirty-four, and by two in the Senate, where the Democrats now held twenty-seven seats to twelve Republicans and one independent. Askew's erstwhile Senate aide, George Sheldon, was elected to the House from Hillsborough County. Enormously important to Askew was Buddy MacKay's election to succeed Jim Williams in a sixteen-county, mostly rural Senate district. He defeated a Republican who exploited "forced busing."[31]

"We felt it was a referendum on the future and we believe the people of Florida spoke very loudly. We're humbled by that vote," Askew said. "I hope we never see such a race again," said Williams. Thomas claimed credit for Askew's having "shifted ever so slightly to the right." Askew had also won the battle of the purse, outspending Thomas $583,629 to $364,808. His campaign reported 8,876 individual contributors, which he took as proof that grassroots campaigns could succeed in Florida. The five campaigns collectively had spent only $1,345,827, but it was the last such gubernatorial campaign in Florida. Two years later, the U.S. Supreme Court ruled mandatory spending ceilings such as Florida's to be unconstitutional. By 2006 the total spending by candidates for governor exceeded $50 million, which was nearly ten times more, adjusted for inflation, than in 1974.[32]

In December, Askew went to the Democratic Party's first national midterm convention, in Kansas City, where he was credited with drafting and persuading delegates to pass a compromise charter guaranteeing full participation for minorities in party affairs without the quotas that had applied in 1972. Organized labor opposed his effort. "The governors," he said in a voice hoarse from a day of talking, "want unity because they want a president in the White House in 1976." He would spend 1975 having to deny repeatedly that he wanted to be that president.[33]

17

"MY SENATE" (1975)

Reubin Askew did not expect that his second term would begin as triumphantly as his first. Enthusiastic, experienced allies such as Richard Pettigrew, Marshall Harris, and Louis de la Parte had left the legislature. Forty-one House members were freshmen. Both chambers now had presiding officers who were eager to cut Askew down to size. "The governor has no more mandate than we do . . . and some of us didn't even get opposition," House Speaker Donald Tucker told the *Miami Herald*. "There are no marriages—to the executive branch or the House. They will stay separate and I suspect at times will strongly disagree," said Senate president Dempsey Barron. To chair the most influential House committees, Tucker chose mostly conservative, pro-Cabinet Democrats who had not held power before. They included appropriations chairman Ed Fortune of Pace, rules chairman Gus Craig of St. Augustine, and natural resources chairman Bill Fulford of Orlando. Tucker rewarded Dick Clark of Miami, who had helped him win the speakership, with the role of House majority leader. Representative Jim Redman and Senator George Firestone, who had pursued corruption in the Cabinet, lost their seats on the Joint Legislative Auditing Committee. Barron said he removed Firestone because the committee had become "involved in the investigation of crime . . . very, very highly improper for the Legislature at any time . . . unless you want to throw away the constitution." Subsequently, Barron and Tucker blocked Firestone's election to the governing board of the National Conference of State Legislatures. Tucker did allow Redman to continue chairing a committee that was considering O'Malley's impeachment, and he initiated the House investigation that forced two supreme court justices to resign, but he disapproved of the close relationship between the auditing committee and special prosecutor Ed Austin. He also had a thin skin when his own conduct was questioned. Tucker retaliated against Robert Johnson, a Sarasota Republican whom he suspected of having him investigated by a grand jury, by assigning Johnson to two of the least desirable committees in the House. He had allowed the minority leader to assign all the other Republicans.[1] In his first speech to the Senate, two weeks after the 1974 general election, Barron harshly criticized the state's environmental agencies and the Department of Health and Rehabilitative Services. "Our biggest, most effective, and most dangerous lobbyist is the bureaucracy itself," he said. He analogized the environmental permitting process to a pinball machine in which "state agencies are the machine's bumpers and flippers, batting the citizen here and there." The citizens Barron had in mind were most often land developers.[2]

Despite springlike weather, fewer than four thousand people witnessed the second inauguration of the first Florida governor to win two full consecutive terms. With the economy in recession, Askew had decided it would be inappropriate to have a parade and inaugural ball. His speech that day was notably brief, lasting only twenty minutes. He referred to the fiscal crisis in saying that "shortfalls in revenue must not bring shortfalls in compassion." Jim Bacchus, his new speechwriter, had crafted the text with the examples of Franklin D. Roosevelt and John F. Kennedy in mind: "We know that the future will not belong to those who cannot find hope, cannot offer hope, and instead reduce the world and all its complex problems into misleading simplicities. The future will belong to those who can fashion vision and conviction and uncommon courage into an unwavering commitment to the great dreams we have always cherished as a people."[3]

Askew categorically rejected higher consumer taxes and said he would "adamantly oppose" a burgeoning movement to legalize casino gambling. Alluding to the Cabinet scandals, he renewed his demand for a more revealing financial disclosure law. "Above all else," he said, "we can rid ourselves once and for all of the caprice and the corruption too often associated with the public realm." Treasurer Tom O'Malley, the only Cabinet member ever re-inaugurated while under indictment, was sitting only a few feet away. He did not applaud.[4]

At a Cabinet meeting two weeks later, O'Malley goaded Askew relentlessly about Don Pride's interim appointment as director of the Florida Bicentennial Commission. An employee who had supported Adams had been asked to resign to make way for the governor's former press secretary, who had lost his race for secretary of state. Askew told O'Malley that the commission was none of his business and refused to debate it with him. He said afterward that he had not known that the former director's job was protected under the career service law, which meant he should have been dismissed only for cause. The man complained unsuccessfully to the ethics commission.[5]

In January, Askew ordered the personnel division to draft and implement affirmative action regulations, but he instructed that there be no quotas. He also disbanded the county patronage committees that had been sources of occasional embarrassment as well as of advice not taken. He was unsure whether the law obliged him to reappoint his department heads, which would expose them to possible rejection by the Senate, and asked the Florida Supreme Court for an advisory opinion. Fatefully for Askew's human services secretary, O. J. Keller, the court held that new appointments were required.[6]

Askew was able to avoid a showdown with Tucker and Barron over their environmental reorganization bill, which proposed a single department dominated by the Cabinet. Pre-session negotiations produced a compromise accommodating Barron's interest in speedier permitting and Askew's objection to a single super-agency. It provided for a governor-controlled Department of Environmental Regulation, and for the Department of Natural Resources to remain under the governor and Cabinet. The bill abolished another Cabinet agency that held title to submerged lands and controlled their development. Barron had confided to Representative Curt Kiser, a leader of House opposition to the single-agency plan, that he was not particularly interested in it; he had endorsed it only as a courtesy to Tucker. As the session approached, it was clear that Askew's intensive lobbying would win enough votes to sustain a veto of any version he did not like. Elaine Bloom, a freshman House member from Miami, helped craft the compromise. It called for a seven-member board appointed by the governor to establish rules and standards for air and water quality and for waste management. It left the Cabinet board in charge of managing lands, parks, and marine resources.[7]

The environmental battle impressed Bloom with what veteran legislators already knew. Askew was "one tough cookie . . . his was the most resolute mind I ever met," she said. Once Askew was comfortable with a position, said former senator Mallory Horne, "he was absolutely intractable. . . . If he ever felt it was a moral issue, it was not negotiable." Buddy MacKay considered him "absolutely unique" in that regard. Although Askew's inflexibility was frustrating at times, it encouraged allies to stay with him in a hard fight. "You could see, 'Hey, this isn't impossible,'" MacKay said. "It wasn't like having a meeting with the governor. It was like a come-to-Jesus meeting, but he had the character for it too, he wasn't hypocritical," said Representative Dick Batchelor.[8]

Askew remembered from his twelve years in the legislature how it flattered members to be asked to meet with a governor, even when they might rarely agree. "We did not always like to admit it, but we really did like it," he said. He often invited legislators to breakfasts and lunch at the mansion as well as to scheduled and impromptu meetings in his office. Tradition held that governors did not lobby in person on the House or Senate floors; he skirted that by routinely sending in signed notes during sessions. He also made evening rounds at receptions and at restaurants that lawmakers frequented. He memorized how they had voted and did not shy from telling them what he thought. Representative George Sheldon, his former aide, felt a tap on his shoulder one night; he turned to face the governor, who said, "George, your mother would not have been proud of you today." Askew did the same to Curt Kiser on another occasion. Summoning freshman representative Bob McKnight after a disappointing vote, Askew slammed his fist on the desk and told McKnight, "You should be ashamed of yourself." Askew's lobbyists stuffed their pockets with two sets of notes signed by the governor. One read "Thanks." If a legislator's vote had been unfavorable, Askew's lobbyist would send in the note that asked "What happened?" Over loudspeakers and, later, closed-circuit television, Askew was able to monitor sessions as if he had been sitting in both galleries simultaneously. He eventually had direct telephone lines to the Speaker's and president's podiums. On a day when Don Tucker thought Askew was making too much use of the technology, the Speaker looked straight at the camera and announced to the entire House, "Governor, I can either keep answering this telephone or I can go back and do what you asked me to do three calls before."[9]

Tucker was not as cordial to the governor in 1975 as he would become later. Addressing the House on the regular session's opening day, he warned Askew to be "very careful" in his use of the veto. "*We* are the selected representatives of the people . . . subject to *their* review *every two years*," Tucker said (emphasis in the original). "I would hope that the favorable vote by the majority will not be overturned because one man in his review doesn't like it." Undeterred, Askew would veto thirty-four bills after the session ended, more than twice as many as the year before. Barron and Tucker would have to wait until 1976 to begin overriding them.[10]

Askew embraced relatively few entirely new proposals when he addressed the opening-day joint session. Among them were hospital and health-care cost containment; legislation to control handguns; a full-time prosecutor for the statewide grand jury; and appointment rather than election of judges, at least at the appellate level. Alluding to the supreme court scandals, Askew's prepared remarks asserted that Florida's nonpartisan judiciary was still too political. "We cannot allow our system of justice to be misused," he said. After Askew overlooked those words in reading the speech, his press office asked the media to emphasize them. The address reflected his concerns over various reorganization schemes, among them a bill to begin breaking up the Department of Health and Rehabilitative Services. A separate department of adult corrections would be a "viable alternative" if it included the parole commission's field staff, he said, but he was unwilling to remove youth delinquency programs from HRS. "Our emphasis in corrections must be on results and not retribution," he said. "And this should be done in the realization that genuine rehabilitation is the best possible protection for the people." He made an exception for mandatory prison terms for using a gun in a crime and subsequently signed that bill into law. The most provocative lines—to legislators' ears, at least—came toward the end.

"I consider my re-election to be a mandate for full financial disclosure. I will do everything I can to fulfill that mandate," Askew said. He called again for ratification of the Equal Rights Amendment and shrugged off an attack of laryngitis to speak emotionally to some two thousand pro-ERA demonstrators outside the capitol. The House complied by a vote of sixty-two to fifty-eight, but the Senate, as anticipated, voted twenty-one to seventeen against the ERA. Askew's intensive lobbying had failed to sway several essential Democrats—among them, Buddy MacKay. He voted for the ERA in subsequent sessions.[11]

The ERA saga bore out the lobbyists' maxim that it is much easier to defeat an issue than to enact it into law. Askew was most effective at discouraging actions he opposed; legislators knew that he could veto their bills if they refused to compromise and that he would need only 14 of 40 senators or 41 of 120 representatives to make a veto stick. But the veto power was useless in his power struggle with Barron over O. J. Keller's reappointment. It resulted in what Askew considered the worst defeat and disappointment of his eight years in office, and led to a coup in the Senate that made Barron the dominant force long after his two-year presidency had ended.

Keller was Askew's most visible, energetic, and popular agency head. He had reformed Florida's juvenile delinquency programs, which had a lurid history of brutality, to the point that one study rated them the nation's best. The reforms displeased some conservative sheriffs, who lobbied the Senate against Keller. All things considered, he was a tempting target of opportunity. Barron's campaign to purge Keller capitalized on an inconclusive House subcommittee investigation into the HRS department's $1.8-million-a-year rentals at Winewood, a private Tallahassee office park. Keller inherited the lease from Emmett Roberts, his predecessor. Roberts's deputy, Damon Holmes, had advised against it because he suspected a conflict of interest on the part of another official involved in the lease. The lease became Keller's liability after his deputy secretary signed a letter of intent to rent additional space. The proposed expansion was untimely, since reorganization would diminish the HRS central office staff. Although the letter was not binding on the state, it helped Winewood secure financing for another building. House investigators were interested less in Keller than in Chester Blakemore,

Askew's recently hired aide for Cabinet affairs. Blakemore had headed the state's leasing agency, the Department of General Services, when it negotiated the first Winewood leases, and he had subsequently been employed by the Winewood developer. A grand jury eventually said the transactions were "colored with acts of influence-peddling," but it indicted no one and criticized the House subcommittee for "prolonging" the investigation.[12]

Although it ended inconclusively, the probe fueled Barron's allegation that Keller was a "poor administrator." The purge culminated in a "hearing" in the Senate chamber that consumed twenty-three hours over two days. For a span of more than four hours, Keller was required to stand at a podium, like a prisoner in a dock, listening to enemies denounce him. Some senators were openly contemptuous of Keller's witnesses. MacKay called it a kangaroo court. At the end, the Senate voted twenty-five to fifteen against Keller's confirmation. Keller conceded that the letter of intent was a mistake but adamantly defended his decision not to fire his deputy over it. "I'm very lucky to have him," Keller said. The "poor administration" issue, echoed by a number of senators who resented Keller's progressive views on crime and punishment, was a pretext. "Nobody could have run HRS well," former senator Louis de la Parte said in a newspaper interview. It appeared to many people that Barron was either settling an undisclosed personal grudge against Keller or simply seizing an opportunity to show Askew who was boss. In an interview for this book, Barron's widow, Terri Jo Rauch, said it was the reorganization controversy that cost Keller his job. According to Rauch, who was on the Senate staff in 1975, Senator Jack Gordon, a Miami Democrat, initiated the anti-Keller campaign. The conservative Barron and the liberal Gordon were unlikely allies on some issues. Gordon, Rauch said, objected that Keller had resisted reorganization; Gordon thought the department head should be fully committed to it. The issue of Keller's "poor administration" was window dressing. By the time Askew and Keller eventually agreed to a reorganization compromise, Keller's confirmation had become—at least to Barron—a power struggle between the governor and the Senate president over who would be king of the hill. "Reubin kept on lobbying until Dempsey blew," said Mallory Horne.[13]

Askew had miscounted the votes, underestimating Barron's determination. The senator's fury erupted at an evening barbecue at George Firestone's lakeside residence. Standing toe-to-toe with Senator Bob Graham, Barron loudly threatened to dismiss him and other committee chairmen in "my Senate" if they voted for Keller rather than fulfill their duty to "uphold the president's philosophy." Not flinching, Graham said he would make up his own mind. After several more "my Senate" remarks, Firestone calmly interjected, "It's the people's Senate." But Barron persisted. "If you're going to vote for the governor and for Keller, you ought to get a job with the governor," he said. Askew had attended the barbecue but had already left. Barron's parting words to him were, "You're gonna lose it, Rube." No one present could recall such a public tirade by any other Florida politician, let alone one witnessed by most of the news bureau chiefs in Tallahassee. None wrote what they had remarked in private—that Barron was intoxicated by more than power that evening. Afterward, Barron said the dismissal threat applied only to senators who voted for Keller out of "friendship." He was referring to Kenneth Myers and Graham. Barron denied a claim by Senator David Lane, a neurosurgeon, that he had threatened to kill a medical malpractice bill that physicians supported if Lane voted for Keller. Lane stood by what he had told the press and voted for Keller; he was one of only three Republicans to do so. The malpractice bill passed unanimously.[14]

The Keller affair gave rise to a coalition of conservative Democrats and Republicans that enabled Barron to control the Senate long after his presidency. "Power changed Dempsey more than anybody I ever saw," remarked Horne. Askew was so outraged by the vote that he was unsure whether he could control his temper, and refused to face the press or even discuss it with his staff. He issued a written statement: "There was no victory today. . . . Florida state government has lost a good and faithful servant. The Department of Health and Rehabilitative Services has lost an able administrator. And thousands upon thousands of disadvantaged and troubled people have lost a friend. . . . By any fair and just standard, Mr. Keller deserved to be confirmed." The ousted secretary was the calmest person around. "I'm not going to sit home and cry," Keller said. "I don't regret a bit having had this job. It's been a fascinating experience." Later that month, he went to the convention of the

American Correctional Association as a president-elect newly fired from his day job. Askew designated Emmett Roberts as acting secretary. Encountering Gordon at a restaurant some years later, Askew remembered the senator's vote against Keller and curtly reminded him of it.[15]

Senator Bob Saunders of Gainesville had voted for Keller. Six days later, he lost something more consequential than a chairmanship. In a surprise coup supported and likely planned by Barron, a majority of Senate Democrats reneged on their word to elect Saunders the next president and designated Lew Brantley of Jacksonville instead. Saunders, who had held written pledges from all but two of his twenty-six Democratic colleagues, was left with only eleven votes. One of the defectors was Sherman Winn of Miami, who had chaired Askew's patronage committee in Dade; Brantley had promised to make him Senate president pro tem. Askew aide Bernie Parrish tried unsuccessfully to talk Winn out of the deal. Barron swiftly heard about it. Lieutenant Governor Jim Williams warned Parrish against going back upstairs because, he told him, Barron had threatened "to knock you on your ass." Askew told Parrish to take the rest of the day off. Addressing the Senate, Barron charged that Askew's lobbyists had threatened Brantley supporters. (Askew, Williams, and the lobbyists denied making any threats.) Giving profane voice to his temper, Barron declared, "Let the word go forth. The governor of Florida will not run the Florida Senate, and let him stay the hell out of our business. If he starts fooling around with me, he ain't seen nothing yet."[16]

Askew called a press conference a day later to reply to what he called Barron's "inappropriate, intemperate and frankly disappointing" remarks. He said he would continue to talk to senators "about anything I want to talk to them about." As for the Brantley-Saunders issue, he said he had talked to only a few senators, mainly allies who were worried and sought his advice. "Frankly, had I been able to do anything about it, I would have done it," Askew said. He reminded the media that Barron had interfered in the executive branch in regard to the Harmon Shields appointment. "I want to say," Askew emphasized in a strong voice, "that the business of the Senate is the people's business. It's the people's Senate." He said he had dispensed with a ceremony in signing the environmental reorganization bill because "it was the wrong time to have a hand-holding session with Dempsey Barron." He chose the moment to warn legislators that he would go to the people with a petition campaign for a constitutional amendment if they did not improve the financial disclosure law. He could not have picked an issue more obnoxious to Barron.[17]

Brantley readily admitted that he had promised chairmanships to senators in exchange for their votes to elect him president. He confirmed also that lobbyists—in particular one whose job was to legalize branch banking in Florida—had helped persuade senators to default on their pledges to Saunders. House majority leader Dick Clark, the banking bill's House sponsor and a friend of the banking lobbyist, was instrumental in Gordon's decision to support Brantley. Gordon thought Brantley had promised him the appropriations chairmanship for 1977–78. When the time came, Brantley put him in charge of finance and taxation. It was a meaningless assignment, as Brantley was not going to let the Senate enact any of Gordon's liberal ideas on taxes. Meanwhile, the branch banking bill became law.

Five of the twelve Senate committee chairmen had voted for Keller. A few days after the vote, Kenneth Myers obeyed a summons to Barron's office. Although he and Barron were friends and shareholders in a Wyoming ranch, Myers expected Barron to fire him as chairman of the health and rehabilitative services committee. Barron sat silently at his desk for what seemed a long time, not looking at Myers. Finally he growled, "Okay, keep your damned committee." Saunders was not so fortunate; Barron split his committee, ways and means, into two parts, leaving Saunders to chair finance and taxation, which had little to do under Barron. He gave Gordon the choice part, appropriations. Graham kept his education chairmanship, but only briefly. When Brantley took over the Senate in November 1976, he moved Graham to the health and rehabilitative services chairmanship, replacing Myers. Myers got the transportation committee, which would not have been his choice. Graham was secretly pleased with his new assignment, believing it would help his campaign for governor.[18]

For the next several years, Graham, MacKay, Ed Dunn, Harry Johnston, and Firestone were the nucleus of a Senate minority known as the "Doghouse Democrats." They had to depend on sympathetic House members to get their ideas written into legislation. On occasion, they had to turn to Askew's office for staff support that Barron was unwilling to provide. Although MacKay's sixteen-county district spanned a fourth of the state, Barron allowed him only one aide and only one office, in his hometown of Ocala. In Gainesville, MacKay's largest city, retired teachers belonging to the League of Women Voters obtained donated office space and furniture and became his volunteer staff for two years. The University of Florida provided telephones. Meanwhile, Dunn persisted without success in trying to reform the Senate rules to limit the power of the presidency.[19]

In a year with few other major enactments, the HRS reorganization bill gave Askew something he wanted: the transfer of the parole commission's field staff to the prison system. To get that, he had to agree to establish the prisons as a separate department. It was the first step in the destruction of HRS. The head of the prisons, Louie Wainwright, stayed on as secretary of the new department. Two parole commissioners sued unsuccessfully to prevent the transfer of their staff. Askew won a modest increase in workers' compensation payments. The legislature agreed to what the ethics commission had defined as its highest priority: a law allowing it to investigate sworn complaints without first referring them to the agency in question. Responding to harsh criticisms of the state's facilities for the mentally retarded, the legislature enacted a "bill of rights" for their residents. It also committed the state to replace some of the institutions with community-based programs. Witnesses said Barron and Tucker nearly came to blows in negotiations over the appropriations bill. As it was about to adjourn a day early, the legislature also revised the financial disclosure law to require officials to identify more of their income sources and debts. "I think it's a nothing bill, unneeded," said Barron, but he let the Senate vote on it rather than risk having Askew call a special session. Askew remained unsatisfied, as the bill did not require anyone to divulge income-tax and net-worth statements. Askew said he was now committed to an initiative campaign. "We will look now to the people in the days ahead for full financial disclosure and possibly for judicial reform," he said.[20]

18

JUSTICE HATCHETT
(1975–1976)

For a long time the Florida Supreme Court had been the least visible branch of the state government. Journalists rarely inquired into the motives or politics behind its decisions. Lawyers who had misgivings shared them only with each other. By the spring of 1975 the court had become not only well known but notorious. It was in the headlines as a select House committee probed for grounds to impeach Justices Joseph A. Boyd Jr., Hal P. Dekle, and David L. McCain. The investigation yielded immediate results in the resignations of Dekle and McCain and the appointment of Florida's first African American justice, Joseph W. Hatchett. It would take another year for the legislature to accept the conclusion that appellate judges should be appointed rather than elected.[1]

House Speaker Donald L. Tucker appointed the committee shortly after a panel of substitute judges chosen by the court voted only to reprimand Dekle and Boyd in the *Gulf Power* affair. The Judicial Qualifications Commission had recommended that the court remove them from office. The substitute panel also dismissed a second JQC case against Dekle, which involved his attempt to fix a circuit court case for one of his campaign supporters. In ruling that the *Gulf Power* mischief deserved only a reprimand, the panel held that a judge should not be removed from office without proof of some "corrupt motive"—in other words, a bribe. Cronyism, however unethical, deserved at most a reprimand. Intense criticism from the legal profession and the media prompted the impeachment proceedings. Tucker appointed Representative William

J. "Billy Joe" Rish of Port St. Joe, a particularly tough-minded legislator, to chair the inquiry. Rish demonstrated that he meant business by hiring Fred Karl as chief counsel. While serving in the Senate, Karl had brought due process and integrity to the consideration of gubernatorial suspensions, which once had been debated behind closed doors and decided on the whim of the senator representing the suspended official's county. Dekle resigned during the committee's methodical but relentless investigation. The committee voted not to impeach Boyd on the condition that he submit to a thorough physical and mental examination. Members assumed that the results would compel Boyd's retirement for disability. The doctors found to the contrary—that Boyd was not only competent but a "highly principled man." He remained on the court twelve more years until his mandatory retirement at age seventy. He boasted of being the only justice who could prove his sanity.[2]

The probe was incomplete when Karl suffered serious complications from elective surgery. Sandy D'Alemberte became chief counsel, and the committee began to investigate McCain on charges of trying to rig cases for friends. The most damaging accusation concerned a telephone call to the Second District Court of Appeal in which he asked for a decision favoring three men who were appealing a bribery conviction. They were officers and members of a labor union local backing McCain's campaign. The district judge whom McCain telephoned testified that he considered it a "personal affront." The committee voted unanimously to recommend McCain's impeachment on multiple charges. McCain resigned a day before the House was expected to vote overwhelmingly against him. The hearings resulted in changes in the constitution as well as in the membership of the court. One amendment that voters ratified in 1976 provided for the appointment rather than election of all judges of the Florida Supreme Court and five district courts of appeal. Another overturned the "corrupt motive" precedent so that judges could be removed for unethical acts short of bribery. It provided for chief circuit judges chosen by seniority to sit in place of the Florida Supreme Court in JQC proceedings involving a justice, and it required all JQC proceedings to become public upon the filing of formal charges.[3]

Askew chose Alan C. Sundberg, a St. Petersburg attorney, to succeed Dekle. The court now had three reform-minded justices: Ben F. Overton,

Arthur England, and Sundberg. There was a surge of applications for the McCain vacancy—fifty-three—and an intense debate within the supreme court nominating commission over how many to recommend to Askew. The result was an eyebrow-raising list of seven nominees rather than the customary three. Two, including Karl, were former legislators. Four were prominent judges. The least-familiar name on the list was that of Hatchett, a federal magistrate at Jacksonville. Only two of the six lawyers on the commission had heard of him before his interview. That interview, according to Robert L. Parks, a commissioner at the time, "was quite an impressive performance." When the members tallied their preferences, Hatchett and four other candidates were tied for third place. It was not possible to recommend merely two; the constitution stipulated at least three. A series of votes failed to break the tie. There was also an unsuccessful attempt to change the commission's vote-counting rules, which would have eliminated Hatchett.[4]

Both sides took for granted that Askew would not pass up the opportunity to appoint Florida's first African American justice. Hatchett's selection was widely anticipated as soon as the nominations were announced, and there were insinuations that he was not the most qualified of the nominees. A *Tampa Tribune* editorial remarked that some nominees did not measure up to others; Askew's staff took it as a veiled objection to Hatchett. Gavin Letts, a highly respected Palm Beach attorney and future appellate judge who had volunteered to investigate McCain for the JQC, wrote to Askew that too many people had been nominated. "I am opposed to all the candidates except the one who is the most judicially deserving, be he, or she, white, red, yellow or black," Letts wrote. He did not say which candidate he considered the most deserving.[5]

Askew received the nominations two days after attending a dinner of the National Association for the Advancement of Colored People at Orlando. He spoke proudly there of his recent black appointees, including a new secretary of community affairs, Bill Ravenell, and Doris Alston, whom he named to a vacancy on the Leon County School Board. There will be "many, many more," Askew said. He took two weeks, longer than with either of his first two supreme court appointments, to deliberate on McCain's successor, and interviewed Hatchett at the governor's mansion before announcing his decision. Askew acknowledged that Hatchett's race "played a major consideration in my determination." Alluding perhaps to the implications of the *Tampa Tribune* editorial and the unpublicized Letts letter, Askew said that he assumed every commission nominee to be "eminently qualified." Hatchett, the son of a Clearwater couple who had worked as a housemaid and a fruit picker, was a 1954 Florida A&M graduate who had studied law out of state at Howard University because African Americans were not allowed to attend the University of Florida law school. In 1959, when he sat for the two-and-a-half-day Florida Bar examination, he was barred from the Miami hotel where the white applicants boarded. Two years earlier, the Florida Supreme Court had blatantly defied a U.S. Supreme Court decision by refusing to desegregate the University of Florida law school. Hatchett would now be sitting on the same bench as B. K. Roberts, the justice who wrote the majority opinion in that infamous 1957 case.[6]

Hatchett was sworn in on September 7, 1975, his voice breaking as he quoted the prophet Micah's admonition to "do justly, love mercy, and walk humbly with thy God." Four years later, President Jimmy Carter appointed him to the Fifth U.S. Circuit Court of Appeals, where he was the first African American to hold that rank in the South. Askew's friend and adviser Ed Price was a member of the federal commission that recommended Hatchett. By then, he had become the only African American to defeat a white candidate in a Florida statewide election other than a party primary, a record that stood until Barack Obama carried the state in 2008. Defending his seat in 1976, Hatchett scored 60 percent of the vote against Harvie S. DuVal, a Dade County circuit judge. DuVal charged that Askew had tampered with the commission to get Hatchett nominated, but he offered no proof and retracted the allegation after Askew and commission chair Dixie Beggs forcefully denied it. DuVal's was the last openly racist campaign in Florida. All but one of the twenty-two counties he carried were rural ones with a history of supporting segregationist candidates. DuVal had scant support in the bar and virtually none in the media following a *St. Petersburg Times-Miami Herald* exposé of his favorable rulings for an attorney who had hosted him on expensive hunting trips. Chesterfield Smith, a former president of the

Florida Bar and of the American Bar Association, chaired Hatchett's campaign committee.[7]

Hatchett's appointment gave the Florida Supreme Court a firm majority committed to reforms. Roberts decided to retire, and Karl was elected in 1976. He was the last person to join the court by election. Ever since, Florida Supreme Court justices and judges of the district courts of appeal have been appointed. The public votes at six-year intervals on whether to retain them in office. None has been defeated. With the court's support, the constitution was amended again in 1980 to restrict the court's discretion in deciding what appeals to accept. The old court often had abused its discretion.

The 1976 legislative debate on exclusive merit selection for the appellate bench was difficult. Many Republicans thought Askew had been appointing too many Democrats to judgeships. Representative Curt Kiser told Askew that the Democratic clerk of court and sheriff in Pinellas County had been pulling political strings with the nominating commission there. Askew took the complaint seriously. His next appointee to the commission was Sallie Wallace, a sister-in-law of one of the county's most prominent Republicans. The commission chairman objected to Askew that she was not a lawyer, but Kiser was satisfied with the results. In the Senate, Republican David McClain of Tampa co-sponsored the merit retention amendment with the ubiquitous Kenneth Myers. "Elections compromise the integrity of the judiciary," Myers said. Bill Nelson, a future U.S. senator, was the lead sponsor in the House. Gus Craig, the House rules chairman, did not want to allow a vote, but Tucker overruled him. Tucker also kept the House from adding a controversial provision to maintain the remaining municipal courts beyond January 1977. When the resolution cleared the legislature on its way to the ballot, Chesterfield Smith said it was "perhaps THE red letter day in Florida's judicial history." The House had insisted, however, on two dubious clauses. One required that there be at least one supreme court justice from each of the five appellate districts. Some legislators resented the fact that Askew's first two appointees, Overton and Sundberg, were both from Pinellas County and that his third, Hatchett, had been born and raised there. The second questionable change required the nominating commissions to propose precisely three—no more, no fewer—candidates for each appellate vacancy. Had this provision been in force in 1975, it probably would have thwarted Hatchett's candidacy. Twenty years later, the constitution was amended again to allow up to six names for each seat. In 2006, when Askew was asked at a public forum what had given him the most satisfaction in office, he replied that it was the Hatchett appointment.[8]

19

TWO INNOCENT MEN AND
A CROOK (1975–1976)

Reubin Askew pardoned Freddie Pitts and Wilbert Lee in September 1975; they were freed after spending twelve years in prison for another man's crime. It was one of the defining acts of Askew's career. Pardons for people still serving their sentences were conspicuously rare; Askew said he knew of only two such instances. Although Pitts and Lee still had an appeal pending at the U.S. Supreme Court, Askew decided he would be shirking a moral duty if he delayed his decision in deference to the judicial process. "I am sufficiently convinced that they are innocent," he announced to the Cabinet. "In good conscience, I did what I think is right." During the previous eighteen months he had read nearly all of the courtroom transcripts and had spent more time, he thought, on this than on any other issue.[1]

Pitts, a twenty-eight-year-old agricultural laborer, and Lee, a twenty-year-old U.S. Army private, were arrested in August 1963. They were beaten and brainwashed into confessing to kidnapping and killing two white attendants at the Mo-Jo service station in Port St. Joe, a paper mill town on the Gulf of Mexico west of Tallahassee. At Port St. Joe, an African American did not count as a human being; it was a place where "you go along with what the white peoples was saying." Lee said later. "I was so lame. So lame. So lame." Nearly three years after Pitts and Lee went to death row at Raiford prison, a white man from Port St. Joe admitted the crime. He was Curtis Adams Jr., who pleaded guilty, in exchange for a life sentence, to a strikingly similar murder in Broward County. Adams then confessed to Warren Holmes, a poly-graph investigator, that he had also committed the Mo-Jo murders. The north Florida prosecutors, unwilling to credit any evidence that they had convicted innocent men, refused to grant Adams immunity to tes-tify in court. It would take Holmes, *Miami Herald* reporter Gene Miller, Dade County public defender Phillip A. Hubbart, and other volunteers another nine years—and some 120 *Miami Herald* articles—to win free-dom for Pitts and Lee. Early in that painfully slow process, Pitts and Lee were granted a new trial because the state had concealed evidence that would have helped them, but they were convicted and condemned again. When Askew began to review the cases, their death sentences had been commuted automatically to life in prison as a result of the 1972 U.S. Supreme Court decision temporarily abolishing capital punish-ment. They had no realistic hope for parole; Florida's Cabinet-appointed parole commissioners were notoriously conservative, highly unlikely to disregard public opinion in the eastern Panhandle, which was intensely hostile to Pitts, Lee, Miller, and the *Miami Herald*.[2]

Miller would win a Pulitzer Prize—his second—for the Pitts-Lee cru-sade. He remarked afterward that he had written *Invitation to a Lynch-ing*, a 1975 book on their case which sold poorly, for an audience of one. He meant Askew; Miller sent the governor a pre-publication copy with an ending worded to goad him into action. Askew said later that the book itself did not convince him "but did open a lot of doors that I could then check out, so it proved helpful to me." The book influenced others, including Askew's third general counsel, Arthur C. Canaday. Canaday went to Tennessee to question Adams's former girlfriend, Mary Jean Akins. She told him—as she had said for years—that Adams had con-fessed the Mo-Jo killings to her before they fled Port St. Joe on the day of the crime. Canaday sent his deputy counsel, Don Middlebrooks, to hear Adams reiterate his confession at Raiford. Eventually, Askew received a remarkable letter from Chris Burkett, a son of one of the Mo-Jo victims, who said he too believed Pitts and Lee to be innocent. The governor and his staff now agreed, but they waited in the hope that the First District Court of Appeal would reverse the second convictions. When it upheld them instead, Askew decided he had to act.[3]

A Florida governor cannot grant clemency on his own authority. It requires the consent of half the Cabinet. In 1975 that meant three votes; Askew could not be sure he had them. He made certain of Attorney General Robert Shevin's support before announcing the intended pardon. Treasurer Philip Ashler, whom Askew had appointed following Tom O'Malley's impeachment, signed soon after Shevin did. Canaday had sent Miller's book to Education Commissioner Ralph Turlington, who found it to be "truly a fascinating story . . . very convincing." Turlington added the decisive fourth (and last) signature five days after Askew's. He resisted heavy pressure from Agriculture Commissioner Doyle Conner to delay or deny his vote. Conner and Comptroller Gerald Lewis publicly disparaged Askew's findings. Secretary of State Bruce Smathers complained that there had not been enough time to review the matter.[4]

Shevin's decision was one of the most courageous and selfless acts in Florida history. The attorney general, who planned to run for governor in 1978, had little to gain and much to lose. Shevin had already suffered withering criticism in the Panhandle for conceding to the Florida Supreme Court in 1971 that Pitts and Lee were entitled to a retrial. "We don't need your breed in a position of vast importance in Florida government," raged the *Panama City News-Herald* in an editorial calling for his resignation. Some people suspected an anti-Semitic implication in the words "your breed." The criticism was ironic, because few Floridians had ever fought crime as passionately and personally as Shevin. He had come home from college on a weekend to find his father, a Miami clothing merchant, fatally beaten by robbers. The Pitts-Lee pardon hurt him in the Democratic gubernatorial primaries three years later. Bob Graham, whose running mate was another senator from the Panhandle, Wayne Mixson, ran far ahead of Shevin in twelve of the region's fourteen counties and won all but Escambia in the runoff. The Panhandle accounted for nearly 40 percent of Shevin's margin of defeat statewide. The Pitts-Lee pardon remained so politically controversial that it took until 1998, twenty-three years after their release, for the legislature to vote to pay them $500,000 each. When Governor Lawton Chiles signed the bill, Lee was overcome with emotion and collapsed into his arms.[5]

In one sense, Pitts and Lee owed their freedom to Tom O'Malley's corruption. O'Malley most likely would have refused to sign the pardon, which Askew did not announce until after O'Malley had been impeached, removed from office, and replaced. Ignoring pressure from the Speaker to finish quickly, Representative Jim Redman and his committee worked patiently to build a massive case for impeachment. Mike Rose, the staff director, took an extraordinary step to make sure that the news media would not overlook or minimize the evidence. The night before the committee was to announce its findings, Rose arranged a secret preview for several influential journalists. He intended to ensure a "rolling crescendo of publicity" that would make it impossible for O'Malley's allies to suppress the case. The well-backgrounded news stories began appearing while the committee was still in session. O'Malley had boycotted the hearings and did not have even an observer present. Before he could react, the momentum for his impeachment was unstoppable.[6]

On June 2, in the last week of the 1975 session, the House voted overwhelmingly to impeach O'Malley on ten of the committee's eleven proposed articles. The vote was 112–3 on one of the strongest charges, which alleged a kickback scheme with his former law partners. He had paid them to be receivers for three insolvent insurance companies. The House also accused him of receiving $71,175 from the partners for clients he sent their way, of taking $1,800 in cash from employees of an insurance company that needed a favorable decision, and of having a secret, one-eighth gift interest in a Fort Walton Beach shopping center for which he approved an insurance company's mortgage loan. The evidence showed that over a two-year period, one in every four insurance companies seeking Florida licensing had hired O'Malley's former partners. O'Malley was the first (and as of this writing, still the only) statewide officer ever to be impeached. The fundamental issue, Redman told the House, was that O'Malley shook down insurance companies while serving as "judge and jury regarding their every business transaction in the State of Florida." Representative Ralph Haben, a committee member, said that O'Malley personally escorted an insurance applicant to meet one of his law partners at a coffee shop. In the day-long debate, only four members did not vote for at least one of the articles. One of them was an insurance agent who abstained.[7]

O'Malley was suspended automatically until the Senate could try him. Askew swiftly appointed Ashler, a retired vice-admiral who had served with him in the legislature, to act in O'Malley's place. Ashler had already taken leave as a vice-chancellor of the Board of Regents to help Askew enact the recommendations of his efficiency study commission. He took the Cabinet post expecting to give it up to someone else—as Askew said he would—in the event the Senate convicted O'Malley and removed him permanently from office. Tall, slim, silver-haired, and still strikingly handsome at the age of sixty, Ashler was often described in the press as suave, debonair, and even "dapper," but the qualities for which Askew chose him were his trustworthiness and his disinterest in running for the office.[8]

The House had done O'Malley a favor in one sense; it gave him an opportunity to trade his resignation for a get-out-of-jail card in the pending state felony charges against him. From special prosecutor Ed Austin's viewpoint, it was worth waiving a jail term to get O'Malley out of office without the expense of a Senate impeachment trial and the risk of more interference by the supreme court. O'Malley now had serious heart trouble, which made a severe prison sentence unlikely. The deal was announced on July 29, 1975. Through an attorney, O'Malley pleaded no contest to a single misdemeanor charge involving the shopping center. He was ordered to pay $500 in court costs. With the consent of Redman's committee, the chief justice dismissed the impeachment case. Although O'Malley claimed he would have been "vindicated" at trial, Austin had the last word. He gave the federal government the evidence it needed to convict O'Malley in a U.S. district court. After a trial and prolonged appeals, O'Malley eventually served two years.[9]

To complete O'Malley's term, Askew said he would appoint someone who would run for the office in 1976, because "I would like to serve with my own Cabinet." Three months later, Ashler obeyed a summons to Askew's office expecting to be told to clean out his desk. Instead, Askew asked him to stay on through the election. He now thought it unwise to appoint someone who would be running for election; in Askew's opinion, there were serious problems in the treasurer's office that needed the immediate attention of someone who was not distracted by a campaign or worried about the outcome. Ashler agreed. "I couldn't do what

I want to do if I were a candidate," he said. The decision bitterly disappointed Jim Apthorp, Askew's chief of staff, who wanted the appointment so that he could run for treasurer from an incumbent's position of strength. Apthorp did not run, and he resigned from the governor's office in January 1977. Former state senator and U.S. congressman Bill Gunter had also sought the appointment. He even organized a petition campaign, which was probably the most counterproductive way to lobby Askew. But Askew had not appointed a rival. Without an incumbent to oppose, Gunter won easily in 1976.[10]

20

SUNSHINE AND STRIFE
(1975–1976)

Reubin Askew had not been bluffing about taking the financial disclosure issue directly to the voters. The Sunshine Amendment initiative he announced in mid-November 1975 made legislators regret that they had not given him what he had asked for. The amendment entailed much more than Askew's core proposal that all constitutional officeholders and candidates be required to disclose their income-tax returns and net-worth statements. The amendment would also bar lawmakers from representing clients before state agencies other than the courts and from lobbying the legislature itself for two years after leaving office. Askew had in mind the example of E. C. Rowell, a former Speaker who was still serving as House rules chairman in 1970 when he arranged to become the trucking industry's lobbyist. Askew's initiative was a hard swallow even for some of the lawmakers who had supported him on disclosure. Senator Kenneth Myers, for one, represented water and sewer companies before the Public Service Commission. Rowell was not the only legislator to return as a lobbyist.[1]

The initiative also gave constitutional status to the ethics commission, required "full and public disclosure" of all campaign finances, provided for financial restitution and loss of pension for crimes involving "breaches of the public trust," and empowered the legislature to enact any additional laws necessary to "preserve the public trust and avoid conflict between public duties and private interests." The pension provision addressed a loophole that had protected Floyd Christian when he was convicted of unauthorized compensation rather than of bribery.[2]

Askew's staff had spent many days drafting the initiative in consultation with Jon Moyle, who would chair the campaign, and with Sandy D'Alemberte, who chaired the ethics commission. Their chief concern was the single-subject limitation on initiatives. They rationalized that "ethics in government" was a single subject. Moreover, it all had to fit on a postcard, which was the most surprising element of Askew's campaign. According to Jim Krog, an Askew aide at the time, the postcard idea came to mind one night as a solution to the problem of sorting signed petitions so that supervisors of elections could verify the signatures easily. The constitution required not only a certain number of signatures—in 1975, that meant 210,537 statewide—but also a minimum number in at least eight congressional districts. The postcard format also lent itself to printing the petition in the newspapers for readers to clip, sign, and mail. Some newspapers complied with Askew's request to print it, but others, including the *Miami Herald*, objected that it would compromise the objectivity of their news pages.[3]

Throughout his administration, Askew cultivated publishers and newspaper editorial boards because "key people of the community all read the editorials." He made it a point to visit them frequently even if he had nothing to ask at the moment. Askew thought he had a good relationship with all but three or four Florida newspapers. If most editors were content, however, their reporters in Tallahassee were not. Askew did not mind what he called a "natural tension" between them, since "the government needs to be checked on." As most capital reporters saw it, he made the checking needlessly difficult. They complained that during his second term he had he had become inaccessible, using his press office, as one writer put it, as "a considerable shield" against them. In August 1975 he met for two and half hours with some forty reporters and said he would try to schedule more individual interviews. He made it plain, however, that he would continue to refuse to respond "cold turkey" to questions on controversial issues.[4]

In November 1975, Askew began the petition drive with a three-day, seven-city campaign tour. He called the initiative "the greatest single step and perhaps the most positive step we can take to restore the confidence of the people." The campaign's fifteen congressional district chairs included ten current or former legislators: Steve Pajcic, Edgar Dunn, Dick Batchelor, Tom Moore, Bob Hattaway, George Firestone, Barry Richard, Richard Pettigrew, Buddy MacKay, and Don Reed, the only Republican. (MacKay said he would have preferred an initiative to reform the legislative process.) Askew had strong support also from Attorney General Robert Shevin, who quickly sent him forty-two petitions signed by Shevin, his wife, and aides and administrators. Even Charley Johns, the onetime Pork Chop Senate president and acting governor, signed one. "We certainly need something done to restore the confidence of the people," he wrote to Askew. When Senate president Dempsey Barron denounced the amendment as "junk," the *St. Petersburg Times* replied by printing the petition on its editorial page.[5]

The League of Women Voters, Common Cause, Democratic committees, teachers unions, and other organizations provided volunteers to circulate the petitions. Most newspapers backed it editorially. There was little organized opposition, but former representative Donald R. Crane Jr. of St. Petersburg continued to argue that Askew wanted too much made public. To be required to expose personal details to "fund solicitors, burglars, even kidnappers," Crane said, would discourage successful people from seeking public office. Askew worried less about Crane and other opponents than about inertia; he had underestimated the difficulty of collecting more than 200,000 valid signatures. He began spending his weekends stumping at shopping centers. It was helpful that 1976 was a presidential election year; Askew sent volunteers to polls at hundreds of selected precincts on the day of the primary, March 9, and scored nearly 70,000 signatures. His success goaded the legislature into persistent attempts to banish petition gathering anywhere near voting venues. Askew detached Krog from his office to manage the campaign for signatures and contributions. Krog worked in rented quarters on the second floor of a vacant bank near the capitol. "Askew was like a laser beam on this thing," said Krog. "He would come upstairs in that ratty old building just to look at what we had on the table. Every day he wanted me to count those suckers; he wanted to know how many we had." Not caring to spend all his time counting, Krog resorted to stacking the arriving petition forms, measuring them with a ruler, and estimating the count for Askew.[6]

The campaign was still short of the signature goal when the legislature convened in 1976, but Barron, Jack Gordon, and other opponents assumed it would succeed. Late in the session, they contrived legislation to supersede the Sunshine Amendment's net-worth and tax-return disclosure requirements. Askew denounced it as a "cynical disregard of the people." Senator Lori Wilson, whom Askew had passed over when he was selecting his running mate in 1974, accused him of acting "like the little boy who pouts." Both houses passed separate versions of the bill by majorities that seemed veto-proof, but Askew thought he could stop it by defeating the conference committee report. "Governor," asked Krog, "when was the last conference report that ever got killed?" Askew knew of none but insisted on trying. Krog, Jim Apthorp, and other Askew staffers staked out the doors to the House chamber. On this occasion, the last day of the session, they were not gentle; the message was blunt: vote against the conference report "if you ever want to speak to this guy [Askew] again." Some legislators were brought to his office to get the message in person. The House, which had voted 102–9 for the initial version, now voted 84–17 to reject the conference report, putting an end to Barron's maneuver. Apthorp assigned part of the credit to Barron himself. Many House members were angry at him because he had abruptly adjourned the Senate in order to force the House to accept the Senate's budget for education, and their resentment spilled over into the disclosure showdown. After the session, Senator Bob Saunders of Gainesville, who had lost the Senate presidency to Lew Brantley, said he would not run for reelection, since he did not want to remain in an environment "where people are considered guilty until proven innocent." Representative Roger Wilson, a Republican from Clearwater, said he would leave also and released an exchange of letters in which Askew refused to debate him. The invasion-of-privacy issue lost some force in June when the Florida Supreme Court unanimously upheld the limited law already in effect. "No court has yet declared that a federal right of privacy overrides a reasonable effort by the state to implement a policy of ethics in government," Justice Arthur England wrote.[7]

On July 29, a day before the deadline, the secretary of state announced that the Sunshine Amendment had enough valid signatures to become Florida's first ballot initiative. It had been a close call; there were only 5,461 signatures to spare. Although the campaign had met the requirements in ten congressional districts, two more than necessary, the margins were perilously thin in three of them. A big question remained: how would the court rule on the issue of a "single subject"?

With former rival John E. Mathews Jr. among his lawyers, Askew won a six-to-one decision on October 11 that the various provisions were "sufficiently related to withstand an attack that they embrace more than one subject." The dissenter was Justice B. K. Roberts, who contended that it should be more difficult to amend the constitution by initiative than by legislative action. An initiative, he had complained during the oral argument, allows "one man in a back room" to change the constitution. The Sunshine Amendment decision would be turned against Askew two years later when the court cited it as precedent for allowing a casino gambling initiative to go on the ballot.[8]

In subsequent cases, the court began to interpret the single-subject rule much more strictly. The justices adopted what one commentator called an "iron rule" that if an initiative affected "more than one function, branch, or level of government," it could not qualify as a single subject. Initiatives flourished nonetheless, with Askew's single-signature form having become the requirement for petition campaigns in Florida. The style did not spread to other states, in part because it is regarded as highly susceptible to fraud. Individual signature sheets make it harder to detect identical handwriting.[9]

Voters approved the Sunshine Amendment on November 2, 1976, by one of the most impressive margins ever recorded in a Florida referendum: 1,765,626 votes yes to only 461,940 no. Every county voted for it. The amendment to appoint all appellate judges carried 1,600,944 to 527,056. Askew won a third victory with overwhelming approval of the amendment reinforcing the discipline of judges, and a fourth when the voters turned down an amendment that would have allowed the legislature to overturn agency rules by resolutions not subject to veto. Another of Askew's long-range goals, an amendment authorizing state bonds for housing, was defeated.[10]

Some provisions of the Sunshine Amendment needed legislation to implement them. Askew sent legislators a letter before the 1977 session inviting them to improve upon the amendment but warning against requiring full disclosure from minor officials and appointees, particularly "in areas in which people serve for little or no pay." Not wanting the ethics commission to implement the amendment administratively, the legislature sent a bill to Askew. The more he and his staff looked at it, the less they liked it. Two Board of Regents members who were his friends said that they would resign if they had to file full disclosure on the same terms as Florida's eighteen hundred county and state constitutional officers. Askew vetoed the bill on the grounds that it went to such "unnecessary extremes" as to compel full disclosure by more than ten thousand people. "It requires the most revealing form of disclosure from public officials who have little power and even less control over the public purse," Askew said. He suspected the legislature of trying to make disclosure so unpopular that it could be repealed. Denying that the two regents influenced his decision, Askew said he would require all his future appointees to state boards to file full disclosure. The veto left it unclear how some provisions would be interpreted or enforced until implementing legislation finally was enacted in 1982.[11]

The Sunshine Amendment was self-executing to the extent that it set an annual deadline for those subject to full disclosure of their income-tax returns and net-worth statements. Most complied, but six state senators—Ken Plante, Phil Lewis, Jack Gordon, Jon Thomas, Bill Gorman, and Dempsey Barron—refused to file pending the outcome of lawsuits that they hoped would overturn the amendment. Six school board members resigned rather than comply, and in September, Askew suspended two others for their failure to file.[12] He contended that legislators had no right to decide for themselves what part of the constitution they should obey, and he challenged the Senate to expel the senators. The Senate ignored him. The ethics commission voted to ask the Senate to act against them, which it refused to do while their appeals were pending. The commission then voted to issue a report accusing the senators of "a breach of public trust," but the First District Court of Appeal ruled that the commission was powerless in the matter. Such a decision from that court surprised no one. In March 1979, after the end of Askew's term, the Florida Supreme Court ruled six to one that the commission indeed was entitled to find "probable cause" that the senators were in violation of the constitution. The court also concluded that the commission had no power to compel the Senate to expel them. In a separate case filed by Senator Kenneth Myers, the court ruled unanimously that the bans on representing clients before state agencies did not apply to legislators who were still serving terms that began before the January 1977 effective date of the Sunshine Amendment. That applied to all members, even those whose terms had begun in November. This was good news to Plante and others who were contemplating retirement in 1978. They would not have to sit out two years before becoming lobbyists. In the case of a circuit judge who had been convicted for dealing in marijuana, the court ruled that the amendment's pension loss provisions required legislation to enforce them. It took the legislature until 1982 to get around to that as well. In 1978 the legislature put a stop to the judge's pension by exercising the impeachment process. In response to another ethics commission probe, the Senate reprimanded Senator Ralph Poston of Miami and fined him $500 in December 1977 for using the influence of his office to promote his private business, a wheelchair ambulance service. Although the penalty was light, it was the Senate's first act of self-discipline in 105 years. The voters were not as forgiving; Poston lost his subsequent reelection campaign.[13]

To Askew's displeasure and a chorus of "we told you so" from opposing legislators, some newspapers made sport of the first financial disclosure filings. One newspaper bordered the data with dollar signs. Another wrote that Representative Elaine Bloom of Miami owned a dog that cost more than the entire net worth of her colleague from Hillsborough, George Sheldon. His balance sheet came to less than the $1,004 value that Bloom assigned to her white toy poodle, Lucky. Bloom had picked the figure out of the air, describing the poodle as a watchdog to discourage burglars. Meanwhile, Richard Pallot, who had been one of the first south Floridians to support Askew's candidacy, resigned as chair of the Business Regulation Board, but he said disclosure was not the reason.[14]

On June 30, 1978, just in time for that year's campaigns, the Fifth U.S. Circuit Court of Appeals upheld the Sunshine Amendment. The opinion, in an appeal brought by the defiant senators, embraced Askew's argument that public trust was more important than the privacy of public officials. "The senators contend," wrote Judge John Minor Wisdom,

> that the Amendment will not stop corruption. They make the reasonable point that few officials are likely to make a public disclosure of illegal income. Yet, the existence of the reporting requirement will discourage corruption. Sunshine will make detection more likely. The interest in an honest administration is so strong that even small advances are important . . .
> We are not insensitive to the senators' dilemma; nor do we doubt the sincerity of their opposition to the Amendment. Their privacy, and the privacy of others included in the Amendment, is severely limited by it. We do not say that it is wise; the people of Florida, by a four to one vote, have done that. We do say that, on its face, it is constitutional.[15]

In January 1979 the U.S. Supreme Court refused to review the decision, leaving Lewis, Barron, and Gordon no choice but to disclose. Plante and Thomas had left the legislature, and Gorman had already filed.[16]

By then, Askew had fought and won another Sunshine Amendment skirmish. Mary Singleton, a former House member from Jacksonville who headed the secretary of state's elections division, refused to require non-incumbent candidates to submit disclosure statements when they filed for the 1978 elections. She cited the lack of implementing legislation. Her decision cost her an opportunity to become Florida's first black Cabinet officer since Reconstruction. When Secretary of State Bruce Smathers resigned to run for governor, Askew appointed Jesse McCrary Jr., an African American former assistant attorney general, to finish his term. McCrary overruled Singleton's interpretation, and she resigned to campaign for lieutenant governor as Claude Kirk's running mate. She was the first black candidate on a gubernatorial ticket, but it was a sad footnote to history because she and the former governor, who was running as a Democrat this time, placed a poor fifth in a six-way primary, receiving only 6 percent of the vote.[17]

That fall, financial disclosure forms revealed that a candidate for appointment to the Public Service Commission had owned stock in a company involved in a fuel overcharge scandal he was investigating as a senior PSC employee. He did not get the appointment.[18] There have been few prosecutions on account of the disclosure provision, but in 1997 a Pinellas County judge resigned after being convicted of falsifying his form. That same year, Sandy D'Alemberte told the Florida Constitution Revision Commission that he had come to regret his role in liberalizing Florida's initiative process. By then there had been successful initiatives to ban commercial fishing nets, restrict tax increases, limit terms in office, and establish a state lottery, as well as costly but unsuccessful campaigns to legalize casino gambling and tax sugar. "First, I was wrong," said D'Alemberte, attributing his mea culpa in part to U.S. Supreme Court decisions that allowed unlimited spending in referendum elections. He had second thoughts about the Sunshine Amendment itself. He agreed that it responded to "a crisis in public confidence" arising from the Cabinet and Florida Supreme Court scandals. But the initiative he helped to draft, he said, "is mostly legislative in content." In other words, the Sunshine Amendment did not belong in a constitution, and D'Alemberte urged the commission to "clean up or repeal" the amendment. The commission did not accept either suggestion.[19]

21

LAME DUCK? (1976)

Although a staff memorandum described Askew's 1976 legislative agenda as "limited in scope . . . stressing primarily the unfinished business of prior years," that was no small order. His specific recommendations to legislators went into a forty-seven-page, single-spaced letter. It dealt with such recurring issues as the Equal Rights Amendment, crime and prisons, transportation, housing, gun control, merit selection of judges, and the budget. The fresh topics included fraudulent land sales that seemed to be beyond the grasp of state regulators. His major new initiative, which was in trouble from the outset, was a wholesale gasoline tax equal at the time to 2.8 cents per gallon that would hasten completion of Florida's interstate highways and support mass transit in urban areas. Prison overcrowding was a crisis. Men were sleeping on mattresses on the floors of reception center cells. The overflow bunked in tents, warehouses, and converted classrooms. Florida prisons were admitting convicts at a rate more than three times that of the state's population growth. There were two and a quarter times more inmates in June 1979 than a decade before. With the count growing by ninety-three a week—"younger, more hardened, and serving longer terms than those who came before," as the *New York Times* reported—Askew proposed five new 600-bed prisons and expansion of two others. Florida now faced a federal judge's order to either release prisoners en masse or build adequate facilities. The state appealed unsuccessfully. Not for the last time, prisons became the top budget priority, yet Askew still opposed more taxes for general revenue. The struggling economy, always a reliable barometer of rising crime, accounted only in part for the prisoner deluge. Florida's prosecutors, judges, and parole commissioners had become sensitive to the public's perception, fed by mass media, that crime was out of control. The parole commission released 32 percent fewer prisoners in 1975 than in the year before, and judges were imposing prison rather than probation in more, not fewer, cases. "This situation," Askew complained, "is neither humane nor necessary."[1]

As the 1976 session was about to convene, several newspapers reflected the dismay of some liberal lawmakers in articles portraying Askew as a dispirited and ineffective lame duck. The *Miami Herald*'s headline was brutal: "The forgotten man . . . Weary Askew falters on eve of new Legislature." Conceding that Askew's program was "guided by restraint," press secretary Paul Schnitt protested to the media that for more than a year the administration had been faced with a rebellious legislature and economic distress. Askew could not afford to pick new fights.[2]

That did not mean shrinking from old ones. In his opening-day address to a joint session, Askew decried what he referred to as "an undeniable hostility against government today, a saddening hostility that is alien to our tradition of confidence as a people and harmful to us at a time when we are badly in need of confidence." To deride government, he said, "may be an easy way to get headlines in the newspapers or a few minutes on the evening news . . . but government will not work if we dislike and abuse it . . . or pretend that we can abolish it." Some in the audience thought the remarks were directed only in part at Senate president Dempsey Barron and applied also to the softer but still unmistakably anti-Washington theme of Jimmy Carter's burgeoning presidential candidacy. Askew did not endorse Carter until he already had the Democratic nomination sewn up.[3]

In words unmistakably meant for Barron and House Speaker Donald L. Tucker, he declared that legislative responsibility "does not extend to unwarranted intrusions and unnecessary invasions into the responsibilities of the executive branch." He announced his "every intention of exercising the lawful and constitutional responsibilities of the office of governor, to their fullest extent, and on behalf of the people of Florida." Askew's reading text at that point bore notes reminding him to speak "slowly and emphatically." At the end of the text, he wrote more instructions to himself: "Long pause. Smile." He concluded with "My best wishes for a good and productive session."[4]

The presiding officers responded with a coordinated campaign to override his 1975 vetoes. The first override to clear both houses required state agencies to estimate the economic effect of any proposed decision. Askew remarked on the irony of his first veto defeat that "virtually every speaker" in the Senate debate had conceded the bill was flawed and needed revision. The legislature, Askew said, "Was more interested in overriding my veto than in asking whether this bill was good for the people of Florida." By the end of the second day of the session, the House and Senate had each voted to override four more vetoes, including controversial proposals to relax certain liquor laws; grant sales tax breaks for boats, yachts, and automobiles purchased for use out of state; and allow landlords instead of sheriffs to serve eviction notices. Apparently forgetting that Askew was listening to the debates, Tucker remarked from the House rostrum, "I probably shouldn't be enjoying this as much as I am." After another round of override votes the second week, including a contractor's claim bill that Askew called a "$1 million rip-off of the people," Tucker agreed to give the furious governor twenty-four hours' notice before taking up any more vetoes. "We've reached a point in time when we should quit casting epithets at one another," Tucker told the House after a private meeting with Askew. "I still respect the governor and personally like him." To Askew's grim delight—and the consternation of airline lobbyists—one of the bills enacted over his veto also repealed four-year-old tax exemptions for leased government property at airports, marine terminals, and other profit-generating sites. Senator Buddy MacKay had slipped that poison pill into the legislation when he saw that the bill could not be defeated. The legislature restored some of the port and airport exemptions later in the 1976 session, but MacKay and Representative Carl Ogden saw to it that restaurants, bars, and other leased ventures not essential to transportation would be taxed on their leaseholds. The override campaign, meanwhile, ran out of steam in late April when Representative Jim Redman led a successful effort to sustain the veto of a bill allowing minors to work in dinner theaters where liquor was served. That upset the momentum; the House then narrowly upheld the veto of $5 million in sales tax exemptions for pollution control equipment; Askew argued forcefully that the state could not afford it. The final score stood at ten of the thirty-four 1975 vetoes overridden and sixteen sustained. Eight did not come to a decisive vote. The vetoes he successfully defended in the House prevented an array of consumer interest-rate increases and killed an attempt to exempt small waste treatment plants from several environmental laws. Once that battle was behind him, Askew kept rather distant from the media as he worked to salvage his stalled program for 1976. There were occasional written statements but only one press conference. Aides said he preferred to work behind the scenes and that in May alone he had fifty House members come to his office, in groups, for sandwiches, soft drinks, milk, and cookies. Askew was aware that many legislators were jealous of his popularity, but as his subsequent vetoes would show, he would concede no ground to them over the powers of the governor's office in regard to environmental protection or public safety. The protracted combat over the 1975 vetoes had not left Askew battle-shy. To the contrary, he vetoed thirty bills that reached his desk after the 1976 session. There would have been another had the House not defeated the attempt to undermine the Sunshine Amendment. Surprisingly, none was brought up for an override attempt during the 1977 session.[5]

Among those he vetoed was a fiercely debated bill to allow residents to shoot intruders anywhere within the "curtilage"—generally speaking, the fenced yards, barns and other outbuildings—surrounding their homes. This was a vast expansion of the existing right to use deadly force in self-defense. As Senator David McClain of Tampa argued in support of the bill, "You've all heard the story that if you shoot someone in your yard you'd better drag them inside the house. Well, this gets us away from that." Opponents dubbed it the "Shoot-the-Avon-lady" bill. In the Senate, only Jack Gordon voted no, apparently unaware that his friend Dempsey Barron was the secret sponsor. Although there was more resistance in the House, it passed there by what appeared to be a veto-proof majority of eighty-two to twenty-three. On the day the Senate approved it, a distraught Florida State University graduate student purchased a handgun and murdered his major professor. Askew remarked sharply that legislators were ignoring his requests for a seventy-two hour "cooling off" period on the purchase of handguns and a ban on the sale of cheap handguns known as "Saturday night specials." Sixteen of the twenty state attorneys asked him to veto the deadly force bill. So did Florida Supreme Court justice Arthur England, in a letter he intended to be confidential. Shevin recommended a veto also, warning that the bill gave private citizens more license to kill than even the police. The attorney general was at Askew's side for moral support when the governor announced his veto and denounced the bill as an ill-conceived overreaction. Representative Charles E. Bennett of Jacksonville, a Florida congressman noted for his high standard of ethics, wrote Askew afterward to praise him for "your personal and political courage in doing things . . . which in your conscience you determined to be the right thing to do." Askew simultaneously vetoed legislation authorizing the death penalty for burglaries involving rape or kidnapping, which he said would encourage criminals to leave no victims alive, and empowering prosecutors to charge juveniles as adults without the approval of a grand jury or a juvenile court. Askew's other notable post-session vetoes included bills to enable the Cabinet to stop the attorney general from filing environmental and consumer protection lawsuits, prevent one agency from taking legal action against another, deny unemployment compensation to people charged but not convicted of crimes, require reconsideration of any state environmental rule stronger than federal law or regulations, allow nonprofit organizations to raise money through raffles, and repeal Miami Beach's rent control ordinance. The landlord lobby had enlisted a north Florida senator, Pat Thomas of Gadsden County, to sponsor the rent control bill. Askew also blocked the farm lobby's bill authorizing the aerial spraying of a fire ant pesticide in violation of federal regulations. The bills he signed included significant reforms in nursing home regulation, a controversial requirement that two doctors certify the need for a late-term abortion, and a little-noticed enactment by Kenneth Myers that provided for "sunset" review of laws regulating businesses and professions. MacKay and Representative George Sheldon eventually took advantage of "sunset" to end the Public Service Commission's oversight of the trucking and bus industries, which the commission had been shielding from competition.[6]

The deadly force bill supposedly originated with the Florida Bar, which lobbied for its passage. Such legislation was completely out of character with the rest of its legislative program, offended some prominent attorneys who asked Askew to veto it, and mystified members of its Board of Governors who could not recall a discussion of the subject, much less a vote to sponsor it. The untold story was that it was actually Barron's bill, a fact that became known only after his death many years later. Although as a Florida attorney Barron was required to belong to the Bar and pay its dues, he disliked its hierarchy and its politics and typically sided with doctors, insurance companies, and business groups which lobbied for restrictions on lawsuits. Hoping to make peace with him, J. Rex Farrior Jr., the Bar's president in 1976, visited Barron's capitol office and offered to help him in any way he could. Suppressing a grin, the Senate president reached into his desk and pulled out the deadly force bill. Farrior was aghast, but he was trapped. By the time the veto message was ripe for action by the 1977 session, the legislators who had sponsored it for the Bar were gone, and the Bar had a new president, Edward J. Atkins of Miami, who was happy to let the matter drop.[7]

Barron may not have wanted his fingerprints on the legislation out of concern that they would guarantee a veto, but it was also his style to try to not be obvious about legislation he wanted to pass lest other lawmakers expect favors in return. In one notable exception during 1976, he forced the universities to accept a modified lottery system for some admissions to their law schools and other highly selective graduate programs. On the other hand, he never hid his opposition to bills or programs he disliked. In the last session of his presidency, he used its powers to reduce the field staff of the Department of Law Enforcement in retaliation for its investigations of public officers. He also made it his personal business to defeat a coalition of Democrats and Republicans who wanted to increase the proposed budget for education. "Just today you told me the education lobby said they have the votes. It's like Reubin Askew on O. J. Keller," he gloated to a reporter. "He doesn't want to beat them, he wants to kill them," observed Republican senator David Lane. Barron perpetuated his power through the coup that made Lew Brantley his successor as president. Although Brantley did not turn out to be quite as compliant as Barron had expected, he did punish the senators who had opposed him and Barron with committee assignments that left them nearly powerless. In the House, Tucker, who expected to run for governor in 1978, kept himself in power by winning a second two-year term as Speaker. He became the first one to succeed himself since 1917. Redman ran against him on a promise to dilute the rules committee's control over floor debate. During the 1975 session, Redman said, not one bill had reached the floor for debate without that committee's approval. Although Redman believed he had enough votes to win, the vote was not even close, fifty-six to twenty-nine in Tucker's favor. The vote was by secret ballot, a policy House Democrats had adopted after Tucker's 1973 contest with MacKay. It became obvious that some members had promised support to both Tucker and Redman in confidence that the secret ballots would conceal their duplicity. "I didn't believe it would be that bad," said Redman, who had expected a margin of only one or two votes either way. In victory, Tucker was generous to Redman, offering him chairmanship of the education committee and of the auditing committee once again, but he was ruthless toward Barry Kutun of Miami, who had given up his own speakership campaign to aid Redman's. Tucker removed Kutun as chair of health and rehabilitative services and took away his seat on the rules committee. He also demoted Carl Ogden of Jacksonville, the finance and tax chair, and Richard Hodes of Tampa, the education chair, who was left without a committee to head for the first time in his ten-year career. The news media pronounced a verdict on the leadership by voting to name Ogden in the House and MacKay in the Senate as the "most valuable" legislators in an annual poll sponsored by the *St. Petersburg Times*. It was the fourth time MacKay won the award, tying him with former senator Louis de la Parte. MacKay would win three more times, and holds the record.[8]

Many of the disaffected House Democrats soon found a partnership with Republicans in what came to be known as the Urban Coalition. The alliance recalled their common ground in the reorganization battle of 1969. Curt Kiser, a coalition leader, said it responded to "a real erosion of respect for an individual member's right to take his position as he sees fit." Sheldon, who had openly supported his delegation colleague Redman for the speakership, felt Tucker's retribution after the session; he was left off the committee that would oversee significant nursing home legislation which he had just guided to passage. The Tampa Bay area, which suffered from serious traffic congestion and had persistent inter-city disputes over water resources, was left with no representative on the natural resources and transportation committees. Tucker retaliated against Tom Moore, another outspoken critic of the House hierarchy and one of only two Democrats in the Pinellas County House delega-tion, by stripping him of his prized seats on the natural resources and elections committees. He reduced the minority office staff from eleven positions to two, prompting Republican leader William James to call him the "most vindictive" of all speakers. James claimed Tucker was retaliating for a budget vote in which Republicans and Democrats had blocked a $1.6 million state land deal that involved a business partner of Tucker.[9]

Tucker at that point was a wounded politician. A sergeant-at-arms whom he had fired told the Republicans that Tucker had spent $8,431 for a desk and credenza for his office in the new capitol building that was under construction. That was more than the average state employee earned in a year, the equivalent of more than $31,000 today. A week before the November election, the Republicans told the *St. Petersburg Times* about the desk and exploited the purchase in a campaign mailing to all voters in Tucker's four-county, heavily Democratic district, which had more state workers than anywhere else in Florida. The Republicans neglected to mention that identical furniture had been purchased for the Senate president's office, a fact apparently unknown even to Brant-ley when he told the newspaper that for such a price, a desk ought to be able to fly. Tucker, who had thought he could coast to reelection against a neophyte Republican candidate, won with only 53 percent of the vote. Such a weak showing at home meant that he would not be a plausible candidate for governor and he refocused his ambitions on Washington. Tucker had been the first Florida politician to endorse the new president, Jimmy Carter, who nominated him for vice-chairman of the Civil Aeronautics Board. Unyielding opposition developed in the Senate Commerce Committee and Tucker withdrew from consideration. The committee never divulged its objections; a newspaper reported that it was particularly concerned with a loan to Tucker in 1975 from a bank whose directors also sat on the boards of two major airlines. Tucker's candidacy also suffered from factors beyond his control. One was a major controversy over the private business ethics of Carter's budget director, Bert Lance, who resigned while Tucker's nomination was pending. The other was that Tucker had no expertise to compare with that of Carter's first CAB appointees, Alfred Kahn and Elizabeth E. Bailey, who were widely respected economists.[10]

Barron had his own unexpected difficulty at the polls. Sam Mitchell, a former House member from Washington County, took enough votes in a three-way Democratic primary to force Barron into a runoff, his first since 1967, against Travis Marchant, a Leon County commissioner. Barron repeatedly accused Askew of meddling in the race. Askew denied it, refusing to say directly which candidate he favored, but remarking that the answer "should be obvious without me saying it." Barron claimed that he was being opposed by "the Miami Beach teachers unions, the governor, and the South Florida trial lawyers," never mentioning the dozens of statewide lobbies that were contributing to him. Although Barron won the runoff with 56 percent, he polled only 45 percent in Leon County. Askew said Barron ought to find a message in his "very tough election." When Barron did, it was not the one Askew had in mind. In 1982, Barron designed a single-member district system for the Senate in which his own constituency no longer included Leon County and its thousands of state employees.[11]

Events unconnected with the 1976 session were significant milestones for Askew. In July, the U.S. Supreme Court upheld the revised death penalty law he had signed into law nearly four years earlier. "I intend to fulfill the responsibilities with which the people have entrusted me as governor, including the signing of death warrants," Askew said in a notably brief written statement of only nine lines. There were seventy-four men on death row, although none had exhausted his appeals. Ironically, the Florida inmate whose case prompted the decision was resentenced to life eleven years later; the state supreme court ruled that his crime was not sufficiently heinous for execution.[12]

In the fall, Askew and the Cabinet had to decide whether to rescind or renew the state's support for the Cross-Florida Barge Canal. A federal judge in 1974 had overturned President Nixon's impoundment of funds, which had stopped construction with a third of the project completed. There had been no work since then, pending Congress's decision whether to appropriate more money. In the end, that would depend upon Florida's recommendation. The canal's fate was all but sealed on September 21 when the Army Corps of Engineers conceded to Askew and the Cabinet that it might cost more money to complete the canal than anyone would save by using it. Hundreds of people, about two-thirds of them environmentalists opposed to the canal, attended two days of hearings in Tallahassee in December. Jay Landers, the secretary of environmental regulation, contended that a twenty-eight mile excavation west of Ocala would be a "substantial serious threat" to contaminate the Floridan aquifer, the state's major natural underground fresh water reservoir. Protection of the aquifer was the *raison d'être* of the Florida Defenders of the Environment, which had been founded in 1969 by Marjorie Carr, a zoologist married to a University of Florida professor. In the ensuing nine years, Carr became the living symbol of opposition to the canal. Hundreds of people stood to cheer her final speech and again an hour later when Askew and the Cabinet voted six to one against completion. Doyle Conner, the agriculture commissioner, cast the only vote for the canal. Five months later, President Carter asked Congress to deauthorize "this ill-advised project," but it took until 1990 for Congress to comply. The canal holdings were returned to the state for recreation. Although the sports fishing lobby successfully lobbied the legislature against removing the Rodman dam and restoring the Ocklawaha River, much of the route eventually became a park—the Marjorie Harris Carr Cross Florida Greenway. It was the most appropriate tribute imaginable for the person who, almost single-handedly at first, had won one of the most significant environmental victories in American history.[13]

22

CULTURE WARS (1977)

In January 1977, LeRoy Collins telephoned Reubin Askew to congratulate him; he had now served as governor longer than the six consecutive years that Collins had. Askew was determined to continue building on that record rather than take the opportunity to go to Washington with President Jimmy Carter, who had expressed interest in appointing Askew to his Cabinet. Askew did agree to accept a part-time, unpaid assignment from Carter as chairman of a new commission to advise him on ambassadorial appointments. He helped Carter also by using his influence as chairman of the National Governors Conference to gather political support for the president's programs, including ratification of a highly controversial treaty that ceded the Panama Canal to the nation of Panama. But with Askew's own career nearing its end, or at least a hiatus, in 1978, when there would be no U.S. Senate seat on Florida's ballot, his staff members began striking out for themselves or hitching their wagons to rising stars. His chief of staff, Jim Apthorp, disappointed that he had not been named to succeed Treasurer Tom O'Malley, left to become an executive with Deltona Corporation, a major land developer. Askew praised him as "one of the finest public servants and able administrators I've ever known in state government," and said he had to work "a lot harder at being governor" after Apthorp left. His new chief of staff would be James Tait, a lawyer and economic adviser who had been one of Speaker Richard Pettigrew's protégés on the staff of the Florida House of Representatives. Askew's general counsel, Arthur Canaday, had resigned to run for the First District Court of Appeal.

After he lost, Askew appointed him to the Industrial Commission, which judged workers' compensation disputes. Don Middlebrooks, his new general counsel, stayed only until August 1977, when he left to join Sandy D'Alemberte's law firm. Bernie Parrish, "more than an aide, more than a friend," resigned to become a lobbyist. With Askew's encouragement, Jim Bacchus had resigned as deputy press secretary to study law at Florida State University, though he continued to write some of Askew's speeches part-time. His staff replacement was Ron Sachs, a former *Florida Alligator* editor at the University of Florida who had defied a law against printing abortion information and challenged it successfully in court. Edward Trombetta, Askew's secretary of commerce, resigned in December 1977 to become a deputy to Treasurer Bill Gunter, whose reelection was virtually certain. Askew recalled Phil Ashler yet again, this time from retirement, to replace Trombetta. Jim Williams resigned as secretary of administration to concentrate on running for governor. He remained lieutenant governor but waived the salary. To have been guardian of the budget, Williams said, was not a job he would recommend "to anyone wanting to build a political base."[1]

Askew had opposed a general sales tax increase for his first six budgets, but he surrendered to necessity in 1977 and asked the legislature for a penny increase, to five cents on the dollar. He intended it largely for education and highways. He conceded that "a sales tax can be a regressive tax" but rationalized that Florida exempted the basic necessities of groceries, medicine, household utilities, and residential rents. The Senate refused even to discuss it; the urban coalition in the House continued to fight for the penny long after Askew had given up. For once, the Senate's powerless "Doghouse Democrats" were on the same side as Senator Dempsey Barron, although not for the same reasons. They argued that a general sales tax increase would preclude genuine tax reform. The compromise budget, enacted during a second special session, was financed with higher taxes principally on cigarettes, alcoholic beverages, and phosphate mining. It also reduced inventory taxes, a step the governor had requested in order to counter the impression that his administration was anti-business. "I don't think there's any question in anybody's mind . . . [that] the Senate wrote the script," exulted Senate president Lew Brantley.[2]

In his opening-day address, Askew mentioned only briefly what would become one of the major disputes and eventual successes of his final two years. He wanted to replace the three-member elected Public Service Commission with a five-person board appointed by the governor and confirmed by the Senate. "This would broaden the range of expertise . . . and provide for better representation of the public," he said. Concerned that the prison situation remained out of hand, he urged the legislature to divert more felons from confinement and enact sentencing guidelines to reduce "unfair disparities . . . in different courts." He recommended that Florida establish a commission to pay the medical expenses of victims of violent crime. (This was enacted; one of the first beneficiaries was a student who survived serial killer Ted Bundy's rampage at a Tallahassee sorority house where two other women died.) Askew's major new tax reform initiative in 1977 was a $50 million plan to offset the impact of property taxes on low-income renters as well as homeowners. It went no further than a subcommittee hearing in the House.[3]

House Speaker Donald L. Tucker agreed with Askew on several issues, notably, overhauling the Public Service Commission, but that was delayed until 1978. The governor had no significant support from Brantley. Askew wanted a law to limit the immunity that prosecutors had to grant to witnesses in criminal cases. Brantley said he agreed with that, but Barron took the occasion to show who still ran the Senate on most days. Barron amended the bill to allow lawyers to accompany clients testifying to grand juries. He said he had been harassed by the federal grand jury that indicted O'Malley. As he expected, the House refused to pass the amended bill. (The limited immunity and lawyer provisions were enacted eventually.) Tucker, whose business affairs had withstood probes by two grand juries, attempted unsuccessfully to abolish their use except for capital indictments.[4]

Askew's veto of the implementing legislation for the Sunshine Amendment (see chapter 20) erased what might have been one of the session's few significant outcomes. One surprising success was the enactment of a state law prohibiting employment discrimination based on age, sex, race, marital status, or disability. It had strong support from major employers, who preferred to deal with the state rather than with the federal Equal Employment Opportunity Commission. The lead sponsor in the Senate, Jack Gordon, was in a Miami hospital recovering from a heart attack when freshman senator Betty Castor of Tampa secured the victory for him on the session's last day.[5]

Once again, the legislature's work was defined in large part by Askew's vetoes—twenty-three this time, none of which was overridden. One of the most important struck down a bill he said would seriously damage the open meetings statute by allowing governmental boards to meet secretly with their attorneys to discuss pending litigation. Assistant Attorney General Sharyn Smith had urged Askew to veto the bill. The local government lobbies persisted until similar legislation was enacted in 1993.[6]

The new House had a record number of women, sixteen; there were now two in the Senate. Castor, a former teacher who had been the first female Hillsborough County commissioner, defeated Senator Julian Lane, a Barron ally, in the 1976 Democratic primary. Askew expressed concern that there were only three African Americans in the House, none in the Senate, and no Hispanics in either chamber. Florida ranked last in the South in black state and local officeholders. Black leaders who faulted the state's multi-member legislative districting found allies in the Republican Party, which had been reduced to twenty-eight seats in the House and ten in the Senate. The African Americans and the Republicans had a mutual interest in single-member districting, as they anticipated it would help them both. Askew unsuccessfully urged the 1977 session to adopt a single-member policy as the standard for the next mandatory redistricting in 1982. "It would be a return to ward politics at its worst," Brantley objected.[7]

The House was about to experience a revolution that would result in single-member districts after all. It began with a skillfully organized coup early in the 1977 session that made Representative J. Hyatt Brown the Speaker-designate to succeed Tucker. Brown, a Daytona Beach insurance executive, had collected seventy commitments from other Democrats, but some were defecting to his remaining rival, Representative Edmund Fortune of Pace. Fortune belonged to Tucker's power structure; most of its members backed him for Speaker, as did many of the special-interest lobbyists. On the afternoon of April 11 and into the night, Brown's closest supporters—a group that included Barry Kutun of Miami, George Sheldon of Plant City, Lee Moffitt of Tampa, Ralph Haben of Palmetto, Sam Bell of Daytona Beach, and Robert McKnight of Miami—quietly began collecting signatures on a petition calling for a party caucus to change the rules and allow an immediate vote to designate the next Speaker. Brown feared his support would erode before the scheduled caucus eight months later. His move was timed to coincide with an annual fish-and-oyster "redneck party" hosted by two conservative lawmakers, where it was assumed most of Fortune's supporters would be relaxed and off guard. "It was almost comical," said McKnight, "all of us in sneakers and dungarees spread out all over town gathering names in the middle of the night." By morning, Brown had the signatures of sixty-one of the ninety-two Democrats. Tucker kept his word to call a party caucus whenever a majority of Democrats demanded one. The caucus voted to designate the next Speaker immediately—sixty-one yes, thirty-one no—and Brown was chosen unanimously a few minutes later. He was now in position to enact the appointment of the Public Service Commission, an issue to which he was as committed as Askew. Moreover, his victory influenced the course of the next decade, reviving the Golden Age in the House. A year later, Brown encouraged Curt Kiser to stage a similar coup and displace the far more conservative Richard Langley as the House's next Republican leader. Kiser, who had planned to run for Congress instead, had sufficient signed pledges in hand before Langley knew what was happening. Brown's speakership began a progressive dynasty in which succeeding Speakers Haben, Mofitt, James Harold Thompson of Quincy, and Jon Mills of Gainesville had all been Brown's lieutenants during or after the coup. Haben entrusted the 1982 redistricting to Moffitt, who held public hearings that he said persuaded him to do away with all of the House's multi-member districts. Barron made a similar decision for the Senate, although his motives appeared more complex.[8]

Following Brown's example, Senator Phil Lewis quickly scheduled a Senate Democratic caucus to declare him Brantley's successor. Buddy MacKay and Barron, in rare agreement, had arranged to elect Lewis because they both trusted him to be fair. But Brantley was still the president; after the 1977 session, he fired the Natural Resources Committee's staff director, environmentalist Jim Lewis, to punish Chairman Guy Spicola of Tampa for passing a safe drinking-water bill supported by Askew and opposed by many lobbyists. When Spicola protested Lewis's dismissal, Brantley sacked him too, moving him to the least-sought chairmanship in the Senate: retirement, personnel, and claims. When Spicola complained that he didn't know "a hill of beans" about those subjects, Brantley fired him again, saying that "he wasn't a good boy." He offered the chairmanship to Castor, who refused to accept it.[9]

Advocates of the Equal Rights Amendment were optimistic that the Senate would ratify it in 1977. Democrat Don Chamberlin, a Clearwater High School history teacher, had defeated Senator Richard Deeb in a 1976 campaign that emphasized Deeb's opposition to the ERA. Jim Glisson, a former Republican who had been reelected as a Democrat from Eustis, said he would switch his vote to favor the ERA. MacKay changed his vote also; he attributed his change of position to a private meeting with women supporters who persuaded him that their legal rights in regard to divorce, inheritance, and other issues should not depend on the vagaries of various states. MacKay's switch went for naught because Pinellas Republican Henry Sayler and Democrat Ralph Poston of Miami changed their votes to oppose the ERA. Despite personal pleas from Vice-President Walter Mondale and former first lady Betty Ford, the Senate voted twenty-one to nineteen against ratification. None of the nine Republicans voted for it.[10]

The ERA was but one battle in an expanding culture war that eventually polarized the major political parties and dogged the rest of Askew's political career. Dade County enacted a civil rights ordinance prohibiting discrimination against gays and lesbians. The entertainer Anita Bryant, a former Miss America runner-up known to the public for her Citrus Commission singing commercial, "Come to the Florida Sunshine Tree," organized a referendum campaign to overturn the ordinance. Responding to a question, Askew told a news conference he would vote to repeal the ordinance if he lived in Dade. "I've never viewed the homosexual lifestyle as something that approached a constitutional right," he said, adding that "I do not want a known homosexual teaching my child." To another question, Askew replied that he would not employ a "known" homosexual on his staff, "and I don't think I have." In fact, there had been several homosexuals in his administration and in his campaigns, even if he did not know who they were. One was in the room that day. He was Dan Bradley, a lawyer serving as Askew's director of pari-mutuel regulation. "I had to loosen my collar to breathe," he said several years later. Bradley announced his homosexuality in 1982 after serving President Carter as president of the Legal Services Corporation.[11]

A coalition of straight and gay citizens led by Marshall Harris defended the ordinance, but Bryant won the 1977 referendum with 69.3 percent of the Dade vote. In Tallahassee, the legislature echoed her bias. It enacted a law against gay marriage and another to prohibit homosexuals from adopting children. There were no votes against the marriage bill in the Senate and only eleven in the House, where merely fifteen House members opposed the adoption bill. In the Senate, Chamberlin—knowing that he would lose the debate and was risking his career—pleaded that the legislation was unnecessary and contrary to the best interests of some children. "It begins a state policy—selective, deliberate discrimination. It picks the fight," Chamberlin said. His colleagues paid tribute to his courage by voting to print his speech in the *Journal of the Senate*, but only four of them—Castor, Gordon, Kenneth Myers, and Lori Wilson—voted against the bill. Chamberlin's vote contributed to his defeat for reelection in 1980. The anti-gay crusade eventually backfired on Bryant; under the political stress, her marriage dissolved and she lost her $100,000-a-year Citrus Commission contract. In 1998, Dade County enacted another anti-discrimination ordinance that survived a referendum challenge. At this writing, a district court has overturned the adoption ban.[12]

The 1977 legislature also required each university to establish a censorship board. It was a spasm of righteous indignation provoked by two events at the University of West Florida: a nude scene in a drama class presentation of the Broadway play *Equus* and a screening of the pornographic film *Deep Throat* in a class on media law. Freshman House member Bill Sadowski of Miami, who had voted against the gay adoption ban, objected that the censorship legislation overreacted "to a dumb decision made by a teacher over in the Panhandle." Askew agreed and vetoed the bill.[13]

The 1977 session was the last in the old Florida capitol, which had been enlarged in stages between 1845 and 1947. Askew and Tucker wanted it torn down upon completion of a new $45 million skyscraper capitol in 1978, arguing that the old building ruined the vista intended by the new capitol's architects. Askew considered the new building "beautiful," a view not universally shared. Howell Raines, the *St. Petersburg Times* political editor, wrote of it as proof that former governor Claude R. Kirk Jr., who had opposed the architectural plan, was not always wrong. Askew would not win on this issue; five of the six Cabinet members adopted a recommendation to keep part of the old domed capitol as it had appeared in 1923. In 1978 the legislature opted to restore the old capitol as it had appeared in 1902.[14]

In September, Askew signed his only death warrant, the first by a Florida governor since Farris Bryant in 1965. Askew refused for years to say why he had selected inmate John Spenkelink, who had killed a traveling companion whom he claimed had abused him. In a 2007 interview with the author, Askew said he thought Spenkelink merited the death penalty because he was a twice-convicted felon who was an escapee from a life sentence in California when he committed the murder. In his seminal book on the Florida death penalty, *Among the Lowest of the Dead*, David von Drehle notes that Spenkelink was the only death row inmate who had no appeal of any kind in progress at the time. Spenkelink alone had refused to join an ultimately unsuccessful class-action lawsuit challenging Florida's clemency process. He did appeal Askew's warrant, winning a series of stays before he was executed under Governor Bob Graham's warrant in 1979. When Askew signed Spenkelink's warrant, Deputy Attorney General Jim Whisenand described the governor as "distraught but not hesitant in any way." A staff member told a reporter that Askew had been having nightmares over what he perceived to be his duty. "I was bothered," Askew once said, "by picking out one as opposed to the others."[15]

Askew was now interested in an ambassadorial appointment after his term ended. During a European trade promotion trip in October 1977, he delivered a major address, which Bacchus wrote for him, at the Swiss Institute of International Studies at Zurich. "The essence of democracy is the dignity of man," Askew said, regretting that it remained "still much more of an ideal in our world than a reality." This was true, he said, "even in the most advanced of the Western democracies. America's love for freedom has sometimes seemed less compelling than America's desire for material and martial might. And America's love for democracy has sometimes been less apparent than the misguided passions some Americans have displayed for accumulating political power. . . . Yet, the outcome of Watergate is lasting evidence of the depth and the durability of democracy in America. . . . There were no tanks at Watergate. There was no coup d'état. Watergate was tragic indeed, but the tragedy ended in a triumph for American democracy."[16]

If Askew had lost the first round in the matter of an appointed Public Service Commission, he had just begun to fight. Public Service Commissioner William Bevis asked to be appointed to the new Crime Victims' Compensation Commission, where he would not have to face another election or continue to quarrel with fellow PSC member Paula Hawkins. Askew seized the opportunity to fill Bevis's vacancy with Robert T. Mann, a former legislator and appeals court judge who had become a University of Florida law professor. Askew said the choice epitomized the "quality" Floridians could expect if all PSC members were appointed. Recalling Mann's years in the legislature, Askew remarked, "If you can think of a proposal back then to reform government, Bob Mann was in on it." As a freshman legislator in 1959, Askew had often relied on Mann's example in voting on issues unfamiliar to him. Most Republican legislators still opposed the bill to appoint the PSC, which they saw as a threat to Hawkins, their only statewide officeholder. There was some truth to that. Although Askew considered her to be honest, a devoted consumer advocate, and "not under the influence of the utilities," he also thought she was overplaying her hand and endangering the electric power industry's ability to raise capital. "When you start voting against almost everything that comes before your commission, you create the image of an unfair regulatory process," Askew said.[17]

The achievements of the 1977 session were so few that some of Askew's allies thought he had lost his energy. Senator Kenneth Myers said it was "late-term-itis . . . he's sort of relaxing a little bit." In actuality, Askew was already preparing for what he anticipated would be the last great struggle of his governorship: to rid Florida of the Cabinet system. The opportunity lay in his duty to appoint a Constitution Revision Commission. In a provision unique to Florida, the 1968 constitution established the commission at prescribed intervals and gave it the power to place amendments directly on the next general election ballot. This was one of the legacies of Governor LeRoy Collins's struggles against the Pork Chop Gang in the 1950s; the initiative process was another. The commission was to meet ten years after the constitution was ratified and every twenty years thereafter. But the drafters had assumed it would be ratified in 1967; the legislature did not adjust the schedule to reflect the year's delay. That created what Askew called a "serious and perhaps irreconcilable" scheduling problem. If the commission did not meet before 1978, it would be impossible for it to put any proposals on the ballot that year. Askew sought an advisory opinion from the Florida Supreme Court that would allow him to appoint the commission in 1977. In effect, he was asking the court to rewrite the constitution. By a vote of five to two it agreed. "We must . . . look outside the document to verify the intent," the court said. Askew had thought of asking the legislature to amend the schedule but decided against it for fear that it would attack his power to appoint commission members.[18]

The court's decision delighted the governor, who took care in appointing the commission chairman and fourteen other members. Although there would be thirty-seven in all, Askew hoped to fashion a voting majority comprising his fifteen, three members chosen by the chief justice, and the attorney general, who was a member ex officio. The balance would be close; Askew assumed that the nine members chosen by the Speaker and the nine appointed by the Senate president would favor the Cabinet. Gus Craig and other conservative legislators, foreseeing that the commission would adopt proposals they disliked, attempted to amend the constitution to give the legislature the last word on commission recommendations. Although seventy House members were listed as sponsors, Askew's lobbying yielded a majority of votes against the amendment. Even so, the debate revealed that many contemporary legislators were no different from the Pork Choppers in their mistrust of the voters. A motion in the House to abolish the revision commission failed by only six votes, fifty-two to fifty-eight. It would not be the last attempt.[19]

Askew's appointees were a who's who of the Golden Age, including Sandy D'Alemberte as chairman; Askew's acknowledged role model, Collins, who had asked for the assignment; Askew's 1970 rival John E. Mathews Jr.; former House minority leader Don Reed; environmentalist Nathaniel Reed; Jon Moyle, Askew's close friend and former Democratic Party chairman; John DeGrove, the professor who had helped to fashion Askew's water-management and land-use legislation; Jan Platt, a crusading member of the Tampa City Council; and two African Americans, Secretary of State Jesse McCrary and Freddie Grooms, a professor. Tucker appointed, among others, his cousin the retired justice B. K. Roberts; House Republican leader Bill James; and W. Dexter Douglass, a Tallahassee attorney who would chair another revision commission twenty years later. Chief Justice Ben F. Overton appointed himself and two other judges, one of whom, Tom Barkdull of the Third District Court of Appeal, had been a member of the first revision commission in the 1960s. In 1997, Barkdull would become the only person to have served on all three commissions. Brantley's appointments included himself and Barron, whose strategy to save the Cabinet would ultimately contribute to defeating the commission's entire agenda.

23

TRIUMPH AND TRAGEDY (1978)

"There's six of them and one of me," Reubin Askew complained to the Constitution Revision Commission at a public hearing in September 1977. He was speaking of Florida's elected Cabinet, which he had defended when he served in the Florida Senate. Less than a decade later, Askew as governor wanted to rid Florida of the Cabinet or reduce it to a fragment. Now that Florida had a strong, activist legislature, he said, it no longer needed the Cabinet to keep watch on the governors. Rather, it was the Cabinet that bore watching. Askew said it had become the tool of powerful legislators and lobbyists, as well as a "committee of competitors," two of whom were running for governor. He found it inefficient, unaccountable to the voters, and guilty of "posturing and political melodrama at the expense of the people." The office of governor, Askew said, "is a victim of Florida's past at a time when Florida needs a vision of the future." As if to confirm his opinion of the Cabinet's true constituency, thirty-five of Florida's most influential lobbyists met in Tallahassee in January 1978 to strategize how to save the Cabinet from the revision commission. "I tell you my damn board room was packed. Everything that operates for profit in the State of Florida was there," said Jon L. Shebel, president of Associated Industries.[1]

Askew had debated with his staff whether to propose abolishing all six Cabinet offices or consolidating them into two, thinking the latter was more likely to succeed. The staff persuaded him to reserve the so-called mini-Cabinet for a fallback position. Senator Dempsey Barron, a member of the commission, had anticipated just such a compromise, which he opposed because he assumed, as Askew did, that the voters would approve it. Barron's strategy to save the Cabinet was to give the voters only an all-or-nothing choice. He struck a private bargain with Sandy D'Alemberte, the commission chairman, to put abolition—but nothing less—on the 1978 ballot. Although D'Alemberte suspected Barron's motives, he felt that he had to take the chance; at the time, he was not sure whether there were enough votes among the thirty-seven commissioners to advance any Cabinet proposal that Barron did not support. On a test vote, twenty-five members opposed a mini-Cabinet and favored abolition. Barron, Senate president Lew Brantley and retired justice B. K. Roberts were among them, which made the strategy transparent. For the moment, Askew's allies on the commission chose not to see it. They envisioned a replay of the 1971 corporate tax referendum in which Askew would triumph once again.[2]

The more Askew thought about it, the more he doubted the outcome of an all-or-nothing choice. With his encouragement, former governor LeRoy Collins and House minority leader Bill James formally proposed a mini-Cabinet compromise. They expected twenty-two votes, but it failed with only eighteen, one short of a majority. D'Alemberte, true to his secret deal with Barron, abstained from casting the nineteenth vote. "I told you that I intended to support the will of the commission, but I also wanted a substantial majority," he said. In the governor's office afterward, D'Alemberte revealed the real reason to Askew and Jon Moyle. They were astounded and furious, but they did not betray D'Alemberte's confidence. Meanwhile, the St. Petersburg Times reported that Barron and Brantley had turned around the votes of three commissioners who had promised Askew they would support the mini-Cabinet. They were a teachers union representative who feared for her job, a trial lawyer sensitive to Barron's threat to prohibit damage awards for pain and suffering, and a Winn-Dixie board member whose son worked for Brantley on the Senate staff. Former House minority leader Don Reed was so disillusioned with the results of his nine months of service on the commission that he attempted to abolish it. He saw that it was as susceptible to lobbying as the legislature.[3]

Lobbyists had been notably effective in fashioning the commission's seventh proposed revision, which dealt with taxes. D'Alemberte admitted that it would make the tax structure "vastly worse," and Askew denounced it strongly. It contained provisions to erode the corporate profits tax and restore $9 million a year in real estate tax exemptions to the Daytona International Speedway, airport restaurants, and other businesses operating for profit on leased government property. In the legislature, Senator Buddy MacKay and Representative Carl Ogden, among others, had fought for years to put such commercial leaseholds on the tax rolls.[4]

Although the odds had lengthened, it still seemed possible for Askew to save the revisions he supported. He would have to take a campaign to the people, as many expected him to do. In February, *St. Petersburg Times* political editor Howell Raines and staff writer Rob Hooker had published a long article critical of Askew's second-term record. They asked whether "Reubin the Bold" had been replaced by "Reubin the Reluctant, the puzzling and remote figure of the second term." They predicted, however, that Askew would assert himself in the constitutional revision process. But Askew was now being distracted by something he detested even more than the Cabinet: casino gambling.[5]

Following Askew's Sunshine Amendment example, south Florida hotel interests organized an initiative campaign to authorize casinos at Miami Beach and along the Broward County coast. Askew turned nearly his full attention to fighting what he considered to be a profound threat to Florida. He cited organized crime, loan sharking, prostitution, drugs, violent crime, fraud, and embezzlement as evils that "seem to swirl around the casino gambling community like moths around a light." No one should believe, he said, that casinos could be "confined to one little corner of the state."[6]

The casino initiative was on his mind in early January when he appointed Janet Reno to replace retiring Dade County state attorney Richard Gerstein. Reno, thirty-nine, a former assistant to Gerstein, became not only Florida's first female chief prosecutor but also the head of the South's largest prosecutorial staff. In 1993, President Bill Clinton appointed her attorney general of the United States. In selecting Reno, Askew once again was his own man. Gerstein had recommended Edward Carhart, his chief assistant; so had the Dade County Grand Jury and even Reno herself. Askew, who was characteristically oblivious to double meaning, told a news conference he decided on Reno because "she stacks up better." Reno was also the candidate whom he knew best; she had been a key figure in the 1972 judicial reform. Although they talked for nearly an hour on the telephone before he got around to offering her the position, Askew said he asked for only two commitments: that she would seek election in the fall and that she would oppose casinos. In March, Askew made his fourth supreme court appointment, choosing James Alderman, a circuit judge from Fort Pierce, to succeed Fred Karl, who resigned for financial reasons after barely a year in office.[7]

Askew's uncompromising morality influenced his refusal to accept the resignation of Circuit Judge Samuel S. Smith of Lake City, who had been convicted in federal court of conspiring to sell fifteen hundred pounds of marijuana that were being held as evidence. To prevent Smith from collecting his $22,000-a-year pension, Askew insisted on Smith's removal through the impeachment process. Smith became the first Florida official to be convicted in a Senate trial.[8]

In late February 1978, Askew left on a trade development trip to Japan and Hong Kong with a delegation of Florida business leaders. Comptroller Gerald Lewis joined the party. Soon after, Lewis's auditors began to scour the travel vouchers of the Commerce Department and the governor's own staff. Lewis was determined to show voters the value of an independently elected Cabinet. He made issues of Askew's $456-a-night hotel bill for three nights in Osaka, the first-class airfares that had been purchased for the governor's party, and an expensive luncheon that only the Florida businessmen had attended. Askew replied that he had tried to minimize expenses by dining in his room one evening on boiled grits and mushroom soup that his security guard had brought from Florida. Lewis, he remarked, had asked to go on the trip and "seemed to enjoy" it. Although Lewis won the publicity war, it did not constitute a major scandal. A Senate inquiry found only $7,628 in questionable expenses. State Attorney Harry Morrison declined to prosecute anyone. It did cost the jobs of several Commerce Department employees and gubernatorial aide Doug Sessions. Sessions volunteered his resignation after Lewis's auditors reported that he had billed the state for a complimentary hotel room at a governors' conference several years before. "If it hadn't been for the governor-Cabinet issue, they wouldn't have been looking," Sessions said.[9]

The last of Askew's speeches to a joint session of the legislature was the longest of them all. It was as much a valedictory as a recitation of the business he still wanted to finish, including appointment of the Public Service Commission and establishment of a state holiday on the birthday of Dr. Martin Luther King Jr. In the decade since reapportionment, Askew said, "we have literally reshaped the face of state government. I think we can say that no one will ever again have to run as fast as we ran in this decade, because hopefully we have insured that never again will state government be allowed to fall so far behind."[10] That assessment was too optimistic. For all that had been done to modernize Florida, one fundamental weakness remained. Even with the addition of Askew's corporate income tax, the revenue base was still inadequate. There had been no proposal to repeal the prohibition on taxing personal income and only one brief, unsuccessful attempt by the House to apply the sales tax to personal and professional services. The state continued to depend on taxes on merchandise and to be vulnerable to recessions.

As the regular session drew to a close, the Senate, having accomplished next to nothing, made a point of swiftly reinstating Franklin County sheriff Jack Taylor, whom Askew had suspended for allowing jail inmates to drink and go on fishing trips in county vehicles. The Senate's hearing officer, D. Stephen Kahn, confirmed that Taylor "runs and ran a loose jail" but advised that nothing was "sufficiently wrongful" to justify the sheriff's ouster. The Senate agreed by a vote of thirty-three to five. Dempsey Barron led the sheriff's defense in a debate memorable for Jack Gordon's quip that "I'm in favor of pilot programs. I think the state of Florida deserves at least one jolly jail." Senator Buddy MacKay, who voted to remove Taylor, heard from Senator Pat Thomas that when a trooper stopped a county truck to find it full of fish and inebriated inmates, the excursion "might have" had to do with a fish fry in Barron's honor.[11]

The regular session's thin record was eclipsed by the stunning results of an ensuing two-day special session. Askew and Representative Hyatt Brown, exerting his influence as Speaker-designate, succeeded in making the Public Service Commission appointive. The outcome humiliated Brantley, who had promised the trucking lobby that the bill would not pass. Askew also obtained legislation intended to preserve the state's claim to hundreds of thousands of acres of so-called sovereignty land, so named because it was under navigable water when Florida attained statehood in 1845. Public ownership was in jeopardy because of a split Florida Supreme Court decision interpreting an arcane 1963 law on land titles. The phosphate lobby opposed Askew on that issue; during the regular session it had managed to block corrective legislation by Representative Sam Bell, which Askew cited as the sole reason for calling a special session. Out of sight, Askew, Brown, Barron, Bell, Speaker Donald L. Tucker, and W. D. Childers, a Democratic senator from Pensacola, were negotiating for much more. The complex deal included some $15 million in tax exemptions for north Florida paper mills and chemical plants, which were important to Barron and Childers; a bill intended to reduce workers' compensation benefits and employers' insurance premiums, which Brantley wanted to pass to help his campaign for mayor of Jacksonville; legislation establishing a nonbinding state comprehensive plan, which mattered greatly to Askew; and a one-year delay in the implementation of a law codifying Florida's evidence rules, which was Barron's personal issue of the moment. As the *Miami Herald*'s Robert Shaw unraveled the events, all of that legislation had been blocked at the close of the regular session because of Brantley's pledge to the trucking lobby, which was happy with the PSC as it was. In the clandestine negotiations, Barron and two other senators who had opposed the PSC bill agreed to change their votes in exchange for the tax breaks. They misled Brantley into allowing a roll call that he thought would kill the PSC bill. Instead, it passed. After the session, Askew and Barron stood arm in arm beaming for photographers. "You know, Reubin," Barron said, "we're the last of the Pork Choppers." Askew agreed. Brantley could only smile wanly. (He lost the mayor's race.)[12]

Askew and Brown needed Representative George Sheldon's support for the deal because he had sustained Askew's veto of a bill repealing the evidence code. Sheldon's price for postponing the code for a year was passage of his bill to repair a nursing home rating system that the Florida Supreme Court had overturned.[13]

Askew described the PSC bill as one of his toughest and most gratifying victories. He said it would "take the complex and technical and controversial issue of establishing utility rates out of the hands of politicians and put it into the hands of competent, qualified individuals." All the same, utility lobbyists retained a strong if indirect influence through the legislature. The bill established a nine-member council, appointed by the Senate president and House Speaker, to nominate candidates for appointment to the new PSC. Brantley's first appointments included the past president of the Florida trucking lobby. He also appointed Childers, who voted for himself as chairman to keep Representative Curt Kiser's hands off the gavel. The council immediately fought Askew by voting to send him names only for the two new seats created by the bill. It reserved the three PSC incumbents or their replacements for the next governor. To one of the new seats Askew appointed Joe Cresse, his budget director, who had helped persuade him of the wisdom of appointing the PSC. It was a popular choice among legislators, who admired Cresse's grasp of economics. A few months later, the nominating council left incumbent commissioner Robert Mann off its interview list. It was an apparent reprisal for his vote to dismiss the PSC's influential general counsel, whom Mann and Paula Hawkins accused of whitewashing an investigation of a fuel overcharge conspiracy involving Florida Power Corporation. Childers's Pensacola haberdasher was among the candidates the council considered preferable to Mann. Under blistering criticism from the media, the commission restored Mann to the list. Governor Bob Graham reappointed him and he served two more years, helping to win a $6 million refund to consumers for the Florida Power scandal. Meanwhile, the legislature's joint auditing committee chose Jack Shreve, a former representative, for the public counsel's job, in which there had been a rapid turnover. Shreve remained until his retirement twenty-five years later. His presentations to the PSC won more than $6 billion in rate reductions and refunds for utility consumers. (In 2010, a nominating council dominated by pro-industry legislators refused to renominate four of the five PSC members who had recently rejected the largest electric rate increases ever sought in Florida.)[14]

Other successes from the 1978 session, as gauged by Askew and his allies, included bills converting the Board of Business regulation into a panel concerned only with pari-mutuel issues, carving a new

Department of Labor out of the Department of Commerce, requiring the parole commission to open its meetings and set presumptive release dates for eligible prisoners, and establishing the Martin Luther King Jr. holiday. His notable vetoes included a bill to limit judges' discretion in sentencing; Askew objected to "equal penalties for unequal offenses." None of his twenty-three vetoes was overridden.[15]

Askew's last months in office, which he spent opposing casinos, would become as intense as his first had been. The pro-casino campaign was in the hands of a professional manager, Sanford Weiner, an undefeated veteran of many California initiatives and of the 1976 New Jersey campaign to authorize casinos at Atlantic City. Florida casino promoters had not bothered with the legislature because they knew Askew would veto any gambling bill and make the veto stick. Constitutional amendments, on the other hand, are not subject to a veto. Operating under the slogan "Let's Help Florida," Weiner brought paid signature solicitors into Florida for the first time. The petition earmarked casino revenue for education and law enforcement. It was a deceptive promise in that it did not guarantee an overall spending increase for either purpose, but the Florida Education Association, a teachers union, took the bait and endorsed casinos as "the only game in town." Askew assumed Weiner would succeed in gathering 256,000 signatures to make the 1978 ballot, and he knew that early voter sentiment favored the initiative. Askew anticipated having to decide whether it would be more important to defeat casinos than to campaign for the revision commission's constitutional proposals. He said that if the casino initiative qualified for the ballot, it would command his attention.[16]

The campaign took an expensive turn when a federal judge, ruling in Weiner's favor, said Florida could not apply its $3,000-per-person political contribution limit to referendum campaigns. Hotel and gambling companies now could stake Weiner to as much as he needed to pay his signature solicitors. (An appeals court upheld the decision two years later.) Two could play that game, of course; in his turn, Askew solicited contributions of $25,000 or more from selected allies. They included the Walt Disney Corporation, which considered gambling incompatible with its image. Much more controversially, eight of the state's newspapers, including the *St. Petersburg Times* and the *Miami Herald*, staked Askew to $150,000 at a time when he had raised no significant funds elsewhere. Although the publishers and senior editors insisted that the contributions would not affect news coverage, many of their rank-and-file journalists were indignant. "I think it is very regrettable that we have let them make an issue of the credibility of the *Miami Herald*," said reporter Patrick Riordan. The National News Council subsequently dismissed a complaint against the *Herald*, finding that its news coverage had not been affected, but it criticized the contributions for jeopardizing public confidence in the media. The ten daily and weekly newspapers owned by *The New York Times* and the Gannett Corporation's three Florida dailies refused to contribute despite personal appeals from the governor to their top executives. In October, Gannett's *Pensacola News-Journal*, Askew's hometown newspaper, became the only major daily to endorse the casino initiative. Its editorial said that casino gambling was necessary "to guarantee the health of Miami Beach." Gannett president Allen H. Neuharth had other issues with Askew, who had passed over his wife, Senator Lori Wilson, for lieutenant governor in 1974. In February 1978, Neuharth delivered a speech to the Economics Club of Tallahassee in which he said that Florida had fallen "tragically behind" other Sun Belt states in search of new industry because of the "lethargy and naiveté of the Askew administration."[17]

The casino initiative qualified for the ballot with 286,165 valid signatures, some 30,000 more than the minimum. Press secretary Paul Schnitt said Askew would "organize the state like it's never been organized before." Although Askew gave most of his attention to the "No Casinos" campaign, he also established a campaign committee in support of the revision commission's eight ballot amendments. But he admitted that the latter effort would be "low-key." Two other anti-casino committees, one financed primarily by pari-mutuels fearful of competition for gambling dollars, also got into the fight. The opposing committees were able to match the casino promoters' advertising spending nearly dollar for dollar. Askew's attacks were unsparing, his language apocalyptic. "Casinos," he said, "are made-to-order fishing grounds for the loan shark." Florida would become like Las Vegas, "an around-the-clock town." He said he could not recall "a time in recent history when the future of the state lay at such a decisive crossroads."

If we take the wrong road and admit casinos to Florida, we will wake up one day to discover that they have infiltrated the politics and lifestyle of this state and have spread their influence to every corner of Florida. Casinos are an invitation to the further expansion of crime at a time when we are fighting to contain crime.... If we do not stop casino gambling now, I firmly believe we will soon have casinos and slot machines from Key West to Pensacola. We will have totally changed the character of this state, and we will have totally lost and reversed the momentum that we have been building for economic development.

Askew was determined to do more than defeat that particular initiative. He wanted to do it soundly enough to inhibit any more attempts in the near future. "He's truly acting like his life is at an end over this issue," Weiner complained.[18]

Askew was in the awkward position of campaigning fiercely against one referendum issue at the same time he was encouraging a yes vote on seven of the eight proposals from the revision commission. Jim Krog, newly detached from the governor's staff to manage No Casinos Inc., devised an alliterative slogan, "No on Nine," that voters easily could mistake to mean no on *all* nine. Steve Uhlfelder, D'Alemberte's former staff director now on the governor's payroll, warned Askew that the intense negativism of his anti-casino campaign would backfire on the amendments he supported. Askew told him that he considered the casino issue more important than anything else. He did not say so publicly, but he acted as if revision had been a lost cause since the defeat of the mini-Cabinet compromise. Two months before the election, a Hamilton poll confirmed Askew's assessment. Only 16 percent of the voters favored doing away with the Cabinet. The polls showed that the tide had turned in Askew's favor on casinos. Let's Help Florida began publishing full-page advertisements claiming that casinos would "hold the line on taxes," triple tourist visits to the state, and add more than $800 million in new payrolls. Two days after Askew spoke against casinos at the state AFL-CIO convention, union delegates heard a pro-casino research firm forecast 89,000 new jobs and then voted to endorse the initiative.[19]

The revision commission had packaged eighty-seven distinct changes into its eight ballot proposals. Most were in Revision 1, which included guarantees of individual privacy and access to public meetings and documents, required judges to favor pretrial release without money bail, and limited Cabinet members to two terms. Revision 2 was a state equal rights amendment. Revision 3, which the commission adopted with surprisingly little discussion, called for single-member legislative districts, a nonpartisan commission for legislative and congressional redistricting, and a ban on gerrymandering designed to favor parties or incumbents. Revision 4, the most controversial, abolished the elected Cabinet. Revision 5 put the appointed Public Service Commission into the constitution, which Askew considered unnecessary. Revision 6, another that had cleared the commission with surprising ease, called for appointment and merit retention of the trial courts in the same manner as the appellate bench. Askew forcefully opposed Revision 7 because of the commission's tax breaks for special interests. Revision 8 created an appointed board of education in place of the Cabinet and gave constitutional status to the existing Board of Regents.[20]

It was the casino issue, Amendment 9, that preoccupied Askew and dominated media coverage of the campaign. His last hope for keeping it off the ballot was dashed in mid-October when the Florida Supreme Court rejected an appeal from the pari-mutuels. The court ruled six to one that the initiative did not violate the one-subject rule even though it both authorized casinos and earmarked revenue. The opinion cited as precedent the court's 1976 decision in favor of Askew's Sunshine Amendment. The court eventually abandoned both precedents.[21]

Askew's campaign alliance with the racetracks underscored the casino lobby's argument that Florida had long since lost its virginity with respect to gambling. The 1931 legislature had authorized pari-mutuel wagering over Governor Doyle Carlton's veto. By 1978 there were thirty-eight horse tracks, dog tracks, and jai alai frontons generating nearly as much tax revenue as Nevada's 1,258 licensed casinos. Askew maintained that pari-mutuels were significantly different from casinos in that they had no stake in the wagers. Casino gamblers bet against the house, but pari-mutuel patrons bet against each other; the racetrack's share and the state's tax come off the top. To the casino supporters and at least some voters, it was a distinction without a difference. Remarking on Askew's plans to join a prominent Miami law firm in 1979, Tallahassee attorney Richard McFarlain, a casino supporter, visualized the former governor in his skyscraper office "looking out at Hialeah horse track, Gulfstream horse track, Biscayne Kennel Club, Flagler Kennel Club, the jai alai, the bingo games, and twenty-five Mafia families, and saying 'I have saved you.'" To Askew, it *was* a matter of salvation—minus the sarcasm. "Before you know it, they'll be asking for legalized prostitution," he said at Gainesville as he began a thirteen-city campaign tour in mid-October.[22]

Askew was on the road when he received word that his brother John, who had been in and out of hospitals with complications from alcoholism, had died at Houston. He continued the campaign until funeral arrangements were complete. Six days before the election, he told the press he would campaign against casinos forever.[23]

On November 7 it appeared that he would never have to. In a statewide landslide for Askew, the voters rejected the casino initiative, 71.4 percent no to 28.6 percent yes. It failed even in Dade County and lost elsewhere by margins of up to four to one. The 2.4 million who voted on the issue were nearly as many as voted in the race for governor.

But the revision commission's amendments all failed also. The margins varied from 50.9 percent against the reapportionment proposal to 74.9 percent against abolition of the Cabinet, which had drawn the most hostile advertising. Business interests, teachers, and professions had contributed $110,000 to Save Your Vote Inc., the pro-Cabinet committee. D'Alemberte said Askew's anti-casino campaign had "brought out voters who were inclined to vote no on anything that had to do with changing the constitution." Had the Ten Commandments been on the ballot, said Curt Kiser, "they would have failed too." No county voted to abolish the Cabinet or in favor of an appointed board of education. Only Volusia supported the appointed PSC. The proposed state equal rights provision had been seen as a test vote on the federal amendment, and its failure in all but five counties, 56.9 percent voting no overall, discouraged Askew from submitting ratification of the federal ERA to a post-election special session.[24]

Although most Florida governors had kept their hands off the election of their successors, Askew announced just before the 1978 primary that he had cast an absentee ballot for his lieutenant governor, Jim Williams. The endorsement came too late to do much good for Williams, who had been desperate to receive it. In private, earlier, Askew had helped persuade Betty Castor to give up her Senate seat to be Williams's running mate. Like Askew in 1970, Williams had been in danger of having to quit the race for lack of a well-known lieutenant governor candidate. Former House Speaker Terrell Sessums had declined, but he recommended Castor and encouraged her to accept. Williams, whom a reporter described as "the candidate of blunt consistency," was characteristically unwilling to make bold promises or run a flashy campaign. The Williams-Castor ticket finished fifth with 12 percent in a field of seven Democratic primary candidates. Even so, they doubled the vote for Claude Kirk, running as a Democrat this time, who had enlisted Tom Adams as his campaign manager. Attorney General Robert Shevin led the gubernatorial primary with 35 percent to Senator Bob Graham's 25.2 percent. Graham had overcome slight name recognition and his reputation as a child of privilege with a series of well-publicized blue-collar "work days" that were as effective as Lawton Chiles's long march of 1970. The media might ignore or barely mention the candidates' speeches, but it seldom failed to cover Graham as the Harvard law school graduate toiled in a laundry or bagged groceries. An iconic campaign poster pictured him sweating over a felled log during his day as a lumberjack. He won the runoff with 53.5 percent of the vote. In November, Graham and running mate Wayne Mixson, a conservative state senator from Marianna, defeated Republicans Jack Eckerd and Paula Hawkins with 55.6 percent of the vote.[25]

When the new legislature met in November to organize, Barron spoke from the Senate floor in praise of Askew. "I want to congratulate you, Rube, on a good job for a kid from Pensacola who used to sell newspapers on the street," he said. A few days later, Askew watched bemused as reporters waiting outside the Cabinet room pounced on the governor-elect rather than on him. "Thank goodness for small favors," Askew said. But his work as governor was not done. In November the Florida Supreme Court unanimously overturned the decision of the governor and Cabinet designating the Florida Keys and the Green Swamp as areas of critical state concern. The court ruled that the legislature had unconstitutionally delegated the authority. Former representative Murray Dubbin, who had co-sponsored the law when he was rules chairman in the House, represented landowners challenging the act. "We could have done it better," he said. During a special session that Askew called on December 6, the legislature restored the environmental protections—but only for a year. It extended them again during its 1979 regular session.[26]

At the age of fifty, after eight years as governor and twenty in public service, Askew confided to his friend Robert Strauss, President Carter's trade representative, that he was virtually broke. He had a daughter about to start college and a son still in high school. He had assumed financial responsibility for his mother and mother-in-law, both of whom were in poor health, and for the mortgage on his mother's home. He had only $14,465 in cash. David Levin offered to meet anyone else's offer to entice Askew back into his law firm, but Askew now had higher ambitions. He followed Strauss's advice to look for a large Florida partnership that would pay him handsomely and indulge his absence if he went to Washington. Through an intermediary, Askew found his new niche at Miami in the South's fastest-growing law firm, which would be renamed Greenberg Traurig Askew Hoggman Kipff Quentel and Wolf. It came with a compensation package of more than $300,000 a year and a rented luxury condominium on Key Biscayne. Partner Melvin Greenberg reminded Askew that he had refused to see him in the governor's office even though he had been one of Askew's first $1,000 contributors in 1970. At the time, Askew explained, the state was investigating one of the firm's clients. "I think almost anybody else would have seen me except you," said Greenberg. "My contribution," Askew said of Greenberg Traurig years later, "was to tell the law firm whom they shouldn't represent." The firm also made a place for Askew's protégé Jim Bacchus, who was about to graduate from law school. He turned out to be the better investment. Long after Askew had left, Bacchus returned to be co-chair of the firm's international division.[27]

In a short farewell speech at Graham's inauguration, Askew said his last day in office was "bright and happy." He was still elated by the magnitude of his victory over casino gambling; he felt "as if I had won re-election without the necessity of serving another term." He talked about the Sunshine Amendment and about the larger purposes he had tried to serve. "The fundamental obligation of political leadership is to lead. It is not enough simply to respond to opinion polls. . . . Mankind has a stewardship to serve on this planet. We serve our God and our destiny by serving one another, not for glory, or for gain, but because our faith tells us that such service is part of our deepest reason for being."[28]

The first Florida governor to serve two consecutive terms had concluded them with a spectacular victory. But unlike the campaigns for the corporate tax, court reform, and the Sunshine Amendment, Askew's anti-gambling crusade had simply preserved the status quo. It did so at a heavy cost: the defeat of constitutional amendments that would have moved Florida forward. Although he expressed regret for the defeat of the revisions he favored, particularly merit selection of judges, Askew never second-guessed his strategic decision. There would be other opportunities to improve the constitution; casinos, he said, would "forever change the perception of Florida as a serious place for investment."[29]

Florida eventually did adopt more than 40 percent of the revision commission's proposals. Among them were a personal privacy amendment that Barron sponsored in 1980; amendments in 1992 to guarantee public records and open meetings and to limit Cabinet members to two terms; and a mini-Cabinet and an appointed board of education proposed by the revision commission of 1998. An initiative organized by Bob Graham in 2002 created a university system board of governors to replace the Board of Regents, which Governor Jeb Bush and the legislature had abolished in 2001. The new board's authority remains unsettled at this writing.[30]

For two of the commission's most important revisions, however, 1978 was an opportunity that evaded recapture. The redistricting amendment, that failed by only 130,647 votes, left the present-day legislature vulnerable to the partisan gerrymandering and polarized politics for which it compares so poorly to the legislatures of the Golden Age. In 2010, however, voters approved initiatives to apply anti-gerrymandering standards to leglislative and congressional districts, but it will be up to the courts to enforce them. The amendment to appoint all judges came within a single percentage point of passing, failing by only 37,182 votes. In 1998 the next revision commission was able to agree only on a local-option version of merit selection. The voters approved that, but when they were asked two years later to exercise the choice, every circuit and every county voted by enormous margins to continue electing judges. By the end of the twentieth century, right-wing and pseudo-populist commentators on talk radio, cable television, and the internet had fomented a nationwide backlash against the judiciary. Some campaigns for circuit judge have become as expensive as races for the legislature. The Florida Supreme Court has had to discipline and even remove judges for unethical campaigns that violated the Code of Judicial Conduct.[31]

A question for historians is whether Askew's victory over gambling was worth the other consequences. The answer would be clearer had the 1978 referendum put a stake through the heart of the gambling industry. But the gambling lobby refused to take no for an answer and produced more casino initiatives in 1986 and 1994. They were defeated, but by noticeably declining margins. The pari-mutuels, suffering from declining attendance, successfully sponsored a 2004 initiative allowing slot machines at racetracks in Broward and Dade counties, subject to local referendums. Although the initiative failed in fifty counties, it passed statewide with 50.8 percent of the vote. Jeb Bush, the governor at the time, opposed it, but he did not campaign against it as Askew had in 1978. By then, there was gambling within commuting distance of every Floridian. The legislature had authorized thirty-one remaining pari-mutuels to simulcast races from other venues and to operate card rooms with progressively higher stakes. Voters overwhelmingly approved a lottery initiative in the same 1986 election that defeated casinos for the second time, and tickets went on sale at nearly every convenience store. Seventeen "cruises to nowhere"—casino ships immune from state regulation and taxation while on international waters—sailed from every major Florida port except those in the Panhandle, where they would have to compete with casinos in nearby Biloxi, Mississippi. Capitalizing on its sovereignty and on the federal Indian Gaming Act, the Seminole Tribe was operating slot machines and card rooms at seven of its reservations. Governors Chiles and Bush rebuffed the tribe's request for a compact that would allow full-scale casinos, but in 2010 Governor Charlie Crist signed a $1 billion compact, negotiated by him and approved by the legislature, that guarantees the Seminoles exclusive rights for five years to operate blackjack and other house-banked card games at five of their reservations. It also gives the tribe a twenty-year franchise to operate Vegas-style slot machines. Competing racetracks were appeased with lower tax rates and, for their card rooms, unlimited stakes and expanded hours.[32]

24

EIGHT YEARS TOO LATE
(1976–1984)

We must take the current when it serves,
Or lose our ventures

—William Shakespeare, *Julius Caesar*, act 4, scene 3

Long after he was out of politics, Reubin Askew met an admirer who told him it was a pity that he had not run for president. "It was," he replied, "the best-kept secret of 1984." Or so it had seemed when the votes were counted. The wry humor aside, the national media had not ignored his three-year campaign for the Democratic nomination. The problem was that much of the coverage was hurtful. There was a condescending, almost mocking tone, depicting him as a Don Quixote who might attain, at best, only the vice-presidency. To potential campaign contributors and voters, it was the equivalent of a "sell" message from a stockbroker. Askew was forced out of the race even before the presidential primary in Florida, the state that had twice elected him governor.[1]

Askew would have had a better reception in 1976, when there were influential people urging him to run. They included Senate majority leader Mike Mansfield, Democratic National Committee chairman Robert Strauss, and former first lady Lady Bird Johnson. Andrew Young, the Georgia congressman and disciple of Dr. Martin Luther King Jr., remarked to journalists that he was advising his friends to support Georgia governor Jimmy Carter "unless Reubin Askew gets in the race." Askew enjoyed the respect of national journalists such as the *Washington Post*'s David Broder and Godfrey Sperling of the *Christian Science*

Monitor, both of whom wrote of him as a leading potential candidate. If Askew did not lack for encouragement from others, he could not find it in himself. He did not believe he was capable of winning the presidency or performing the duties of the office. When he finally concluded that he did have that "right stuff," it was eight years too late.[2]

So Askew left it to Jimmy Carter to catch the electoral tide that would carry a southern politician to the White House for the first time since the Civil War.[3]

Carter sensed that the Watergate scandals had cast a pall over all Washington politicians, creating an opportunity for an outsider to promise reforms. Carter understood also that for him to defeat George Wallace in a major southern primary would establish his credentials with moderates and liberals nationwide. Although Askew could have entered the 1976 race on the same terms and with more support than Carter had at the outset, he did not believe he was ready.[4]

Askew steadfastly rebuffed everyone who tried to persuade him otherwise. Before signing up with Carter, pollster Pat Caddell had met with Damon Holmes and two other Askew aides in Washington to make a case for Askew's candidacy. Askew's response was fast and final: "I'm not only closing the door, I'm slamming it," he said. On Labor Day of 1975, David Levin went to the governor's mansion to plead with his former law partner that he was needed in the White House. Levin had used the same approach when Askew was reluctant to seek a second term as governor. This time, though, it did not work. "David," Askew said, "if you love me, you won't ask me to run."[5] Carter, too, had been skeptical of his own potential. But as Senators Edmund Muskie, George McGovern, Hubert Humphrey, and Henry Jackson paid courtesy calls to Atlanta during their campaigns for the 1972 Democratic nomination, Carter took their measure and decided that "I knew as much as they did." He began to prepare his 1976 campaign while McGovern was still running against President Richard Nixon, even though he and his closest aides knew that what they had in mind was audacious. "The first time we talked about it, it was embarrassing," said his chief of staff, Hamilton Jordan. Soon after, at the 1972 meeting of the Southern Governors Conference, Carter lunched with Askew aides Jim Apthorp and Bernie Parrish and tried to recruit them to run his 1976 campaign in Florida. They declined.

It struck Parrish as "the most foolish thing we've ever heard." They did not think Carter could win Florida, much less the presidency.[6]

As Carter's intentions became apparent, the news media wrote that he and Askew might be rivals for the nomination. Events at the 1973 meeting of the Southern Governors Conference spiced the speculation. Askew was seeking the vice-chairmanship, which would make him chairman a year later, but Carter supported Dolph Briscoe of Texas. The media interpreted it as an attempt by Carter to edge Askew out of the "New South" limelight. What seems to have happened was that when Carter endorsed Briscoe he did not know that his staff had promised his support to Askew. Briscoe put out the fire by withdrawing in Askew's favor, but the two staffs continued to be wary of each other. Carter's aides confided to the Atlanta press corps that their greatest fear was of Askew entering the presidential race.[7]

Carter's strategy concentrated on shedding his underdog image by winning Florida's primary, which he did on March 9, 1976, with 34 percent to 32 for George Wallace and 10 for Senator Henry Jackson. Nine other candidates—none of whom had campaigned in Florida—split the rest. From that day forward, Carter was the front-runner for the nomination. His victory over Arizona representative Morris Udall in Wisconsin four weeks later was narrow, but it fatally wounded the campaign of his only liberal competitor. "I watched Carter doing what I knew Askew could do," said Jim Bacchus, who had turned down an offer to join Carter's campaign press staff.[8]

Askew endorsed no one in the Florida primary. Five weeks later, and only twenty-two minutes before the deadline, he went to the Florida Democratic Party headquarters to register as a convention delegate for Jackson, who was still contesting Carter in other primaries. Upon being asked for his reaction, Carter could not hide his irritation. "I think it's about time he made up his mind," Carter said. By then, Carter was all but assured of the nomination, and in one sense he had Askew to thank for it. Had Askew been a candidate, Carter could not have won the Florida primary. Had Askew declared his preference for Jackson before the Florida primary, it could have cost Carter enough votes to give Wallace the plurality. Askew accepted the inevitable and endorsed Carter after he had won eighteen of thirty primaries, including Texas and Ohio, and Jackson and Wallace had conceded.[9]

Carter's election as president overcame whatever resentment he may have had toward Askew. Had he wanted to, Askew could have joined the new administration. Preferring to finish his term, he turned down an inquiry about heading the FBI. Upon completing his term in Tallahassee, Askew finally was interested in national politics. He looked for an influential position, such as an ambassadorship, that would give him the foreign-policy credentials he lacked. Robert Strauss, who was about to become the president's special Middle East envoy, recommended Askew to succeed him as U.S. trade representative. "You're my ticket out of this job," he told Askew, warning him that it was the toughest "but most interesting" assignment in Washington. By then, Askew had gathered the self-confidence he needed to run for president; Carter's success may well have contributed to that. Askew even alluded to a possible candidacy in his farewell Tallahassee press interview in December 1978. "Some of the things that concerned me in 1972 no longer concern me in terms of my own ability," he said. By 1979, Carter saw his strength waning in Florida, which he had won over President Gerald Ford in 1976; an appointment for Florida's popular former governor might help reverse the tide.[10]

The trade representative is an ambassador with cabinet rank, requiring confirmation by the Senate. The mission, as Askew described it in his testimony to the Senate Finance Committee, was "to improve our export performance and to make America more competitive in the world marketplace." The hearing would have been uneventful but for Askew's 1977 support of Anita Bryant's anti-gay campaign. He reiterated his bias under pointed questioning from Senator Robert Packwood of Oregon. "I would not have a known homosexual on my staff, simply . . . by virtue of the tremendous problems it presents in dealing with public constituencies," Askew said. Although he agreed to respect federal regulations that prohibited discrimination against gays in the civil service, those did not apply to the exempt positions of his most important subordinates. Leaders of three gay rights organizations testified strongly against Askew's confirmation. Richard Cohen of the *Washington Post* wrote a scathing column which concluded that "people like Askew" should "keep out of public life and stay in the closet with their prejudices." None of the hearing was covered by the television networks or the wire services. The committee and the Senate approved Askew without dissent.[11]

Askew was sworn in to office by Joseph Hatchett, whom he had appointed to the Florida Supreme Court and who was now a judge of the Fifth U.S. Circuit Court of Appeals. Conspicuously absent from among the more than three hundred guests at the Rose Garden ceremony was Askew's onetime aide George Sheldon. The White House had withdrawn Sheldon's invitation because he was supporting Senator Edward M. Kennedy of Massachusetts against Carter for the 1980 Democratic nomination. Askew's newest protégé, Bacchus, took leave from their law firm to be his special assistant in Washington. It was a priceless apprenticeship in the arcane world of international trade law and diplomacy. After two terms in Congress (1991–95), Bacchus was appointed the U.S. representative on the appellate court of the World Trade Organization and eventually became co-chair of Greenberg Traurig's global practice group.[12]

Askew rented an apartment in Arlington, commuted on weekends to a new home in Kendall, an upscale Miami suburb, and was soon deeply involved in a trade issue with serious domestic political consequences. Rising oil prices in 1979 and 1980 triggered double-digit inflation in the industrialized countries. Their central banks responded with record-high interest rates that led to the most serious recession since the 1930s. As new-car sales fell in the United States, smaller, more fuel-efficient Japanese models more than doubled their market share. The United Auto Workers, joined by Ford Motor Company, pressed Congress for import restrictions in the form of domestic content legislation. Askew opposed them in testimony to Congress and in a side-by-side "debate" in the May 12, 1980, issue of *U.S. News* with UAW president Douglas Fraser. Askew asserted the administration's position that the legislation would cost American consumers $100,000 for each job that it created. "If you held back imports, you would either force consumers to buy larger, less efficient cars, or make them defer buying until other small cars are available, so the benefits could be substantially outweighed by the consumer cost, the inflationary impact and increased consumption of gasoline," Askew said. To accommodate the political pressure on

Washington, the Japanese government committed itself to encourage its auto manufacturers and parts companies to invest in U.S. facilities and said it would urge its manufacturers to use "prudence" in selling in the United States. The agreement helped the Carter administration hold the line against protectionist legislation in 1980, but that success was short-lived because Carter was defeated for reelection. Ronald Reagan's victory brought to Washington an administration and a Congress that pressured the Japanese manufacturers into "voluntary" export limitations which significantly increased the price of the cars they sold in the United States. As for Askew, his defense of free trade had earned him no friends in organized labor.[13]

Askew also secured Japan's promise of cooperation in opening government procurement—primarily Japan's telecommunications agency—to foreign competition. To get the Japanese ambassador's agreement, Askew needed time alone with him, out of earshot of Japan's senior trade minister, who opposed what Askew wanted. Askew arranged to ride with the ambassador in George Steinbrenner's limousine to a New York Yankees baseball game. He knew that there was no room for the trade minister. Japan agreed also to reduce tariffs and other obstacles to American tobacco products.[14]

Askew held the position for fifteen months, leaving Washington when Carter did in January 1981. He had intended to relinquish the office in any event, because it paid only $66,000. He would return to a law firm salary of more than $300,000, which he needed to pay substantial medical bills for his mother and mother-in-law. He was now thinking seriously of running for president in 1984. At a farewell press interview in December 1980, a Washington journalist asked whether that might be his intent. Bacchus was elated to hear Askew say, "I'm unwilling to preclude it."[15]

For 1984 there was a large field of better-known potential Democratic rivals, led by Walter Mondale, Carter's vice-president. As Askew acknowledged retrospectively, there was "very little encouragement" for his own candidacy other than from a faithful cadre of longtime aides. Jim Krog became his campaign manager. Bacchus spent his days practicing law and his nights as Askew's research department, speechwriter, and press secretary. Doug Sessions was the chief fund-raiser. Donald

Middlebrooks served as the campaign's legal adviser. Don Pride, the first staffer to have dreamed of an Askew presidency, was out of the action now; he had become a newspaper editor in Massachusetts. Pride's son Damon became Askew's traveling aide. Although Askew ultimately had forty paid staffers, every other major candidate employed more.[16]

Neither Askew nor any of his inner staff had any experience in a national campaign, a circumstance that the national media took into account in dismissing his prospects. It was as if it were 1970, when he was "Reubin Who?" Once again, he heard the beat of a different drummer. "Jimmy, we're going to do this the right way or not at all," Askew told Bacchus in February 1981, a month before his first organizational meeting. For Askew, "the right way" meant eschewing the political committees that presidential candidates typically established as legal subterfuge for their undeclared campaigns. Askew decided instead to report all the contributions he raised and the money he would spend "testing the waters" before formally declaring his candidacy. He broke ground by asking the Federal Elections Commission for guidance. David Broder, the *Washington Post*'s senior political writer, was so impressed with the unusual candor that he put aside a resolution "not to write about the 1984 presidential race until that calamity is upon us." Askew, he wrote approvingly, "is apparently going to say what he thinks and not be coy about what he is doing."[17]

While Askew was preparing his campaign, a paper presented to the Southern Political Science Association ranked him as one of the ten outstanding governors of the one thousand chief executives of American states in the twentieth century. George Weeks, the paper's author, had excluded such well-known former governors as Carter and Reagan. "It was based not only on successes within the states but also on having influence beyond their states," he explained. Weeks said had never heard "such a sustained and warm ovation" as the one Askew received at his last meeting of the National Governors Association in 1978. Weeks, chief of staff to Michigan governor William G. Milliken, had conducted his study while he was a graduate student at Harvard University, which gave rise to a persistent misperception that the university itself had certified Askew's stature. But only a few newspapers took note of Weeks's paper, and among those that did it was a one-day story. Most of the journalists who would cover the long campaign cared only about national politics and were disinterested in state government. Some who thought Carter had failed as a president regarded Askew's state government credentials as a liability, not an asset. During his appearance on *Meet the Press* in October 1982, the first question, from an NBC News reporter, asked Askew why he thought that "the Democratic Party or the country in general is ready for another former southern governor with management experience." Askew said that his visits with voters in every state had made him confident they would judge the candidates "on not where they are from but what they say and what they have to offer." Broder, a panelist, put the issue starkly: "Are you another Jimmy Carter?" No, Askew said; his federal experience, he pointed out, was more than either Carter or Reagan had before their inaugurations. Sensing what Broder meant, Askew added that he would not manage the White House and congressional relations in the ways that Carter had. In another exchange with Broder, he called for increasing the Social Security retirement age and limiting the program's annual cost-of-living adjustments. The newsman could not hide his astonishment at hearing such talk from the former governor of a state whose economy depended upon Social Security.[18]

Askew's campaign was as unconventional as his candor. He held only one news conference during the fifteen months before he declared his candidacy. He shunned routine political events, such as a California state party convention and even an AFL-CIO conference near his Florida home, to which other candidates flocked. "I can't pull away from the pack if I run with them," he said. "I have to build my own constituency. . . . If I have to respond to every event, I can't have my own schedule and do the things I have to do." On another occasion he said that did not want to "peak too early." He need not have worried about that. When Askew advertised a free continental breakfast at Manchester, New Hampshire, in June 1982, only one person showed up. Among the thousands of people he encountered aboard scores of commercial airline flights, few had a clue to the identity of the tall, handsome fellow passenger who cheerfully volunteered to help them stow their luggage in the overhead bins. Nor did they guess the reason; ever fastidious, Askew was seeing to it that *his* suit bag would be on top. "You may be wrinkled,

Bacchus," he told his companion, "but how many people will vote for a man whose suit isn't pressed?" As he had done in Florida, Askew voluntarily disclosed his federal form 1040, which showed $312,000 in 1982 gross income. The net taxable amount was reduced by $101,458 in deductions, including $70,000 in medical expenses for his mother and mother-in-law. The syndicated columnist Jack Anderson wrote favorably of Askew's financial disclosure, but few other journalists seemed to notice.[19]

Askew formally declared his candidacy on February 23, 1983, with a short speech and news conference at the National Press Club in Washington. His only promise, he said, was that he would not belong "to any one person" or "any one group." He said to the American public what he had told George Sheldon in 1970 and Bacchus in 1981: "I don't want to become president if, to get elected, I have to tie my hands so tightly that I won't be free to govern the right way." He said he would risk losing some votes "by being candid about the hard realities of the world transition." Emphasizing his commitment to free trade, he declared that "we can't remain strong ourselves, and we can't lead the world safely if we leap into the quicksand of protectionism." He called for a "new union" of labor and management to make American industry more competitive. Belatedly, he announced that he was accepting no contributions from political action committees. That had been his policy from the beginning, but he had rejected Bacchus's advice to publicize it, which allowed Mondale and Senator Gary Hart to beat him to the punch. Five more candidates would enter the race: Senators John Glenn of Ohio, Alan Cranston of California, and Ernest Hollings of South Carolina; Rev. Jesse Jackson; and former senator George McGovern. The *New York Times* led its Askew story with the "new union" theme but buried it on page 20 with the deprecating comment that "Some Democratic leaders believe that Mr. Askew is, more realistically, a candidate for the vice-presidential nomination on a ticket that might benefit from a Southerner with somewhat more conservative views than the standard-bearer." The newspaper reported that Robert Strauss had attended the press conference "to give him support," but minimized the significance by saying that Strauss's Dallas law firm reportedly had a member active in every Democratic campaign.[20]

Askew recognized three significant obstacles. The first was that the Democrats were not a united party but rather a coalition of interest groups in which organized labor was the most prominent. As governor, Askew had fought to raise unemployment and workers' compensation payments, had supported collective bargaining for public employees, and had established Florida's separate Department of Labor and Employment Security. That was in the past, however, and Askew was alone among the Democratic candidates in opposing the protectionist legislation that labor favored. "Askew has to be ranked an extreme long shot," wrote *Washington Post* economics columnist Hobart Rowen. "But at least Askew knows what it means to stick to a principle." Askew's second problem was the disproportionate influence of Iowa's caucuses, the opening event of the 1984 campaign, and of the New Hampshire primary a week later. Although they would allot barely 1 percent of the convention delegates, they had (and still have) enormous symbolic significance to the media. As a dark-horse candidate, Askew needed to run respectably in both states or his race would be over. He thought the free trade issue would help him in Iowa, where farmers feared that their export crops would bear the brunt of any international trade war over foreign cars and steel. But to win in Iowa required turning out the most people willing to attend caucuses on a cold winter night, which was labor's strength. Askew's third great concern was the national media, which for the most part prefers to cover the "horse race"—who seem to be winning and losing, and above all who is raising the most money—than to report in depth on what the candidates stand for. When the polls rather than the principles become the story, the media are merciless to the trailing candidates. The early *New York Times* article minimizing Askew's chances was just one of many. Two weeks later, *Newsweek* wrote that "everyone predicts . . . he loses at the Democratic convention." By early June 1983, Askew was outspokenly critical of the media bias. Howell Raines, who had joined the *New York Times*, wrote that Askew was "voicing the frustration shared privately by other second-tier candidates. . . . They blame the press and the polltakers for skewing the campaign process by judging the candidates on their national name recognition." Trying to lighten the situation a few days later at a "roast" for Morris Udall, Askew quipped that he was such a dark horse that the only newspaper to report his announcement was the *Daily Racing Form*. Even when Askew led in an early New Hampshire straw poll, the *Washington Post* minimized the achievement in a story that was critical of straw polls and suggested that Askew owed his victory to the free tickets he had distributed for the picnic where the poll took place. "Askew has been having a hard time shedding the image of a very dark horse," remarked Robert MacNeil of the *MacNeil/Lehrer Report* at the outset of an August 24, 1983, public television broadcast that gave Askew a rare opportunity to talk about issues. Even that interview closed with the persistent question: was he really aiming for the vice-presidency? No, Askew said; under "no circumstances" would he accept it.[21]

The domestic content controversy was not the only issue that set Askew apart from his Democratic rivals. He was cool to the "nuclear freeze" movement for an international moratorium on the production and deployment of nuclear weapons. He was unwilling to endorse repeal of the "right to work" provisions of the anti-labor Taft-Hartley Act. He called for temporarily reducing Social Security and government pension cost-of-living increases. Among the eight Democrats, he was the only one who opposed abortion on demand and advocated a constitutional amendment to overturn *Roe v. Wade* and allow states to enforce their own laws once again. Unlike many right-to-life militants, he supported abortion in cases of rape, incest, and severe health problems. The militants had no alternative in the Iowa Democratic caucuses, and the national media noticed that many of them were backing Askew's candidacy. "It was painful to see how he was treated as an anti-abortion fringe candidate," said Phil Gailey, a Georgia-born reporter covering the Iowa campaign for the *New York Times*. Unfortunately for Askew, many of the anti-abortion Iowans would be participating in the state's Republican caucuses rather than in the Democratic Party's.[22]

Askew's fund-raising went well at first, with $1.3 million, most of it from Florida, raised by June 1983, and his penny-pinching left him in reasonable shape for the run-up to Iowa even as some rivals were laying off members of their larger staffs. Mondale was far ahead of them all, however, and was setting a trap in Askew's home state. In October 1983, Askew campaigned strenuously to win a straw vote at the Florida Democratic convention in Hollywood. The poll would not select any delegates, but it was hugely significant to the news media. Although Askew won the straw vote with a 45 percent plurality, much of the media wrote of it as if he had lost and said that Mondale, with 35 percent, was the true winner. Mondale's surge owed largely to efforts on his behalf by the AFL-CIO and the National Education Association. Mondale and organized labor were not Askew's only home-state problems; there were nearly 2 million new voters in Florida since he had last run for governor. Earlier that day, three Florida newspapers reported a poll showing Mondale ahead among actual Florida Democratic voters by 32 percent to Askew's 26. Amidst the dour coverage, the *Washington Post*'s editorial board came to Askew's defense. "A win is a win," it said, adding that "not every former governor could win such an endorsement from his state party."[23]

Askew did not hide his disgust with the media coverage. It boiled over on a day when he had spoken on the concept of national service to an enthusiastic college student audience. Roger Mudd of CBS News was waiting to interview him afterward. "I thought to myself, finally somebody is going to ask me something right," Askew said. But Mudd was interested only in the polls; he wanted to know whether Askew considered himself "washed up." As Askew recalled the incident, "I'm spending two and a half years of my life in a motel room, 350,000 miles; it really got to me. I looked straight into the camera. I said, 'Not any more than you were, Mr. Mudd, when you got passed up for [CBS Evening News] anchor.' I pointed my finger and said, 'Now, let's see you run that little piece.'" Mudd did not.[24]

The campaign would continue into the snows of Iowa and New Hampshire, where scores of Floridians, including Governor Bob Graham, stumped in support of Askew. But the Florida straw poll had been fatal. "We knew we were close to finished," Bacchus said of it later. Askew was able to raise only $50,000 in contributions during the last quarter of 1983 and went into the final weeks of the Iowa campaign unable to broadcast his prepared television ads. Mondale swept Iowa with 48.9 percent of the caucus votes. Askew, who needed desperately to be in the top four, came in sixth with only 2.5 percent, ahead of only Jackson and Hollings, neither of whom had campaigned there. "I was reaching out to the forgotten majority in Iowa tonight, and I think a lot of them forgot to vote," Askew said. The media and even Askew himself began to predict that he would drop out if he did as poorly in New Hampshire. He tried to lower expectations by saying his goal was only to do better than John Glenn, who had finished fifth in Iowa.[25]

Although snow and sleet fell in New Hampshire on the day of the primary, Askew refused Bacchus's entreaties to wear a hat as he stalked the streets searching for more hands to shake. "If I wear a hat," he said, "the press will say that the candidate from Florida couldn't stand the weather up North." The reporters were interested only in the opinion polls predicting—accurately—that he would finish last. The great upset for which Askew had been hoping favored Hart instead. When the polls closed, Askew had merely 1,025 votes, the fewest of the eight serious candidates. Myra McPherson, the *Washington Post* reporter who called Bacchus for Askew's comment, could not help laughing into the telephone. Bacchus rebuked her and hung up.[26]

Cranston quit the next day. Askew and Hollings left the race two days later. Opinion polls showed Askew running a poor second to Mondale in Florida. Askew accused the media of having discouraged potential campaign contributors. He insisted he could still have won the Florida primary but only at the cost of substantial debt, and was unwilling to ask Floridians to vote for him when he knew he was "out of it." He endorsed none of his rivals in the remaining primaries, but he did attend the party convention in San Francisco to demonstrate support for Mondale, the nominee, who lost all but Minnesota and the District of Columbia to incumbent Ronald Reagan in November. Askew returned to Miami to practice law. Bacchus changed law firms and moved his family to Orlando, his hometown, to prepare to run for Congress, where he served from 1991 to 1995. For the *Orlando Sentinel*'s Sunday magazine, Bacchus wrote an eloquent postmortem on the presidential campaign. The title told it all: "The Good Fight: 3 Years, 300,000 Miles, 3,000 Votes."[27]

25

THE SHORTEST CAMPAIGN
(1987–1988)

By 1987, the disappointing presidential campaign well behind him, Reubin Askew had moved his family and his law practice to Orlando, where the Greenberg Traurig law firm opened a branch office. Much of the work involved municipal bond issues, with which Askew was not comfortable. Clients commonly expected political assistance as well as legal advice, but he was unwilling to lobby or contribute to their campaigns. Still, he thought he was through for good with seeking and holding office. Suddenly, Lawton Chiles, "The Walking Senator," turned everything upside down by walking away from his career. Chiles had been reelected with nearly two-thirds of the votes in 1976 and 1982, even though he limited his contributions to $30 per person the first time and to $300 the second. He was strongly favored to win a fourth term in the U.S. Senate in 1988 despite a likely challenge from a Republican with a famous name: U.S. representative Connie Mack, whose grandfather had managed the Philadelphia Athletics baseball team. No one else knew it, but Chiles was suffering from severe clinical depression that subsequently required treatment with Prozac. On December 7, 1987, barely twelve hours after notifying his family and staff, Chiles announced he was ending his reelection campaign and would retire from the Senate when his term ended a year later. Immediately, Askew's telephone began ringing nonstop. Florida Democratic Party chairman Charles Whitehead, fearing the loss of a seat long thought to be safe, was among the first to urge Askew to step in for Chiles. Bob Graham, Florida's junior U.S. senator since the 1986 election, also called. Law partner Robert Traurig was enthusiastic. The *Daytona Beach News Journal*, the first daily that had endorsed Askew in 1970, editorialized that he should run for the Senate. "We weren't sure," recalled Donna Lou Askew. "We had been out long enough that we had adjusted to life outside politics." This time, however, Askew would not have the luxury of time to think it through. There was pressure for him to decide quickly so that the Democratic primary would not become a free-for-all. Dan Mica, a congressman from West Palm Beach, leaped into the race and refused to back out when Askew let it be known on December 14 that he would run. Buddy MacKay, serving his third term in the U.S. House of Representatives, had run for the Senate in 1980 and was interested in doing so again, but he gladly made way for Askew and began planning a campaign for governor in 1990.[1]

The news conference at which Askew made his formal announcement on December 21 illustrated how politics had changed since he had last appeared on a Florida ballot. Candidates were now routinely asked about drugs, sex, and other aspects of their private lives. Admissions of marijuana use had derailed a U.S. Supreme Court nominee, Douglas Ginsburg. Chiles and Mack had both admitted to experimenting with marijuana. Gary Hart had withdrawn briefly as a candidate for president in 1988 after the *Miami Herald* exposed an extramarital affair. "I have never taken any illegal drug in my life," said Askew, adding that he had always been true to his wife. "I wish," he said wistfully, "that these had been the tests in 1984." Tom Fiedler, the *Miami Herald*'s political editor, wrote that "Santa has brought the Democratic Party a substitute" for Chiles and referred to Mack as the GOP's "designated martyr."[2]

Invasion of privacy was not the most drastic feature of the new politics. Askew and Chiles had won their 1970 campaigns under strict state and federal spending limits. In 1976 the U.S. Supreme Court struck down those laws. For the 1988 campaign, Askew calculated that he would need to raise nearly $6 million, more than ten times the cost of his 1974 reelection as governor. Five of his twenty-one salaried staffers were assigned to fund-raising. It was the aspect of politics he found most distasteful; it was also the one that would demand most of his own time. "It's not a very good system where a person runs for the United States Senate by becoming a professional beggar," Askew said at a West

Palm Beach reception where he raised $50,000. He had never needed or sought money outside Florida when he was running for governor. He had refused to accept political action committee contributions in his presidential race. This time, he reluctantly accepted money from PACs and from non-Florida donors. He collected $70,000 in one evening at a $1,000-a-head reception at the Georgetown home of Democratic Party doyenne Pamela Harriman, who for his sake put aside her policy against taking sides in a Democratic primary.[3]

In early March 1988, when he had yet to campaign publicly, a four-newspaper poll showed Askew leading Mica for the nomination 62 percent to 16 and comfortably ahead of Mack, 55 percent to 26. By May he had raised more than $1 million. But Askew was beginning to doubt his own desire to be a senator. At Naples, an audience of senior citizens expected to hear rousing campaign oratory from him. He surprised them with what a friend described as "the finest nonpartisan, nonpolitical speech" Askew had ever made. The candidate explained to the friend that he was thinking of quitting the race. Another old acquaintance who attended the event described Askew in private conversation as disconsolate over "a system that made him compromise his principles." Shortly before he decided to quit, Askew had experienced an epiphany. He had telephoned a friend to ask for money. When the man's wife said he was too ill to come to the telephone, Askew asked her, "Can he write?" When she said he would sign a check for $1,000, Askew responded, "Could he make it $2,000?" The blatant begging was still on Askew's mind as he left the campaign event at Naples and drove by himself to Miami. He telephoned a warning to Whitehead. He called Donna Lou to fly to Miami so that he could tell her in person. Late that night, he firmed up his decision to abandon the race. Jim Bacchus was the first to know. "I asked him if there was any point in our discussing it," Bacchus said. "But I could tell by the tone in his voice that there wasn't." Even so, he tried. Bacchus pleaded to Askew that he was popular enough to run an inexpensive race, a "front-porch" campaign such as William McKinley's in 1896. Don Pride made the same argument. He had just quit a fairly new job covering politics for the *Charlotte Observer* to be Askew's campaign press secretary. Askew agreed that he could win the race on a reduced budget. In that event, he thought, he would rule out running for reelection so that he would not have to spend six years soliciting more millions of dollars. But when he discussed that scenario with Donna Lou, she cautioned him that the Democratic Party and individual supporters would not accept his decision to be a one-term senator. They would pressure him to run again as relentlessly as they had in the days after Chiles bowed out.[4]

The stunning news that he would withdraw from the race leaked before Askew could announce it. He confirmed the rumors in a two-page statement in which he said that "something is seriously wrong with our system when many candidates for the Senate need to spend 75 percent of their time raising money. It's just not right." An underlying reason, however, was that he was unhappy at the prospect of sacrificing family time once again to the demands of politics. "I'm not prepared to reassume all the demands of elective office," he said. "Public service has been my life. . . . Yet I also know that there are other important things in life." He spoke of treasuring his once-a-week lunch break with Donna Lou, "the only respite from the consuming demands of the campaign . . . demands [that] don't end on election day." His decision, he said later, "was based on the assumption that I would win, not that I would lose." His most vivid memory of the campaign was of seeing people only "with my hand out" for money.[5]

Askew had tipped off Buddy MacKay, whom he encouraged to run in his stead. He promised to ask his own contributors to redirect their donations to MacKay. MacKay agreed to run with Askew's endorsement, but he did not inherit the uncomplicated Democratic primary campaign that Askew would have had against Mica. With Askew out of the way, Treasurer Bill Gunter, who had run unsuccessfully for the U.S. Senate in 1974 and 1980, could not resist the opportunity to try again. It meant there would be a costly runoff barely a month before the general election. Pat Frank, a state senator from Tampa, got into the Democratic primary also. So did Claude Kirk and a sixth candidate whom hardly anyone knew or would remember. After trailing Gunter in the primary, MacKay won the runoff with 52 percent, but it left his campaign nearly broke. Meanwhile, Mack had won the Republican primary in a landslide and had money to spare. He defeated MacKay in November, but by a margin of merely 33,612 votes out of more than 4 million cast. It was the closest general election Florida had seen; MacKay might even have won it but for three circumstances beyond his control. The first was that Michael Dukakis, the Democratic presidential nominee whose name appeared on the line above MacKay's, gave up on Florida and withdrew his staff and advertising from the state. The second was that a PAC representing foreign car dealers spent some $300,000 on "independent" ads attacking MacKay on television. The experience was ironic as well as bitter, because MacKay, like Askew, had opposed legislation to discriminate against auto imports. MacKay alleged illegal collusion with Mack's campaign, which employed the same advertising firm and political consultant as the car dealers' committee. But the Federal Election Commission, paralyzed by equal numbers of Democratic and Republican members, refused to order the ads off the air and eventually dismissed the complaint, eighteen months after the election. The third circumstance was a suspect vote count that foreshadowed Florida's disputed presidential race of 2000. Although exit polls had MacKay winning the election, he lost when the actual votes were reported. He believed that there were systemic undercounts in four of his strongest counties. MacKay's loss was not the only disaster for the Democrats that day. The Republicans also picked up MacKay's congressional district along with Gunter's seat on the Cabinet. Some dismayed Democrats blamed Askew for all the dominoes that fell. Had he stayed in the race, they said, MacKay would have kept his seat in Congress and Gunter would have remained in the Cabinet. It was, of course, conjecture not subject to proof.[6]

Within a week of his decision to leave the race, Askew was out of a job as well. He resigned from Greenberg Traurig before the firm could hold a partners' meeting that likely would have asked him to leave. The partners had reasons to be resentful. The firm had been paying Askew's salary while he campaigned. A senior partner, Marvin Rosen, had been one of his chief fund-raisers. The partners and spouses had individually contributed $22,600 to the campaign. Askew sensed also that they were unhappy with his endorsement of MacKay, who was affiliated with a rival law firm in Miami. Rosen, for one, made it his business to endorse Gunter, not MacKay. Some partners may not have understood that

Askew would have had to leave the firm to be seated in the Senate. Its rules, unlike those of the House at the time, forbade significant outside employment.[7]

Askew had made no secret of his dissatisfaction with the municipal bond business. To Bacchus, it seemed that Askew had "confused his desire to get out of the full-time practice of law with a desire to run for the Senate." It took Askew several more months, Bacchus said, "to realize that he didn't want to do that, either." In a reversal of their roles of 1978, Bacchus brought Askew into the Orlando office of the younger man's new law firm, Akerman, Senterfitt. Askew's status there would be "of counsel," which meant that he would not share in the partnership's income or decisions. He would be paid only a beginning associate's salary, but he would be at liberty to do other things. Askew would soon return to public service, as a teacher rather than a practitioner. In August 1990 he signed on to teach a graduate class in public administration at Florida Atlantic University. Within a year, he had a $100,000 salary and tenure in the university system; the rapid ascent annoyed some other professors. He eventually taught at least a semester at every university in the state system. At this writing, he holds the eminent scholar chair at Florida State University's Reubin O'D. Askew School of Public Administration and Policy. He is also the convener of an annual statewide conference on public policy that has been held since 1994 by the Askew Institute on Politics and Society at the University of Florida. Askew's post-political career has fulfilled a prediction by former governor LeRoy Collins, who wrote in August 1988 that he understood Askew's reluctance to become a freshman senator at the age of sixty. "Askew has done a great deal for Florida," he said in his weekly column in the *St. Petersburg Times*. "If I judge correctly," Collins concluded, "Reubin Askew is not ready to hang up his spurs. I think he just feels that he owes it to his wife, to his friends, and to himself to serve in other ways, private and public ways in which he can be himself."[8]

26

EPITAPH FOR THE GOLDEN AGE

The Golden Age of Florida politics, which had burst into being with the dramatic reapportionment of 1967, faded away in the ensuing twenty years. Although Reubin Askew's first term was unquestionably the high point, there continued to be significant progress, if at a slower pace and with less intensity, for a decade after he left office. The momentum owed to the leadership of younger politicians who took their inspiration from him, much as he had taken his from LeRoy Collins. Writing of his protégé in 1988, Collins remarked that "Floridians always will remember the standards he made and set as hallmarks for our state's future—responsible citizenship, clean government, effective government, protection of the Florida environment, ever-improving public and private education, and liberty and justice and opportunity for all people." Although Askew's direct involvement in Florida government was in the past, his presence continued to be felt. As historian David Colburn wrote, "No prominent candidate would run for the governorship in the next two decades without referring to Askew's legacy. Moreover, all subsequent Democrats through 2000 were influenced by his leadership style and his programs, and many pursued political office because they had been motivated to do so by his example."[1]

In 1980, backed by Speaker Hyatt Brown, Representative George Sheldon and Senator Buddy MacKay used Senator Kenneth Myers's "sunset" law to repeal economic regulation of the trucking and bus industries. As expected, competition flourished and prices fell. Florida's example was emulated by other states and the federal government. Significant growth-management legislation finally was enacted during Governor

Bob Graham's administration (1979–87). Although the House remained the more liberal chamber during the renaissance that had begun with Brown's coup to secure the speakership, the Senate under President Harry Johnston (1985–86) set the stage for a tax reform that was as dramatic as Askew's and could have yielded much more money. The unforeseen consequence was that the effort tolled the end of the Golden Age.

Askew and allies such as Richard Pettigrew, Don Reed, Buddy MacKay, Nathaniel Reed, and Curt Kiser shared a belief, regardless of party, that the American political process was inherently good. In his eulogy for Senator Edward M. Kennedy of Massachusetts, President Barack Obama talked wistfully of "an age when the joy and nobility of politics prevented differences of party and philosophy from becoming barriers to cooperation and mutual respect, a time when adversaries still saw each other as patriots."[2] Askew's improbable election victory in 1970 and his overwhelming reelection four years later reflected a kindred spirit among the people of Florida. On those occasions, it was possible for a governor to be elected owing no one but the people who had voted for him because they admired his independence and his courage.

A mere generation later, that spirit has vanished. As Florida politics became sharply polarized and partisan, government itself became an enemy in the eyes of the state's new political elite and the voters who responded to their propaganda. At his second inauguration, in January 2003, Republican Governor Jeb Bush dreamed aloud of a day when the state office buildings around him would be "empty of workers, silent monuments to a time when government played a larger role than it deserved or could adequately fill."[3]

The last days of the Golden Age occurred during the 1985 and 1986 legislative sessions, which saw the enactment of a state comprehensive plan and a growth-management act described as the "most ambitious city planning agenda ever to become law." The legislature also enacted Johnston's bold proposal to "sunset" the entire sales tax at the end of the 1986–87 fiscal year. The device would force the next session to consider the tax reforms considered necessary to finance the infrastructure and government services comprehended by the state plan and growth management. For the first time since the original sales tax in

1949, every exemption would be on the table. Johnston hoped also to be the governor who would oversee that process, but he ran third in the Democratic primary to succeed Bob Graham, who was term-limited. Representative Steve Pajcic of Jacksonville defeated Attorney General Jim Smith in a runoff that reopened the liberal-versus-conservative fault line in Democratic politics that had been so destructive to Robert King High's campaign in 1966. Once again, a Republican governor who had not served in the legislature—Tampa mayor Bob Martinez—had to deal with a House and Senate still controlled by the Democratic Party. He was not confrontational like Claude Kirk and found the legislature receptive to environmental legislation to safeguard water and preserve sensitive land and continue programs that Graham had begun. Martinez—unlike Kirk—was even initially enthusiastic about tax reform. In his opening-day address to the 1987 session, he urged the legislature to apply the sales tax to advertising, legal fees, and other personal and professional services as well as to the merchandise that had been Florida's primary revenue source since 1949. "If we are to make our tax system more fair over the long term, then we must extend the sales tax to services," Martinez said. The legislature complied, but the good intentions vanished in the face of fierce opposition from the media, the real estate industry, and other professions averse to adding taxes to their invoices. The tax had barely gone into effect when Martinez panicked and the legislature followed him in retreat. They repealed the new taxes on services, replacing them with a sixth cent on merchandise. "Once again we are falling back on the most regressive tax we have," lamented Senator Jeanne Malchon, a St. Petersburg Democrat. From that point, said Jim Bacchus, "it has all been downhill." Bacchus had been general counsel to the State Comprehensive Plan Committee and had drafted its report documenting the need for the tax reform. "The decision to repeal the services tax . . . rather than simply fine-tune it was, to my mind, the beginning of the end of what had previously been a remarkable generation of progress for Florida. Since that fateful decision, Florida has gone backward," Bacchus said.[4]

In a prophetic article written before the debacle of 1987, two of the legislature's leading staff fiscal experts warned that without broad tax reform, subsequent recessions would render the State Comprehensive

Plan "all but destroyed," and that policy making would "degenerate into an annual exercise in crisis management." The recessions of 1991 and—especially—2008 bore them out. The state government's fiscal weakness compelled local governments to keep raising property taxes despite a historic collapse in the housing market, which was accompanied by rampant mortgage foreclosures, declining taxable values, and steeply rising property insurance rates. Florida had staked its future on an economy so dependent on growth that historian Gary Mormino likened it to a Ponzi scheme. In August 2009 the University of Florida's Bureau of Economic and Business Research announced that for the first time since 1946 the state that had once gained 700 residents a day was now losing population. It estimated a decline of some 58,000 in the previous year.[5]

Lawton Chiles, recovered from his clinical depression, defeated Martinez in the November 1990 gubernatorial election, and Buddy MacKay returned to Tallahassee as Chiles's lieutenant governor. The day they took office, a recession forced Chiles to impose draconian budget cuts. He tried in vain to renew legislative interest in taxing services. A decade later, so did John McKay, a Republican Senate president. McKay's effort was stifled by Governor Jeb Bush and the House leadership. Bush's idea of reform, carried out by party-line votes in a legislature now controlled by Republicans, was to repeal Florida's only state tax on accumulated wealth, the annual intangibles levy on stocks and bonds. It had yielded nearly $1 billion in the peak fiscal year of 1997–98. The Institute on Taxation and Economic Policy, a liberal Washington advocacy group, now ranks Florida second-worst in the nation, behind only the state of Washington, in the degree to which its taxes are "regressive"—imposing a heavier burden on the poor than on the wealthy. As of 2009, the poorest 20 percent of Floridians, with income averaging $10,500 a year, were found to be paying 13.5 cents of every dollar in state and local taxes. The wealthiest 1 percent, earning on average $2.4 million a year, contributed only 2.6 cents of every dollar, which compared to 3.6 cents before the intangibles tax was repealed. The burden on the middle class, however, was up significantly since the institute's last measure, in 1995, from 7.7 cents in tax for every dollar earned, to 9.2 cents in 2007. Although Florida politicians often campaign on the premise that taxes are too high, the institute's survey found that thirty-five states levy even more on the middle class; only the thinly populated states of Alaska, Nevada, New Hampshire, South Dakota, and Wyoming asked less of their wealthiest residents.[6]

More than three decades after the flowering of the Golden Age produced Askew's corporate income tax, there has not been another successful effort to make Florida taxes either less regressive or more responsive to the needs of the state. The services tax debacle of 1987 was a conspicuous failure. All the while, the legislature has regularly added more exemptions and credits to the corporate tax code. By 2008 these loopholes totaled an estimated $1.6 billion, nearly as much as the entire $2 billion actually collected. In 2003 the *St. Petersburg Times* found that although 2 percent of the companies doing business in Florida were paying 98 percent of the tax, many of the largest paid nothing. Only two states had more generous shelters. Florida's corporate tax had become "a voluntary tax. Accountants and lawyers control it," one expert told the newspaper. In 2009 a Senate committee held hearings on a bold proposal to recapture taxes from corporations sheltering assets in out-of-state subsidiaries but took no action on it.[7]

A decade into the twenty-first century, Florida is suffering the economic version of a perfect storm: population growth no longer nourishes construction, and the service sectors and tax revenue have declined sharply. That the state was particularly ill-suited to weather a recession owed much to the political changes that had made Tallahassee nearly unrecognizable to veterans of the Golden Age. In their happier and productive era, neither party had expected unflinching discipline from its legislators. But in 1999, the first year the Republicans owned the governor's office as well as both houses of the legislature, the minority Democrats managed to prevail on only four of eighty-one partisan roll calls. Bush and the Republican legislative leaders sensed neither necessity nor moral imperative to compromise with the Democrats on any major issue. In 2001 the Republicans deliberately repoliticized the judiciary through legislation empowering Bush and his successors to appoint all nine members of every judicial nominating commission. Only seven of the seventy-seven House Republicans and none of the twenty-five Senate Republicans bucked the party line. Democrats held firm in the House but not in the Senate, where four backed the Republican bill that gravely compromised one of Askew's greatest achievements. The legislation was seen as a reaction to the Florida Supreme Court's split decision to order a manual recount of Florida's decisive votes in the 2000 presidential race between the governor's brother George W. Bush and Democrat Al Gore. With one exceptional interval, under Speaker Allen G. Bense in 2005 and 2006, the House has remained intensely partisan. The Senate has been less so, a consequence of the fact that its members serve larger districts and of its history of coalitions dating to Barron's conservative reign. But even in 2005 the parties split dramatically over a Republican bill abolishing the runoff primary that had made possible the careers of LeRoy Collins, Reubin Askew, Lawton Chiles, and Bob Graham. Only ten Republican legislators voted no. Because winner-take-all primaries tend to empower the ideological extremes in political parties, the Florida Legislature is likely to become even more partisan in the near future. At this writing, changing leadership in the Senate implies a significantly more conservative posture.[8]

The urban and suburban politicians who succeeded the Pork Chop Gang in 1967 brought to Tallahassee a unique force of pent-up energy and enthusiasm that could not have sustained itself indefinitely. It was not inevitable, however, that so much of their progress would be undone eventually. Calculated decisions rather than a series of accidents sabotaged the progressive, bipartisan spirit that characterized the Golden Age. The most significant of these were the out-of-control campaign spending unleashed by the U.S. Supreme Court, single-member districts, computerized gerrymandering, the abuse of power by presiding officers, the term limits imposed by a 1992 initiative, and an increase in partisanship nationally, exemplified by Newt Gingrich, Speaker of the U.S. House of Representatives. Some Golden Age veterans even fault the tightening ethical standards that discouraged lobbyist-funded weekends where legislators and their families socialized. And in one critical respect, the Republicans simply did well at what the Democrats largely neglected: building their bench strength with promising young successors to their aging politicians. When Governor Chiles died during his last month in office in December 1998, writer Patsy Palmer remarked on the end of a "Long Generation" of mostly male, mostly white, mostly Democratic politicians who had governed Florida for nearly half a century. Many of the "Long Generation"—among them her husband, Sandy D'Alemberte—also shared an experience largely unknown to their present-day successors: military service. It was a leveling, democratizing factor that inspired their ability to work together.[9]

A series of U.S. Supreme Court decisions, beginning with *Buckley v. Valeo* in 1976, made it impossible to enforce Florida's spending limitations on candidates or restrict "independent" expenditures by special-interest political committees. (A highly controversial split decision by the Supreme Court in 2010 opens the door for corporations and unions to spend unlimited funds to oppose or support candidates irrespective of any state's legal limits on direct contributions.) In 2006, legislative campaigns raised more than $47 million; forty-two House candidates spent more than $200,000 each. The candidates for governor in 2006 spent $42.4 million; Republican Charlie Crist won the spending race and the election with $19.8 million. Adjusted for inflation, that was more than five times what it had cost Askew to win in 1970, and it does not count what independent committees may have spent on Crist's behalf. Campaign money has become a domestic arms race vastly enhancing the influences of special-interest lobbies. Much of the money is collected through the political parties or by legislators campaigning to be Speaker and Senate president. Their control of the money helps them to enforce voting discipline on their members—to the benefit of the contributors. "We turned a 600-pound gorilla over to the lobbyists," said MacKay. The profusion of money became the root of another evil: dirty campaign tactics. In one example among many, a circular attacked a physician legislator as "Dr. Date Rape" based on his professional objection that legislation criminalizing use of the drug Rohypnol would also interfere with legitimate medical uses. Such slurs were unthinkable in the early 1970s. The legislator won that election, but soon afterward he changed his registration to the party that had slandered him.[10]

After observing the legislature's 1986 session, Rutgers University political scientist Alan Rosenthal, who had watched Florida closely for years, identified some of the forces that were about to lower the curtain on the Golden Age. "As a result of single-member districts and other factors," he wrote, "the national trend is toward more self-interested and parochial legislators." He noted that incumbents, fortified by their superior ability to raise campaign funds, rarely faced serious challenges; except in reapportionment years, nearly half of the House members ran unopposed. Although partisanship was a "new and significant phenomenon in Florida" and in legislatures nationally, "the Florida Legislature is not really a partisan place—at least not yet," Rosenthal wrote. But in 1992, the voters approved a term-limits initiative allowing only eight years for representatives and eight to ten years for senators, which a decade later left the House barren of experienced leadership. Despite the massive reapportionment turnover in 1967 and 1968, the early Golden Age legislatures were capably led by seasoned presiding officers and committee chairs. Under term limits, most Speakers now ascend to the podium after only six years of legislative experience and have secured their victories with the votes of colleagues who barely know them. Legislators have been campaigning for Speaker even before taking their seats in the House. "Term limits have created an urgency to claw your way to the top in the way that becomes the name of the game—more than keeping your party in power and sticking together to make it happen," says Ken Plante, once a senator, now a lobbyist. But although term limits guarantee that each seat will be vacated by a time certain, competition remains low. Many potential challengers prefer to wait for open seats rather than oppose incumbents. From 2000 through 2006 only five incumbents lost reelection campaigns. In 2008, a year in which term limits affected thirty-one seats, nearly twice as many—comprising a majority of the House—were effectively uncontested in November. Incumbents retained fifty of those. It was not that the voters were either satisfied or apathetic, but that they had been made impotent by the gerrymandering of districts to preclude effective competition.[11]

The single-member districting systems in force since 1982 achieved the sponsors' stated goals of dramatically increasing African American and Hispanic membership. More women were elected as well. But the system also served purposes that were not so lofty. The Senate's 1982 plan was designed to return all the members of Dempsey Barron's ruling coalition. Over the long range, particularly in 1992, the Republicans leveraged the Voting Rights Act, the U.S. Justice Department, and the Florida Supreme Court to accelerate and amplify their eventual takeover of the legislature. According to Tom Slade, a former senator who chaired the Florida Republican Party as it won majorities in the legislature: "The Republicans wanted more predominantly white districts and the African Americans wanted more predominantly black districts. Every time you created an African American district, you created two Republican districts. Pretty soon white Democratic members of the legislature got to be pretty scarce. All I did was ride the wave that had been created by serving the selfish interests of the Republicans and African Americans."[12]

Charles Reed, who served as chancellor of the Florida university system during this era of legislative transition, observed the effects of the new districting when he tried to interest a respected Dade legislator in creating a hospitality program at Miami's Florida International University. "That university is not in my district. I don't care what happens there," the legislator replied.[13]

Because each member necessarily had to serve a relatively broad constituency, multi-member districts had a moderating effect on the legislature. In his old four-county Senate district, said Bob Johnson, a Republican from Sarasota, "You had to know agriculture, you had to know migrant labor, you didn't just please the people on the beach." Repeal of the runoff primary law also contributed to increased partisanship; a winner-take-all primary in a multi-candidate field tends to favor political extremes. In consequence of such changes, the Florida Legislature of the twenty-first century is characterized by a rigidly conservative majority, a liberal minority, and relatively few members in the middle. In the 1970s, Askew had to reach out to Republicans to enact much of his program; bipartisanship was a virtue born of necessity. But at the turn of the century, the virtue lacked necessity.[14]

For those who recall the Golden Age with nostalgia, the future is not encouraging. It is true that American politics are inherently cyclical and that the Florida Democrats show signs of becoming a stronger and more effective minority. Even so, none of the dozens of people I interviewed for this book could foresee another Golden Age. "So much of what we despair has been institutionalized," said Bob Graham. "You sit down with a lot of legislators, and five minutes into any conversation you're talking about fund-raising. It's so ingrained, it's part of the lifestyle. I think the single-member districts, term limits, and then the partisanship in the legislature, which is really a reflection of the partisanship in society, have all tended to make the legislature less public-policy oriented and more focused on the particular aspirations of moneyed interest groups."[15]

It is improbable that Reubin Askew could have been elected governor in the face of the circumstances that confront candidates today. It is even more unlikely that he—or anyone like him—would make the attempt. Prospects for effective campaign finance legislation are nonexistent under the U.S. Supreme Court's credo that paid political advertising is protected speech.

As governor, Askew had struggled to control prison construction by emphasizing alternatives to incarceration. The Graham administration dealt with severe overcrowding through early releases. Afterward, as politicians flocked to the simplest but potentially most costly ideas for coping with crime, Florida began to build prisons at breakneck speed, adopted more of the mandatory minimum sentences that Askew had discouraged, enacted sentencing guidelines that sharply curtailed judicial discretion, abolished parole, and required that inmates complete 85 percent of their sentences. On March 15, 2010, Florida had 101,517 convicts, about five times as many as in 1978. Prison spending grew to 10 percent of its budget, more than that for universities. Florida ranked third in the nation in that statistic, compared to a national average of 6.7 percent. The state's population as a whole had merely doubled during the interval. Its incarceration rate ranked eighth, with 535 of every 100,000 adults in jail or prison compared to 447 nationally. In 2009, when twenty-seven states reduced their prison counts, Florida's still increased slightly. Concerned over the ingravescent expenses, which according to the re-offender rates are throwing good money after bad, business lobbies have begun calling for a revived emphasis on education, job preparation, and other rehabilitative efforts reminiscent of the Askew years. Governor Crist, who as a legislator was so zealous to punish prisoners that the author nicknamed him "Chain Gang Charlie," agreed that it was time to change direction and proposed no new prisons in his budget for fiscal year 2011.[16]

The state's commitment to growth management, already crippled by economics, was pronounced dead in 2009 when Crist signed legislation relieving most developers of the responsibility to pay for roads to serve their projects or to submit large ones to scrutiny for their effect on neighboring communities.[17]

Among the few enduring achievements of the Golden Age is the Myers Act, which provided for medical treatment rather than incarceration for alcoholics. Myers left the Senate in 1978, disappointed only that he had been blocked from its presidency. Some years later, he received a 2 A.M. telephone call from a man who told him the Myers Act had saved his life. Noting the hour, Myers asked if the caller indeed was sober. "Yeah," he replied, "I was just thinking about it and wanted you to know I'm home and okay." Such a conversation, Myers said, "Makes you feel it was worthwhile getting involved." Myers died as he had lived—in the act of doing a kindness for others. He was taking some fruit to the workers roofing his house on a blistering summer day in 2007 when he slipped on a stairwell and fell to his death. The Myers Act was one of some 150 progressive laws that constitute his legacy.[18]

A Few Last Words about Some Others

Louis de la Parte, the unwavering champion of Floridians in need of the government's help, had endured Alzheimer's disease for nearly twenty years when he died in 2008, never comprehending why Lawton Chiles—who knew of his illness and wept over it—had not appointed him to head the Department of Health and Rehabilitative Services. In 1996, while he was still able to appreciate the honor and enjoy the day, the state rededicated the mental health facility he had established at the University of South Florida, renaming it for him.[19]

Jim Redman survived cancer for twenty-six years after leaving the House in 1978. He was remembered as the conscience of the legislature. He died of his illness on the same day that Tom Adams, whom he had attempted to impeach, perished in a traffic accident while driving his youngest son to college. Speaking at a memorial service for the lieutenant governor who had run against him, Askew said they had long since renewed their friendship. "One of the main reasons our administration was able to get off the ground running was we were able to attract so many of Tom's able staff to the governor's office," he said.[20]

Most Democrats remembered Don Reed as a Republican leader who never took politics personally. He applied the same attitude to his subsequent career as a lobbyist. In 1989, *St. Petersburg Times* reporter Lucy Morgan exposed a provision that Reed and another lobbyist had slipped into an eighty-seven-page bill for the benefit of a corporate client. The publicity doomed their amendment, costing them a $1 million contingency fee. Reed took it matter-of-factly. "Lucy doesn't understand that we're not mad at her," Reed said over dinner with the author. "We know that she was just doing her job." Having survived a heart transplant, Reed died of a stroke in 1996. Claude Kirk attended the funeral.[21]

The Equal Rights Amendment fell three states shy of the necessary thirty-eight. In 1979, just before the Florida Senate voted it down for the last time, Dempsey Barron, still leading the opposition, refused to take a telephone call on the issue from President Jimmy Carter. But in 1992, four years after he had been defeated for reelection, Barron expressed regret for the defeat of the ERA. He said he had changed his mind because women in the armed services had fought and died for the United States in the liberation of Kuwait.[22]

Reubin Askew has often said that the worst experience of his eight years as governor was the Senate's 1975 rejection of his Health and Rehabilitative Services secretary, O. J. Keller. Keller never forgave Barron for that, but Askew did, long before the former senator's death from Alzheimer's and Parkinson's diseases at the age of seventy-nine, in July 2001. In May of that year, Florida State University honored Barron and his wife, Terri Jo, for a $3 million contribution to improve the quality of life for Floridians with neurological disease. Askew led the list of dignitaries at the ceremony and lingered long after. When nearly everyone else had left, Askew walked over to Barron, who had remained in his chair, unable to speak. The former governor leaned down, whispered a farewell to the man who had been his colleague and his nemesis, and kissed him on the forehead.[23]

ACKNOWLEDGMENTS

The inspiration for this book owes to the veterans of the Golden Age who attended the reunion described in chapter 1. It occurred to me there that contemporary Floridians should know there was a time in their state's recent history when progressive politics and legislative courtesy were not contradictions in terms. I am grateful above all to my wife, Ivy, my muse and best editor, who toiled a semester in the dungeons of academia to subsidize much of the research. I deeply appreciate the time and courtesy on the part of all those who graciously granted interviews or bore patiently my frequent telephone calls and e-mails: Jim Apthorp, Phil Ashler, Donna Lou Askew, Kevin Askew, Reubin Askew, Jim Bacchus, Martha Barnett, Dick Batchelor, Jim Bax, Bill Birchfield, Elaine Bloom, Hyatt Brown, Arthur Canaday, Ed Carhart, Betty Castor, Don Chamberlin, David Coburn, Don Crane, Paul Danahy, Sandy D'Alemberte, Lance deHaven-Smith, Pete Dunbar, Virginia Ellis, Art England, Greg Favre, Bill Fleece, Phil Gailey, Bill Gillespie, Bob Graham, Ralph Haben, Marshall Harris, Lee Hinckle, Damon Holmes, Mallory Horne, Jim Joanos, Bob Johnson, Greg Johnson, O. J. Keller, Linda Keever, Fred Kimball, Claude Kirk, Curt Kiser, Jim Krog, Jay Landers, Phil Lewis, Buddy MacKay, Hugh MacMillan, Charlotte Maguire, Sheila McDevitt, Richard McFarlain, George McGovern, Judge Donald Middlebrooks, Jim Minter, Ed Montanaro, Ken Myers, Jon Moyle, Bill Nelson, Ben Overton, Hallie Page, Steve Pajcic, Bob Parks, Bernie Parrish, Dick Pettigrew, John Phelps, Ken Plante, Ed H. Price Jr., Don Pride, Terri Jo Rauch, Charles Reed, Nathaniel Reed, Janet Reno, Barry Richard, Mike Rose, Marvin Rudnick, Paul Schnitt, Fred Schultz, Doug Sessions, Terrell Sessums, George Sheldon, Myrna Shevin, Jack Shreve, Tom Slade,

Jim Smith, Sharyn Smith, John Sowinski, Gene Stearns, Jim Tait, Ralph Turlington, Bonnie Williams, Jim Williams, Lori Wilson, and Ken Woodburn. This book is my memoir as well as theirs, and where an event is told without attribution it is because I witnessed it as a journalist. Similarly, the conclusions are my own.

I owe special thanks to Julian Pleasants and Gary Mormino for their invaluable historical advice and suggestions and for Dr. Pleasants' superior interviews, which are on file at the University of Florida's Sam Proctor Oral History Collection; to Don Pride for essential photographs; to Anne McKenzie of the Florida Legislative Research Center and Museum and to Mike Vasilinda for access to the museum's priceless interviews of Jim Redman, Warren Henderson, and other principal figures; to Cynthia Barnett and Lucy Morgan for notes and interviews they shared; to Terrell Sessums and George Sheldon for loans of their House and Senate *Journals*; to John Phelps for his insights on legislative history; to Francine Walker of the Florida Bar; to Boyd Murphree, Miriam Gan-Spalding, Holly Sinco, Eden Andes, Krissi Demnman, and Valerie Emhof, the ever-patient, unfailingly helpful staff at the State Archives of Florida; to Jane Healy and Nancy Kunzman of the *Orlando Sentinel*; to Randy Schultz and Gwen Surface of the *Palm Beach Post*; to Ben Montgomery of the *St. Petersburg Times*; to my exacting copy editor, Jonathan Lawrence; and to Mary Mellstrom, my friend at the *St. Petersburg Times* news library, who always found an answer even when I came up empty-handed elsewhere.

NOTES

Abbreviations Used in the Notes

House *Journal*   Florida Legislature. House of Representatives. *Journal of the House of Representatives*. Tallahassee, 1967–79.

RG   Record Group

SAF   State Archives of Florida, Tallahassee

Senate *Journal*   Florida Legislature. Senate. *Journal of the Senate*. Tallahassee, 1967–79.

Chapter 1. The Big Bang

1. *St. Petersburg Times,* October 27, 2002.

2. Ibid., February 26, 2004 (Byrd quote); Colburn and deHaven-Smith, *Florida's Megatrends,* 74.

3. *St. Petersburg Times*, October 27, 2002.

4. Ibid.; Crane interview; Fleece interview.

5. *New York Times*, January 1982; Bass and De Vries, *Transformation of Southern Politics*, 24.

6. Maggiotto, "Impact of Reapportionment," 393; R. Askew interview by Pleasants.

7. Key, *Southern Politics*, 83–105; Kallina, *Claude Kirk*, 11; MacKay interviews.

8. R. Askew interviews by the author (Johnson quote); Allen Morris, syndicated column, date unknown; *St. Petersburg Times*, December 7, 1962, November 26, 1971.

9. *Swann v. Adams*, 385 U.S. 440 (1967), 263 F.Supp. 225 (1967).

10. Klas, "Lawmakers Getting the Boot"; Florida Legislature, House, *People of Lawmaking*; Graham interview by Vasilinda; N. Reed interview by the author.

11. Bass and De Vries, *Transformation of Southern Politics*, 110; Harris interview; Pettigrew quoted in Rosenthal, "State of the Florida Legislature," 404; MacKay interviews.

12. Rosenthal preface in Smith, *Strengthening the Florida Legislature*, v; Bass and De Vries, *Transformation of Southern Politics*, 110; Askew text, box 2, RG 65, SAF.

Chapter 2. Claudius Rex (1966–1970)

1. R. Askew interviews by the author; Nordheimer, "Florida's 'Supersquare.'"

2. Kallina, *Claude Kirk*, 48–49; *St. Petersburg Times*, January 4, 1967; *New York Times*, January 4, 1967; *Miami Herald*, April 25, 1969.

3. Kallina, *Claude Kirk*, 23, 52, 86; Bass and De Vries, *Transformation of Southern Politics*, 117.

4. Colburn and deHaven-Smith, *Florida's Megatrends*, 10; *St. Petersburg Times*, March 19, 1969; Morris, *Florida Handbook* (30th ed.), 717; Morris, *Florida Handbook* (15th ed.), 570; *Swann v. Adams*, 385 U.S. 440 (1967); Morris, *Reconsiderations* (3rd ed.), 58–59.

5. Kirk interview by Pleasants.

6. Kallina, *Claude Kirk*, 27–28; Ed H. Price Jr., "The Birth of a Bonddoggle," *Tampa Tribune*, October 24, 1965; Turlington interview by Doherty; R. Askew interviews by the author; *St. Petersburg Times*, September 2, 1965.

7. Kallina, *Claude Kirk*, 32–37; Colburn, *Yellow Dog Democrats*, 57–60; Morris, *Florida Handbook* (15th ed.), 682.

8. Plante interview; R. Askew interviews by the author.

9. Maguire interview; de la Parte quotes from Bax interviews; Crew and Smith, "Research Note—Rating the Governors," 28–30; Michael Barone, Grant Ojifusa, and Douglas Matthews, *The Almanac of American Politics—1976* (New York: Dutton, 1975), 160.

10. Kallina, *Claude Kirk*, 61–5.

11. N. Reed interview by the author; N. Reed interviews by Pleasants; Kallina, *Claude Kirk*, 152.

12. Kallina, *Claude Kirk*, 30–32; N. Reed interviews by Pleasants; D. Reed interview by Bass and De Vries.

13. Kallina, *Claude Kirk*, 161; N. Reed interviews by Pleasants.

14. Kallina, *Claude Kirk*, 109; N. Reed interview by the author; N. Reed interviews by Pleasants.

15. Kallina, *Claude Kirk*, 160–63; D. Reed interview by Bass and De Vries; Carter quoted in *St. Petersburg Times*, March 7, 1968.

16. Pettigrew interview; Kallina, *Claude Kirk*, 20, 77; *St. Petersburg Times*, May 3, 8, December 7, 9, 20, 1967.

17. *St. Petersburg Times*, July 13, 1968, November 11, 1969, September 30, 2009; Kallina, *Claude Kirk*, 118–19, 145–48; Bass and De Vries, *Transformation of Southern Politics*, 119; N. Reed interview by the author.

18. D. Reed interview by Bass and De Vries; Schultz interview by Vasilinda.

19. Dunbar interview.

20. Myers interview; *St. Petersburg Times*, July 11, 16, 1967; Turlington interview by the author.

21. *St. Petersburg Times*, June 6, 24, 28, 1967; Kallina, *Claude Kirk*, 90; Turlington interview by the author; R. Askew interviews by the author.

22. *St. Petersburg Times*, July 3, June 27, August 5, 1967; Dunbar interview.

23. *St. Petersburg Times*, February 1, 2, 1968, July 24, 1991; Kallina, *Claude Kirk*, 92–100; *New York Times*, February 18, 1968.

24. *St. Petersburg Times*, June 12, 23, 25, 1968; *St. Petersburg Independent*, June 19, 1968.

25. Kallina, *Claude Kirk*, 123; *St. Petersburg Times*, July 4, October 17, December 12, 1968; *Tampa Tribune*, July 4, 1968.

26. Morris, *Florida Handbook* (29th ed.), 676, 690, 718; Dyckman, *Floridian of His Century*, 240–51; Dyckman, *Disorderly Court*, 27; *St. Petersburg Times*, November 6, 7, 1968.

Chapter 3. The Double Cross (1969–1970)

1. Schultz quoted in *Florida Times-Union*, December 4, 2004; D. Reed interview by Bass and De Vries; Dunbar interview; James interview.

2. Morris, *Reconsiderations* (2nd ed.), 30–21; Pettigrew interview; *St. Petersburg Times*, March 30, 1967; Opinion 67-5, March 6, 1967, withdrawn by the Florida Bar Board of Governors on February 12, 1999.

3. *St. Petersburg Times*, March 19, 20, April 16, 1969; Pettigrew interview.

4. *St. Petersburg Times*, March 19, July 22, 1969, January 27, March 9, April 12, 1972.

5. Schultz interview by Vasilinda; *Miami Herald*, April 18, 1969.

6. Kallina, *Claude Kirk*, 129; *Orlando Sentinel*, April 12, 13, 16, 19, 27, 1969; *St. Petersburg Times*, April 20, 25, 1969; *Miami Herald*, April 24, 25, 1969.

7. D. Reed interview by Bass and De Vries; *St. Petersburg Times*, April 25, 26, 1969; *St. Petersburg Evening Independent*, April 25, 26, 1969; *Miami Herald*, April 25, 26, 1969; Linda Gardner to Reubin Askew, June 6, 1969, folder 9, box 4, RG 497, SAF; James interview; *Orlando Sentinel*, April 26, 1969; Kallina, *Claude Kirk*, 131–37; Kirk interview by Pleasants.

8. *Tampa Tribune*, April 25, 1969; *St. Petersburg Times*, April 26, 1969, September 10, 1970; *Orlando Sentinel*, April 26, 1969; *Kirk v. Brantley*, 227 So. 2d 278 (1970); D. Reed interview by Bass and De Vries.

9. *St. Petersburg Times*, May 1, 9, 15, 1969; Joanos interview; Pettigrew interview; Schultz interview by the author.

10. *St. Petersburg Times*, November 11, 12, 1968, April 20, May 1, November 9, 1969; Pettigrew interview.

11. Joanos interview; *St. Petersburg Times*, June 6, 7, 19, 1969; *In re Advisory Opinion to the Governor*, 223 So. 2d 35 (1969).

12. *St. Petersburg Times*, June 4, 20, 1969.

13. Ibid., June 8, 1969.

14. Ibid., June 25, 1969, April 11, 1970.

15. *Miami News*, January 21, 1970; Kallina, *Claude Kirk*, 17–75; *St. Petersburg Times*, April 7–21, 1970; *Caroline Harvest v. Board of Public Instruction, Manatee County, et al.*, 429 F.2d 414, 312 F.Supp. 269 (1970); *Swann et al. v. Charlotte-Mecklenburg Board of Education, et al.*, 402 U.S. 1 (1971).

16. Kallina, *Claude Kirk*, 17–75; *St. Petersburg Times*, April 11–14, 1970; Kiser interview by the author; Kirk interview by the author.

17. Kallina, *Claude Kirk*, 187; *St. Petersburg Times*, April 21, 1970; Morris, *Handbook* (15th ed.), 541.

18. *St. Petersburg Times*, April 13, 16, 1970; D. Reed interview by the author.

19. *St. Petersburg Times*, May 10, June 4, 11, 12, 1970; *Palm Beach Post-Times*, May 16, 1970; G. Johnson interview.

20. *St. Petersburg Times*, June 5, 20, 1970; *Tampa Tribune*, June 28, 1970; *New York Times*, August 16, 1970; *In re Advisory Opinion to the Governor*, 239 So 2d. (1970).

21. R. Askew interviews by the author; *St. Petersburg Times*, June 4, 1970; *Deeb v. Adams*, 315 F.Supp. 1299 (1970); *Stack v. Adams*, 315 F.Supp. 1295 (1970); *Clements v. Fashing*, 457 U.S. 957 (1982).

Chapter 4. A Mother's Son

1. Schnitt interview; R. Askew interviews by the author; R. Askew interview by Pleasants.

2. Schnitt interview; R. Askew interviews by the author; R. Askew interview by Pleasants.

3. R. Askew interviews by the author; R. Askew interview by Sellers; R. Askew interview by Pleasants.

4. Ibid.

5. Ibid.

6. Harris interview; R. Askew interviews by the author.

7. R. Askew interviews by the author.

8. R. Askew interviews by the author; R. Askew interview by Pleasants; *Tampa Tribune*, January 4, 1971; Myers interview.

9. Pleasants interview.

10. DeHaven-Smith interview; R. Askew interviews by Pleasants; *Tampa Tribune*, January 4, 1971.

11. Don Pride, e-mail to the author, October 8, 2009; Schultz interview by Vasilinda; E. W. Hopkins Jr. quoted in *Tampa Tribune*, January 4, 1971; R. Askew interview by Pleasants; R. Askew interviews by the author; R. Askew interview by Sellers.

12. R. Askew interview by Pleasants; R. Askew interviews by the author; R. Askew interview by Sellers; Godown, "A Talk with Reubin Askew."

13. Dyckman, *Floridian of His Century*, 50, 109; R. Askew interview by Sellers; FSU University Council minutes, May 7, 1951, copy in possession of author.

14. R. Askew interviews by the author; R. Askew interview by Pleasants.

15. R. Askew interviews by the author; Birchfield interview; Pettigrew interview; Bax interviews.

16. R. Askew interviews by the author; D. L. Askew interview; Bacchus interview.

Chapter 5. Reubin Who? (1968–1970)

1. Bill Moyers, multiple sources, confirmed in e-mail to the author, April 11, 2001.

2. Bass and De Vries, *Transformation of Southern Politics*, 123–24 (Caddell quote); Clotfelter and Hamilton, "'New Faces,'" 6.

3. Steve Pajcic, "The Economic Desirability of a Corporation Income Tax for Florida" (senior thesis, Princeton University, 1968), 1–158; Pajcic interview.

4. G. Johnson interview; Stearns interview; Talbot D'Alemberte, e-mail to the author, May 20, 2008.

5. Slade interview; Allen Morris column, date unknown, copy in author's possession; *Gainesville Sun*, November 28, 1999.

6. *Gainesville Sun*, November 28, 1999; R. Askew interviews by the author; *St. Petersburg Times*, April 27, 1970; R. Askew interview by Pleasants; Nordheimer, "Florida's 'Supersquare.'"

7. Nordheimer, "Florida's 'Supersquare'"; Horne interview; Morris interview.

8. R. Askew interview by Pleasants; Meiklejohn, "Rube."

9. R. Askew interviews by the author; Apthorp interviews; *Gainesville Sun*, November 28, 1999.

10. Hooker, "Most Powerful People in Florida"; R. Askew interviews by the author; *St. Petersburg Times*, November 4, 1970.

11. Moyle interview by the author; Stearns interview; Mack Humphrey to Reubin Askew, November 4, 1970, folder "Democratic Party," box 2, RG 497, SAF.

12. *Gainesville Sun*, November 28, 1999; Sheldon interview.

13. *St. Petersburg Times*, June 3, October 20, November 26, December 29, 1969, July 15, 18, 1970; Bacchus, "Cracker Catharsis," 19.

14. Sheldon interview; *Gainesville Sun,* November 28, 1999.

15. Graham interview by Vasilinda; *St. Petersburg Times*, July 17, 1970.

16. Elmer Rounds quoted in Dyckman, "The Reubin Askew Years"; Godown, "A Talk with Reubin Askew"; R. Askew interviews by the author; *St. Petersburg Times*, August 6, 7, 1970.

17. R. Askew interviews by the author; *St. Petersburg Times*, October 1, 1970; Florida Secretary of State, *Tabulation of Official Votes, Florida Primary Election, 1970*; *Palm Beach Post*, August 3, 1970; Slade interview; campaign statement, August 25, 1970, copy in author's possession.

18. G. Johnson interview; Stearns interview; *Tampa Tribune*, August 27, 1970; *St. Petersburg Times*, September 3, 1970; *Miami Herald*, September 13, 1970.

19. Trippett, "He Won in a Walk," 46–47.

20. *Tampa Tribune*, August 29, 1970; *St. Petersburg Times*, August 30, 1970; Florida Secretary of State, *Tabulation of Official Votes*.

21. Florida Secretary of State, *Tabulation of Official Votes*; Meiklejohn interview.

22. *Miami Herald*, September 10, 1970; *St. Petersburg Times*, September 15, 27, 1970; *Tampa Tribune*, September 22, 1970; R. Askew interviews by the author.

23. Associated Press, October 21, 1970; Morris, *Florida Handbook* (15th ed.), 534–37;

Miami Herald, September 30, 1970; Hagaman interview; *St. Petersburg Times*, October 25, 27, 1970.

24. Askew campaign statement, September 14, 1970, copy in author's possession; R. Askew interviews by the author; *Gainesville Sun*, November 28, 1999.

25. Bass and De Vries, *Transformation of Southern Politics*, 124; R. Askew interviews by the author; *St. Petersburg Times*, November 2, 1970.

26. Florida Secretary of State, *Tabulation of Official Votes, November 3, 1970, General Election.*

27. *Tampa Tribune*, November 3, 1970; *St. Petersburg Times*, November 3, 1970.

Chapter 6. Baptism by Fire (1970–1971)

1. R. Askew interviews by the author; Smith interview; Ed H. Price Jr. to James Apthorp, January 26, 2004, copy in author's possession.

2. *St. Petersburg Times*, December 13, 1970; Pride interview by the author; Ed H. Price Jr. to author, March 5, 2007; Apthorp interviews.

3. Apthorp interviews; R. Askew interview by Pleasants; R. Askew interviews by the author.

4. R. Askew interview by Pleasants; *Tampa Tribune*, January 3, 1971; Smith interview.

5. *St. Petersburg Times*, July 25, October 3, November 18, 1970; Gillespie interview; Pettigrew interview; Stearns interview.

6. *Tampa Tribune*, January 1, 1971; Dyckman, *Disorderly Court*, 37–38; Young interview.

7. *Tampa Tribune*, January 3, 1971; Floyd T. Christian to Reubin Askew, January 12, 1971, folder 10, box 2, RG 942, SAF; Barnett, "Icon," 19; *St. Petersburg Times*, December 29, 1970, January 2, 1971; Apthorp interviews.

8. Governor David Sholtz (1933–37) had Jewish parentage but professed Christianity. Gary Mormino, e-mail to the author, December 9, 2008.

9. Kirk text, folder January 1971, box 1, RG 67, SAF; *Tampa Tribune*, January 10, 1971; R. Askew interviews by the author.

10. Apthorp interviews; Stearns interview; Stearns e-mail to the author, February 2, 2007; *Tampa Tribune*, January 6, 1971.

11. Arthur J. England, e-mail to the author, July 14, 2008; *In re Advisory Opinion to the Governor*, 243 So. 2d 753 (1971); *Tampa Tribune*, January 13, 16, 23, 1971.

12. Art. XI, secs. 2, 5, constitution of 1968; *In re Advisory Opinion to the Governor*, 243 So. 2d 753 (1971); Askew text, box 1, RG 65, SAF; Dyckman, *Disorderly Court*, 3.

13. Greg Johnson, "A Corporate Profits Tax in Florida," January 25, 1971, copy in author's possession; *Tampa Tribune*, January 18, 27, 1971; Price interviews; G. Johnson interview; Apthorp interviews; Stearns interview; Dyckman, "The Reubin Askew Years."

14. *Tampa Tribune*, January 31, February 1, 1971; *City of Miami Beach v. Berns*, 245 So. 2d 38 (1971).

15. *Tampa Tribune*, February 1, 4, 5, 7, 14, 1971; House *Journal*, February 2, 1971, 98, and February 3, 1971, 102–3; Birchfield interview; Parrish interview; *St. Petersburg Times*, February 19, 1971.

16. *New York Times*, January 13, 1971; *Time*, February 1, 1971, http://www.georgia encyclopedia.org/nge/Article.isp?id-h-676.

17. *St. Petersburg Times*, February 13, January 16, 19, 1971; *Tampa Tribune*, January 16, 19, May 6, 1971; statement, folder "February 1971," box 1, RG 67, SAF; R. Askew interviews by the author.

18. *St. Petersburg Times*, May 6, July 31, 1971.

Chapter 7. "Curse You, Red Baron" (1971)

1. *Tampa Tribune*, March 3, 6, 12, 21, 1971; *St. Petersburg Times*, March 17, 1971; Askew's speech, box 1, RG 65, SAF; see Trippett, *The States*, regarding special interests as the legislature's "true constituency."

2. House *Journal*, April 6, 1971, 57–62, 66.

3. Ibid.; *St. Petersburg Times*, May 7, 17, 1971.

4. *St. Petersburg Times*, April 22, 23, 1971; House *Journal*, April 22, 1971, 245–46; Dunbar interview.

5. *St. Petersburg Times*, April 25, 30, 1971; Amlong, "Law Is Just a Four-Letter Word."

6. *St. Petersburg Times*, April 24, May 5, June 27, 28, 1971; remarks to Florida Press Association, folder "May 1971," box 1, RG 67, SAF; House *Journal*, May 6, 1971, 420.

7. Executive order establishing the nominating councils, folder "August 1971," box 1, RG 67, SAF; Young interview.

8. *Tampa Tribune*. January 16, 20, February 12, 1971; *St. Petersburg Times*, April 2, 30, July 7, 1971; Gene Stearns to William Hamilton, August 18, 1971, folder "Corporate Profits Tax Correspondence Out G-Wi," box 1, RG 939, SAF; Woodburn interview; *New York Times*, May 6, 1971; Paul Schnitt, e-mail to the author, March 24, 2006.

9. Tom Adams to Mallory Horne, Mallory Horne to Tom Adams, May 28, 1971, folder "Adams 1971–72(7)," box 1, RG 942, SAF.

10. R. Askew interviews by the author; R. Askew interview by Pleasants; folder "April 1971," box 1, RG 67, SAF; *St. Petersburg Times*, April 3, 18, 21, 1971.

11. *St. Petersburg Times*, April 14, May 7, 23, 30, June 3, December 13, 1971, March 26, 1972; D'Alemberte interview.

12. *St. Petersburg Times*, April 27, May 11, 19, June 4, 11, 1971; official history of mental health legislation, http://www.dcf.state.fl.us/mentalhealth/laws/histba .pdfput, accessed January 6, 2009.

13. *St. Petersburg Times*, April 9, May 26, June 16, 1971; *Florida Tax Handbook*, 136; House *Journal*, April 8, 1971, 83; MacKay interviews.

14. *St. Petersburg Times*, April 13, June 23, 1971; veto messages, folder "1971," box 1, RG 947, SAF; D'Alemberte interview; Pettigrew interview; Stearns interview.

15. Veto messages, folder "1971," box 1, RG 947, SAF.

16. *St. Petersburg Times*, May 11, October 9, 24, 1971; *New York Times*, October 17, 1971.

17. *St. Petersburg Times*, June 27, 1971, December 3, 1996; D. Reed interview by Bass and De Vries; Dunbar interview; Stearns interview. Voting statistics were compiled from the 1971 House *Journal*; a partisan vote is defined as one in which a majority of one party opposes a majority of the other.

18. Schultz interview by the author; T. Terrell Sessums to the author, October 30, 2007.

Chapter 8. "And Rightly So" (1971)

1. Don Pride, e-mail to the author, January 11, 2009; Peggy Peterman, "Three Who Led," *St. Petersburg Times,* February 21, 1993; Pride interview by the author; Page interview.

2. *Swann v. Charlotte-Mecklenburg Board of Education*, 402 U.S. 1 (1971); *St. Petersburg Times*, April 30, August 4, 1971; "Busing: Stop and Go," 47.

3. *St. Petersburg Times*, October 11, 1970; Askew statement regarding Charlotte-Mecklenburg decision, folder "April 1971," box 1, RG 67, SAF; *Tampa Tribune*, August 19, 1971; Don Pride to Reubin Askew, undated memorandum in Pride's personal files, copy in author's possession; R. Askew interviews by the author; Roland Page column, *Gainesville Sun*, December 1978 (date unavailable).

4. Commencement address, University of Florida, August 28, 1971, "as-delivered" text in Don Pride's personal files.

5. Ibid., emphasis added.

6. Page column, *Gainesville Sun*; R. Askew interviews by the author.

7. *St. Petersburg Times*, August 29, 1971; *Miami Herald*, August 29, 1971; *Florida Times-Union*, August 29, 1971; *New York Times*, September 1, 1971; *St. Petersburg Times*, September 20, 1971.

8. Dyckman, "The Reubin Askew Years"; Stearns interview; Apthorp interviews.

9. *St. Petersburg Times*, October 14, November 9, 1971; Askew remarks to PTA Congress, box 3, RG 65, SAF; *New York Times*, November 19, 1971.

Chapter 9. "Some Nut with a Huey Long Outlook" (1971)

1. Jim Smith to Reubin Askew et al., August 26, 1971, folder "Corporate Income Tax," box 1, RG 686, SAF; Greg Johnson to Reubin Askew, August 5, 1971, folder 3, box 9, RG 942, SAF; R. Askew interview by Pleasants.

2. R. Askew interview by Pleasants; press statement, September 8, 1971, box 1, RG 66, SAF; *Greenhut v. Knott*, 247 So. 2d 517 (1971); Charlie Harris to Reubin Askew, September 13, 1971, folder "General Correspondence 1971," box 1, RG 942, SAF.

3. *St. Petersburg Times*, October 30, 1971; R. Askew interviews by the author; R. Askew interview by Pleasants; *Miami Herald*, October 1, 1971; *St. Petersburg Independent*, October 29, 1971.

4. "Ax the Tax" pamphlet, folder 19, box 4, RG 942, SAF; Ben Duncan to Reubin Askew, folder "Corporate Profits Tax," box 1, RG 939, SAF; Askew speech to bankers, box 2, SAF 65; *St. Petersburg Times*, October 10, 20, 21, 22, 28, 1971; folder "Corporate Profits Tax Correspondence Out A–F," box 1, RG 939, SAF; Alan Lindsay to Reubin Askew, June 7, 1971, and Robert J. Bishop to James Apthorp, September 15, 1971, folder 19, box 4, RG 942, SAF; Donald H. Reed Jr. to Reubin Askew, October 21, 1971, folder 18, box 12, RG 942, SAF.

5. Askew speech to Associated Industries, box 2, RG 65, SAF.

6. *St. Petersburg Times*, October 13, 28, 1971; Floyd Christian to Mel Turner, October 20, 1971, folder "Cabinet," box 1, RG 497, SAF.

7. Dyckman, "The Reubin Askew Years"; *St. Petersburg Times*, October 27, 31, November 1, 3, 1971; *Miami Herald*, November 3, 1971.

8. *St. Petersburg Times*, November 1, 3, 1971; *Miami Herald*, November 1, 3, 1971.

9. *Miami Herald*, November 3, 1971; *St. Petersburg Times*, November 4, 5, 1971; Bob Bentley to Reubin Askew, November 2, 1971, folder "A–B," box 1, RG 497, SAF.

10. *St. Petersburg Times*, November 4, 13, 1971; Thomas F. Fleming Jr. to Jim Smith, February 11, 1972, folder "Corporate Income Tax," box 1, RG 686, SAF.

11. *New York Times*, December 24, 1971; Alvah Chapman Jr. to Reubin Askew, November 16, 1971, Askew to Chapman, November 19, 1971, folder "Corporate Profits Tax Correspondence Out A–F," box 1, RG 939, SAF.

12. Transcript, box 3, RG 65, SAF; Don Pride, e-mails to author, January 25, 2009.

13. Transcript, box 3, RG 65, SAF; Don Pride, e-mails to author, January 25, 2009.

14. Lorna Allen to Reubin Askew, November 23, 1971, file "Florida Council of 100," box 2, RG 686, SAF; Joint statement, August 10, 1971, folder "August 1971," box 1, RG 67, SAF.

Chapter 10. Promises Fulfilled (1971)

1. Reubin Askew to John Culbreath, November 16, 1971, folder "Corporate Profits Tax Correspondence Out A–F," box 1, RG 939, SAF.

2. D'Alemberte interview.

3. Ibid.; R. Askew interview by Pleasants; D'Alemberte, e-mail to the author, January 25, 2009, *St. Petersburg Times*, September 5, 1970.

4. D'Alemberte interview; Birchfield interview.

5. House *Journal*, December 9, 1971, 115; Senate *Journal*, December 9, 1971, 69; *St. Petersburg Times*, December 10, 1971; House *Journal*, December 10, 1971, 116; *Tampa Tribune*, March 23, 1996; Chesterfield Smith to Reubin Askew, December 13, 1971, folder "S," box 3, RG 497, SAF.

6. *St. Petersburg Times*, December 3, 1971; Talbot D'alemberte, e-mail to the author, January 9, 2009; House *Journal*, December 9, 1971, 115; Don Reed to Reubin Askew, December 22, 1971, folder 18, box 12, RG 942, SAF.

7. Senate *Journal*, November 29, 1971, 5; House *Journal*, December 7, 1971, 67; *St. Petersburg Times*, December 9, 1971.

8. *St. Petersburg Times*, November 11, 1971; *Newsweek*, January 13, 1972; *New York Times*, December 24, 1971.

9. Greg Johnson to Reubin Askew, December 21, 1971, file "Special Session 1971 General Correspondence, box 2, RG 686, SAF; *St. Petersburg Times*, November 9, 14, 15, 1971.

10. *St. Petersburg Times*, August 30, October 26, November 24, 1971.

Chapter 11. Bus Wreck (February–April 1972)

1. *St. Petersburg Times*, February 15, March 1, 1972; Dent, *Prodigal South*, 247.

2. Senate *Journal*, February 1, 1972, 42–47; *St. Petersburg Times*, February 2, 1972; Barnett, *Mirage*, 53–54.

3. Senate *Journal*, February 1, 1972, 42–47; *State ex rel. Shevin v. Yarborough*, 257 So. 2d 891 (1972).

4. Senate *Journal*, February 9, 1972, 107–9; House *Journal*, February 10, 1972, 249–51; *St. Petersburg Times*, February 11, 1972.

5. House *Journal*, February 14, 1972, 135–37; *St. Petersburg Times*, February 15, 18, 22, 1972; R. Askew interview by Range; Dyckman, "The Reubin Askew Years."

6. Askew speech, http:///www.floridamemory.com/OnlineClassroom/Reubin Askew/speech.18cfm, accessed November 30, 2006.

7. *New York Times*, February 22, 24, 1972; R. Askew interview by Denham; *Meet the Press*, March 5, 1972; "Letter from Barry Goldwater," March 6, 1972, http://www.floridamemory.com/OnlineClassroom/ReubinAskew/Goldwater1.cfm, accessed November 30, 2006; *St. Petersburg Times*, February 26, 1972.

8. *Miami Herald*, April 29, 1972; Hagaman and Sanford contributions, folder "Campaign Treasurer's Preelection Report," box 1, RG 87, SAF; *St. Petersburg Times*, February 24, March 3, 11, 13, 14, 1972; R. Askew interview by Vasilinda.

9. Florida Secretary of State, *Tabulation of Official Votes* for presidential primary, March 14, 1972; *Tampa Tribune*, March 25, 1972; *St. Petersburg Times*, March 15, 16, 1972; Mormino, "When Florida Counted"; House *Journal*, March 15, 1972, 665.

10. Senate *Journal*, March 14, 1972, 429–31, 433; *St. Petersburg Times*, February 13, March 3, 16, 17, 1972; House *Journal*, February 7, 1972, 223.

11. House *Journal*, February 23, 1972, 408–10, and March 3, 1972, 554–66.

12. Ibid., March 2, 1972, 524–25; *St. Petersburg Times*, March 3, 1972.

13. *State v. Barquet*, 262 So. 2d 431 (1972); *St. Petersburg Times*, February 16, 18, 1972.

14. *St. Petersburg Times*, February 25, March 17, 1972; Senate *Journal*, March 16, 1972, 452.

15. Dyckman, "The Reubin Askew Years"; Don Pride to Reubin Askew, March 31, 1972, and Eugene Stearns to Reubin Askew, May 18, 1972, copies in author's possession; Stearns e-mail to the author, February 27, 2007; R. Askew interview by the author; Parrish interview; Apthorp interviews; Stearns interview; Smith interview.

16. *St. Petersburg Times*, March 29, April 2, 1972.

17. Ibid.; *Trombetta v. State*, 339 F.Supp. 1359 (1972), 353 F.Supp. 575 (1973); *New York Times*, May 4, 2003.

18. House *Journal*, March 16, 1972; Senate *Journal*, April 7, 1972, 917; *St. Petersburg Times*, April 11, 1972.

19. Minter interview; *St. Petersburg Times*, March 30, July 18, 1973.

20. *St. Petersburg Times*, March 30, April 8, 1972; DeGrove interviews; Graham interview by the author; Crane interview; Shreve interview.

21. Gregory Johnson to Reubin Askew, July 28, 1972, folder 18, box 3, RG 942, SAF.

22. Gregory Johnson to Reubin Askew, July 5, 1972, folder "J," box 3, RG 497, SAF.

Chapter 12. The Politics of 1972

1. *Miami Herald*, July 23, 1972; R. Askew interviews by the author; Nordheimer, "Florida's 'Supersquare'"; *Meet the Press*, March 5, 1972.

2. *New York Times*, April 16, 1972; McGovern interview; Mansfield, "All the Governor's Men"; *Miami Herald*, July 23, 1972; R. Askew interview by Pleasants; R. Askew interviews by the author; Don Pride to Reubin Askew, June 7, 1972, copy in author's possession.

3. Askew's notes, box 7, RG 65, SAF; Paul Schnitt, e-mail to the author, March 24, 2006.

4. R. Askew interview by Pleasants; Newell and King, "Keynote Address," 347–48.

5. R. Askew interviews by the author; R. Askew interview by Pleasants; D'Alemberte interview; *Miami Herald*, July 23, 1972.

6. Newell and King, "Keynote Address," 349; *St. Petersburg Times*, July 12, 1972.

7. Newell and King, "Keynote Address," 353.

8. R. Askew interview by Pleasants.

9. Ibid.; Newell and King, "Keynote Address," 355; E. J. Speed to Reubin Askew, July 12, 1972, copy in author's possession; Robert Bowden to Reubin Askew, July 20, 1972, folder 17, box 4, RG 497, SAF.

10. George McGovern, "Help Wanted," *New York Times,* August 29, 2008; Pride interview by the author; Parrish interview; *St. Petersburg Times*, July 26, 1972.

11. *Miami Herald*, July 26, 1972; *New York Times*, August 2, 1972; Don Pride to Reubin Askew, August 3, 1972, copy in author's possession; Pride interview by the author.

12. G. Johnson interview; Page interview; *St. Petersburg Times*, August 28, September 25, 1972.

13. McGovern interview.

14. James Apthorp to Reubin Askew, May 31, 1972, folder 15, box 2, RG 942, SAF; *St. Petersburg Independent*, May 17, 1972, *St. Petersburg Times*, June 2, 1972; news conference transcript, box 1, RG 66, SAF.

15. *Miami Herald*, May 14, 1972, January 14, 1973; Jane Love to Reubin Askew, April 26, 1972, box 15, RG 942, SAF; *St. Petersburg Times*, July 23, 1972; press release, folder "January 1973," box 2, RG 67, SAF.

16. Dyckman, *Floridian of His Century*, 102; Edgar M. Dunn Jr. to Reubin Askew, May 17, 1972, William L. Reed to Reubin Askew, October 16, 1972, and Robert A. Murphy to Edward A. Miller, July 18, 1972, folder "Willis McCall," box 7, RG 947, SAF; *St. Petersburg Times*, October 24, November 19, 1971, May 19, August 21, November 8,

1972, November 28, 1999; R. Askew interviews by the author; *Daniels v. State*, 354 So. 2d 395 (1971).

17. *Furman v. Georgia*, 408 U.S. 238 (1972); *St. Petersburg Times*, July 8, 10, 1971; press releases, folder "August 72," box 2, RG 67, SAF.

18. Muskogee speech, box 5, RG 65, SAF.

19. Press releases, folder "July 1972," box 2, RG 67, SAF; Morris, *Florida Handbook* (15th ed.), 549; Hawkins interview.

20. Pettigrew interview; *St. Petersburg Times*, November 9, 1972, April 1, 1973; Price interviews.

21. Gregory Favre, e-mail to the author, February 26, 2009.

22. Text of Askew speech, box 13, RG 65, SAF.

23. Senate *Journal*, November 28, December 1, 1972, 7–8, 35–40; House *Journal*, December 1, 1972, 51; *St. Petersburg Times*, November 29, December 1, 2, 9, 1972; E. Harris Drew to Reubin Askew, December 7, 1972, and Askew to Drew, December 13, 1972, folder "D," box 1, RG 497, SAF.

24. *State v. Dixon*, 283 So. 2d 1 (1973); *Proffitt v. Florida*, 428 U.S. 242 (1976); Skene, "Review of Capital Cases," 267.

25. *Washington Post*, December 10, 11, 1972.

Chapter 13. Down on the Farm (Spring 1973)

1. R. Askew interviews by the author; Amlong, "Reubin Askew"; K. Askew interview.

2. R. Askew interviews by the author; *Ft. Lauderdale News*, February 14, 1973; Hayes interview.

3. *Ft. Lauderdale News*, February 14, 1973; *St. Petersburg Times*, February 15, 1973; *Miami Herald*, March 25, 1973.

4. *Ft. Lauderdale News*, February 14, 15, 23, 1973; Hayes interview; *St. Petersburg Evening Independent*, February 16, 17, 1973; speech text, February 13, 1973, box 6, RG 65, SAF.

5. Parrish interview.

6. *St. Petersburg Times*, February 24, 1973; *Florida Times Union*, February 24, 1973; *Ft. Lauderdale News*, February 24, 1973; transcript and notes for press conference, February 23, 1973, box 1, RG 66, SAF.

7. Kennison, *Report*, 2; *Miami Herald*, February 25, 1973; *Orlando Sentinel*, February 25, 1973; *Fort Lauderdale News*, February 26, 1973; *Tampa Tribune*, March 1, 19973; *Pensacola News-Journal*, March 2, 1973.

8. *Pensacola News-Journal*, February 28, 1973.

9. *St. Petersburg Times*, March 1, 1973; Conley M. Kennison to James L. Redman, September 24, 1973, folder 3, box 2, RG 942, SAF.

10. *St. Petersburg Times*, March 3, 1973; *Miami Herald*, June 28 1974.

11. Ed H. Price Jr. to the author, March 19, 2007; *St. Petersburg Times*, March 8, 14, 15, 1973; Kennison, *Report*, 11; *Miami Herald*, March 16, 1973.

12. *St. Petersburg Times*, March 30, 1973; House *Journal*, June 1, 1973, 1185–1203; Richard T. Mounts memo to file, March 20, 1973, copy in author's possession.

13. *Miami Herald*, March 25–30, 1973; House *Journal*, April 3, 1973, 4–9.

14. House *Journal*, April 3, 1973, 4–9, and April 17, 1973, 216–17; *St. Petersburg Times*, March 29, 1973.

15. Speech to legislature, April 3, 1973, and speech to Florida Education Association, March 29, 1973, box 7, RG 65, SAF.

16. Rudnick interview.

17. *St. Petersburg Times*, April 6, 8, 10, 11, May 3, June 10, 1973; *District School Board of Lee County v. Askew*, 278 So. 2d 272 (1973); C. B. Reed interview.

18. *St. Petersburg Times*, June 3, 1973; *Miami Herald*, June 8, 1973; Sessums interview; Harris interview.

19. Pettigrew interview; *State ex rel. Szabo Food Services Inc. v. Dickinson*, 286 So. 2d 529 (1973).

20. Statement, folder "April 1973," box 2, RG 67, SAF; *St. Petersburg Times*, April 12, 26, May 17, 2003; Rose interview; Redman interview.

21. House *Journal*, May 17, 1973, 627, 633, and June 1, 1973, 1185–1203; *St. Petersburg Times*, May 18, June 1, 1973; Askew speeches, folder "May 1973," box 2, RG 67, SAF.

22. *St. Petersburg Times*, May 13, 1973; MacKay interviews.

23. *St. Petersburg Times*, May 23, June 10, 1973; veto message, folder "1973," box 1, RG 947, SAF.

24. *St. Petersburg Times*, April 11, 1973; press release, folder "May 1973," box 2, RG 67, SAF; *Florida Baptist Witness*, May 24, 1973; form letter, folder "1973," box 1, RG 947, SAF.

Chapter 14. Scandals in the Capitol (1972–1975)

1. *St. Petersburg Times*, December 2, 1972; R. Askew interview by Pleasants; R. Askew interviews by the author; Don Pride, e-mail to the author, April 9, 2009.

2. *Miami Herald*, September 10, 1973; R. Askew interview by Pleasants; *St. Petersburg Times*, July 29, 1973.

3. R. Askew interviews by the author.

4. *St. Petersburg Times*, June 1, 1974.

5. Ibid., November 20, 1973, February 6, 7, 10, 1974; Associated Press, September 20, 1980; *United States v. Shields*, 675 F.2d 1152 (1982); R. Askew interviews by the author.

6. R. Askew interviews by the author; Hilliard, "Welcome to Barron Country."

7. *St. Petersburg Times*, July 29, August 6, 1973; Paul A. Skelton Jr. to Oliver J. Keller, August 6, 1973, folder 1, box 8, RG 942, SAF.

8. Howard Jay Friedman to Floyd Christian, August 10, 1972, and Floyd Christian to Terrell Sessums, September 6, 1972, folder 11, box 1, RG 302, SAF; Rose interview; *St. Petersburg Times*, January 1, 13, 27, February 28, 1974; R. Askew interviews by the author.

9. *St. Petersburg Times*, April 18, 26, 1974.

10. Ibid., April 22, May 18, 19, 1974; *Pensacola News-Journal*, May 18, 1974.

11. *In re Executive Assignment of State Attorney*, 298 So. 2d 382, (1974); *St. Petersburg Times*, August 6, 7, 1974; Dyckman, *Disorderly Court*, 70–72; Askew press statements, folder "July 1974," box 3, RG 67, SAF.

12. *St. Petersburg Times*, August 27, 28, October 19, 1974.

13. Dyckman, *Disorderly Court*, 73–75; *St. Petersburg Times*, April 5, September 17, 1975.

14. *St. Petersburg Times*, June 26, 1975; Askew press statements, folder "April 1975," box 3, RG 67, SAF; R. Askew interviews by the author.

15. Dyckman, *Disorderly Court*, 73–75; *St. Petersburg Times*, September 30, 1974; *Ocala Star-Banner*, January 12, 1977.

Chapter 15. Scandals in the Court (1973–1976)

1. Dyckman, *Disorderly Court*, 1–15; *St. Petersburg Times*, December 15, 1973.

2. Dyckman, *Disorderly Court*, 1–15.

3. *Gulf Power v. Bevis*, 296 So. 2d 482 (1974).

4. *State ex rel. Turner v. Earle*, 295 So. 2d 609 (1974); Dyckman, *Disorderly Court*, 85; *St. Petersburg Times*, May 29, 1974.

5. Dyckman, *Floridian of His Century*, 256–7; *St. Petersburg Times*, May 29, 1974; Canaday interview; Chesterfield Smith to Reubin Askew, February 18, 1974, folder 3, box 13, RG 942, SAF.

6. Speech text, October 17, 1974, box 11, RG 65, SAF.

Chapter 16. Only in Florida (Politics of 1974)

1. Moyle interview by Bass and De Vries; *St. Petersburg Times*, February 24, 1974.

2. *St. Petersburg Times*, October 22, 1974; *Miami Herald*, September 6, 1974.

3. *St. Petersburg Times*, January 31, 1974.

4. *Gainesville Sun*, January 29, 1974; *St. Petersburg Times*, September 20, 1973, August 7, 14, 1974, January 19, 1975; press releases, folders 7, 8, box 4, RG 942, SAF; *Gainesville Sun*, November 24, 1973; miscellaneous memoranda, folder "January 1975," box 3, RG 67, SAF.

5. *St. Petersburg Times*, April 7, 1974; House *Journal*, April 2, 1974, 2–12.

6. *St. Petersburg Times*, April 23, May 22, 30, 1974.

7. House *Journal*, April 23, 1974, 436–42; MacKay interviews; Horne interview; Williams interview.

8. House *Journal*, April 15, 1974, 318–20; Senate *Journal*, May 31, 1974, 958; Gillespie interview.

9. Crane interview; House *Journal*, April 25, 1974, 463, April 29, 1974, 490, and May 30, 1974, 1152; *St. Petersburg Times*, May 31, June 13, July 14, 1974; *Miami Herald*, June 2, 1974.

10. Danahy interview; House *Journal*, April 29, 1974, 490, and May 30, 1974, 1152, 1185; *St. Petersburg Times*, April 24, May 30, 31, June 1, 6. November 7, 1974; *Miami Herald*, June 2, 1974.

11. *St. Petersburg Times*, May 16, 1974; Harris interview.

12. *Miami Herald*, June 2, 1974.

13. *In re Advisory Opinion (Civil Rights)*, 306 So. 2d 520 (1975); *New York Times*, April 6, 2007.

14. Press release, folder "October 1973," box 2, RG 67, SAF; *Miami Herald*, June 26, 1974.

15. *St. Petersburg Times*, April 11, 23, 1974; Adams statement, copy in author's possession; undated Askew staff memorandum, folder "January 1974," box 3, RG 67, SAF; Meiklejohn, "Rube"; Parrish interview.

16. *St. Petersburg Times*, April 23, 1974; *Tampa Tribune*, April 22, 1974.

17. *St. Petersburg Times*, May 7, June 29, August 1, 13, 15, 26, 1974; *Clearwater Sun*, June 16, 1974; *Miami Herald*, June 28, 1974.

18. *St. Petersburg Times*, May 15, 27, 1974.

19. Ibid., May 16, 27, June 17, 1974; speech text, box 10, RG 65, SAF; R. Askew interview by Bass and De Vries.

20. R. Askew interviews by the author.

21. *St. Petersburg Times*, July 24, August 1, 23, 1974; *Orlando Sentinel-Star*, July 25, 1974; Pride interview by the author; R. Askew interviews by the author; Morris, *Florida Handbook* (15th ed.), 542.

22. Apthorp interviews; Bacchus interview; R. Askew interview by Pleasants; Middlebrooks interview.

23. Parrish interview; statement, September 10, 1974, box 2, RG 66, SAF; *St. Petersburg Times*, August 24, September 15, 1974; Florida Secretary of State, *Tabulation of Official Votes*, 1974 primaries.

24. Dyckman, *Disorderly Court*, 78–81; *St. Petersburg Times*, September 10, 1974.

25. Morris, *Florida Handbook* (15th ed.), 538–41.

26. Speech in Austin, box 11, RG 65, SAF.

27. Ibid.; *Tampa Tribune*, September 25, 1974; *St. Petersburg Times*, October 4, 17, 1974; *Evening Independent*, October 14, 1974.

28. *St. Petersburg Times*, September 27, October 6, 1974; press conferences transcript, folder September 1974, box 3, RG 67, SAF.

29. *St. Petersburg Times*, October 30, November 1, 1974; *Tampa Tribune*, October 31, 1974.

30. *Miami Herald*, November 1, 1974; *Orlando Sentinel-Star*, November 3, 1974; *St. Petersburg Times*, November 5, 1974.

31. *St. Petersburg Times*, November 4, 7, 10, 1974; Florida Secretary of State, *Tabulation of Official Votes*, 1974 general election; MacKay, *How Florida Happened*, 35–36.

32. *St. Petersburg Times*, November 6, 1974; Morris, *Florida Handbook* (15th ed.), 541; campaign finance data, https://doe.dos.state.fl.us/elections/resultsarchive/index.asp, accessed April 15, 2009.

33. *St. Petersburg Times*, December 9, 1974.

Chapter 17. "My Senate" (1975)

1. *Miami Herald*, November 10, 1974; *St. Petersburg Times*, November 17, 20, 21, December 5, 1974, October 21, November 30, 1975.
2. Senate *Journal*, November 19, 1974, 4–5.
3. *St. Petersburg Times*, January 8, 1975.
4. Ibid.
5. Ibid., January 22, June 20, 1975.
6. Ibid., January 1, 16, 1975; R. Askew interview by Pleasants; *In re Advisory Opinion*, 306 So. 2d 509 (1975).
7. *St. Petersburg Times*, April 6, 1975; Kiser interview by the author; Bloom interview.
8. Bloom interview; Horne interview; MacKay interviews; Batchelor interview.
9. R. Askew interview by Pleasants; R. Askew interviews by the author; McKnight, *Golden Years*, 75.
10. House *Journal*, April 8, 1975, 10; *St. Petersburg Times*, April 9, 1975; House *Journal* (bound volume 1975), 1274.
11. *St. Petersburg Times*, April 9, 1975; House *Journal*, April 8, 1975, 3–8; Senate *Journal*, April 25, 1975, 161.
12. *St. Petersburg Times*, July 23, 1972, April 15, 23, 1975, October 30, 1975.
13. Ibid., April 6, May 16, 17, 1975; Rauch interview; Horne interview.
14. *St. Petersburg Times*, May 12, 13, 14, 1975.
15. Ibid., May 17, 1975; Horne interview; Gordon interview.
16. *St. Petersburg Times*, May 22, 1975; Parrish interview.
17. *St. Petersburg Times*, May 24, 1975.
18. Ibid., July 15, 1975; Myers interview; Graham interview by the author.
19. MacKay interviews.
20. *St. Petersburg Times*, June 6, 1975; *Miami Herald*, June 6, 1975.

Chapter 18. Justice Hatchett (1975–1976)

1. Dyckman, *Disorderly Court*, 107–31.
2. Ibid.
3. Ibid., 108–34.
4. Parks interview.
5. Dyckman, *Disorderly Court*, 108–34; Parks interview; *St. Petersburg Times*, July 3, 1975; Gavin Letts to Reubin Askew, June 28, 1975, folder "Supreme Court Appointments Miscellaneous," box 21, RG 138, SAF.
6. Speech, June 21, 1975, box 12, RG 65, SAF; *St. Petersburg Times*, July 8, 9, 1975; Hatchett biography, http://www.floridasupremecourt.org/about/gallery/hatchett.shtml, accessed May 5, 2009; *State ex rel. Hawkins v. Board of Control et al.*, 93 So. 2d 354 (1957).
7. *St. Petersburg Times*, September 8, 1975, March 11, 1988, September 18, 2003; Dyckman, *Disorderly Court*, 135–42.

8. Kiser interview by the author; Lloyd M. Phillips to Reubin Askew, July 17, 1975, folder "Sixth Circuit Judicial Nominating Commission," box 17, RG 136, SAF; McDevitt interview; *St. Petersburg Times*, May 19, 26, 28, November 3, 1976.

Chapter 19. Two Innocent Men and a Crook (1975–1976)

1. *St. Petersburg Times*, September 11, 1975; R. Askew interview by Pleasants.

2. Miller, *Invitation to a Lynching*, 147, 311–13.

3. R. Askew interview by Pleasants; Middlebrooks interview; Canaday interview; Turlington interview by the author; *Miami Herald*, June 17, 2005.

4. Turlington interview by the author; *St. Petersburg Times*, September 16, 1975; *Miami Herald*, September 20, 1975.

5. Miller, *Invitation to a Lynching*, 236–38; Florida Secretary of State, *Tabulation of Official Returns*, 1978 primary and second primary elections; *St. Petersburg Times*, May 2, 1998.

6. *St. Petersburg Times*, May 16, 23, 26, 1975; Rose interview.

7. House *Journal*, June 2, 1975, 1052–61, 1193–1259; *Miami Herald*, November 7, 1974.

8. *St. Petersburg Times*, June 4, 1976; Ashler interview; R. Askew interviews by the author.

9. *St. Petersburg Times*, July 30, 1975; Dyckman, *Disorderly Court*, 74–75.

10. Transcript, October 30, 1975, box 2, RG 66, SAF; statement, folder "January 1977," box 4, RG 67, SAF; *St. Petersburg Times*, November 1, 1975.

Chapter 20. Sunshine and Strife (1975–1976)

1. For the text of the Sunshine Amendment see article II, section 8, Constitution of Florida, as amended in 1976.

2. Ibid.

3. Moyle interview by the author; Krog interview; R. Askew interviews by the author; Don Shoemaker to George Firestone, January 7, 1976, folder "Sunshine Amendment Correspondence," box 1, RG 87, SAF.

4. *St. Petersburg Times*, August 28, 1975; R. Askew interview by Pleasants.

5. *St. Petersburg Times*, June 14, November 20, 1975, January 14, 15, 1976; Askew remarks at campaign kickoff event, folder "November 1975," box 4, RG 67, SAF; Charley Johns to Reubin Askew, January 28, 1976, folder "I–J," box 2, RG 97, SAF.

6. Krog interview; *St. Petersburg Times*, November 1, 1976.

7. Krog interview; *St. Petersburg Times*, April 23, May 28, June 5, July 7, 1976; Lori Wilson statement, June 3, 1976, folder "1976 Legislative Session," box 3, RG 80, SAF; House *Journal*, June 4, 1976, 1306–9; *Goldtrap v. Askew*, 334 So. 2d 20 (1976).

8. *St. Petersburg Times*, July 30, October 7, 1976; *Weber v. Smathers*, 338 So. 2d 819 (1976), *Floridians Against Casino Takeover v. Let's Help Florida*, 363 So. 2d 337 (1978).

9. *Fine v. Firestone*, 448 So. 2d 994 (1980); Rutherford, "The People Drunk," 76–78; Kimball interview.

10. Florida Secretary of State, *Tabulation of Official Votes*, general election, November 1976.

11. *Miami Herald*, January 16, 1977; folder "March 1977," box 4, RG 67, SAF.

12. Executive order 77-51, September 19, 1977, quoted in Senate *Journal*, April 11, 1978, 106.

13. *Florida Commission on Ethics v. Plante*, 369 So. 2d 332 (1979); *Myers v. Hawkins*, 362 So. 2d 926 (1978); *Williams v. Smith*, 360 So. 2d. 417 (1978); *St. Petersburg Times*, December 14, 1977, May 13, 1978; *Boca Raton News*, September 13, 1978.

14. *St. Petersburg Times*, July 1, August 2, 3, 1977; Elaine Bloom, e-mail to the author May 23, 2009.

15. *Plante v. Gonzalez*, 575 F.2d 1119 (1978).

16. *St. Petersburg Times*, January 23, April 11, 1979.

17. Ibid., July 20, 21, 25, 26, 1978; Florida Secretary of State, *Tabulation of Official Votes*, 1978 primary election.

18. *St. Petersburg Times*, October 1, 1978.

19. D'Alemberte, "Essay," 23.

Chapter 21. Lame Duck? (1976)

1. *St. Petersburg Times*, August 10, 1975; Askew statement, December 2, 1975, and Hugh MacMillan memorandum, December 17, 1975, file "December 1975," box 4, RG 67, SAF; *New York Times*, October 24, 1975; prison population statistics, www.dc.state.fl.us/oth/timeline/pop.html, accessed May 27, 2009.

2. *St. Petersburg Times*, April 6, 1976.

3. Askew text, folder 76-11, box 13, RG 65, SAF; *St. Petersburg Times*, June 10, 1976.

4. Askew text, folder 76-11, box 13, RG 65, SAF.

5. *St. Petersburg Times*, April. 17, 20, 24 29, 1976; House *Journal* (bound volume 1976), 1449; Senate *Journal* (bound volume 1976), 799–80.

6. *St. Petersburg Times*, May 20, June 3, June 6, 11, 19, 1976; *Miami Herald*, June 24, 25, 1976; veto messages, folder "1976," box 2, RG 947, SAF; Charles E. Bennett to Reubin Askew, July 1, 1976, folder "A–B," box 1, RG 497, SAF.

7. *St. Petersburg Times*, May 16, 2009.

8. Ibid., January 15, 16, April 30, May 1, 14, 17, 19, June 2, July 14, November 17, 1976, August 26, 1980; Horne interview.

9. *St. Petersburg Times*, April 22, May 24, December 10, 1976.

10. Ibid., October 29, 1976, October 4, 6, 1977; Kiser interview by Vasilinda; *Boca Raton News*, November 3, 1976, *Washington Post*, September 14, October 4, 1977, *New York Times*, September 22, 1977.

11. *Tallahassee Democrat*, September 8, 26, 29, 1976; news conference transcripts, September 14, 30, 1976, box 3, RG 66, SAF.

12. *Proffitt v. Florida*, 428 U.S. 242 (1976); *Proffitt v. State*, 510 So. 2d 896 (1987); July 2 statement, folder "July 1976," box 4, RG 67, SAF.

13. *St. Petersburg Times*, December 17, 18, 1976, May 24, 25, 1977; *New York Times*, December 18, 1976; Noll and Tegeder, *From Exploitation to Conservation*, 1–38.

Chapter 22. Culture Wars (1977)

1. Interview with President Jimmy Carter, the American Presidency Project, October 28, 1977, www.presidency.ucsb.edu/ws/index.php?pid=30255&st=Askew&st1=, accessed December 1, 2006; *Washington Post*, February 3, December 1, 3, 1977; *St. Petersburg Times*, September 9, 10, 1977; R. Askew interviews by the author; folders "June, October 1976" and "January, August 1977," box 4, RG 67, SAF; Middlebrooks interview; Tait interview; *St. Petersburg Times*, December 1, 1977.

2. House *Journal*, April 5, 1977, 19–30; *St. Petersburg Times*, May 28, June 25, 28, 1977.

3. House *Journal*, April 5, 1977, 1–15; folder "March 1977," box 2, RG 67, SAF; *St. Petersburg Times*, February 12, 1978.

4. *St. Petersburg Times*, April 16, 1977; House *Journal*, April 5, 1977, 11, and April 27, 1977, 373.

5. *St. Petersburg Times*, June 4, 5, 1977.

6. Veto message, June 29, 1977, box 3, RG 947, SAF; Sharyn Smith, e-mail to the author, June 19, 2008; Weitzel, *The White Paper*, 22.

7. *St. Petersburg Times*, November 8, December 12, 1976, January 2, 1977.

8. Ibid., April 13, 18, 1977, April 27, 1978; Kiser interview by the author; Brown interview; Mills interview.

9. *St. Petersburg Times*, April 20, 21, July 13, October 12, 13, 1977.

10. Ibid., April 9, 14, May 28, 1977; Senate *Journal*, April 13, 1977, 143–46; MacKay interviews.

11. *St. Petersburg Times*, April 30, 1977; *Lakeland Ledger*, April 1, 1982.

12. Senate *Journal*, May 9, 1977, 354; House *Journal*, May 30, 1977, 839–40; *St. Petersburg Times*, May 4, 1977; *Los Angeles Times*, August 31, 1980; *New York Times*, December 3, 1998; Chamberlin interview; *Miami Herald*, January 26, 2010.

13. *St. Petersburg Times*, April 8, 9, September 4, 1977.

14. R. Askew interviews by the author; R. Askew interview by Pleasants; Morris, *Florida Handbook* (29th ed.), 268–78.

15. *St. Petersburg Times*, September 12, 17, 24, 1979; von Drehle, *Among the Lowest*, 434; R. Askew interviews by the author; R. Askew interview by Pleasants

16. Text, folder 77-36, box 15, RG 65, SAF.

17. *St. Petersburg Times*, December 9, 1977; R. Askew interview by the author.

18. *St. Petersburg Times*, August 7, 1977; *In re Advisory Opinion*, 343 So. 2d 17 (1977).

19. House *Journal*, May 24, 1977, 699–700, and May 25, 1977, 719; *St. Petersburg Times*, May 26, July 2, 17, 1977.

Chapter 23. Triumph and Tragedy (1978)

1. Text, September 1, 1977, folder 77-30, box 14, RG 65, SAF; *St. Petersburg Times*, January 22, 1978.

2. D'Alemberte interview; R. Askew interviews by the author; R. Askew interview by Pleasants; *St. Petersburg Times*, January 11, 1978.

3. D'Alemberte interview; Moyle interview by the author; R. Askew interview by Pleasants; *St. Petersburg Times*, April 16, 23, 28, 1978.

4. *St. Petersburg Times*, May 5, October 24, 1978.

5. Raines and Hooker, "Reubin Who?" 8–10.

6. Askew statement on casino gambling, folder 78-11, box 15, RG 65, SAF.

7. *Miami Herald*, January 5, March 16, 1978; *St. Petersburg Times*, January 14, 1979; assorted correspondence regarding Gerstein vacancy, box 21, RG 138, SAF; Reno interview.

8. Morris, *Florida Handbook* (30th ed.), 134.

9. *St. Petersburg Times*, May 2, 19, 21, June 14, September 11, 1978; *Tallahassee Democrat*, May 10, 1978; *Ocala Star-Banner*, May 19, 1978; Sessions interview.

10. Senate *Journal*, April 4, 1978, 2–9.

11. Ibid., June 2, 1978, 779–83; *St. Petersburg Times*, June 3, 1978; *Tallahassee Democrat*, June 3, 1978; MacKay, *How Florida Happened*, 51–52.

12. *Odom v. Delta Corp.*, 341 So. 2d 977 (1976); House *Journal*, June 7, 1978, 1–2, and June 8, 1978, 3–28; *St. Petersburg Times*, May 26, June 8, 1978; Shaw article quoted in Morris, *Reconsiderations* (3rd ed.), 145–50.

13. House *Journal*, June 7, 1978, 1–2, and June 8, 1978, 3–28; Sheldon interview.

14. *St. Petersburg Times*, March 25, July 8, 18, September 20, 23, 26, 27, 28, November 30, 1978, March 6, 1979, September 12, 1981, September 25, 2003; Askew statement, June 27, 1978, folder "June 1978,", box 5, RG 65, SAF; R. Askew interview by Pleasants; *Miami Herald*, July 1, 2010.

15. *St. Petersburg Times*, June 3, 4, 1978; veto messages, folder "1978," box 3, RG 947, SAF.

16. *St. Petersburg Times*, February 5, April 2, May 21, 27, October 31, 1978; Askew statement, April 21, 1978, folder 78-32, box 16, RG 65, SAF.

17. *Let's Help Florida v. Smathers*, 453 F.Supp. 1003 (1978); *Let's Help Florida v. McCary*, 621 F.2d 195 (1980); *St. Petersburg Times*, February 10, April 21, August 29, 30, September 5, 24, October 31, December 7, 1978.

18. *St. Petersburg Times*, June 25, August 3, 8, October 31, 1978; Askew statement, August 5, 1978, folder "August 78," box 5, RG 67, SAF; *Washington Post*, October 19, 1978.

19. Krog interview; D'Alemberte interview; Uhlfelder interview; *St. Petersburg Times*, August 24, September 5, 14, 21, 1978; pro-casino advertisements, folder "September 78," box 5, RG 67, SAF.

20. Askew text, September 16, 1978, folder 78-48, box 16, RG 65, SAF; Reubin Askew to Robert Pittman, September 26, 1978, box 18, RG 122, SAF; *St. Petersburg Times*, September 30, 1978; Uhlfelder and Buzzett, "Constitution Revision Commission," 24.

21. *Floridians against Casino Takeover v. Let's Help Florida*, 363 So. 2d 337 (1978).

22. Gannon, *New History of Florida*, 290, 395; *St. Petersburg Times*, September 30, October 11, November 2, 1978.

23. *St. Petersburg Times*, October 21, November 2, 1978.

24. Florida Secretary of State, *Tabulation of Official Returns*, general election, November 1978; *St. Petersburg Times*, November 8, 9, 12, 1978.

25. Florida Secretary of State, *Tabulation of Official Returns*; *St. Petersburg Times*, March 26, August 10, 1978; Castor interview; Sessums interview; *Ocala Star-Banner*, August 6, 1978.

26. *St. Petersburg Times*, November 22, 23, 26, December 7, 1978; *Askew v. Cross Key Waterways*, 372 So. 2d 913 (1978); House *Journal*, December 6, 1978, 11, and May 14, 1979, 515–19.

27. R. Askew interview by Morgan; Morin, "Askew and the Upstarts," 10–12, 14–17; R. Askew interview by the author; Bacchus interview.

28. Farewell speech, folder 79-1, box 16, RG 65, SAF.

29. R. Askew interviews by the author.

30. Uhlfelder and Buzzett, "Constitution Revision Commission," 24; Florida Constitution Revision Commission, http://www.law.fsu.edu/crc/library.html.

31. Dyckman, *Disorderly Court*, 168–72.

32. Florida Secretary of State, *Tabulation of Official Returns*; Florida Senate, *Legalized Gambling in Florida*, 1–14; *St. Petersburg Times*, May 7, 2009; *Miami Herald*, April 28, May 6, 2010.

Chapter 24. Eight Years Too Late (1976–1984)

1. Remarks at dedication of Reubin Askew Student Life Building, Florida State University, October 6, 2006.

2. Blanton, "Quest of the White House," 13; R. Askew interviews by the author; Raines and Hooker, "Reubin Who?" 7; Broder, 39; *Christian Science Monitor*, June 7, 1973.

3. Woodrow Wilson, although born in Virginia, was elected president from the governorship of New Jersey. Vice-President Lyndon Johnson, a Texan, succeeded to the presidency on the death of President John F. Kennedy.

4. R. Askew interviews by the author.

5. Ibid.; Raines and Hooker, "Reubin Who?" 8–10; Holmes interview.

6. Carter interview; Parrish interview; Anderson, "Peanut Farmer for President," 80.

7. *St. Petersburg Times*, February 14, 1999; Gailey interview.

8. *St. Petersburg Times*, March 11, April 8, 1976; Bacchus interview.

9. *St. Petersburg Times*, April 18, June 10, 1976; Carter interview.

10. R. Askew interviews by the author; *Tallahassee Democrat*, December 31, 1978; *Miami Herald*, August 7, 1979; *Washington Post*, August 9, 1979.

11. U.S. Congress, Senate, *Hearing on the Nomination of Reubin O'D. Askew*, 31–44; *Washington Post*, September 23, 1979.

12. *St. Petersburg Times*, October 4, 1979, *Washington Post*, October 13, 1979; Bacchus biography, www.gtlaw.comPeople/JamesBacchus, accessed September 8, 2008.

13. William Duncan, presentation at Ohio State University, November 10, 1995, http://www.jama.org/library/position111095.html; *New York Times*, November 18, 1980; *U.S. News*, May 12, 1980; Cohen.

14. R. Askew interviews by the author; R. Askew interview by Pleasants; *New York Times*, November 22, 1980.

15. Blanton, "Quest of the White House," 13; Bacchus, "Good Fight," 11; *Washington Post*, July 1, 1983.

16. R. Askew interview by Pleasants; Bacchus, "Good Fight," 11; Bacchus interview; Stavro, "Askew Plans to Pinch Pennies," 44.

17. *Washington Post*, September 9, 1981, March 23, 1983; Bacchus, "Good Fight," 11; Federal Election Commission Advisory Opinion Number 1981-32, October 2, 1981.

18. *St. Petersburg Times*, December 8, 1981; *Meet the Press*, October 17, 1982.

19. *Washington Post*, January 7, March 21, July 1, 1983; Bacchus, "Good Fight," 21.

20. Text of candidacy speech, www.4president.org/speeches/askew1984 announcement.htm, accessed November 30, 1976; *New York Times*, February 24, 25, 1983; R. Askew interview by Pleasants.

21. "The Darkest of Dark Horses"; *New York Times*, June 1, 1983; *The MacNeil-Lehrer Report*, transcript 2015, June 16, 1983, and transcript 2063, August 24, 1983; *Washington Post*, July 19, 1983.

22. *Washington Post*, January 30, 1984; Gailey interview.

23. Stavro, "Askew Plans to Pinch Pennies," 44–45; Reubin Askew interview, *MacNeil/Lehrer Report*, transcript 2063, August 24, 1983; *New York Times*, October 24, 1983; *Washington Post*, October 24, 15, 1983.

24. R. Askew interviews by the author.

25. Ibid.; *St. Petersburg Times*, February 21, 23, 1984; *Washington Post*, February 24, 1984; *Gainesville Sun*, February 23, 1984.

26. Bacchus, "Good Fight," 10–11; *St. Petersburg Times*, February 29, 1984; *Gainesville Sun*, March 4, 1984.

27. *Washington Post*, March 2, 1984; Bacchus, "Good Fight," 10; R. Askew interviews by the author; Bacchus interview; *Lakeland Ledger*, July 19, 1984.

Chapter 25. The Shortest Campaign (1987–1988)

1. *Daytona Beach News Journal*, December 10, 1987; *St. Petersburg Times*, December 15, 1987; *New York Times*, April 14, 1990; R. Askew interviews by the author; D. L. Askew interview; K. Askew interview.

2. *St. Petersburg Times*, December 22, 1987; *Miami Herald*, December 27, 1987.

3. Undated campaign document, copy in author's possession; *Palm Beach Post*, March 25, 1988; *Tampa Tribune*, April 27, 1988; *St. Petersburg Times*, April 15, 1988; R. Askew interview by Morgan.

4. R. Askew interviews by the author; *St. Petersburg Times*, March 8, June 14, 1988; *Washington Post*, May 25, 1988; *Miami Herald*, May 15, 1988.

5. Statement, May 7, 1988, copy in author's possession; R. Askew interviews by the author; Askew remarks at University of Central Florida, March 27, 2006.

6. MacKay, *How Florida Happened*, 114–17; *St. Petersburg Times*, May 17, 1990; Morris, *Florida Handbook* (29th ed.), 685, 688; Florida Secretary of State, *Tabulation of Official Returns*, general election 1988.

7. *St. Petersburg Times*, May 12, 1988; R. Askew interviews by the author.

8. *Miami Herald*, May 15, 1988; R. Askew interviews by the author; Bacchus interview; *Tallahassee Democrat*, April 2, 1991; *St. Petersburg Times*, August 15, 1988, April 27, 1994.

Chapter 26. Epitaph for the Golden Age

1. *St. Petersburg Times*, August 15, 1988; Colburn, *Yellow Dog Democrats*, 97.

2. *New York Times*, August 29, 2009.

3. *St. Petersburg Times*, January 8, 2003.

4. Morris, *Florida Handbook* (29th ed.), 329; Jim Bacchus, e-mails to the author, August 25, 2009; Neils, "Pain in Paradise," 14, 20–22; *St. Petersburg Times*, December 11, 13, 1987.

5. Zingale and Davies, "Florida's Tax Revenues," 461; Mormino, "So Many Residents," 40; *New York Times*, August 30, 2009; Grunwald, "Is Florida the Sunset State?"; Padgett, "Behind Florida's Exodus."

6. Davis et al., *Who Pays?* 2, 14–118.

7. Freedberg, "Loophole Inc."; Florida Legislature, House and Senate, *Florida Tax Handbook*, 2008, 50–53; *Miami Herald*, April 6, 2009; Mary Ellen Klas, e-mail to the author, September 8, 2009.

8. House *Journal* (bound volume 1999); House *Journal*, March 22, 2001, 331–32; Senate *Journal*, May 4, 2001, 1505–6, and April 28, 2005, 669.

9. Haben interview; Harris interview; Krog interview; Palmer, "Sunset of the 'Long Generation.'"

10. *Citizens United v. Federal Election Commission*, 130 S.Ct. 876 (2010); Department of State, campaign finance database; MacKay interviews; *St. Petersburg Times*, November 19, 1996.

11. Rosenthal, "State of the Florida Legislature," 409–14; Klas, "Lawmakers Getting the Boot"; Plante interview.

12. Slade interview.

13. C. B. Reed interview.

14. B. Johnson interview.

15. Graham interview by the author.

16. Prison statistics, http://www.nicic.org/Features/StateStats/?State=FL, accessed September 8, 2009; Division of Economic and Demographic Research; C. Barnett, "Prison Reform"; *St. Petersburg Times*, June 1, 2009, March 17, 2010.

17. *St. Petersburg Times*, June 1, 2009.

18. Myers interview; *St. Petersburg Times*, August 4, 2007.

19. *St. Petersburg Times*, November 21, 1996, October 3, 2008.

20. Ibid., May 31, 2006.

21. Ibid., May 25, 26, 1989, December 3, 1996.

22. Ibid., January 2, 1980; Rauch interview.

23. Keller interview; *St. Petersburg Times*, May 7, 2001; McFarlain interview.

BIBLIOGRAPHY

Interviews

Apthorp, James. Interviews by the author. January 28, May 9, 2007.

Ashler, Phil. Interview by the author. February 21, 2007.

Askew, Donna Lou. Interview by the author. July 15, 2008.

Askew, Kevin. Interview by the author. May 22, 2007.

Askew, Reubin O'Donovan. Interviews by the author. February 15, May 9, August 29, September 5, 19, 2007, July 15, 2008.

———. Interview by Jack Bass and Walter De Vries. July 8, 1974. Southern Oral History Program, Southern Historical Collection, University of North Carolina.

———. Interview by James M. "Mike" Denham. October 19, 2006. Oral History Collection, Lawton M. Chiles Center for Florida History, Florida Southern College.

———. Interview by Lucy Morgan. January 7, 2005.

———. Interview by Julian Pleasants. May 8–9, 1998. University of Florida Sam Proctor Oral History Collection (FP 1).

———. Interview by Peter Range. March 2, 1972. Transcript in Don Pride's personal possession.

———. Interview by Robin Sellers. February 19, 2007. Florida State University Reichelt Oral History Program.

———. Interview by Mike Vasilinda. May 9, 2001. Florida Legislative Research Center and Museum.

Bacchus, James. Interview by the author. September 9, 2008.

Batchelor, Dick. Interview by the author. March 17, 2008.

Bax, James. Interviews by the author. June 26, July 17, 2008.

Birchfield, Bill. Interview by the author. April 4, 2007.

Bloom, Elaine. Interview by the author. April 27, 2009.

Brown, J. Hyatt. Interview by the author. June 16, 2008.

Canaday, Arthur. Interview by the author. July 8, 2008.

Carter, Jimmy. Interview by the author. September 18, 2007.

Castor, Betty. Interview by the author. August 15, 2008.

Chamberlin, Don. Interview by the author. June 30, 2009.

Crane, Donald R., Jr. Interview by the author. August 12, 2008.

D'Alemberte, Talbot. Interview by the author. March 30, 2007.

Danahy, Paul. Interview by the author. April 1, 2009.

DeGrove, John. Interviews by Cynthia Barnett. December 1, 8, 2001. University of Florida Sam Proctor Oral History Collection.

deHaven-Smith, Lance. Interview by the author. August 19, 2008.

Dunbar, Peter. Interview by the author. June 30, 2007.

Fleece, William R. Interview by the author. July 2, 2007.

Gailey, Phil. Interview by the author. July 23, 2009.

Gillespie, William. Interview by the author. August 15, 2007.

Gordon, Jack. Interview by Mike Vasilinda. October 10, 2002. Video. Florida Legislative Research Center and Museum.

Graham, Bob. Interview by the author. March 21, 2007.

———. Interview by Mike Vasilinda. February 14, 2005. Video. Florida Legislative Research Center and Museum (FLRCM).

Haben, Ralph. Interview by the author. August 13, 2008.

Hagaman, Lloyd C. Interview by Ben Houston. July 1, 2000. University of Florida Sam Proctor Oral History Collection.

Harris, Marshall. Interview by the author. September 25, 2007.

Hawkins, Paula. Interview by Julian Pleasants. November 11, 1997. University of Florida Sam Proctor Oral History Collection.

Hayes, John. Interview by the author. March 2, 2009.

Holmes, Damon. Interview by the author. October 30, 2006.

Horne, Mallory. Interview by the author. May 2007.

James, Bill. Interview by Mike Vasilinda. July 23, 2003. Video. Florida Legislative Research Center and Museum.

Joanos, James. Interview by the author. March 21, 2007.

Johnson, Bob. Interview by the author. August 4, 2007.

Johnson, Greg. Interview by the author. April 19, 2007.

Keller, Oliver J. Interview by the author. October 15, 2007.

Kimball, Fred. Interview by the author. August 18, 2008.

Kirk, Claude R., Jr. Interview by the author. February 5, 2009.

———. Interview by Julian Pleasants. October 29, 1998. University of Florida Sam Proctor Oral History Collection (FP 74).

Kiser, Curt. Interview by the author. February 15, 2007.

———. Interview by Mike Vasilinda. June 25, 2004. Video. Florida Legislative Research Center and Museum.

Krog, Jim. Interview by the author. January 18, 2007.

MacKay, Kenneth H. "Buddy," Jr. Interviews by the author. August 9, 2007; September 20, 2008.

Maguire, Charlotte. Interview by the author. July 31, 2007.

McDevitt, Sheilah. Interview by the author. June 30, 2008.

McFarlain, Richard. Interview by the author. May 2001.

McGovern, George. Interview by the author. September 8, 2008.

Meiklejohn, Don. Interview by the author. September 3, 1970.

Middlebrooks, Don. Interview by the author. July 10, 2008.

Mills, Jon. Interview by the author. June 30, 2008.

Minter, Jim. Interview by the author. July 29, 2008.

Morris, Allen. Interview by Jack Bass and Walter DeVries. May 16, 1974. Southern Oral History Program, Southern Historical Collection, University of North Carolina.

Moyle, Jon. Interview by the author. April 4, 2007.

———. Interview by Jack Bass and Walter De Vries. May 17, 1974. Southern Oral History Program, Southern Historical Collection, University of North Carolina.

Myers, Kenneth. Interview by the author. February 8, 2007.

Page, Hallie. Interview by the author. December 22, 2008.

Pajcic, Steve. Interview by the author. April 17, 2007.

Parks, Robert L. Interview by the author. May 6, 2009.

Parrish, Bernie. Interview by the author. April 4, 2007.

Pettigrew, Richard A. Interview by the author. February 3, 2007.

Plante, Kenneth. Interview by the author. July 17, 2008.

Price, Ed H., Jr. Interviews by the author. December 27, 2006, September 6, 2008.

Pride, Don. Interview by the author. October 30, 2006.

Rauch, Terri Jo Barron. Interview with the author. October 25, 2008.

Redman, James L. Interview by Mike Vasilinda. December 13, 2001. Video. Florida Legislative Research Center and Museum.

Reed, Charles B. Interview by the author. January 8, 2008.

Reed, Don. Interview by Jack Bass and Walter De Vries. May 23, 1974. Southern Oral History Program, Southern Historical Collection, University of North Carolina.

———. Interviews by the author. Undated.

Reed, Nathaniel. Interview by the author. September 4, 2008.

———. Interviews by Julian Pleasants. November 2, December 18, 2000. University of Florida Sam Proctor Oral History Collection.

Reno, Janet. Interview by the author. February 9, 2007.

Rose, Michael. Interview by the author. January 3, 2008.

Rudnick, Marvin. Interview by the author. December 20, 2007.

Schnitt, Virginia Ellis. Interview by the author. January 3, 2008.

Schultz, Frederick B. Interview by the author.

———. Interview by Mike Vasilinda. October 9, 2001. Video. Florida Legislative Research Center and Museum.

Sessions, Doug. Interview by the author. May 22, 2007.

Sessums, Terrell. Interview by the author. September 26, 2007.

Sheldon, George. Interview by the author. May 4, 2007.

Shreve, Jack. Interview by the author. May 7, 2007.

Slade, Tom. Interview by the author. June 2, 2008.

Smith, James C. Interview by the author. March 26, 2007.

Stearns, Eugene. Interview by the author. February 19, 2007.

Tait, Jim. Interview by the author. February 17, 2007.

Turlington, Ralph. Interview by the author. May 14, 2008.

———. Interview by Peter Doherty. April 12, 1996. Florida State University Reichelt Oral History Project.

Uhlfelder, Steve. Interview by the author. March 20, 2008.

Williams, James H., Jr. Interview by the author. April 6, 2009.

Woodburn, Ken. Interview by the author. July 12, 2007.

Young, Burton. Interview by the author. May 16, 2005.

Published Sources

Amlong, William R. "Law Is Just a Four-Letter Word: Ramblings on a Tallahassee Cowboy." *Miami Herald Tropic* magazine, April 19, 1981, 9–14.

———. "Reubin Askew: The Unlikely Politician." *Miami Herald Tropic* magazine, February 11, 1973, 24–31, 40.

Anderson, Patrick. "Peanut Farmer for President." *New York Times Magazine*, December 14, 1975, 15, 69, 71, 76, 80.

Askew, Reubin O'D. "To the Editors." *New Republic*, December 13, 1982.

———. "Tribute: Talbot D'Alemberte." *Florida State University Law Review* 16 (Spring 1989): 897–98.

"Askew of Florida." *New Republic*, March 4, 1971, 5–7.

"Askew Recalls His Sudden Rise to the Governor's Office." Excerpt of Askew interview with Julian Pleasants. *Gainesville Sun*, November 28, 1999.

Bacchus, James. "Cracker Catharsis: The Tenacity of Tin Cup Tom." *Florida Magazine* (*Orlando Sentinel*), July 15, 1973, 18–23.

———. "The Good Fight: 3 Years, 300,000 Miles, 3,000 Votes." *Florida Magazine* (*Orlando Sentinel*), July 15, 1984, 10–22.

Barnett, Cynthia. "Icon: Nathaniel Pryor Reed." www.floridatrend.com.december 2007.

———. *Mirage: Florida and the Vanishing Water of the Eastern U.S.* Ann Arbor: University of Michigan Press, 2007.

———. "Prison Reform: A Course Correction." http://floridatrend.com, accessed May 4, 2009.

Barrilleaux, Charles J., and Robert E. Crew Jr. "Legislative and Congressional Candidate Characteristics, 1978–1990, and Legislative Campaign Spending, 1974–1986." In *Reapportionment and Representation in Florida*, ed. Susan A. MacManus, 403–19. Tampa: University of South Florida, 1991.

Bass, Jack, and Walter De Vries. *The Transformation of Southern Politics: Social Change and Political Consequence since 1945*. Athens: University of Georgia Press, 1995.

Blanton, Donna. "Reubin Askew in Quest of the White House." *Florida Magazine* (*Orlando Sentinel*), February 7, 1982. 13, 17–18.

Broder, David. "The Democrats' Dilemma." *Atlantic*, March 1974, 39–41.

"Busing." *New Republic*, May 1, 1972.

"Busing: Stop and Go." *Newsweek*, August 16, 1971, 11–12.

Buzzett, Billy, and Steven J. Uhlfelder. "Constitution Revision Commission: A Retrospective and Prospective Sketch." *Florida Bar Journal* 71 (April 1997): 22.

Clotfelter, James, and William R. Hamilton. "'New Faces': An Alternative to Racism and 'Limousine Liberalism'?" *South Today*, June 1971, 6–7.

Cohen, Stephen D. "The Route to Japan's Voluntary Export Restraints on Automobiles." Working Paper no. 20, School of International Service, American University, http://www.gwu.edu/~nsarchiv/japan/scohenwp.htm, accessed July 27, 2009.

Colburn, David R. *From Yellow Dog Democrats to Red State Republicans: Florida and Its Politics since 1940*. Gainesville: University Press of Florida, 2007.

Colburn, David R., and Lance deHaven-Smith. *Florida's Megatrends: Critical Issues in Florida*. Gainesville: University Press of Florida, 2002.

Colburn, David R., and Richard K. Scher. *Florida's Gubernatorial Politics in the Twentieth Century*. Tallahassee: University Presses of Florida, 1980.

———. "Race Relations and Florida Gubernatorial Politics Since the *Brown* decision." *Florida Historical Quarterly* 55 (October 1976): 153–69.

Collins, LeRoy. "State Political Power Bases Are Shifting." *St. Petersburg Times*, April 18, 1976.

Congressional Quarterly. *Presidential Elections, 1789–2000*. Washington, D.C.: CQ Press, 2002.

Crew, Robert, and David L. Smith. "Research Note—Rating the Governors: An Assessment of Florida's Chief Executives in the Twentieth Century. *Political Chronicle* 4 (Fall–Winter 1992): 27–30.

D'Alemberte, Talbot "Sandy." "Essay: The 1997–1998 Constitution Revision Commission: Reflections and Commentary from the Commission's First Chairman." *Florida State University Law Review* 25 (Fall 1997): 18–23.

"The Darkest of Dark Horses." *Newsweek*, March 7, 1983, 35.

Davis, Carl, Kelly Davis, Matthew Gardner, Robert S. McIntyre, Jeff McLynch, and Alla Sapozhnikova. *Who Pays? A Distributional Analysis of the Tax Systems in All 50 States*. 3rd ed. Washington, D.C.: Institute on Taxation and Economic Policy, 2009. www.itepnet.org/whopays.htm.

Dennis, John. "Jimmy Carter's Fierce Campaign." *Nation*, May 17, 1975, 592–96.

Dent, Harry S. *The Prodigal South Returns to Power*. New York: Wiley, 1978.

"Dent in a Hard Hat." *New Republic*, November 14, 1970.

Dietsch, Robert W. "Florida's Woebegone Economy: Trouble in Fantasyland." *New Republic*, July 17, 1971, 13–14.

Dyckman, Martin A. *Floridian of His Century: The Courage of Governor LeRoy Collins*. Gainesville: University Press of Florida, 2006.

———. *A Most Disorderly Court: Scandal and Reform in the Florida Judiciary*. Gainesville: University Press of Florida, 2008.

———. "The Reubin Askew Years." *St. Petersburg Times*, December 24, 1978.

———. "Women: Rising to Power; Janet Reno: 'Strong Enough to Take on the World.'" *St. Petersburg Times*, March 14, 1993.

Edwards, Mickey. *Reclaiming Conservatism: How a Great American Political Movement*

Got Lost—and How It Can Find Its Way Back. New York: Oxford University Press, 2008.

Florida Legislature. House. *Journal of the House of Representatives.* Tallahassee, 1967–79.

———. *The People of Lawmaking in Florida, 1822–2008.* April 2008.

———. Speaker's Advisory Committee on the Future. *The Sunrise Report.* March 1987.

Florida Legislature. House and Senate. *Florida Tax Handbook.* http://edr.state.fl.us/reports/taxhandbooks/taxhandbook2008.pdf.

Florida Legislature. Senate. *Journal of the Senate.* Tallahassee, 1967–79.

———. *Legalized Gambling in Florida: The Competition in the Marketplace.* November 2006.

Florida Trend. Perspective. March 1973, 13.

"Four Men for the New Season." *Time,* May 31, 1971.

Freedberg, Sydney P. "Loophole Inc.: A Special Report on Florida's Corporate Income Tax." *St. Petersburg Times,* October 26, 2003.

Gannon, Michael, ed. *The New History of Florida.* Gainesville: University Press of Florida, 1996.

Godown, Jan. "A Talk with Reubin Askew." *Florida State University's Research in Review* (Spring and Summer 1998), www.rinr.fsu.edu/springsummer98/features/askew.html.

Grunwald, Michael. "Is Florida the Sunset State?" *Time,* July 10, 2008, www.time.com.

Herzberg, Donald G., and Alan Rosenthal, eds. *Strengthening the States: Essays on Legislative Reform.* New York: Doubleday, 1971.

Hilliard, Ardith. "Welcome to Barron Country." *The Floridian, St. Petersburg Times,* April 29, 1979.

Hooker, Robert. "Who Are the 10 Most Powerful People in Florida?" *St. Petersburg Times,* November 27, 1977.

Kallina, Edmund F., Jr. *Claude Kirk and the Politics of Confrontation.* Gainesville: University Press of Florida, 1993.

Karl, Frederick B. *The Power to Suspend: An Important Process for Fighting Corruption in Public Office.* Self-published, 2006.

Keever, Lynda. Viewpoints. July 2001, www.floridatrend.com/articleasp?aid=43361.

Kennison, Conley M. *Report to Governor Reubin O'D. Askew on the Employment and Expense Records of Roger A. Getford, Jr. Social Security Number xxx-xx-xxxx Employed by State of Florida Department of Commerce.* Tallahassee: State of Florida Department of Administration, Division of Personnel, 1973.

Key, V. O., Jr. *Southern Politics in State and Nation.* New York: Vintage, 1949.

Klas, Mary Ellen, "Lawmakers Getting the Boot." *Miami Herald,* June 1, 2008.

Kraft, Joseph. "The Cast." *New York Times Magazine,* November 17, 1974, 32.

Landers, Jay. "Right-Sizing Starts at the Top." *Florida Trend,* November 1991, 28–32.

MacKay, Kenneth H. "Buddy." "Sandy D'Alemberte: Florida's Catalyst." *Florida State University Law Review* 16 (Spring 1989): 915–18.

———. *How Florida Happened: The Political Education of Buddy MacKay.* With Rick Edmonds. Gainesville: University Press of Florida, 2010.

MacManus, Susan A., and Ronald Keith Gaddie. "Reapportionment in Florida: The Stakes Keep Getting Higher." In *Reapportionment and Representation in Florida*, ed. Susan A. MacManus, 457–75. Tampa: University of South Florida, 1991.

Maggiotto, Michael A., and Manning J. Dauer, Steven G. Koven, Joan S. Carver, and Joel Gottlieb. "The Impact of Reapportionment on Public Policy: The Case of Florida, 1960–1980." Reprinted from *American Politics Quarterly* 13 (January 1985). In *Reapportionment and Representation in Florida*, ed. Susan A. MacManus, 387–402. Tampa: University of South Florida, 1991.

Mansfield, William. "All the Governor's Men." *Florida Trend*, March 1975, 24.

———. "How Askew Passed Up No. 2 Spot—The Meeting in Collins' Basement." *Miami Herald*, July 23, 1972.

McKnight, Robert W. *The Golden Years: The Florida Legislature, '70s and '80s*. Tallahassee: Sentry Press, 2007.

McWilliams, Carey. "The Winner in Florida." *Nation*, March 27, 1972, 386–87.

Meet the Press. National Broadcasting Company. March 5, 1972. Typescript at box 4, record group 497, Florida State Archives, Tallahassee.

———. June 8, 1975.

Meiklejohn, Don. "Rube." Unpublished manuscript, n.d. Personal papers of Don Pride.

Mello, Michael, and Ruthann Robson. "Judge over Jury: Florida's Practice of Imposing Death over Life in Capital Cases." *Florida State University Law Review* 13 (Spring 1985): 31–71.

Miller, Gene. *Invitation to a Lynching*. Garden City, N.Y.: Doubleday, 1975.

"The Mod Populist." *Newsweek*, January 13, 1972, 15–16.

Morin, Richard. "Reubin Askew and the Upstarts: How the South's Hottest Law Firm Lured the Man Who Couldn't Be Bought." *Miami Herald Tropic* magazine, February 11, 1979, 10–12, 14–16.

Mormino, Gary. "When Florida Counted: 1972." *Tampa Tribune*, June 22, 2008.

———. "So Many Residents, So Few Floridians." *FORUM* 33, no. 1 (2009): 38–40.

Morris, Allen, comp. *The Florida Handbook*. Tallahassee: Peninsular Publishing Co., 1947–. Published biennially. Later editions compiled with Joan Perry Morris.

———. *Reconsiderations: Second Glances at Florida Legislative Events*. 2nd ed. Tallahassee: The House of Representatives, 1982.

———. *Reconsiderations: Second Glances at Florida Legislative Events*. 3rd ed. Tallahassee: The House of Representatives, 1985.

Neils, Parker. "Pain in Paradise: Florida's Failed Fix-All." *Florida State University Research in Review* 17, no. 3 (2008): 12–33.

Newell, Sara Arendall, and Thomas R. King. "The Keynote Address of the Democratic National Convention, 1972: The Evolution of a Speech." *Southern Speech Communication Journal* 39 (Summer 1974): 346–58.

Noll, Steven, and M. David Tegeder. *From Exploitation to Conservation: A History of the Marjorie Harris Carr Cross Florida Greenway*. August 1993. http://www.dep.state.fl.us/gwt/cfg/pdf/history_report.pdf.

Nordheimer, Jon. "Florida's 'Supersquare'—A Man to Watch." *New York Times Magazine*, March 5, 1972, 11, 52–57.

Packer, George. "The Ponzi State." *New Yorker*, February 9–16, 2009, 80–93.

Padgett, Tim. "Behind Florida's Exodus: Rising Taxes, Political Ineptitude." *Time*, September 4, 2009. www.time.com.

Palmer, Patsy. "The Sunset of the 'Long Generation.'" *Perspective. St. Petersburg Times*, December 20, 1998.

Palmer, R. Scott, and Barbara M. Linthicum. "The Statewide Prosecutor: A New Weapon against Organized Crime." *Florida State University Law Review* 13 (Fall 1985): 653–80.

Paulson, Darryl. "Campaign Finance in Florida: Who Gave It, Who Got It, Who Knows?" In *Money, Politics, and Campaign Finance Reform Law in the States,* ed. David Schultz, 213–37. Durham, N.C.: Carolina Academic Press, 2002.

Pelham, Thomas G., William L. Hyde, and Robert P. Banks. "Managing Florida's Growth toward an Integrated State, Regional, and Local Comprehensive Planning Process. *Florida State University Law Review* 13 (Fall 1985): 515–98.

Prier, Eric. *The Myth of Representation and the Florida Legislature: A House of Competing Loyalties, 1927–2000.* Gainesville: University Press of Florida, 2003.

"Put Limits on *Auto Imports*?" *U.S. News and World Report*, May 12, 1980.

Raines, Howell and Robert Hooker. "Reubin Who?" *The Floridian, St. Petersburg Times*, February 12, 1978.

"Reubin Askew's Lonely Run for President." *U.S. News and World Report*, September 26, 1983, 41.

Rosenthal, Alan B. *The Decline of Representative Democracy: Process, Participation, and Power in State Legislatures.* Washington, D.C.: CQ Press, 1998.

———. "The State of the Florida Legislature." *Florida State University Law Review* 14 (Fall 1986): 399–431.

Rutherford, Thomas. "The People Drunk or the People Sober." *St. Thomas Law Review* 15 (Fall 2002): 64–199.

Sanders, Randy. *Mighty Peculiar Elections: The New South Gubernatorial Campaigns of 1970 and the Changing Politics of Race.* Gainesville: University Press of Florida, 2002.

Sandon, Leo. "Reubin O'D Askew: The Courage to Persevere." Seminar reading, Collins Center for Public Policy. Tallahassee, 1989.

St. Angelo, Douglas. "Florida." In *The Political Life of The American States*, ed. Alan Rosenthal and Maureen Moakley, 153–60. New York: Praeger, 1984.

Shafer, Byron E., and Richard Johnston. *The End of Southern Exceptionalism: Class, Race, and Partisan Change in the Postwar South.* Cambridge: Harvard University Press, 2006.

Skene, Neil. "Review of Capital Cases: Does the Florida Supreme Court Know What It's Doing?" *Stetson Law Review* 15, no. 2. (1986): 264–354.

Smith, C. Lynwood, Jr. *Strengthening the Florida Legislature: An Eagleton Study and Report.* New Brunswick: Rutgers University Press, 1970.

Stavro, Barry. "Reubin Askew Plans to Pinch Pennies to the Presidency." *Florida Trend*, September 1983, 43–48.

Trippett, Frank. "He Won in a Walk." *Look*, January 12, 1971, 46–47.

———. *The States: United They Fell.* Cleveland: World Publishing, 1967.

Troxler, Howard. "Dreaming." *St. Petersburg Times*, May 9, 2009.

U.S. Congress, Senate, Committee on Finance. *Hearing on the Nomination of Reubin O'D. Askew to be Special Representative for Trade Negotiations.* 96th Cong., 1st sess., 1979, 1–44.

Von Drehle, David. *Among the Lowest of the Dead: The Culture of Death Row.* New York: Times Books/Random House, 1995.

Weitzel, Pete. *The White Paper: A Narrative History of Open Government in Florida.* Tallahassee: First Amendment Foundation, 2006.

Whitney, Elizabeth. "5 Florida Superflacks." *The Floridian, St. Petersburg Times,* June 2, 1974.

Wieck, Paul R. "Wallace Mischief: Florida Shambles." *New Republic*, March 11, 1972.

Williams, Roger M. "Gov. Claude Kirk: Having Fun with Florida." *Nation*, August 17, 1970.

Woodburn, Ken. "A Brief History of Florida's Environmental Movement: Four Decades of Increasing Awareness." Originally published in the *Tallahassee Democrat.* http://myflorida.com/fdi/fscc/news/state/woodburn.htm, accessed September 9, 2006.

Zingale, James A., and Thomas R. Davies. "Why Florida's Tax Revenues Go Boom or Bust and Why We Can't Afford It Anymore." *Florida State University Law Review* 14 (Fall 1986): 433–60.

INDEX

Cross-Florida Barge Canal, 13–14, 58, 81; 232–33

Dade County (now Miami-Dade County), 98, 190, 239–40, 260
Dade County Bankers Association, 96
Dade County Grand Jury, 247
Dade jetport, 13
D'Alemberte, Talbot "Sandy," 50, 85–86, 103–4, 140, 181, 188, 204, 216, 256, 287; and Constitution Revision Commission, 223, 246–47
Danahy, Paul, Jr., 181
Daniel, Welborn, 134, 148
Daniels, Jesse, 145, 179–80
Dauer, Manning J., 4–5
Davis, J. E., 98
Davis, Robert L., 98
Daylight saving time, 177
Daytona Beach News-Journal, 59, 276
Daytona International Speedway, 247
Deadly force bill, 227, 229
Death penalty. *See* capital punishment
Deeb, Richard, 123–24, 125, 239
DeGrove, John, 135, 244
deHaven-Smith, Lance, 43
Dekle, Hal P. *See* Supreme Court, Florida: ethics investigation
Delta Tau Delta, 44
Deltona Corporation, 234
Democratic Party, Florida, x, 3–4, 10–11, 272–73, 283, 286–87
Democratic National Committee, 150, 191
Democratic National Convention (1972), 139–42
de la Parte, Louis, Jr., 11, 12, 21, 114, 230; death of, 291; and HRS department, 166, 178, 198, 291; reorganization act of 1969, 12, 28, 29; and tax reform, 68, 73, 79, 99, 106
Dent, Harry S., 123, 124
Department of Business Regulation, Florida, 75, 143–44, 251
Department of Commerce, Florida, 248, 252. *See also* Adams, Tom: as lieutenant governor
Department of Community Affairs, Florida, 30, 144, 205
Department of Education, Florida, 157

Department of Environmental Regulation, Florida, 194–95
Department of General Services, Florida, 199
Department of Health and Rehabilitative Services, Florida, 30, 166, 178, 202
Department of Health, Education, and Welfare, U.S., 33
Department of Justice, U.S., 33, 288
Department of Labor, Florida, 252
Department of Law Enforcement, Florida, 12, 144
Department of Pollution Control, Florida, 30
Department of Natural Resources, Florida, 30, 82, 107, 125, 143
Department of Revenue, Florida, 30, 157
Department of Transportation, Florida (previously State Road Board), 30, 67, 107
Desegregation: busing issues of 1971–72, 89–93; Manatee County schools, 32–33, 128; Volusia County schools, 32; university system, 46
Development Commission, Florida, 15–16
De Vries, Walter, 6
Dickinson, Fred O. "Bud," Jr., 25, 29, 97, 113, 143, 156; corruption charges, 164, 171
Division of Youth Services, Florida, 12
Divorce legislation, 85–86
Dixie Hollins High School, 92–93
Domestic content legislation, 266, 279
Douglass, W. Dexter, 244
Dozier, Beverly, 186
Drew, E. Harris, 6, 146, 147–48, 181
Dubbin, Murray, 103, 104, 258
Dughi, Donn, 111
Dukakis, Michael, 279
Dunbar, Peter, 17
Dunn, Edgar M., Jr., 66, 144–45, 180, 201–2, 217
duPont, Alfred I., estate of, 72, 95. *See also* Ball, Edward
DuVal, Harvie S., 206
Duval County, 60, 90, 98, 130, 134

Eagleton, Tom, 141–42
Earle, Lewis, 35
Eckerd, Jack, 32, 34, 60, 96, 188, 257
Eckerd Corporation, 99
Economy, Florida, 283, 284

Economy, U.S., 255

Education, Florida, financing of, 18, 19, 35, 157, 182; and teacher strike of 1968, 19. *See also* desegregation

Elections and referenda: (1950), 45; (1960), 10; (1964), 10; (1966), 4–6, 9, 10, 49; (1967), 4–5; (1968), 21–22, 49; (1970), 28, 29, 33–34, 35–37; 49–64, 154; (1972), 98–99, 147, 163; (1974), 176–77, 183–91; (1976), 206, 219; (1978), 222, 231, 252–56, 257; (1986), 283; (1988), 275–79; (1990), 284; campaign costs of, 289–90; and Florida Elections Commission, 161, 279; independent expenditures, 279; 1972 presidential primary, 87, 23–24, 127, 129; 1976 presidential primary, 264; 1984 presidential primary, 272–73, 275; and resign-to-run law, 36–37; runoff primary, abolition of, 286; and spending limits, 36, 276. *See also* campaign reform

Ellis, Virginia, 48, 162

Ellison, Ernest, 159, 167

Employment discrimination, 236–37

Energy legislation: *See* Public Service Commission

England, Arthur J., Jr., 71, 72, 133, 156, 161, 205, 218, 228; Supreme Court campaign, 177, 187–88

Environmental protection, 35, 134–35

Environmental reorganization, 124–25, 130, 182

Equal Rights Amendment, 6, 133, 149, 156, 182, 197, 239, 256, 292

Ervin, Richard, 72, 177, 182, 187

Escambia County, 99, 190

Ethics in government, Florida Ethics Commission, 180–81, 215, 220–21. *See also* Askew, Reubin: gubernatorial administration of, ethics/financial disclosure in government; "Sunshine Amendment"

Everglades, and jetport, 125

Evidence code, 250

Faircloth, Earl, 50, 54, 60–61

Farrior, J. Rex, Jr., 229

Fascell, Dante, 62

Favre, Gregory, 100, 148

Federal Communications Commission and "fairness doctrine," 96

Federal Elections Commission, 268

Ferguson, Chester, 53

Ferré, Maurice, 54

Fiedler, Tom, 276

Financial disclosure: *See* ethics in government; "Sunshine Amendment"

Fifth U.S. Circuit Court of Appeals, 206, 221–22, 266

Firestone, George, 99, 168, 192, 199, 201–2, 217

First District Court of Appeal, 169–70, 210, 220

Fishing, 30, 97, 165, 223, 233

Fleece, William, 74, 126

Fleming, Thomas, 99

Florida, history of, ix–xxi

Florida, population of, ix

Florida Alligator, 23

Florida Atlantic University, 280

Florida Bankers Association, 72, 96

Florida Baptist Witness, 161

Florida Bar, 96, 229; role in judicial appointments, 68, 81; ethics opinions of, 24

Florida Blue Key, 47

Florida Chamber of Commerce, 73

Florida Defenders of the Environment, 233

Florida East Coast Railroad, 72

Florida economy, 6

Florida Education Association, 18, 19, 252

Florida Flambeau, 45

Florida Handbook, 51

Florida Keys, protection of, 134–35, 147, 257–58

Florida League of Conservation Voters, 63

Florida National Banks, 72, 96

Florida Petroleum Marketers Association, 169

Florida Power Corporation, 251

Florida PTA Congress, 93

Florida Sheriffs Bureau, 12

Florida State Prison, 11, 71–76

Florida State University (formerly Florida State College for Women), 44, 83, 292; alumni association, 47; Askew school, 280; college of law, 158

Florida Student Government Association, 45

Florida Times-Union and *Jacksonville Journal*, 95, 98

Horne, Mallory, 24, 29, 51, 147–48, 152, 165, 179, 188, 195, 198

House of Representatives, Florida: impeachment proceedings in, 171, 173–74, 212, 221, 248; prayer controversy, 130; speaker selection, 67–68, 181, 192, 230, 237–38. *See also* Legislature, Florida

Hubbart, Phillip A. *See* Lee, Wilbert

Hugli, Robert, 67

Humphrey, Hubert, 129, 130, 138, 263

Hunt, H. L., 33

Hussein, King of Jordan, 138

Industrial Commission, Florida, 235

Institute on Taxation and Economic Policy, 284–85

Insurance industry, agents, and regulation, 25, 30, 76. *See also* O'Malley, Thomas

Internal Improvement Fund, Florida, 66, 125

Invitation to a Lynching. See Lee, Wilbert

Iowa caucuses, 271, 273

Islandia, 13

Issues and Answers, 139

Jackson, Henry M., 127, 263, 264

Jackson, Jesse, 270, 273

Jacksonville, 10, 77, 86, 92, 95, 104, 250

James, Bill, 27, 231, 244, 246

Japan: automobile industry (export limits), 267; import restrictions, 267

Joanos, Jim, 28

Johns, Charley, 69

Johnson, Beth, 11, 54, 289

Johnson, Bob, 82–83, 193

Johnson, Dewey, 4, 103, 179

Johnson, Gregory, 35, 56, 58, 67, 72–73, 94, 99, 107, 135–36, 140, 142

Johnson, Haynes, 137

Johnson, Lady Bird, 262

Johnson, Lyndon, 11, 49, 315n3

Johnston, Harry, 201–2, 282–83

Jordan, Hamilton, 263

Journal of the House of Representatives, 130

Judicial Qualifications Commission, Florida, 173, 174, 182

Judiciary, Florida: appointments to, 68, 81, 174, 203, 204–6, 207–8, 219, 260; nonpartisan elections of, 36, 78; and judicial

nominating commissions, 174–75, 207–8; politicization of, 285–86, reorganization of, 102–5, 129

Kahn, Alfred, 232

Kahn, D. Stephen, 249

Kallina, Edmund F., Jr., 9

Karl, Fred, 25, 83, 104, 128, 133, 179, 204, 205, 207, 248

Keen, Florence, 187

Keller, O. J., 166, 178, 194, 196–200, 292

Kennedy, David, 57, 164, 183

Kennedy, Edward M., 141, 266, 282

Kennison, Conley M., 153, 154, 159

Kershaw, Joel Lang, 130

Key, V. O., Jr., 3

Kilpatrick, James J., 127

King, Dr. Martin Luther, Jr., state holiday, 249

Kirk, Claude R., Jr.: administration of, 8–9, 11–20; on busing for desegregation, 89, 82; and Cabinet system, 14–15, 19–20, 31; campaigns of, 10–11, 32, 60–63, 222, 257, 278; on capitol building, 241; on education and teachers' strike (1968), 13, 18–19; and environmental protection, 12–14; expenditures of, 15, 16; "farewell" address, 70; and "Governor's Club," 16, 36; inauguration, 8; investigations of, 15–16; judicial appointments by, 68; and legislative pay raise (1969), 25–28; legislative relations of, 9, 14, 18–19, 27–28; and Manatee school desegregation issues, 32–33; progressive instincts of, 11, 12; vetoes by, 11, 18, 19, 26, 28, 35, 36; vice presidential ambitions of, 16; "war on crime" of, 8, 12

Kirk, Erika Mattfeld, 8, 15

Kiser, S. Curtis "Curt," 33, 179, 194, 195, 207, 230, 238, 251, 256, 282

Kovachevich, Elizabeth, 83

Krentzman, Ben, 32–33

Krog, Jim, 216, 217–18, 254, 267

Ku Klux Klan, 177, 186

Kutun, Barry, 230, 238

La Croix, David, 173

Lake County, 144–45

Lamoreaux, Cappy, 67

Martin A. Dyckman's investigative reporting for the *St. Petersburg Times* earned several important honors, including the American Bar Association Silver Gavel and the Distinguished Service Award of the Florida Society of Newspaper Editors. In 1984 the Florida Bar Foundation recognized his writing on judicial reform with its Medal of Honor Award. Mr. Dyckman is also the author of *Floridian of His Century: The Courage of Governor LeRoy Collins* and *A Most Disorderly Court: Scandal and Reform in the Florida Judiciary.*

Florida has emerged today as a microcosm of the nation and has become a political bellwether in national elections. The impact of Florida on the presidential elections of 2000, 2004, and 2008 suggests the magnitude of the state's influence. Of the four largest states in the nation, Florida is the only one that has moved from one political column to the other in the last three national elections. These developments suggest the vital need to explore the politics of the Sunshine State in greater detail. Books in this series will explore the myriad aspects of politics, political science, public policy, history, and government in Florida.

The 57 Club: My Four Decades in Florida Politics, by Frederick B. Karl (2010)

The Political Education of Buddy MacKay, by Buddy MacKay, with Rick Edmonds (2010)

Reubin O'D. Askew and the Golden Age of Florida Politics, by Martin A. Dyckman (2011)

Immigrant Prince: Mel Martinez and the American Dream, by Richard E. Fogelsong (2011)